Organization Theory

Organization Theory

A PRACTICE-BASED APPROACH

Ulla Eriksson-Zetterquist • Tomas Müllern • Alexander Styhre

OXFORD
UNIVERSITY PRESS

OXFORD
UNIVERSITY PRESS

Great Clarendon Street, Oxford OX2 6DP

Oxford University Press is a department of the University of Oxford.
It furthers the University's objective of excellence in research, scholarship,
and education by publishing worldwide in

Oxford New York

Auckland Cape Town Dar es Salaam Hong Kong Karachi
Kuala Lumpur Madrid Melbourne Mexico City Nairobi
New Delhi Shanghai Taipei Toronto

With offices in

Argentina Austria Brazil Chile Czech Republic France Greece
Guatemala Hungary Italy Japan Poland Portugal Singapore
South Korea Switzerland Thailand Turkey Ukraine Vietnam

Oxford is a registered trade mark of Oxford University Press
in the UK and in certain other countries

Published in the United States
by Oxford University Press Inc., New York

British Library Cataloguing in Publication Data

Data available

Library of Congress Cataloging in Publication Data

Data available

Typeset by Techset Composition Pvt Ltd., Salisbury, UK.
Printed in Italy on acid-free paper by L.E.G.O. S.p.A.—Lavis TN

ISBN 978-0-19-956930-4

10 9 8 7 6 5 4 3 2 1

Acknowledgements

The work on this book has been a rewarding group process, and we would like to express our gratitude to many people that have contributed to the intellectual process of writing the book. We would like to give a special thanks to Francesca Griffin, our commissioning editor. You have really helped in structuring our book as a textbook—your insights and belief in our ideas has been very helpful. Your detailed comments at the end of the writing process helped us focus our attention on the most important issues. We are also thankful for the numerous comments from the anonymous academic reviewers—your comments have been very useful and you have challenged us to develop our manuscript to fit the expectations of active teachers in the field of organization theory.

Brief table of contents

List of cases   xiv

Guided tour of pedagogical features   xvi

Guided tour of Online Resource Centre   xviii

CHAPTER 1   Introduction: The practical value of organization and management theory   1

PART I   MANAGING SYSTEMS AND TECHNOLOGY   17

CHAPTER 2   Organizational boundaries and structures   19

CHAPTER 3   Information technology and business systems   47

CHAPTER 4   Operations management in day-to-day work   75

PART II   MANAGING PEOPLE   105

CHAPTER 5   Finding people and motivating them to make the best of their potential   107

CHAPTER 6   How to lead in an organization   135

CHAPTER 7   Coping with external influences in organizations   165

PART III   MANAGING CHANGE AND PROCESSES   193

CHAPTER 8   Managing innovation in and between organizations   195

CHAPTER 9   Balancing radical change and continuous improvement   217

CHAPTER 10   Managing learning and knowledge in and between organizations   241

References   271

Glossary   289

Index   295

Detailed table of contents

List of cases   xiv

Guided tour of pedagogical features   xvi

Guided tour of Online Resource Centre   xviii

CHAPTER 1   Introduction: The practical value of organization and management theory   1

The production and distribution of organization and management theory   2

The pedagogic features of the book   3

Historical overview of management practice and management innovations   7

Summary and conclusions   14

PART 1   **MANAGING SYSTEMS AND TECHNOLOGY**   17

CHAPTER 2   Organizational boundaries and structures   19

Introduction   21

Why are organizational structures important?   23

Elements of structures   27

Transcending the formal boundaries of a complex organization   39

Summary and conclusions   44

Study questions   44

Literature recommendations and further readings   45

CHAPTER 3   Information technology and business systems   47

Introduction   49

Organizing and technology   49

The Industrial Era to the twentieth century   54

The sociotechnical movement   56

The results from the studies of the sociotechnical system   58

Technology transforms the organization's structure   60

Technology and open systems   62

Organizations with several technologies   63

Information technology   64

A new perspective on technology   67

Computerization movements   70

Summary and conclusions   72

Questions   72

Literature recommendations and further readings   72

CHAPTER 4   Operations management in day-to-day work   75

Introduction   77

The engineering revolution: Scientific management and Taylorism   78

Labour process theory and industrial sociology: Studies of work   85

Work organization   89

Management control and resistance   96

Organization routines, rules, practices   100

Summary and conclusions   102

Study questions   102

Literature recommendations and further readings   103

PART II   MANAGING PEOPLE   105

CHAPTER 5   Finding people and motivating them to make the
best of their potential   107

Introduction   109

Recruitment   109

The Hawthorne Study   111

Part 1 of the Hawthorne Study: The Relay Assembly Room   113

Part 2 of the Hawthorne Study: The Interview Study   114

Part 3 of the Hawthorne Study: The Bank Wiring
Observation Room   115

Results and criticism of the Hawthorne Study   117

Motivation in work life   118

Content-oriented motivation theories   119

Process-oriented motivation theories   123

Challenging motivation theories   126

New ways of understanding work motivation   127

Human Resource Management (HRM)   128

HRM and the organization   130

Diversity   131

Summary and conclusions   132

Study questions   133

Literature recommendations and further readings   133

CHAPTER 6   How to lead in an organization   135

Introduction   137

Leadership in its organizational context   138

Leadership theory—contemporary approaches   144

Gender, intersectionality, and leadership   153

Leadership in the middle   158

Summary and conclusions   162

Study questions   162

Literature recommendations and further readings   162

CHAPTER 7   Coping with external influences in organizations   165

Introduction   167

Decision-making in organizations   168

Institutional theory: How organizations are determined by
norms and practices in their environments   176

The concepts of culture and organization culture   184

Summary and conclusions   191

Study questions   191

Literature recommendations and further readings   191

PART III   MANAGING CHANGE AND PROCESSES   193

CHAPTER 8   Managing innovation in and between organizations   195

Introduction   197

Defining innovation   197

The innovation phases   202

The social nature of innovation   203

Systemic view of innovation   208

Innovation and organization forms   209

Summary and conclusions   214

Study questions   215

Literature recommendations and further readings   215

CHAPTER 9   **Balancing radical change and continuous improvement**   **217**

Introduction   219

Change as a planned process—traditional views   221

Change as an emergent process—the view of institutional theory   225

The new institutional theory   226

Scandinavian institutionalism   227

Types of change in organizations   228

Resistance to change—why change efforts often fail   234

Summary and conclusions   238

Study questions   239

Literature recommendations and further readings   239

CHAPTER 10   **Managing learning and knowledge in and between organizations**   **241**

Introduction   242

Theoretical perspectives on learning   243

Learning on the individual level   247

Learning in organizations   251

The concept of knowledge   256

Three views of knowledge in organizations   257

Situated and local knowledge   258

Knowledge management in organizations: Knowledge work and knowledge workers   260

Learning from risks   262

Risk in organizations: Background and definitions   262

Learning from risk management and disasters   264

Summary and conclusions　　267

Study questions　　268

Literature recommendations and further readings　　268

References　　271

Glossary　　289

Index　　295

List of cases

CASE STUDIES

CHAPTER 1	Oracle completes acquisition of Sun	1
CHAPTER 2	Intel—formal structure, boundaries, and situational demands	19
CHAPTER 3	Introduction of e-business at Volvo Car Company and Ford	47
CHAPTER 4	Toyota revolutionizes operations management through small means	75
CHAPTER 5	Recruiting and training future managers	107
CHAPTER 6	Ericsson—a meeting between different leadership philosophies	135
CHAPTER 7	Managing the portfolio of innovations in the pharmaceutical industry	165
CHAPTER 8	Managing innovation work in industry–university collaboration	195
CHAPTER 9	Healthy Eyes for Life	217
CHAPTER 10	The Melfi Model—a learning factory	241

MINICASES

CHAPTER 2	The organizing of a megacompany—the case of Walmart	24
	Karolinska University Hospital in Sweden	32
	Tata Motors in India	35
	Sustainable structures	40
	General Electric—the boundaryless organization	43
CHAPTER 3	New technologies and organizing	52
	Jute weaving industry	57
	Zara goes online	65
	Women and deskilling in clerical work	67
	Apple and the introduction of the iPad	68
CHAPTER 4	General practitioners and nurses struggle over professional authority and jurisdiction	81
	Singing to prevent strain	85
	TQM outside of the manufacturing industry	92
	TQM as a business strategy in Nissan	93
	Actual control in everyday work	98

CHAPTER 5	The legacy of the Hawthorne Study at ADM	112
	HRM practices at Rolls-Royce Motor Cars	121
	Motivation in movies	125
	HR practices in networked organizations—the case of IKEA	128
	Diversity management at McKinsey & Company	132
CHAPTER 6	Irene Rosenfeld of Kraft Foods	137
	Lou Gerstner and the promise of the new economy	148
	Anita Roddick and Body Shop	148
	Steve Jobs at Apple	151
	The lemon-yellow dress	158
CHAPTER 7	The Cuban crisis in movies	173
	Implementing a CSR strategy in Petrobras	181
	Accounting procedures as institutions	183
	Exporting the Japanese model to the West	189
	Aligning business objectives and traditional family values in an Israeli textile factory	190
CHAPTER 8	Innovation at Nokia—the case of Ovi store	199
	The challenge of establishing the idea in pre-existing social institutions and practices	204
	Edison and recorded music	207
	Innovation at Google	211
CHAPTER 9	Mastering technology through continuous improvement at Shimano	220
	Changes related to environmental issues	227
	Changing the culture in mergers and acquisitions	231
	Using microsystems to foster a culture of improvement	233
	Rapid change and sustainability in the Emirates	234
CHAPTER 10	Harvard Medical School (HMS)	250
	Learning at Shell	254
	Knowledge management practices at Huawei	261
	The organizational process that risks leading to a major accident	265
	Formal and ephemeral organizations for earthquake assistance	266

Guided tour of pedagogical features

Organization Theory is a pedagogically rich learning resource. This 'Guided tour of pedagogical features' will show you how to make the most of your text by illustrating each of the features used by the authors to explain the key concepts of organization theory.

The authors use an innovative case-based approach to organization theory. This will enable you to recognize and practise the skills you will need for exams, and help you to think about how you might apply organization theory in a real-life business situation.

Each chapter starts with a real-life problem faced in an organization and follows this throughout the chapter. Wellknown organizations such as Ericsson, Intel, AstraZeneca, and Fiat are employed in these **chapter-opening cases**, alongside smaller organizations, to provide a wide range of examples.

Keep this case in mind while you are reading the chapter, as a lens through which to view the various theories you encounter. The authors will frequently refer back to the chapter-opening case using '**link boxes**'.

At the end of the chapter the theoretical perspectives are summarized in a **conclusion**, and the opening case is referred back to once again, completing the learning loop.

Bearing this one case in mind throughout the chapter helps to join up your learning and show you the full picture. However, in order to provide a wider range of examples, a large number of **minicases** from other businesses and organizations are also supplied throughout the book. They provide different perspectives, giving a more nuanced overall understanding of organization theory.

Every key theoretical concept is thus illustrated through either the chapter-opening case study or the minicases.

Other features are also used to guide and support your learning:

Chapter guides at the start of each chapter provide a bulleted outline of the main concepts and ideas. These serve as helpful signposts to what you can expect to learn from each chapter.

> **Questions** ❓
>
> As the VCC and Ford case shows, introducing new technological systems is a complex process—in what ways does it transform social life in an organization?
>
> When introducing new technology (in this case a new e-Business system) an important question is—how can the organizational structure be designed to provide the best use of the new technology?
>
> Important questions based on the case are also how the new technology is constructed by its users, how it affects various processes of organizing, and other dimensions of the interplay between the social and the technological.

Definition boxes highlight and define key terms when they first appear in the text, as well as being collated in an end-of-book glossary to enable you to locate definitions easily.

> **DEFINITION BOX** ✔
>
> **Functional foremanship**
>
> The predominant managerial model in Taylor's day was the unitary leadership model, which assumes that each individual reports to only one manager in the line organization, creating an unbroken chain of command. This model is very straightforward and has, over the years, carried a lot of practical appeal. Taylor's idea of functional foremanship radically challenged this idea by arguing that an individual worker could report to up to 6–7 different foremen. Depending on the complexity of the managerial tasks, more than one foreman might be needed to supervise the worker. When implemented this often created friction between the managers and often led to compromises. One such compromise that gained a lot of attention and was later incorporated in the contingency framework was Harrington Emerson's idea of the *staff and line organization*. In his modification of Taylor's ideas the chain of command in the line organization is preserved and the technical expertise needed

End-of-chapter study questions allow you to check your understanding by working through them after you have read each chapter.

> ❓ **Study questions**
>
> 1. Describe the major features of the machine bureaucracy, as described by Henry Mintzberg.
> 2. Discuss different definitions of formal organizational structures offered in the chapter.
> 3. Many different, concrete, elements of structure have been suggested in the literature. Describe some of them and discuss their significance for understanding today's organizations.
> 4. Describe the basic idea of the divisional structure.
> 5. Discuss the basic ideas of Contingency theory and how it improved upon previous theories.
> 6. Describe some of the seminal studies made in the Contingency theory. Discuss also some of the criticism towards this theory.

Literature recommendations and further readings are provided in the form of an annotated list of recommended reading on each subject, which will help guide you through further reading on the subject area.

> **Literature recommendations and further readings** 🖽
>
> Organization theory is a very rich field and books and articles on the role and functioning of organizational structures are not lacking. More than 25 years after its first publication, *Structure in fives*, by Henry Mintzberg (1983), still gives a pedagogical introduction to the ideas of Contingency theory. The original classics by authors such as Burns and Stalker (*Management of innovation*, 1962), Lawrence and Lorsch (*Organization and environment*, 1967), Thompson (*Organizations in action*, 1967), and Woodward (*Industrial organization*, 1965), still makes up essential reading for the interested student of organizational structures and come highly recommended. A good overview of the latest advancements in the field of organizational structures is given in the book *Innovative forms of organizing*, edited by Whittington and Pettigrew (2003).

Guided tour of Online Resource Centre

http://www.oxfordtextbooks.co.uk/orc/erikssonzetterquist/
To support this text there is a range of web-based content for both students and registered adopters.

For students

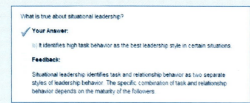

Multiple-choice questions
Test your knowledge and understanding using these instantly marking questions, with feedback and page references back to the textbook if you need to recap your studies.

Further reading and research
Web links to sites such as company websites and news stories are provided to keep you up-to-date on the latest developments. Links to professional websites relevant to each chapter direct you towards valuable sources of information and certified associations.

'What happened next?'
Appropriate cases from within the textbook will be updated on the Online Resource Centre.

For registered adopters

OUP's Online Resource Centres are developed to provide lecturers and students with ready-to-use teaching and learning resources. They are free of charge, designed specifi cally to complement the textbook and offer additional materials which are suited to electronic delivery. Using an Online Resource Centre saves you time by providing you with ready-made teaching and testing materials, while facilitating blended learning and enhancing the student experience.

If you are thinking of adopting this book and would like to take a look at the resources available to lecturers, please contact your local sales representative (via **www.oup.com/uk/ orc/findrep/**) to request an inspection password.

If you have already adopted this book, please register for access to the online resources. Contact your local sales rep and also complete our simple online registration form (follow the links from **http://www.oxfordtextbooks.co.uk/orc/erikssonzetterquist/**). You can choose your own username and password, and access will be granted within 48 hours (subject to verification). All the resources can be incorporated into your institution's existing virtual learning environment by downloading all linking to these – meaning everything is in the same place for quick and easy access.

If you would like advice or help at any point, please contact our ORC helpdesk at: orc.help@oup.com.

PowerPoint® slides

A suite of PowerPoint® slides are provided, complete with notes, in order to save you time in lecture preparation. These are fully customizable.

Leadership and organizational structures

- Decentralization – decision-making authority is spread in the organization and leads to demands for more democratic leadership
- Projects – the growing use of projects leads

Seminar exercises

One seminar exercise is provided per chapter, based around topics such as case analysis, role play or company research. These are complete with discussion questions and teaching notes.

Seminar exercises: teaching notes

Teaching notes for Jill and the meeting

The case is intended for a classroom discussion on leadership and the challenges meeting managers in concrete situations. In the classroom discussion special emphasis can be put on trying to understand the situation and the conflict between Jill and James, and the weak support she seems to have for implementing the new system. In the case description a number of observations can be made on the behaviour (or lack of behaviour) of different individuals in the meeting. The different leadership theories presented in chapter 6 are applicable and could be covered in the discussion. Try, for instance, to characterize Jill's leadership style. The case does also opens up for a discussion on gender and how gender patterns can interfere with leadership processes.

Test bank

A suite of questions, with feedback and page references back to the textbook, is provided for your use in formative or summative assessment.

What information can be drawn from a formal organizational chart? Pick the correct alternative.

- ○ a. Organizational charts show how many subordinates managers on different levels have.
- ○ b. They show the number of decision making levels in the company.
- ○ c. Organizational charts provide information on the name of all managers in the company.

Feedback

0.0% a. It does usually not provide that kind of detailed information.
　　　Page reference: 23

CHAPTER I
Introduction: The practical value of organization and management theory

Oracle completes acquisition of Sun

Redwood Shores, CA—27 January 2010

'Oracle Corporation (NASDAQ: ORCL) announced today that it had completed its acquisition of Sun Microsystems, Inc. Combination of the local entities worldwide will proceed in accordance with local laws.'
(information retrieved from http://www.oracle.com/us/corporate/press/044428)

The press release above mentions a significant event in the IT industry, when two large organizations, Oracle and Sun, merged into one. Formally Oracle acquired Sun, and the new company operates under the name Oracle. For most people this is not an important event. Both Oracle and Sun are fairly anonymous companies for the larger public, even though the Java technology developed by Sun is definitely better known. But for the employees in the two former organizations, and for those that are active within the IT-industry, the decision to acquire Sun was highly important. A decision to merge together two companies gives rise to a highly complex process that touches upon most aspects of the daily life in and around a large organization. The acquisition also has consequences way beyond the formal boundaries of the two organizations—it, in fact, transforms the whole IT-industry. An acquisition process such as this has consequences for the formal structure and systems employed in the two parties:

- It will necessarily touch upon the technologies used in the two, formerly independent, companies.
- It will transform the management of people and processes.
- It poses a challenge to managers on different levels to adapt to new and changing circumstances; and so on.

Source: information retrieved from http://www.oracle.com/us/corporate/press/044428

This book deals with practical challenges such as the one briefly described above, and it rests firmly on the idea that managers, on a daily basis, encounter problems, challenges and opportunities relating to the ways their organization functions or should function. In the next section we will introduce the pedagogical idea of the book and what makes it different from many other textbooks on organizations.

The production and distribution of organization and management theory

This book is a textbook in organization theory, or, to use a more recent term, management theory, aimed at introducing the elementary theoretical frameworks employed in research on organizations. Like many other textbooks, this book is trying to strike a balance between academic rigour and detailed theoretical accounts on the one hand and, on the other hand, practical relevance. Over the years, like perhaps no other academic institution, the business school has been subject to criticism regarding the overarching ideology guiding and structuring business and management school research. Practitioners tend to think that business school research is too theoretical and removed from day-to-day managerial work; researchers representing other scientific disciplines often 'accuse' business school research of being neither of practical relevance nor of any broader theoretical interest. Grey (2001:27) wrote:

'Business schools, more perhaps than any other part of universities, experience a curious dual insecurity. On the one hand, they fear, and have often experienced, the scorn of other, more traditional academic subjects. On the other hand, they often stand accused of being less relevant to business needs and concerns.'

At worst, these two forms of critique are at least partially true. At best, they demonstrate an ignorance regarding the scope and breadth of the research produced in business schools today. The first thing to notice when addressing the debate regarding business school research is that the discussions have been just as animated within the business schools as elsewhere. There have been numerous worried editorials published, conference panels organized, and journal papers written, testifying to the need to problematize and debate the content and orientation of business school research. Other contributors to the special issue called for the need for more thorough theoretical work (Kilduff and Kelemen, 2001), the use of specific research methods such as action research approaches or other 'experimental methods' (Hatchuel, 2001), or more systematic reflection and critical accounts of industry (Grey, 2001; see also Grey, 2004). In the US, a similar debate has been initiated from time to time, for instance by Jeffrey Pfeffer, one of the leading researchers in the field and professor at the Graduate School of Business at Stanford University. In a series of papers Pfeffer (1993, 2008) and Pfeffer and Fong (2002), argued that the lack of practical relevance is a major obstacle for the advancement of business school research. Rather than indulging in overtly theoretical accounts of organizational activities, Pfeffer and colleagues called for a new research agenda that is closer related to the needs and demands of the practicing manager.

Notwithstanding all this criticism regarding the business school research tradition and its alleged lack of relevance, the growth of the number of business titles published and the amount of students enrolling on business school education programs suggest another perspective. For instance, the mere growth of business titles in the academic and 'semi-academic' press (i.e., so-called 'popular management literature') is remarkable:

In 1991, McGraw Hill published 25 (business) titles; in 1996, it published 110 titles. Marketing budgets at the esteemed ... Harvard Business School Press are estimated to

have almost doubled in the last four years. In the UK alone, 2,931 business titles were published in 1996, compared with a paltry 771 in 1975.
(Crainer, 1997:38, cited in Thrift, 1998: 174)

In terms of student attraction, for instance in Australia, business schools today account for the largest number of students graduating from university. In the new millennium, an increasing number of students want to do business and be part of the world of business. Traditional prestigious domains, such as engineering, are today struggling to attract students and engineering school faculty tend to deplore the gradual but still significant lowering of the standards in student populations regarding skills; for example in mathematics. In Thomas Frank's (1997) apt phrase, the world of business has orchestrated a 'conquest of cool'. Today, what Thrift (2005: 6) has called the '*cultural* circuit of capitalism', *comprising* 'business schools, management consultants, management gurus and the media', has also contributed to the interest for entrepreneurship and enterprising activities. Magazines and public competitions in, for instance, entrepreneurial activities have created a new sense of the world of business as being a domain of creativity and self-fulfilment.

Recently Pfeffer and Sutton (2006) argued for a more evidence-based approach in the field of management. They try to strike a balance between academic rigour and practical relevance in arguing for more scientific evidence in the practice of management. In many ways, they argue, practitioners rely on rumours, half-truths, and poorly supported convictions, at the same time that academics have big problems reaching decision-makers with their knowledge. This opens up for some highly relevant and important questions concerning knowledge in the management field, questions that form the backbone of this textbook on organization theory:

• Is there knowledge available concerning the operations of modern day organizations?

• Does this knowledge match the quality demands from both practitioners and academics?

• Is available knowledge used to guide managers in their day-to-day management of their organizations?

• Does the managerial agenda influence the research being done at business schools?

As these, and similar, questions indicate we are seeking to reconcile theory and practice, to bridge rigorous theoretical constructs and practice-relevant ideas. We firmly believe that a modern textbook on organization theory needs to take these questions seriously, and in the next section we present the pedagogical idea of the book.

The pedagogic features of the book

It is against this background—the need to bridge organization theory and practice—that this textbook is being written. Contrary to the harshest critics of business school research, we do not think that research in the domain of organization theory is neither irrelevant nor theoretically unsophisticated. Like in all scientific disciplines, the research produced is of varied quality, and there is no reason to believe that business school researchers are less equipped to provide intriguing research results. The relevance of business school research is also a standing topic of discussion that is largely contingent on what one is hoping to learn from business school research. If one expects business school researchers to be capable of de-contextualized formulations of 'best practice' in a specific field, then one may end up dis-gruntled but if one assumes that there are some valuable things to be learnt from collaborating with business school researchers, then one may find new perspectives and models that can further guide everyday work in organizations.

This book is however by no means an attempt at praising business school research or to join forces with its detractors. Instead, it is a textbook that in its own way is taking the question regarding the practical relevance of organization and management theory seriously. That is, rather than just assuming that a box of theories regarding the nature and functioning of organizations is easily digested by a novice reader, we have tried to connect practical cases and theories and models more closely. Rather than starting off with a series of theories (say, on **innovation** management) and then illustrating the theories with empirical cases, each chapter starts with a highly relevant practical question and thereafter, a series of relevant theories and models are addressed to advance a more detailed understanding of that specific problem. To provide an introduction to the style chosen and explain the pedagogical outline, this first chapter outlines how this book is different. Rather than being *functionally* organized into thematic chapters, the textbook is structured in accordance with the overarching princi-ple that virtually *all* firms or organizations are facing similar problems on a generic level. Such problems and challenges are addressed in the cases used in the book. For instance, all organizations:

Need to monitor and control their structure and form,

Are engaged in employing, training, and leading co-workers who need to be motivated and given the opportunity to develop themselves professionally during the work life,

Use various forms of technologies and machinery in the production of goods and services being sold in the market, and so forth.

In this book, we have identified nine different generic processes or procedures that need to be managed and organized. These nine issues of concern are the 'drivers' of the book, not the theoretical domains or theories.

We have classified the nine issues according to a simple logic that hopefully creates a clear path through the different chapters. Beyond this introductory chapter, the book is divided into three parts:

· Part I: Managing systems and technology

· Part II: Managing people

· Part III: Managing change and processes

The book starts from the basic observation that it makes sense to talk about an organ-ization as something more than simply a group of people working together to achieve a com-mon goal (this formulation, by the way, is a good example of an established definition of the concept *organization*). Instead, we start with the premise that organizations are systems, that is, they 'behave' in ways similar to other systems, be it simple systems such as mechanical objects or more complex systems such as living, biological species. With the focus on organizations as systems it makes sense to talk about the structural features of the system, what we often refer to as the formal structure, and the boundaries to anything that exists outside the system (as we will see in Chapter 2, this distinction between the organization and its environment is far from easy to draw).

Describing organizations as systems implies that they have certain properties that separate them from their environment. A formal structure is one important element in the systemic character of organizations, and this is discussed in Chapter 2 of the book. Within the formal boundaries of the organization certain technologies are being used and in Chapter 3 we highlight the transforming effect of technology in general, and information technology in particular. A discussion on the systemic nature of organizations would not be complete without a discussion on the underlying reasons for building organizations—to carry out work. Chapter 4 takes a closer look at the managerial issues relating to the day-to-day management of the operations—the actual practices that constitute the organizing.

The second part of the book groups together a number of managerial challenges that emanates from the fact that organizations consist of people interacting to, hopefully, reach common goals. In this book, we have identified three major challenges that are covered in Part II. The first two are intimately related and deal with people's motivation to work (Chapter 5) and the fundamental role of leadership in tapping in to the motivational processes of individuals (Chapter 6). In Chapter 7 we take a closer look at decision-making processes in organizations.

The third and last part of the book deals with the managing of change and processes in organizations. Here we have grouped together managerial challenges that deal with the ongoing development and change of organizations. Questions concerning innovation (Chapter 8), improvement and change (Chapter 9), and learning within and between organizations (Chapter 10) are high on the managerial agenda and there is a rapidly growing stream of research covering the more dynamic aspects of organizing, that is, how organizations are capable of responding to external changes in the environment.

The outline of the book, with the three parts and the different chapters within each part, departs from the traditional logic of textbooks on organization theory. It is important to recognize that the book and the different chapters are built around practical issues rather than theories. This structure might cause some confusion for the reader prepared to meet the traditional presentation of theories in the field. To emphasize the strong link to theory that we have in the book, Table 1.1 below summarizes the chapters in which the established theoretical fields are presented. The reader should, however, be aware that a certain theory can be used in more than one chapter and the table only indicates where the major presentation of that particular theory is being done.

The presentation of theories of organization and management

In order to facilitate learning each chapter follows the same structure. Each chapter opens with a case based on a practical issue of relevance for management practice in today's industry. The case is followed by questions aimed to help the student organize the reading throughout the chapter. We then present the relevant theories pertaining to the practical issue and

Table 1.1 Theoretical areas addressed in the book

Area	Chapter	Area	Chapter
Organizational structure	Chapter 2	Charismatic leadership	Chapter 6
Bureaucracy	Chapter 2	Transformational leadership	Chapter 6
Environment	Chapter 2	Post-materialist values	Chapter 6
Contingency theory	Chapter 2	Diversity	Chapter 6
Divisional structure	Chapter 2	Gender and leadership	Chapter 6
Configurational approach	Chapter 2	Intersectionality	Chapter 6
Organizational boundaries	Chapter 2	Middle management	Chapter 6
Collaboration	Chapter 3	Decision-making	Chapter 7
Technology	Chapter 3	Institutional theory	Chapter 7
Sociotechnology	Chapter 3	Organization culture	Chapter 7
Technology and structure	Chapter 3	Innovation management	Chapter 8
Information technology	Chapter 3	Organization form and innovation	Chapter 8
Scientific management and Taylorism	Chapter 4	Network organization	Chapter 8
Labour process theory	Chapter 4	Planned change	Chapter 9
Work organization	Chapter 4	Emergent change	Chapter 9
Total Quality Management (TQM)	Chapter 4	Institutional theory and change	Chapter 9
Business Process Re-engineering (BPR)	Chapter 4	Radical change	Chapter 9
Management control	Chapter 4	Continuous improvement	Chapter 9
Organization routines and rules	Chapter 4	Learning	Chapter 10
Hawthorne studies	Chapter 5	Behaviourism	Chapter 10
Motivation	Chapter 5	Cognitive theory	Chapter 10
Recruitment	Chapter 5	Situated learning	Chapter 10
Human Resource Management (HRM)	Chapter 5	Risk and learning	Chapter 10
Leadership in organizations	Chapter 6	Learning from catastrophes	Chapter 10
Situational leadership	Chapter 6	Knowledge and knowledge management	Chapter 10

use the introductory case to enlighten issues specific to the theoretical approach at hand. The latter will be found in what we call *link boxes* in which we reflect upon the theories out of the contemporary practice presented in the case. In addition, *minicases* are used to further exemplify how theory may serve to shed light on contemporary managerial issues. Each chapter ends with a summary and a conclusion, suggestions for further readings and study questions.

As the book is organized around practical issues and managerial activities rather than chronologically or conceptually, the reader will find some of the theoretical perspectives presented in more than one part of the book. In order to outline the various themes and theories, we present a table providing an overview of the themes discussed in the various blocks and chapters. Table 1.1 is structured chapter-wise and it is noteworthy that it does not suggest that theories are to be conceived of as a 'box of tools' that can be easily disentangled and understood in isolation from one another. On the contrary, the various theories of organization and management are interrelated in manifold and complex ways and in many cases, specific theories are developed as responses to previous theories (e.g., the so-called Human Relations School, namely, scientific management), but for the sake of clarity and didactic reasons, the various theories and theoretical perspectives are listed as if such a compartmentalization is possible. Therefore, the reader is asked to think of theories as being inherently related rather than freestanding contributions.

Historical overview of management practice and management innovations

Organization theory, as a field of research and study, has its roots in the period around the turn of the twentieth century, but individual organizational practices can of course be traced much further back. As background for the subsequent discussions in this book we provide a brief overview of the practices and processes that led to the growth of contemporary organizations and to the study of organization theory. Even if the history of organizations can easily be compared in age with that of Bible tales or the story of the Pyramids, we focus on the more recent past, namely, organizing during the Industrial Age and the growth of the modern corporation and during the recent post-industrial era characterized by an increased importance of service industries and knowledge-intensive and creative work.

As a result of social and intellectual changes in the seventeenth and eighteenth centuries, new ways of conceiving of the world were gradually established. By the Enlightment, scientific thinking and rational reason received a prominent role in Western societies. In addition, the French revolution brought forward new ideals regarding constitution and equality. By the middle of the 1800s—the century of industrialization and substantial urbanization—new organizational forms were established. In the military, people had a long tradition of organizing in the sense of placing people and objects in the right place at the right time (Czarniawska, 2002). It took time, however, before that knowledge spread to companies because people in military circles didn't describe their organization methods in a way that was understandable to company organizers (George, 1972). Another organizing form came from the Catholic Church that had built a hierarchical structure of the Pope, the cardinals, the bishops, and other church officials, dating from the year 1054. Through the church mass, the clergy communicated with the religious community.

While the Church, the military, and some elements in society knew how to organize and lead, their experiences were not transferable to the factory system (Wren, 1972). The reasons were many. First, the factory system and capitalism were doctrinally separate from the Church (where it was considered un-Christian to earn money from others) and politically separate from the military. Second, the entrepreneurs who drove capitalism generally had no military experience. A third reason was that it would be a long time before companies had a hierarchy equivalent to those of the older organizations. Small companies were generally 'flat hierarchies' directly monitored by the owner and a few foremen that managed the day-to-day work. While the Church had developed a rather sophisticated international bureaucratic organization, companies in the first half of the nineteenth century were still relatively small.

The beginning of industrialization

In connection with the growth of the nation-state, countries began to develop along organizational lines. In the beginning, countries were even linked to the economic system that became more trend-setting during the Middle Ages through mercantilism since, for the first time, it was permissible to accumulate capital in the Christian world. This change of attitude about money laid one of the foundation stones that led to the creation of large companies that could grow through industrialization (Weber, 1904).

During the 1700s a new view of people began to appear in Western philosophy—a view generally attributed to The Age of Enlightenment—that had been foreshadowed in the 1600s by developments in the natural sciences when more and more people began to focus on material progress and scientific evidence. Whereas people previously were considered fixed in society on the basis of their religion, their guilds or other social connections, according to this new outlook they now could change their social position. Leading thinkers began to believe that people's fundamental driving force was to improve their own lot in life. People began to view humanity's efforts to seek satisfaction and happiness in life as natural and inevitable. A good society was a society that gave its citizens the opportunity to pursue this course. The implications were not that people are selfish, unpatriotic or irreligious; rather they are simply striving after their own growth and development (Reich, 2000). In short, it was no longer considered greedy to earn money for one's own self-interest (Hirschman, 1977). This idea was supported by Adam Smith, among others.

At the beginning of the 1500s the production system consisted of manual labour by which people produced only as much as they needed for themselves. Production became more efficient with the craft system that developed in England, especially the system for turning wool into cloth. This occurred at the same time as the enclosure movement in agriculture occurred (when landowners forced their farmer-tenants from their farms by fencing in common land). As a result, clothing manufacturers could employ the sudden surplus of farmers in the cottage industries of cloth making. In its turn, this work created different work tasks in the cloth industry (carding, spinning, and weaving) that were *separated*, thus *routinizing* each task.

There are various reasons that explain why this system was gradually industrialized. One reason was that it was difficult to control the workers who sat in their own homes and handled the wool. They could easily steal raw materials under a system where there were no controls. At the same time, as the technical knowledge developed so that more expensive machinery and equipment were needed, more capital was required to buy the necessary tools. Previously the farmers in the cottage industries owned their tools and the clothing manufacturers owned the product; under the new system, the manufacturers owned both. There then developed a new economic doctrine of *laissez-faire* (in French, 'allow to do') that proposed that the marketplace should be free of government control and that private ownership was a natural and absolute right.

Challenging mercantilism and its support of monopolies, Adam Smith, published his book, *The Wealth of Nations*, in 1776. Under monopolies, while the merchants' profits certainly increased, only a few people reinvested their proceeds. With no competition, there was no reason to invest in improved and more efficient production techniques. Smith believed that free trade was preferable to mercantilism's 'favourable balance of trade'. Since mercantilism unavoidably contributed to high prices in a country, people of that country would trade in foreign markets for what they needed. Mercantilism also made it unattractive for other countries to trade with that country. Smith claimed that the wealth of nations would increase most rapidly if private citizens were allowed to act in accordance with their own self-interests. Therefore the State, in adopting a *laissez-faire* policy, should not intervene in the marketplace. Smith thus advocated the natural freedom of a simple and clear economic system with free competition where all actors in the marketplace would trade in the most mutually beneficial way, 'led by an invisible hand.'

According to Smith, the core of the market mechanism was *specialization* and *manpower*. Smith wrote:

'The greatest improvement in the productive powers of labour, and the greater part of the skill, dexterity, and judgement with which it is anywhere directed or applied, seem to have been the effects of the division of labour.'
(Smith, 1776: 3).

Smith's pin factory example is well-known. According to Smith, an unspecialized pin-maker, not trained to the trade, could produce 20 pins in a day. By a division of labour, separating the 18 pin-makers' tasks, up to 48,000 pins could be produced in a day. Specialization meant that one worker would draw out the metal wire, a second worker would straighten the wire, a third would cut it, a fourth would point it, a fifth would grind the pin top to make it ready for the head, and so forth, until finally the last of the 18 tasks, placing the pins in paper, was completed. Although the pin factory was a unique case, Smith believed that by division of labour productivity could be increased in other areas of industry.

It is often assumed that Smith wrote about many of management's main problems. There are even readers who believe that he was referring to something other than what we now call the division of labour. According to Wren (1972), Smith dealt foremost with the theory of how specialization could lead to an increased number of products, and it was only later that people came to regard specialization as a function in itself. Another objection is that Smith wrote about handcraft production, which is different from the much more complex production of factories. This conclusion, however, is contradicted by the fact that Smith called attention to the division of work in the entire factory.

Technological innovation

Technological innovation is often pointed to as a critical factor of the Industrial Revolution. However, there were a number of contributing factors. Between the 1500s and the 1700s in England, as agricultural methods improved, farmers could produce more. More food led to a rapid increase in the population that in its turn led to an increase in the workforce (in which many were out of work because of the land enclosures). At the same time, trade increased and a surplus of capital began to build up. Similarly, society's structure changed as political institutions recommended the *laissez-faire* doctrine, the judiciary advocated the rights of possession and John Calvin's theology, which supported individualism, dominated religious institutions.

Technological innovations, such as the Spinning Jenny, the Flying Shuttle, the printing press, and the steam engine, were manufactured in factories. These machines had been previously used as work tools, but there was a difference between tools and modern, factory-made machinery. As Max Weber (1978) explained, tools served people, but in order for the modern machinery to work, people themselves were placed in service to the machines. During the 1700s, however, the modern factory—characterized by common ownership where the factory owner owns the workplace, the equipment, raw materials and the brand—developed in only a few places.

As a consequence of the technical innovations there was a great need not only for labour but also for new ways-of-working (Wren, 1972). In former times, workers had the right of self-determination, worked independently, and lived close to Nature. Now the industrialized system required a so-called psychological adaptation from them so that they would fit into the new work environment (Dillard, 1967). Workers no longer controlled the means of production and instead sold their wage-labour, resulting in the final separation between labour and capital. Children were placed under the supervision of foremen, and discipline for all wage earners was introduced. Wages were low because the 'natural wage' was considered the amount necessary only for a minimum existence. Unions were illegal. With the introduction of artificial lighting in factories, working hours were increased from 14 up to 18 hours a day. In addition, the unregulated workplace meant that people worked in horrific conditions.

Industrialization and organization

Thus, it is clear that an 'employee', in the sense we mean today, is a recent phenomenon that first arose at the end of the 1800s (Jacques, 1996). The first step to becoming an employee was the craft system where the worker changed from an independent craftsman to a wage earner (George, 1972). Yet the development of the employee didn't happen overnight, but rather occurred gradually in different countries and in different ways. The manager and management developed in a similar fashion.

Technological innovations in machinery created a need for factories, and factory operations required management and organization. The expanding markets required more manpower, more machinery, greater production capability and, of course, more capital to finance the expansion. More people (i.e., men) in authority were needed who could supervise the workers and the factory operations. The division of labour and the specialization of the workforce also required control and coordination of the work efforts. This led to the origin and growth of the factory system with its need for management and leadership (Wren, 1972). As the factories grew, entrepreneurs found that they could not control all activities by themselves, and so began the delegation of responsibility to managers.

As the leadership experiences of the military and the Church were irrelevant for the factory managers, they soon developed their own leadership styles of solving problems as they arose. James Montgomery, an English mechanic who wrote on factory management in the early nineteenth century, is generally cited as the first person to prepare written directions on what a manager should do. According to Montgomery, the manager's responsibilities were to be just, impartial, firm, decisive, and always alert in order to prevent problems in production (Wren, 1972). Specifically, the manager should determine the quality and quantity of the work, repair machinery, control costs, and be reasonably strict in disciplinary matters concerning the employees.

The labour force was recruited from people who were part of the rural urban drift but also from people growing up as a result of the rapid increase in the urban birth rate. These needed to be trained since there was a scarcity of factory-educated personnel. Training was a problem because most people in these early days were illiterate. Therefore these first managers used drawings, oral instructions, and demonstrations to teach workers through trial and error. For those workers who came from the multi-task agricultural environment, the work requirements in the factories were more specialized as well as 'deskilling'. The workers also had to develop the disciplined habits typical of the factory system's ways-of-working that meant, among other things, being on time and staying at one's workstation.

Working conditions were generally grim. In many factories at the beginning of the 1800s women and children made up to 75% of the workforce. Children could begin work as early as five years of age. Sometimes they worked up to 14 hours a day in the factory and, unsurprisingly, often fell asleep at work. Robert Owen, a nineteenth-century English social reformer and factory owner, tried to improve production in his factory by providing education and healthcare for children, limiting their work hours, and building homes for workers. He also designed a subtle work incentive system using coloured codes at each workstation to encourage employees to monitor their own productivity.

Controlling the work in factories was a problem for management. Double-entry bookkeeping, as an accounting system, was first described by Luca Pacioli in 1496, but few people knew about it, and fewer understood it. Even when wages, materials, and revenues were accounted for, there was no coordination with costs through the profit and loss calculation and with product management.

Consistent with the ideas of the Enlightenment, the systematic scientific method was promoted. Charles Babbage, a nineteenth century English inventor and mechanical engineer, believed that technical discoveries should assist people in achieving something. With the help of the scientific method he developed a way to *observe factories* that was the forerunner of time and motion studies. The factory observer should study a factory's operations using a list of questions, for example, on the use of materials, the normal spoilage, costs, prices, the end market, the workers and their wages, the skills required, and the work cycle. Furthermore, Babbage, like Adam Smith, advocated the division of labour that he believed could reduce the time it took to learn a new skill, reduce materials spoilage, reduce time wasted by moving between work stations, require fewer production tools, and increase workers' skills as they repeated the same process. The profit-sharing system is rooted in an idea promoted by Babbage who thought productivity would improve if workers' wages were linked to the factory's profits (Wren, 1972).

The growth of the large and modern corporation

Before the American Civil War (1861–1865), American employers took very little notice of the welfare and working conditions of their employees. It was not until after 1870 that British industrialists, such as Owen, Montgomery and Cadbury who had articulated ideas about taking care of workers, received any attention. Before 1840 companies were relatively small, with few middle managers. The top managers at this time were still owners of companies, either as partners or as majority shareholders (Chandler, 1977).

The construction of the Erie Canal in New York State between 1815 and 1825 was a major project that, for the first time in US history, required an administrative structure to control costs efficiently and to properly assess the work of managers and employees. In part, these management experiences from the Erie Canal construction benefited the subsequent construction of the railroads. The large and expensive railroad projects were the first major undertakings in the USA where people could try different leadership styles. Since there were many shareholders, the projects required many managers in charge of extremely complex and varied administrative tasks. As Chandler (1977) describes, the railroad companies became the first organizational structures with carefully defined lines of responsibility and authority as well as clear lines of communication between the head offices, the department offices, and the field units. Henry Varnum Poor, a nineteenth century business writer who focused on the railroads, was an early advocate of three principles he thought railroad managers should follow: organization through careful division of labour, clear communication, and good information (Barley and Kunda, 1992). Daniel McCallum, a nineteenth century railroad engineer, was another early manager in the railroad industry. He developed the first formal organization plan and claimed that good management was based on good discipline, detailed work descriptions, frequent and exact performance reports, and specific lines of authority. McCallum also thought wages and promotion should be based on merit. By requiring employees to wear uniforms, he believed people could recognize degrees of authority, thus limiting the possibilities for employees to work in their own self-interests (Barley and Kunda, 1992).

In the railroad projects, between 1850 and 1860, a flood of financial and statistical data were developed that could be used to control and evaluate the work of the various managers. Between 1870 and 1880 these measures were standardized as management tools useful in increasing efficiency and productivity in the rail transport industry. In the long run, these tools led to better use of railroad technology with bigger engines, larger carriages, and better signal systems. Full-time, salaried managers with special skills and education were needed by the railroads as well. As administrative hierarchies were created to manage these construction projects, railroad managers realized they could make a career in these companies. This possibility separated them from other top managers on agricultural plantations or in the textile industry. The result was a more professional view of work in railroad management, and an increase in professionalism among its managers (Chandler, 1977).

In the years between 1880 and 1890, making improvements in industrial settings became something of a trend. Cornelius Vanderbilt, the nineteenth century shipping and railroad entrepreneur, built a railroad empire in the USA as a founder of one of the first modern corporations. However, he also supported the YMCA (Young Men's Christian Association) because it provided railroad workers with physical and spiritual assistance and even discouraged alcohol consumption. Other industrialists, in an effort to improve the lives of their workers, built libraries and recreational halls, offered education to workers and their families, founded social clubs and made their factories cleaner and more aesthetic.

Yet, as companies grew, the problems between managers and workers also grew. Face-to-face meetings were rare. At the same time, owing to the need for more workers, more immigrants with different customs and behaviours and even different ideas about work, were employed (Barley and Kunda, 1992). Between 1868 and 1879, industrial wages in the USA declined by 25%. The unions' membership increased in the opposite direction (Jacques, 1996). The combination of the increased number of immigrants with socialist ideas, lower wages and the growth of the unions led to confrontations in the marketplace.

Now the employers, when faced with conflict, began to understand the divisions in a workplace system that was built on cooperation. There also arose a movement that was intended to improve the lot of the workers rather than to improve their workplace conditions (Barley and Kunda, 1992). Companies had become a central part of workers' lives (e.g., as the company built houses, schools, churches, libraries, etc., for workers). Such efforts were designed to maintain order in society so that the industrial work would be performed peacefully. The goal of management had turned to changing the workers.

At the end of the 1880s, mass production was introduced in the USA. One notable example of mass production was the Ford River Rouge Complex in Michigan where cars were manufactured on an assembly line. Mass production involved using work processes where technology allowed several production processes to be performed under the same roof (e.g., manufacture of cars or revolvers). The first modern managers, who saw how to improve the organizational design with the help of better production flows, better production processes, and various innovations in managing the work, came from companies that used mass production. While fewer workers were required to produce the same amount in this manufacturing system, more managers were needed to supervise the different processes.

Turning to 1900

Together these developments caused the USA, from the 1890s forward, to become the world's leading industrialized nation. In 1913, the USA had 36% of the industrial production in the world, Germany had 16%, and England had 14% (Chandler, Jr. 1990). The difference among the three countries was that it was only in England, with its smaller investment in industry, that the company founders and their families continued to dominate management. Germany, which grew most rapidly when industrialization began, developed in a way similar to that of the USA. In these two countries, entrepreneurs invested in large manufacturing units and personnel in order to take advantage of large-scale production. Efficient methods of organizing, both of the physical facilities and of employee relationships, were developed. In the development of thinking around management and control of organizations and companies before the 1900s, the emphasis was on technology over organizing principles. Management was more concerned with finance, production processes, marketing and labour than with rational methods. It is only with Taylor's scientific management theories that the rational manager appeared on the organizational scene. In the 1800s, the tools, technologies, and strategies of modern management had not yet emerged.

The problem of worker challenge vs. worker monotony continued being a concern for both industry and researchers during the 1920s. During the First World War, industry realized it must increase its productivity radically in order to satisfy the war machine. In 1915, when the workday for women in a war materials factory was twelve hours, there were enormous problems because of the number of work accidents. Following a decision by a company committee with responsibility for employees' health, the workday was reduced to ten hours per day, which halved the number of accidents. The goal for researchers and company managements was to find the maximum productivity level, and that required reducing employees' work challenges as well as their fatigue. It was understood that there was a complicated connection involved, and so doctors and biologists were employed to research the physiological aspects related to the percentage of lactic acid in overexerted muscles. Further, because of the practice of *scientific management*, together with modern production techniques, employees had lost control over their work that had become repetitive and tedious. This loss of control led first and foremost, to the situation where employees were bored by the work's monotony rather than challenged by its tasks. Yet studies showed that employees in certain factories found their work tasks utterly boring, while in other factories, with the same work tasks, the employees were happy and content (Mayo, 1933). Not just the nature of the work, but also the social conditions relative to the length of the workday and the compensation system, among other things, seemed to influence employees' opinions about their repetitive work.

Concurrently, personnel management was becoming an established and professional group category. Personnel managers had shown that if employment conditions improved, productivity levels might also increase and personnel turnover might be reduced in certain companies by up to 300% annually (Gillespie, 1991).

Summary and conclusions

The history of the management practices and management innovation shows that changes in management practice are dependent on a series of interrelated social, cultural, technological, economic, and juridical changes. New technologies such as the railroad or new spinning technologies in the textile industry created economies of scale which brought larger factories which in turn increased the demand for a middle management organization tier and the creation of a capital market separated ownership from the control of the organizations and firms. International migration and urbanization brought new categories of workers to the towns and cities, demanding new organization of work, no longer relying on the century-long tradition of master-apprentice training but on an effective division of labour. The history of management practices and management innovation thus suggests that management thinking is both the effect of complex social changes at the same time as managerial practice is itself playing an active role in forming the history. For instance, the idea of separating ownership from control, of central importance for the modern economy and the financial markets, helped provide capital for new industries as money was generated, e.g., the American railway industry could be channelled into new ventures. In other words, management practice and management innovation need to be understood in a historical context.

Take your learning further

online resource centre

http://www.oxfordtextbooks.co.uk/orc/erikssonzetterquist/

Visit the Online Resource Centre which accompanies this book to enrich your understanding of this chapter.

Students: explore web links and further reading suggestions. Keep up to date with the latest developments via 'What happened next' updates to appropriate cases from within the book.

Lecturers: you will find seminar exercises and teaching notes, for use in class or assessment.

PART I
MANAGING SYSTEMS AND TECHNOLOGY

CHAPTER 2 Organizational boundaries and structures   19

CHAPTER 3 Information technology and business systems   47

CHAPTER 4 Operations management in day-to-day work   75

CHAPTER 2
Organizational boundaries and structures

Intel—formal structure, boundaries, and situational demands

Intel Corporation, the worlds largest producer of microprocessers, has a corporate level structure reflecting their large product groups, a so called *divisional structure*. In 2008 Intel was formally organized in 6 divisions: Digital Enterprise, Flash Memory, Digital Home, Mobility, Digital Health, and Channel Platforms. The Digital Enterprise Group is the largest with 55% of consolidated net revenue in 2008, followed by the Mobility Group as second largest with 42% of net revenue. The Digital Entreprise Group has, however, shrunk from 65% in 2005 and 72% in 2004, while the Mobility Group is gaining ground (up from 29% in 2005 and 20% in 2004). These figures reflect the major challenges for a company like Intel with rapid technological and market-related changes, creating issues in designing the formal organization in a way that enables the company to deal with the changes and demands they face. On 27 December 2008 the company had 83,900 employees and net revenues of 37.6 billion dollars. The research and development budget was 5.7 billion dollars (2008) with more than 50% of sales in the Asia-Pacific region (2008).

Intel's customers range from original equipment manufacturers (OEMs) and original design manufacturers (ODMs) who make computer systems, handheld devices, and telecommunications and networking communications equipment, to PC and network communications product users who buy PC components, board-level products, networking, communications, and storage products (2006 Annual Report Intel Corporation).

Intel has its production facilities concentrated in Arizona, New Mexico, Oregon, Massachusetts, California, and Colorado, with 68% of the wafer manufacturing (microprocessors, chipsets, NOR flash memories and communications silicon fabrication) in the mentioned facilities. Thirty two per cent (32%) of the manufacturing is conducted at facilities in Ireland and Israel. The manufacturing organization has to continually adapt to technological changes with new generations of manufacturing process technology being launched at a rapid pace. The start-up costs for preparing a factory for a new manufacturing process technology is high, but it is believed that the benefits from moving to faster microprocesses (e.g., by utilizing less space per transistor, reducing heat output from each transistor and improving power efficiency) outweighs the start-up costs. Manufacturing is primarily done by Intel themselves, and the use of subcontractors is limited to manufacturing board-level products and systems. Intel also follows a strategy of using multiple suppliers to reduce the dependence on a single supplier for critical materials and resources. After the manufacturing process, most components are subject to further assembly and test.

The microprocesser was invented in the late 1960s (Intel was founded in 1968) and the effectiveness of them has followed a stable pattern, known as Moore's law. Intel's co-founder Gordon Moore predicted already in 1965 that the number of transistors on a chip would double about every second year, a prediction that still holds up to this day. Change is thus a fact of life for Intel, and a relentless focus on research and development has been necessary to survive in this highly competitive and dynamic market.

The formal structure on the corporate level is, however, only one part of the full story of Intel's organizational structure. Below the divisional structure the company has to deal with a number of tensions and challenges in its day-to-day operations. There are, for instance, a number of tensions inherent in managing Moore's law, and Intel needs to build a flexible and boundary spanning structure that enables the company to draw on resources both internally and externally. This can not be done in a traditional *machine bureaucracy*. At the same time Moore's law forces the company to run an extremely efficient production process, in order to cut the cost of producing semi-conductors.

Intel is well known for its cutting-edge manufacturing processes, and a good example is the Fab 32 (a Fab is a manufacturing unit in Intel) in Chandler, Arizona, that opened in the second half of 2007. Fab 32 was developed to introduce the 45 nm process technology, being the second factory to produce 45 nm chips. The factory is a highly automated unit with around 1,000 employees working in such positions as process, automation, yield engineers and senior manufacturing technicians. When launching these plans in 2007, Intel was already planning for the next step—to introduce the new 32 nm manufacturing technology during 2009. Paul Ottelini (the CEO of Intel) explains Intel's manufacturing philosophy in the following way:

> 'For Intel, manufacturing is a key competitive advantage that serves as the underpinning for our business and allows us to provide customers with leading-edge products in high volume'
> (www.intel.com/pressroom/archive/releases/20050725corp.htm)

Once a factory is designed and operating, its formal structure and mode of operating fits with the machine bureaucracy model of organizing. At the same time a unit like Fab 32 requires a high level of flexibility and a high level of interaction between manufacturing, marketing, and research. Intel therefore has to incorporate seemingly conflicting ways of organizing in the same company and to manage the coordination issues and problems based on these different orientations. Intel uses a factory strategy called 'Copy Exactly' to solve the problem of getting production facilities up to speed quickly.

> 'The 'Copy Exactly' strategy creates great flexibility for Intel's factory network. Because each fab is nearly identical, wafers can be partially completed in one fab and finished in another, yet yield at the same level as if the wafer were built in only one factory'
> (www.intel.com/pressroom/archive/backgrnd/copy_exactly.htm)

Source: Information for the Intel case was compiled from the 2008 and 2009 annual reports, and from corporate information available at www.intel.com. Andy Groves' autobiography, *Only the Paranoid Survive*, has also provided information for this case study.

Questions

Considering the complex and dynamic environment in which Intel operates—how should they design their formal organizational structure for long term survival?

What are the primary design principles that Intel could use to ensure that the organization achieves a balance between order and flexibility?

What are the managerial challenges involved in making a planned formal structure work in practice?

Introduction

This chapter introduces the reader to a key area of organization theory—the role and significance of formal organizational structures in managing operations within and outside the boundaries of the organization. The case introduction and the questions posed above show that formal structures do matter for managers, but that the solutions and descriptions offered by traditional textbooks on organization theory are not always relevant in today's business environment. This chapter will deepen the understanding of the managerial challenges introduced in the Intel case above, while at the same time thoroughly introducing the reader to theories on organizational boundaries and structures.

The questions above touch upon many of the major concepts and theories in the field of organization theory, and managers in Intel, and, in fact, any serious student of the functioning of organizations, will have to face more detailed questions such as:

How should the company be organized to meet conflicting demands internally and externally?

Should decision-making rights be widely distributed in the organization or should decisions be taken centrally?

What is the external boundary of the formal organization, and how should it be managed? Should temporary hired personnel, consultants, strategic partners and long-term suppliers be included in the formal structure, and to what extent should they take part in internal processes?

How should the formal structure interact with internal processes?

What balance should the company have between in-house activities and outsourcing?

What is the optimal balance between a stable structure and an agile structure?

Intriguing questions, and with no clear-cut answers.

Many of the challenges found in Intel are consequences of the sheer size of the company, but they will also be found in small and medium sized companies. The constant struggle to make sense of the variety of products and product groups in the formal structure is an issue most companies have to face. In the case of Intel, they have been subject to rapid changes in the balance between product groups, and the current structure with 6 groups reflects one type of logic. The choice of structural logic is a major theme in this chapter, where different types of logics are presented and put in a historical context. The chapter expands on the idea that the formal structure is designed to match situational demands, or as Lawrence and Lorsch (1967) put it:

> What kind of organization does it take to deal with various economic and market conditions?

This matching between formal structure and situational demands is illustrated in the link box below.

LINK BOX

Keeping up with changes at Intel

The Intel case from the chapter introduction above illustrates how dependent a company is on meeting external demands. These demands emanate from customers, suppliers, competitors, and other stakeholders and they constantly put pressure on the company to react and deal with the demands. Intel is operating at the crossroads of several industries and in the meeting of different technologies, including information technology, telecommunications, entertainment and media. The market scene is constantly changing and Intel is working relentlessly to keep up with, or preferably to be ahead of, the changes. Companies such as Apple, Google, Microsoft, Nokia, and many others provide both threats as well as opportunities for Intel. A highly relevant and important question is how to design the organization to meet these demands. The speed of change in these converging industries is very high and this puts special pressure on companies like Intel to organize in a flexible way to be able to meet all the different changes they are facing. The factory network described in the case is just one out of many examples of how this is done on an operational level, but, as implied in the quote from Lawrence and Lorsch (1967), it takes much more to design an effective structure. Organizations often face seemingly conflicting demands and they have to take different measures to meet them. Intel is a good example of a company that has, so far, succeeded in balancing between different demands for order, stability, and effectiveness on the one hand, and flexibility, entrepreneurship, and rapid growth on the other hand. Balancing these seemingly conflicting demands is at the very core of the most successful companies. While building a highly successful production organization, as in the factory network, they simultaneously manage to maintain a high degree of flexibility in their operations.

Reflection point: What are the major trends and changes that influence a company such as Intel?

This chapter will:

- Introduce the reader to the role and functions of organizational structures.
- Discuss different theoretical approaches to the analysis of organizational structures.

- Describe contingency and configurational approaches to the design of formal structure, and introduce the concept of fit between the organization and its environment.
- Discuss and problematize the concept of organizational boundaries

Why are organizational structures important?

Above, we introduced the idea that a company has a formal organizational structure which, properly designed, is instrumental in meeting different demands placed on the company. This simple starting point for the chapter is, however, not unproblematic. Organization theory has struggled over the years to locate and identify the object of study—organizations. It might seem straightforward to describe the organization by looking at the formal organizational chart. A complete organizational chart tells us at least three important things about how the organization is planned to work:

- It indicates the general lines of authority in the company and gives us some information about the degree of centralization/decentralization.
- It shows the general logic for grouping the company into units on different levels.
- It shows the number of decision-making levels (the hierarchy) in the company.

The organizational chart depicts the *formal organizational structure* in the company, but this is only part of the story of the functioning of organizations. Throughout the history of organization theory numerous attempts have been made to single out the features of organizations. A number of different approaches can be identified:

- Organizations as structures: Highlighted here are, for instance, important features such as rules and standards, hierarchic ordering of positions, unit grouping, and decision-making authority.
- Organizations as behavioural patterns: Here, important aspects include sharing goals, coordinating behaviour, dealing with stakeholders and coalitions.
- Organizations as cultures: In this perspective, focus is put on shared understandings, myths, artefacts, and ideologies.

Depending on which of the approaches the student of organizations take, the description and understanding of organizations will differ. In this chapter we will take a closer look at the first approach—organizations as structures. The dominant paradigm has, for the last 50 years, understood organizational structures to be 'blueprints' for how to coordinate human effort to reach a common goal. The blueprint can be more or less instrumental in reaching this goal and in meeting the situational demands placed on it. This paradigm has been given different names and is still a vibrant voice in the discussions in boardrooms. In the 1960s this paradigm was launched as the *general system theory* (Bertalanffy, 1968), and in a more narrow formulation as *contingency theory*. Even though **open system** theory and contingency theory have been heavily criticized they are still important parts of textbooks in organization theory, and they carry a lot of significance for practitioners even though the detailed prescriptions proposed by the pioneers in the 1960s and 1970s haven't stood the test.

MINICASE

The organizing of a megacompany—the case of Walmart

The specific structural features of any organization reflect a number of factors inside and outside the organization. These factors are referred to as contingency factors (these will be discussed in depth later in this chapter). Throughout the history of organization theory size has been singled out as one of the primary factors to consider when designing the formal structure of a company. This is especially evident in very large organizations, for instance, in megacompanies. Consider the example of Walmart, currently the largest company in the world, when measured by revenues (http://money.cnn.com/magazines/fortune/global500/2010). By the end of 2009, they employed no less than 2.1 million persons with revenues of up to a staggering 408 billion USD. How can such a huge company be organized? Walmart is a US based retail chain that operates a number of different types of stores and warehouses. Even though the company is firmly rooted in the US they are in the middle of a rapid expansion internationally. In fact, more than 30% of revenues come from the operations abroad, and the foreign operations are put together in a separate division called Walmart International. For the US operations the company is organized in two separate divisions. Walmart Stores is by far the largest and accounts for around 67% of the annual revenues. It houses the different retail formats such as the Discount Stores and the Supercenters, both of which are familiar signs in any American city. The second division is called Sam's Club which houses a chain of warehouse clubs, open to members. A huge company such as Walmart needs to rely on a finely tuned combination of decentralized operations (each store or warehouse operating as an 'independent' unit) at the same time as overall operations are tightly controlled. Walmart, like many huge retailers, has, for example, developed a highly effective logistical system to make sure that goods are bought at lowest possible prices, and delivered to stores and warehouses when needed without carrying big stocks of inventory.

Joan Woodward (1965: 10) gave the following definition of a formal structure in an organization:

> 'Formal organization is the stable and explicit pattern of prescribed relationships inside the firm; it covers a defined system of jobs, each of which carries a definite measure of authority, responsibility and accountability, the whole being consciously designed to enable those employed to work together in accomplishing their objectives.'

The importance of formal structures resides in how useful they are in guiding/controlling behaviour. This clearly reflects a managerial point of view borrowed from earlier theories inherent in the machine bureaucracy model of organizations described below. People like F.W. Taylor, H. Fayol, and F.B. Gilbreth (all practitioners with ambitions to generalize on their practical ideas) popularized the idea that organizations can, and should, be treated and managed in the same way as mechanical systems. They can be designed in purposeful ways and be properly managed by people employed to govern and take decisions. This is bluntly put by Taylor (1911: 9–10):

> 'The writer asserts as a general principle that in almost all of the mechanic arts the science which underlies each act of each workman is so great and amounts to so much that the workman who is best suited to actually doing the work is incapable of fully understanding this science, without the guidance and help of those who are working with him or over him, either through lack of education or through insufficient mental capacity.'

The idea of scientific approaches led Taylor and others to formulate general principles of management that they thought were applicable to any situation. The work of Taylor and others as it pertains to how to operate the firm will be presented in more depth in Chapter 4. Taylor has, however, a few things to say about the structuring of organizations. His major theoretical contribution to this part of organization theory is without doubt the idea of *functional foremanship*, which was an attempt to deal with the problem of the foreman's limited expertise in all areas of supervision. Following the idea of specialization, he suggested that the foreman's authority should be limited to his or her area of expertise, leading to a situation where a worker could have more than one foreman depending on the complexity of the situation and the expertise of the foreman.

DEFINITION BOX

Functional foremanship

The predominant managerial model in Taylor's day was the unitary leadership model, which assumes that each individual reports to only one manager in the *line organization*, creating an unbroken chain of command. This model is very straightforward and has, over the years, carried a lot of practical appeal. Taylor's idea of functional foremanship radically challenged this idea by arguing that an individual worker could report to up to 6–7 different foremen. Depending on the complexity of the managerial tasks, more than one foreman might be needed to supervise the worker. When implemented this often created friction between the managers and often led to compromises. One such compromise that gained a lot of attention and was later incorporated in the contingency framework was Harrington Emerson's idea of the *staff and line organization*. In his modification of Taylor's ideas the chain of command in the line organization is preserved and the technical expertise needed for supervising workers is collected into special staff units, formally outside the strict line organization.

The classical organization theories of Taylor, Fayol, and others, trying to state general principles of management and organizing, were soon challenged from different perspectives. The idea of organizations as structures that are deliberately designed to meet certain goals was challenged by the *Human Relations School* with a growing awareness of the informal and non-planned aspects of organizations and formal structures (Roethlisberger and Dickson,

1939). With the open system view, the emphasis on finding one best way of organizing was challenged and with contingency theory, the ambition was rather to identify which structural features were best adapted to fit a specific environmental situation.

During the formative period of the 1950s and 1960s, organization theory was transformed into a scientific discipline where organizations and formal structures were subject to more rigorous research, as compared to the anecdotal evidence offered by Taylor, Fayol, and others in the early years. The interest of scholars and managers moved away from trying to find general principles on how to organize work, which was a major preoccupation of Taylor. Reflecting the growing size and the more complex competitive reality of many companies, focus shifted towards finding the *determinants of organization structure* (Scott, 2004). Compared to the global setting and turbulent market conditions of most large companies today, the competitive landscape of the 1950s was very tranquil and it made a lot of sense, at the time, to try to identify stable determinants of structures (Walsh, Meyer, and Schoonhoven, 2006).

Formal structures are described above as prescriptive tools for managing in organizations and are believed to have important roles in coordinating human effort towards common goals. Any organization needs to find the design principles that fit their specific circumstances, and this is illustrated using the example of Intel in the link box below.

LINK BOX

Dividing by output

A good example of a prescriptive design principle in the Intel case from the chapter introduction is how the company is divided into six semi-autonomous parts or divisions. Dividing a company in semi-autonomous units by markets or products/product groups is, by far, the most common way of designing the overall structure of companies. The logic of dividing according to markets and/or products is simple—you put decision-making closer to the customer/market. Today, the issue is not whether you should have a divisional structure or not, but rather which markets and/or product groups to focus on. The divisional way of dividing the company tells us a lot about how top management in Intel view the company, for instance, what the strategic priorities are at the moment. In the Intel case the design principle used for dividing the company is the major product groups, what is referred to as grouping by *output*. Intel is not different from many other companies in using their major product areas as the basis for dividing the organization in logical parts. The two major units are Digital Enterprise and the Mobility Group (55 and 42 per cent of 2008 net revenues respectively). The DE group incorporates a large number of product offerings that are built into desktop and nettop computers, as well as servers, workstations, and other products making up the infrastructure of the Internet. A division in a large company, such as Intel, can thus consist of a large number of different products. This indicates that it takes a lot of strategic thinking to decide on how to divide the company into logical units. Numerous studies (see for instance Whittington *et al.*, 1999) show that most larger companies have a divisional type of formal structure, and there are a number of different varieties available to choose from.

Reflection point: Dividing a large organization into coherent divisions is a common practice, but the specific type is up to the company to decide. How has Intel managed to split their organization into divisions?

This assumption inherent in both the machine bureaucracy model and contingency theory is not without problems. Irregardless of which perspective on organizations is being taken, any student of organizations and organization theory will have to face the basic difficulty of moving between individual level and the group level, be it small groups with intensive interaction between the members, larger groups where people share a number of features without working in the same company, or large collectives with less commonalities between the members (e.g., all people in Ukraine). If, for instance, an organization is defined by a shared purpose or goal, this leads to the important question—whose goal? As Katz and Kahn (1966), March and Simon (1958), Cyert and March (1963) and others have convincingly argued, there is no shortcut between the goals of individuals and the supposed goal of the organization. Katz and Kahn (1966: 19) make it part of their effort of defining organizations to warn against this trap.

> The fallacy here is equating the purposes or goals of organizations with the purposes and goals of individuals.

Elements of structures

In the previous section, the role and importance of formal organizational structures were introduced. Organizational structures can be described in various ways and there are different theoretical approaches taken to this. Based on Max Weber's ideas on the ideal type of bureaucracy, a number of features of formal structures were suggested in the first half of the twentieth century. Max Weber suggested the *monocratic bureaucracy* to offer the highest degree of effectiveness, being superior in terms of precision, stability, discipline, and reliability (Weber, 1978: 223) and described a number of features of this ideal type. Important to Weber was the use of goal or value-based rules, systems of rules rather than piecemeal rules, legal authority as superior to other forms of authority (e.g., traditional authority), and obedience based on membership (Weber, 1978: 217).

DEFINITION BOX

The machine bureaucracy

The machine bureaucracy is described by Henry Mintzberg (1983: 164) in the following way:

Highly specialized, routine operating tasks,
Very formalized procedures in the operating core,
A proliferation of rules, regulations, and formalized communication throughout the organization,
Large-sized units at the operating level,
Reliance on the functional basis for grouping tasks,
Relatively centralized power for decision-making,
An elaborate adminstrative structure with a sharp division between line and staff.

Weber's work on bureaucracy sparked a lot of sociological research and the idea of pure bureaucracy was criticized by renowned sociologists such as Talcott Parssons and Robert Merton. In his 1963 book, *The Dynamics of Bureaucracy*, Peter M Blau studied both manifest and latent consequences of bureaucracy, and showed that while consequences are sometimes functional for the organization, they are often dysfunctional. In his book *Social Theory and Social Structure*, Robert Merton (1968) described the dysfunctional aspects of bureaucracy and the inadequacy of bureaucracies to deal with changing circumstances, the so called *trained incapacity*. Through the internalization of rules and the increased use of categorization in decision-making, individuals become more and more rigid in their behaviour which eventually leads to an inability to deal with new situations that do not fit the prescriptions of the rules and pre-defined categories. In a similar way, Alvin Gouldner, in his *Patterns of Industrial Bureaucracy* (1954), described another dysfunction of bureaucracy referred to as the specification of *minimum level of acceptable performance*. By adapting specific rules, Gouldner noticed that this tended to conserve workers apathy by showing them exactly how much work needed to be done to *avoid* punishment.

From the sociological research on bureaucracy, following on the initial work done by Max Weber, a number of important elements of organizational structures can be identified. It is not an overstatement to say that the reliance on rules is a trademark of the bureaucratic model of formal structures. The work of sociologists such as Merton, Selznick, and Gouldner has shown how rules operate in practice and the anticipated and unanticipated consequences of applying rules to create control in organizations. The work of Weber on bureacracy also influenced a different trend in the development of organization theory with a focus on behavioural aspects of organizations. This was implied already in Chester Barnard's book *The Functions of the Executive* from 1938. Despite the title the book deals extensively with the problems of managing formal organizations and has inspired researchers to study the behavioural and psychological aspects of organization, rather than just formal aspects. In a crucial formulation Barnard (1938: 82) defined the basic elements of organizations in a way that emphasized the behavioural aspects:

- Persons that are willing to communicate with each other,
- Persons with a willingness to contribute action,
- Persons with a common sense of purpose,

The late 1950s saw the publication of a number of important books that have since become classics in the field of organization theory. Selznick, in his 1957 book *Leadership in Organizations*, criticized the bureacratic model of organizations, with its emphasis on formal systems of rules and objectives. His major contribution to organization theory was to describe organizations as *institutions*.

> 'An **"institution"**, on the other hand, is more nearly a natural product of social needs and pressures—a responsive, adaptive organism.'
> (Selznick, 1957: 5)

It was perfectly clear to Selznick that a formal organizational chart could, at best, prescribe a framework within which a much more rich and complete set of human behaviours took place, and that there was a complex set of interlinks between formal structure, organizational behaviour and the environment of which the organization was a part. In a similar fashion, March and Simon, in their 1958 book *Organizations*, explored the behavioural aspects of organizations. In their seminal book they criticized the assumptions of traditional organization theory where the human organism was viewed as a simple machine. March and Simon discussed a number of shortcomings in this machine model, several of which touched upon behavioural and psychological aspects of organizations. They were deeply troubled by the observations of Merton and others concerning dysfunctions of bureaucratic organizations and offered their own set of concepts to further explore the shortcomings of traditional theories. An important concept discussed by March and Simon (1958) was *motivation* which is directly drawn from Chester Barnards ideas of finding a balance between inducements and contributions.

'The net satisfactions which induce a man to contribute his efforts to an organization result from the positive advantages as against the disadvantages which are entailed.'
(Barnard, 1938: 140)

Lawrence and Lorsch, in their 1967 book *Organization and Environment*, studied the extent to which organizations were faced with different environmental demands and how these environmental demands related to the internal functioning of effective organizations. They were, in particular, interested in the two concepts *differentiation* and *integration*. Based on the open system theory view that organizations must be understood from a systemic perspective, they argued that any organization needs to solve two sets of challenges: how to divide the tasks of the organization and how to obtain integration between them.

The concepts of differentiation and integration are central to Lawrence and Lorsch's analysis. They describe how organizations differ in how they respond to environments through differentiation and integration. The two concepts are operationalized in the following way (Lawrence and Lorsch, 1967: 9ff):

DEFINITION BOX

Differentiation

- Differences among managers in different functional jobs in their orientation toward particular goals,
- Differences in the time orientation of managers in different parts of the organization,
- Differences in the way managers in various functional departments typically deal with their colleagues, that is, with their interpersonal orientation,
- Formality of structure.

DEFINITION BOX

Integration

- The quality of the state of collaboration that exists among departments that are required to achieve unity of effort by the demands of the environment.

One of the first and most elaborate attempts to formalize the study of organizational structures was the beforementioned study by Joan Woodward (1965). In her book *Industrial Organization* she described a number of structural components in a formal organization, such as:

- The number of distinct managerial levels between the board and the operators (what we usually refer to as the hierarchy),
- Span of control of chief executive and first-line supervisor (span of control means the number of persons reporting directly to the manager),
- Horizontal grouping into departments (the size of departments and the principles for grouping),
- Ratio of staff to industrial workers.

In an even more ambitious attempt to formalize the study of organizational structures, the so-called Aston School conducted a number of well-known studies during the 1960s and early 1970s which were reported in a series of articles in the top-ranked journal, *Administrative Science Quarterly*. In their 1963 article *A Conceptual Scheme for Organizational Analysis*, members of the Aston group (Pugh *et al.*, 1963) lay the foundation for a long series of influential articles. In this article they criticized both the Bureaucratic School of Weber and the Human Relations School of Mayo and others for not giving adequate attention to the comparative analysis of an extended range of structural factors in different firms. Six primary dimensions of strucutral factors were singled out:

- Specialization (division of labor within the organization),
- Standardization of procedures and roles,
- Formalization (the extent to which communications and procedures in an organization are written down and filed),
- Centralization (the locus of authority to make decisions affecting the organization,
- Configuration (the system of relationships between positions or jobs described in terms of the authority of superiors and the responsibility of subordinates),
- Flexibility (changes in organizational structure, measured in the amount, speed, and acceleration of change).

In the link box below the dimensions are illustrated with the Intel case that opened this chapter.

LINK BOX

Dimensions of structural factors at Intel

Parts of the six dimensions of structure described by Pugh *et al*. (1963) can be applied to the case of Intel. Centralization is represented by the corporate level, which governs the organization and makes decisions for the business as such. There are obviously many ways in which the six dimensions of structure can be combined to form a coherent overall structure, and it takes a detailed analysis to capture them all. A quick look at the organizational chart of Intel can, however, tell us a lot about parts of the structural dimensions. The degree of centralization is hard to tell from the general structure of the organization, but the divisional structure suggests that Intel is trying to minimize centralization and decentralize decision-making to divisions, and most probably even lower in each division. This is also something that is suggested in the literature as a way to deal with a dynamic environment. The tricky part comes when semi-independent units should be coordinated to reach common goals. This can be done by standardization. An example of standardization is the structure for establishing, manufacturing, and enrolling subcontractors. The market in which Intel operates requires the organization to have structures to handle flexibility, in order to reorganize as the market changes. In order to shed light on structures concerning formalization and configuration, more internal information describing the situation would be required. The six dimensions reflect the time in which they were described, the 1960s and early 1970s. The modern day company is using a variety of 'new' tools to make the formal structure work, for example, by integrated business information systems, formalized supply chains, and also by deliberately working with the culture of the organization.

Reflection point: The six dimensions discussed above are useful to 'put words' on the formal structure of an organization. Pick an organization you are familiar with—how is it formally organized?

The formal structure of companies, as shown in organizational charts, usually follows a certain logic. Mintzberg (1979) refers to this logic as designing the superstructure of the organization. The process of designing the superstructure goes from designing individual positions in the company to grouping them together in homogeneous groups. This process of grouping together towards higher levels of abstraction creates a hierarchic order in the company, and an organizational chart traditionally depicts the company as a hierarchic structure.

> 'Given a set of positions, designed in terms of specialization, formalization, and training and indoctrination, two obvious questions face the designer of organizational structure: How should these positions be grouped into units? And how large should each unit be?'

(Mintzberg, 1983)

Mintzberg suggested that the grouping of positions and units into larger wholes was a fundamental means of coordinating efforts in organizations, and that there was a need for finding a logic for this grouping. He proposed six different bases for grouping into larger units:

- **Knowledge** and skills (e.g., medical specialities in a hospital),
- Work processes and function (usually follows the production logic such as the assembly line),
- Time (e.g., different shifts in a factory),

- Output (creating units based on what they produce),
- Client (e.g., client-based project teams in an advertising agency),
- Place (creating units based on where people are working).

The principle of grouping by knowledge and skills is illustrated in the minicase below.

MINICASE

Karolinska University Hospital in Sweden

Karolinska is the most prestigious university hospital in Sweden and it provides highly specialized care, not only for the inhabitants in Stockholm, but to patients all over the country and abroad. Besides the clinical part of the organization being responsible for the health care of the patients, the organization Karolinska also contains a highly successful research organization called Karolinska Institutet (KI). Although formally responsible for research, KI is intertwined with the clinical departments at the hospital, and physicians and other professionals work between the two units. The medical services at the hospital are organized into 69 units or departments that illustrate Mintzberg's grouping by *knowledge and skills*. The department structure also illustrates a far reaching *differentiation*. A major problem in such a specialized organization is achieving *integration* between specialized units. When a patient requires care from more than one department, an integration problem arises. The more specialized the department, the higher the need for integration. How, then, can a hospital achieve the necessary integration without sacrificing the necessary specialization? Karolinska, like many other hospitals, has tried to introduce an intermediate level between the specialized departments/clinics and the hospital management. This level is often referred to as a division or a centre. At Karolinska, seven such divisions were introduced and the different departments were grouped based on similarity. As an example the Head division housed such clinics as Neurology, Psychology, Neurophysiology, and Geriatrics.

Information about the organizational structure at Karolinska is retrieved from www.karolinska.se/en/Karolinska-University-Hospital

The structural features of the contingency movement, and the models suggested by Mintzberg, all build on the assumption that the organization is a coordinated whole, with clear boundaries to the environment, and where the formal structure is the most important aspect of the organizing of activities in the firm. The last two decades have, however, given us numerous examples of other, less hierarchic, logics of designing the superstructure. In an ambitious attempt to take the contingency view on formal structures into the new millenium, the so-called Innform (Innovative forms of organizing) programme made a large empirical study covering changes in formal structures during the period of 1992 to 1996 (Pettigrew, Massini, and Numagami, 2000; Whittington *et al.*, 1999). Compared to the Aston School and all of the studies described above, the Innform program realized that the study of formal organizations could not only emphasize structural components from an internal perspective.

In a large survey, three groups of organizational features were studied: Structures (decentralization, hierarchic layers, and project-based forms), processes (horizontal flows of information and interaction, new HR-practices, and information technology), and boundaries (downscoping, strategic alliances, and other forms of external cooperation, and outsourcing).

The study showed that organizations have made clear, even though not revolutionary, changes in the formal structures. Perhaps most striking was the growing use of projects as a means of increasing flexibility and stimulating goal-oriented, temporary efforts. At the same time the survey showed that large companies in Europe, Japan, and the United States were still dominated by the *divisional structure*.

'Thus in the mid-1990s, seventy-five (75) per cent of the top 100 French firms, seventy (70) per cent of the top 100 German firms, and eighty-nine (89) per cent of the top UK firms, were divisionally organized (Pettigrew *et al.*, 2000: 259).'

DEFINITION BOX

Divisional structure

The divisional structure is a corporate level superstructure organized around output, clients, and/or place. The divisional structure is nowadays often organized around larger organizational units such as business areas, business units, groups, and similar concepts.

Contingency theory

Even though there had been a number of influential scholarly attempts at defining and understanding the functioning of organizations (most notably Max Weber's work on bureaucracy and Chester Barnard's (1938) study of organizations as adaptive systems), it wasn't until the open system view, and contingency theory, that organization theory took off as an academic discipline.

DEFINITION BOX

New organizational research

In a review of 'new organizational research' from the early 1960s, disciplines such as anthropology, sociology, business administration, management, industrial management, and social psychology were well represented. The 'new organizational research' was made out of six more famous books on the subject, as a result of which all authors were or would later become influential. The reviewer, Dwight Waldo (1961), pointed out that the studies not inspired by anthropology smelled strongly of American factories. In retrospect, perspectives focusing on structures in factories came to dominate the field until the mid-1970s, and then anthropology, under the label of culture studies, and institutional theory studies were once again taken into consideration.

With the attempts at linking structural features (see the section above) to environmental features, managers were also provided with a more refined set of tools as compared to the one-best-way of Taylor and the like. Joan Woodward's study of industrial firms in the UK and how they linked formal structure to technology spawned a lot of interest among practitioners and helped give emphasis to a number of pressing issues in companies.

On a general level it makes intuitive sense that internal factors, that can be influenced and manipulated by managers, are adapted to factors outside the company that influence it. The major challenge for any theory that aspires to study this is to determine what the relationship between organization and environment looks like. How, more specifically, does the environment influence the organization, and how could/should managers react to environmental demands? What environmental factors or demands are necessary to consider? Furthermore, are there specific measures that are more successful than others in meeting specific environmental demands? These, and other questions, were adressed by the contingency theory movement.

Contingency theory started as a reaction to previous theories on organizations. As was described above, a number of different schools of thinking characterized the field until the mid-1950s. With different theoretical and practical motivations, they all shared the view that the company could be viewed as a homogeneous whole, and that the environment surrounding the company was not important to consider, at least not as a factor influencing the choice of formal structure. Contingency theory challenged two important assumptions in earlier theories:

1. There is one best way of organizing a company. This is an important cornerstone of both the academic work of Max Weber and the practical work of Frederick Taylor and Henri Fayol. The work of both the Human Relations School (which will be further discussed in Chapter 5) and the functionalist theories of Chester Barnard and others already challenged this assumption in the 1930s, but it was one of the more important ideas of contingency theory to argue that, depending on environmental characteristics, different structural features were appropriate—there simply was no one best way of organizing.

2. The choice of formal structure is not influenced by the environment. Contingency theory challenged the assumption that organizations are closed systems that can be organized without explicitly accounting for environmental characteristics and how they influence the company. A variety of explicit connections between different environmental characteristics and structural features were proposed, discussed and tested, and many of these connections were also formulated as prescriptions which created a lot of interest among practitioners.

At the same time contingency theory also shares some basic assumptions with earlier theories and one of the most important is:

3. Organizations can be deliberately organized and it rests in the hands of managers to choose formal structure, and make it work.

Based on these assumptions a number of studies were conducted from the end of the 1950s up until the mid-1970s. It is widely acknowledged that the contingency program was marked by theoretical as well as methodological problems (see more below), but this must not hide the fact that some of these studies have had immense impact on making the study of organizational structures into a scientific discipline in its own right. In an early article Dill (1958: 409) summarized the vision of the contingency movement in the following way:

> Administrative science needs propositions about the ways in which environmental factors constrain the structure of organizations and the behavior of organizational participants.

Dill was preoccupied with the demands of the so called *task environment* and how it influenced the autonomy of top managers. In a case study of two Norwegian firms, he showed how the structure of the task environment, the accessibility of information about the environment, and the managerial perceptions of the meaning of this information, all influenced the autonomy of managerial personnel. Dill's study spawned a strong interest in the environment and how managers could balance demands from the environment with structural measures. Dill also laid the foundation for an interest in a cognitive perspective in organization theory. His study also led to an interest in the environment as a source of *uncertainty*. The role of uncertainty was emphasized in a number of influential studies in the 1960s and 1970s. The interest in **uncertainty** as a central environmental variable was focused on two dimensions (Duncan, 1972):

- Stable—dynamic: the degree to which important factors in the environment remain the same over time or, if they change.
- Simple—complex (also labelled homogeneous—heterogeneous): the number of important factors that decision-makers take into consideration.

Uncertainty was, without doubt, the most important environmental factor studied by contingency theorists. This reflected a growing dissatisfaction with traditional bureaucratic models of organization and a growing realization that the environment matters and that a dynamic and heterogeneous situation put a lot of demands on the organization. The minicase below illustrates a situation marked by high degrees of uncertainty (dynamic) and heterogeneity (complex).

Tata Motors in India

MINICASE

The world scene for producing and selling cars is subject to radical changes. When Toyota succeeded General Motors as the largest producer of cars, few were surprised when the traditional domination of American car manufacturers was broken, this had been foreseen for quite some time. But, perhaps even deeper changes were awaiting. Consider the example of Tata Motors, which is a part of the global giant, the Tata Group (employing more than 350,000 people). For the general public outside India, Tata Motors is probably most well known for buying Jaguar and Land Rover. Their decision to design and build a car that would be sold for just above $2,000 USD was met with a lot of scepticism in the automotive industry. In January 2008 the new car was unveiled at the Auto Expo, and in March 2009, the new car made its commercial debut. The idea of building a car with a very low retail price is challenging, to say the least. It requires a new way of thinking concerning design and production, and to keep up with today's demanding customers, it is not enough just to produce low quality products. For a company owning high profile brands such as Jaguar and Land Rover this would be devastating. After launching the car in March 2009, many observers claimed that Tata could, potentially, alter the way the automotive industry had traditionally viewed car manufacturing. The idea of producing small, light, and cheap, without sacrificing too much of quality could be the role model for the future production of cars.

Three examples of influential studies drawing on the ideas of Dill and others concerning uncertainty (it should be mentioned that Dill was not explicitly using the concept of uncertainty) are presented as bullet points below:

- Burns and Stalker (1961): Based on 20 case studies in different industries, they proposed two different types of organizational systems, each being effective under certain circumstances. The first, labeled mechanistic, was appropriate for a company operating under stable conditions, and the second, labeled organic, was more useful in situations of change. Their book has been a continuous source of inspiration in its basic argument that high levels of uncertainty need to be met with higher degrees of decentralization and other measures, to make the organization react more quickly—to create an organic structure.

- Galbraith (1973): In a more theoretical fashion Galbraith argues that the higher the uncertainty an organization is facing, the more information it has to process between decision-makers during execution of tasks to achieve a certain level of performance. There are, according to Galbraith, two basic ways of dealing with the information processing needs in an organization—either you reduce the need for information processing, for example, by creating slack resources and self-contained tasks, or you increase the capacity to process information by investing in information systems and creating lateral relations. In this way, Galbraith helped pave the way for a closer link between organization theory and informatics and information system theory. The first way has many similarities with Burns and Stalker's suggestion that decentralization is a good measure to meet uncertainty.

- Thompson (1967): Thompson was concerned with how organizations are designed to meet different degrees of uncertainty. Uncertainty, to Thompson, stems from technology and the environment, and it includes aspects such as the type of technology employed, interdependencies among tasks performed, the power of, and dependence on, competitors and other external actors, and stability and homogeneity of the environment. In his book, Thompson develops and discusses more than 80 propositions, most of which deal with the influence of different aspects of the environment on the formal structure, and how it is managed.

The book by Thompson (1967) illustrates an important problem in the contingency framework—the fact that there is a complex interplay between different environmental variables, on the one hand, and between environmental variables and the structure and functioning of organizations on the other hand. In Thompson's case he points at the links between *technology* and uncertainty, with technology being both an internal variable (e.g., the specific tools, machines, and processes used in the company) and external (e.g., the broader technological trends and factors influencing the company).

Common to most early attempts at studying the impact of the environment on the choice of formal structure, was the assumption that the environment should be treated as an exogeneous variable. That is, it was assumed to be outside the control of managers in the single company to influence and change the environment—the formal structure was therefore unidirectionally shaped by the environment. This assumption was soon challenged by different authors, and in an early article, John Child (1972) argued that the organizational structure was only partially determined by the environment, and that managers had considerable leeway in deciding how to deal with the environment. This was referred to as *the strategic-choice* approach and it put top decision-makers as important links between the organization and the environment.

The configurational approach

Defining and describing basic elements of formal structures was a major preoccupation in the contingency movement as described above. In the early 1970s, the contingency theory was subject to severe criticism from different perspectives. Three major streams of criticism emerged. In the first stream, it was argued that the basic tenets of contingency theory were sound, but that single studies had both theoretical and methodological flaws. A good example of this type of criticism was the different attempts to replicate earlier studies on the links between production technology, formal structure, and firm performance (e.g., Aldrich, 1972; Cullen, *et al.*, 1986; Grinyer and Yasai-Ardekani, 1980).

The second stream of criticism focused rather on the underlying assumptions of contingency theory and argued that there were fundamental problems in the assumptions. In an influential article, Pennings (1975) argued that the contingency argument of a causal chain of influence between environment and structure and organizational effectiveness, where the latter was contingent upon the structure being consistent with the environment, was problematic. An even more severe critique focused on the lack of clarity in the contingency theory arguments (Schoonhoven, 1981: 350).

'Although the overall strategy is reasonably clear, the substance of the theory is not clear. The lack of clarity is substantially due to the ambiguous character of the 'theoretical' statements.'

A third stream of criticism focused on the inability of contingency theory to understand the complementarities between structure, environment, and corporate strategy. The links between strategy and structure were described by Chandler in his book *Strategy and Structure: Chapters in the History of the American Industrial Enterprise* (1962). Chandler's basic argument was that the business structure is, over time, determined by the choice of strategy, and that both strategy and structure are in turn determined by how the company applies its resources to market demand. Even though heavily criticized, the argument that strategy drives structure helped broaden the scope of organizational analysis to also incorporate the strategic intent of the company.

In the 1980s, a new stream of research picked up on the ideas of contingency theory and tried to adress some of its shortcomings, in particular, the third problem above. In the so-called *configurational approach* Miller (1986; 1996), Miles and Snow (1978), and others aimed at describing the complementarities between strategy, structure, and environments, and how organizations could be described as design types, configurations, or archetypes (Hinings and Greenwood, 1988; Miller and Friesen, 1978; Miller, 1986; Mintzberg, 1979). Miles and Snow (1978) were strongly influenced by Child's (1972) ideas on strategic choice, and in their book, they argued that organizations act to create their environments, and that major decisions taken by top management in fact define the relationship with the environment. A similar argument was made by Karl Weick (1969) in his idea of *environmental enactment*, which points at the cognitive limitations among decision-makers to respond to a virtually unlimited number of possible factors. The process of defining and choosing which factors to 'see' and respond to, was called enactment by Weick. Through strategic choices, and the process of enactment, the organization's structure and internal processes are shaped. Miles and Snow, in that way, further developed Chandler's argument of a conceptual relationship between strategy and structure. They, however, had a very different view on strategy compared to Chandler, and strongly emphasized the processual nature of strategy. In quoting Mintzberg (1978), they viewed strategy as a pattern or stream of larger and smaller decisions taken over time (Miles and Snow, 1978: 7). They further argued that there is an interplay between strategy and structure/process and that the latter can act as constraints on the strategy, rather than the other way around. In their study they arrived at four basic configurations, or *strategic types*, three of which were labelled stable forms of organization—the Defender, the Analyzer, and the Prospector—and one as unstable—the Reactor.

In addition, Mintzberg's well-known categorization of organizational structures into 5 types (the simple structure, the machine bureaucracy, the professional bureaucracy, the divisionalized form, and the adhocracy) was used by Miller (1986) to describe the bridges between strategy and structure, and how these relate to the environment. He identified four organizational structures that fit with strategic types, and the environments in which these archetypes could flourish:

- The simple structure was connected to a niche differentiation structure,
- The machine bureaucracy was associated with a strategy favouring cost leadership,
- The organic structure was linked to a strategic type called innovative differentiation,
- The divisionalized structure was connected to a conglomerate strategy.

One of the major achievements of the configurational school was to take the contingency view of organizational structure from the piecemeal description found in the Aston School, and in numerous other studies in this tradition, to a more holistic view based on Mintzbergs design types or similar archetypes. In its view on structure, per se, it still relies heavily on the dimensions developed by Lawrence and Lorsch (1967), Burns and Stalker (1962), and the Aston School (Pugh *et al.*, 1968). The result of this can be summarized as:

> Environmental fit demands that organizations match their structures and processes to their external settings.
>
> (Miller, 1992: 159)

As stated, even when taking the environment into consideration, the focus in this tradition is mainly on the internal structures and processes, emphasizing the organization as an entity with boundaries, yet influenced by the environment.

Transcending the formal boundaries of a complex organization

The Intel case, from the introduction of the chapter, was used to highlight a number of important organizing challenges, primarily focusing on Intel's internal structure and how it relates to different situational demands. A closer look shows that the company is highly dependent on a number of external relations that are not formally part of the Intel structure, but nevertheless are crucial for them. Following is a brief summary of some of the more important agreements, partnerships and joint projects signed by Intel during 2007.

LINK BOX

Intel—crossing the boundaries of the formal organization

When the Intel case was introduced in the beginning of the chapter, the focus was on the corporate structure of the company. A basic assumption was that Intel could be described as an integrated whole, with clear boundaries to the environment. Developments after the turn of the millennium have indicated that the company/environment interface is by no means clear and easy to depict. Following is a series of press releases issued by Intel that clearly show that the company is involved in a large number of activities where the boundary between the company and its environment is hard to delimit.

22 January 2007—Sun Microsystems, Inc. and Intel Corporation announced a broad Strategic alliance centered on Intel's endorsement of the Solaris Operating System and Sun's commitment to deliver a comprehensive family of enterprise and telecommunications servers and workstations based Intel Xeon processors.

27 March 2007—Intel Corporation announced the 44 companies receiving Intel's Preferred Quality Supplier award for outstanding commitment to quality and performance excellence. These suppliers provided products and services deemed essential to Intel's business success in 2006.

25 April 2007—Intel Corporation announced a new program that will help resellers worldwide market innovative Intel-based products in a more quick and cost-effective manner. The company has created a new virtual marketing storefront for its reseller channel and has also collaborated with Google to create an advertising program where resellers can place online ads.

30 May 2007—Broad adoption of NAND flash memory technology in the PC platform received a boost with the formation of the Non-Volatile Memory Host Controller Interface Working Group. The Working Group is chaired by Intel Corporation with core contributors including Dell Inc. and Microsoft Corp.

12 June 2007—Intel Corporation and Google joined with Dell, EDS, The Environmental Protection Agency, HP, IBM, Lenovo, Microsoft, Pacific Gas and Electric, World Wildlife

Fund, and more than a dozen additional organizations announcing their intent to form the Climate Savers Computing Initiative.

25 June, 2007—Intel Corporation and CableLabs, the technology consortium of cable operators, announced today that the two companies have signed an OpenCable Platform Agreement and will include support for the OpenCable Platform in future Intel consumer electronic system-on-a-chop products.

The press releases for the link box were retrieved from **www.intel.com.**

Reflection point: How is Intel to manage this variety of external relationships?

It is obvious from the examples above that a company like Intel is not self sufficient in terms of acquiring and utilizing resources necessary to survive and prosper in a global market. They rely on a vast number of external partners and actors to bring in competencies, experiences, financial resources, market presence, and other necessary resources and capabilities. In the contingency framework, this was considered to be part of the external environment, something the organization had to *adapt* to. The notion of adaptation implied that the environment was treated as exogenous to the organization—it was there independent of the actions of the organization. The Intel press releases above make it obvious that the company today manages the environment in a much more proactive way. They not only try to influence external actors, but actively bring them into the company. This has some interesting consequences for how we describe and understand organizations and organizational structures, and it certainly calls into question where the boundaries between the organization and the environment are located. An intriguing example of how linked an organization can be to what happens outside the boundaries is given in the minicase below.

MINICASE

Sustainable structures

Within the traditional business model informing organizational theory as well as business life, an organization is responsible for what happens within its boundaries. The classical value chain model, formulated by Michael Porter (1985), is an example of this, focusing on activities such as production, administration, and distribution of products. What is of interest from this perspective, is what happens within the organization. The external world is something the organization surely needs to adapt to, but it is not something that is deliberately considered a part of what constitutes the organization. Consider the following example from CocaCola. When planning for production and selling of CocaCola in India and China, the CocaCola Company estimated the water needed for production of one litre of CocaCola to be 3.3 litres of water. Even though that amount is fairly large in an already drought-ridden area of the world, the figures seemed plausible in relation to production of soda drinks. External consultants were hired to confirm the estimation, but they came up with a water demand of approximately 230 litres. The explanation can be found in what is to be considered as being within the value chain and the boundaries of the organization.

For example, since production of soda drinks requires sugar, estimates should include water required for the production of sugar, and therefore higher figures would be obtained.

Sugar production, beginning with the watering of young plants, requires a much larger amount of water than that needed for just producing the final product. When faced with these numbers, CocaCola had to reassess their strategies for entering those markets, taking into consideration the issue of sustainability in social, economic, and environmental aspects within the production beyond their own boundaries.

This chapter ends with reflections on three important developments beyond the contingency and configurational approaches drawing on the Intel example.

Complementarities in action

How can we make sense of the wide variety of strategic external relations in the press releases above? From the 1970s and onward, more and more emphasis has been put on the external relations of companies, what is referred to as *interorganizational* relations. Companies to a growing extent, engage in interorganizational relations that can take different forms. They range from informal contacts and joint projects, over strategic alliances, networks and joint ventures, to mergers and acquisitions. Interorganizational relations can thus take many different forms, from very loosely connected to highly formalized forms.

An important question is how the proliferation of external relations can be connected to the formal structure of Intel as discussed in the beginning of the chapter. It is obvious that organization theory has moved away from the simplified descriptions of organizations in both the machine model and the contingency framework, setting aside the notion of one company—one formal structure. Rather, a company like Intel, as well as other companies, face a complex set of internal and external demands, which have to be met by combining different forms of organizing.

The argument that organizations need to be able to combine different resources and orientations has been put forward by several authors (Dosi, Nelson and Winter, 2000; Nohria and Ghoshal, 1997). In the context of organizational structures, it has been proposed by Whittington and Pettigrew (2003) that organizations need to find complementarities between different aspects of structure, internal processes, and boundaries. In essence, this means that there seems to be a performance premium for companies that manage to combine the different resources, values, and structures to create a way of organizing that handles the complexity in the environment at the same time as they make it harder for competitors to imitate the company.

Collaborating and competing—the dual character of organizational boundaries

The open system view has inspired a lot of research on the role of external agents in shaping the organization and its structure. In the *stakeholder management* approach, different categories of external actors are identified and analyzed, and appropriate actions to meet their demands are developed and implemented. Traditionally, the open system view envisioned that the company should balance all the different demands, and that there was an optimal set of actions that could satisfy all demands. Pfeffer and Salancic (1978) viewed this rather as a process of prioritizing the most pressing demands. In the stakeholder approach there are generic roles taken by external actors—competitors, suppliers, governmental agencies, pressure groups, customers, and so on.

There is nowadays a growing awareness that the generic roles are not that generic. It is perfectly possible to be fierce competitors on the market at the same time as you cooperate on finding technological standards. This is perhaps most obvious in the high-tech industries in which Intel and other companies are working. The high degree of uncertainty, with many different actors, a rapid pace of change, and the fusion of technological standards (where, for instance, information technology merges with communication technology and entertainment industries), forces the companies to take a pragmatic view on competing and cooperating.

The organizational challenges are however tremendous—how do you cope with moving between cooperating and competing? How do you develop internal structures, processes, and standards to let the competitors in at the same time as you strive to keep them out? It is important to realize that there is no such thing as the perfect structure—regardless of whether you choose a unitary and hierarchic structure, or if you follow the example of Intel to build a more complex structure, you need to combine it with a variety of internal processes and a lot of managerial efforts to constantly monitor and develop activities in the company. Finding a well-matched structure is not the final solution to deal with environmental demands.

Community building to create and sustain identity

This chapter has introduced the idea that companies need to design and develop formal structures that enable them to cope with demands from the external environment, but also with internal demands. It should be clear by now that it is not enough for a company to have a well designed internal structure (even though it helps). It takes a dedicated staff of managers to make the structure work, and part of these managerial challenges are discussed in Chapter 6.

The organizing of companies is also achieved by factors that are only partially in the control of managers. Coordination of both day-to-day business as well as more strategic and long-term activities is influenced by how people relate to each other in the company and how they manage to create shared patterns of understanding, social identities and shared values. From the 1980s, much interest has been devoted to phenomena and concepts such as corporate culture, corporate identity, branding, and corporate ideology. There is a growing recognition that formal structures, as presented in this chapter, are not enough to manage organizations. Organizations are social entities with people acting and interacting. In relating to each other, within the single organization, and also between organizations, they develop shared patterns of understanding. Many managers have started to understand the importance of creating (or at least trying to create) *communities* of employees, customers, and other stakeholders where a feeling of pride, belonging and identification are conveyed. This was a clear ambition in General Electric under the leadership of Jack Welch as described in the minicase below.

General Electric—the boundaryless organization

A general argument in this part of the chapter is that the definition of the boundaries of a single organization is open to question. This realization was important for General Electric, under Jack Welch, when they launched the idea of the boundaryless organization. Welch, and his management team, struggled to make sense of one of the world's largest organizations and to create a pragmatic approach to continuous change and process orientation. As a part of realizing the vision of the boundaryless organization, a process-based management system was launched in the early 1990s. It was evident from the very beginning that this new system was more than a change of hardware and organizational structure. It, more than other things, required a change of mindset. The new system challenged established power structures and it took a lot of hard work to create the cultural revolution that was needed to get closer to the vision of the boundaryless corporation. The continued development of GE into the new millennium has proved that the idea of the boundaryless organization was more than a fad. With more than sixty per cent (60%) of their sales outside the US, a major challenge is to create an organization that is able to balance the global perspective with local adaptation. This is evident in the recent expansion in China, where GE applies their 'company to country' strategy, to build on local capabilities and to develop local resources.

More information on the boundaryless organization is available in Robert Sinter's book, *Jack Welch & the G.E. Way: Management Insights and Leadership Secrets of the Legendary CEO*. Information on the recent development of GE was retrieved from **www.ge.com**.

MINICASE

In addition, the understanding of the relationship between environment and the organization has been challenged within neo-institutional theory. Being part of an environment, the environment comes to shape the organization and, vice versa, the organization shapes the environment (DiMaggio and Powell, 1983). Within this tradition, the structures of the organization have been shown to be an outcome of external pressures and a way to respond to demands of being seen as a modern organization, governed by rational ideas. Being able to show a certain structure, makes the organization appear as a rational organization, which hereby can be judged as a legitimate entity, worthy of sustained financial and other support. Just having certain structures provides the organization with the ability to survive, suggested Meyer and Rowan (1977). Even though the structures are loosely coupled or even ceremonial, the crucial part is that the organization can show they exist. Within this tradition, loosely coupled structures, which do not necessarily influence daily operations, become an advantage, providing the organization with legitimacy without disturbing the informal structures. Seen from this perspective, the boundaries between the organization and the environment will become further soluble.

There is a growing recognition that companies are arenas for complex processes of sensemaking, conflict and learning, and that these processes interact with the formal structures discussed in this chapter. A number of these factors are discussed in subsequent chapters, with identity being discussed in Chapter 6 on leadership, culture in Chapter 7 on the managing of organizations, and learning being covered in Chapter 10.

Summary and conclusions

This chapter opened with a case description from Intel that showed some of the complexities involved in creating a logical and flexible formal structure. Organizing a company such as Intel is a constant struggle to create and order in both a complex and dynamic environment. The formal structure is one of the important tools that top management can use to make sure that the operations of thousands of employees are coordinated and well adapted to realizing the strategic goals of the company.

Organization theory has gone from a fairly mechanical, deterministic, and closed view on organizational structures, to a much more open view that stresses the importance of flexibility and openness to the surrounding environment. In fact, the whole idea of the organization as something delimited and separate from its environment has been called into question with the advance of new and innovative forms of organizing. In this chapter, we have described the major theoretical developments in the twentieth and twenty-first centuries, with an emphasis on the open system view that was introduced in organization theory in the 1960s.

? Study questions

1. Describe the major features of the machine bureaucracy, as described by Henry Mintzberg.
2. Discuss different definitions of formal organizational structures offered in the chapter.
3. Many different, concrete, elements of structure have been suggested in the literature. Describe some of them and discuss their significance for understanding today's organizations.
4. Describe the basic idea of the divisional structure.
5. Discuss the basic ideas of Contingency theory and how it improved upon previous theories.
6. Describe some of the seminal studies made in the Contingency theory. Discuss also some of the criticism towards this theory.
7. Discuss the recent trends that make it more complicated to locate the boundaries of formal organizations.

Literature recommendations and further readings

Organization theory is a very rich field and books and articles on the role and functioning of organizational structures are not lacking. More than 25 years after its first publication, *Structure in fives*, by Henry Mintzberg (1983), still gives a pedagogical introduction to the ideas of Contingency theory. The original classics by authors such as Burns and Stalker (*Management of innovation*, 1962), Lawrence and Lorsch (*Organization and environment*, 1967), Thompson (*Organizations in action*, 1967), and Woodward (*Industrial organization*, 1965), still makes up essential reading for the interested student of organizational structures and come highly recommended. A good overview of the latest advancements in the field of organizational structures is given in the book *Innovative forms of organizing*, edited by Whittington and Pettigrew (2003).

Take your learning further

online resource centre

http://www.oxfordtextbooks.co.uk/orc/erikssonzetterquist/

Visit the Online Resource Centre which accompanies this book to enrich your understanding of this chapter.

Students: explore web links and further reading suggestions. Keep up to date with the latest developments via 'What happened next' updates to appropriate cases from within the book.

Lecturers: you will find seminar exercises and teaching notes, for use in class or assessment.

CHAPTER 3
Information technology and business systems

Introduction of e-business at Volvo Car Company and Ford

At the end of the 1990s, questions about the new economy were on everyone's mind. With the help of the new solutions, made possible by the development of information technology (IT) and the Internet, companies and organizations could streamline their operations and still be even more productive and profitable. The only question was how to implement the technology. One person who asked how his company could be a part of the new economy was Jacques Nasser, the CEO of Ford Motor Company (Ford), the car manufacturer. For ideas, Nasser turned to McKinsey & Company, the management consulting firm that, after its typical ninety-day investigation, came back with the answer: e-Business! There were a number of plusses associated with changing Ford's purchasing system to a company-wide, electronic solution. For example, the new system would result in:

- Easier connections than EDI (the previous technical solution),
- Lower costs than the present method,
- True market prices,
- Fewer purchasing transactions,
- A worldwide supplier base,
- Improved communications,
- And much more.

Jacques Nasser explained the benefits to Ford:

> The purpose of the e-Business system is to introduce a more modern way of working by means of e-tools. The basic idea is that FMC should have a common purchasing process worldwide. When the system is introduced, everyone within the FMC group all over the world should be able to work in the same way and use the same system.

The introduction of e-Business was therefore thought to be the solution to a series of problems. Ford would finally become a part of the modern economy while at the same time it would realize large efficiency gains in various areas.

One of the first Ford subsidiaries to implement e-Business was the Volvo Car Company (VCC) in Sweden that had been purchased by Ford in 1999. The VCC purchasing department looked forward to the new system with high expectations. Their current system was out-of-date, difficult to work with, and, above all, difficult for new employees to learn. However, at the same time, some of those responsible for systems and IT at VCC were more sceptical. With the efficiency gains expected from the new system, people would certainly have more time for strategic thinking, but the new system also meant changes in the work assignments for the purchasing agents, particularly with regard to increased control over their activities.

Parallel with these management changes, the work continued with developing the e-Business solution. The work was performed with the help of consultants and purchasing agents from their respective areas of the two companies. At VCC, these people met once a week to review the changes needed to make the system compatible with their existing systems and routines. These changes were sent to the software programme supplier who was developing the technical solution. Because the e-Business solution had originated in an American corporation in another area of industry, the changes were extensive. For a company, like VCC, that bought parts for car production in many of the world's currencies, a comprehensive currency exchange software programme was required. Additionally, the system had to accommodate the purchase of the many differentiated parts that are part of car production as well as various sales tax and value-added tax calculations. For example, the production of rear view mirrors in the 56,000 different variations of Volvo cars manufactured meant everything from their design and colour to the warning text 'objects in the rear view mirror may appear closer than they are' had to be considered. The work proceeded slowly and, in 2005, the media reported that the cooperation with the e-business system deliverer, Oracle, had to be terminated. This particular e-Business solution was never going to be implemented, although VCC and Ford continued to work toward a common solution.

At Ford, people had worked towards a comprehensive purchasing solution for the entire company, including its subsidiaries. In addition, the old purchasing system at VCC had to be changed. Until 1999, VCC had used the purchasing system of its parent company, AB Volvo, and when the Ford-VCC solution with Oracle proved unsuccessful, it was easy for VCC to continue with the AB Volvo system that AB Volvo had continued to develop after the Ford purchase of VCC. The solution for VCC was to adopt the new system that had been developed by AB Volvo which required only minor changes in order to introduce this provisional purchasing system. Hereby they received an updated software system for the purchasing processes which will continue to be developed until the next outstanding technological solution is found.

Information for the Volvo/Ford case was mainly compiled through original research by Ulla Eriksson-Zetterquist and Kajsa Lindberg. A thorough analysis is available in Eriksson-Zetterquist & Lindberg, 2002. Information on the e-business platform at VCC is available at **www.volvoit.com.** General information on Volvo Car Company is available at **www. volvocars.com.** The study by Ratnasingam (2001) of Ford's adoption of an EDI system has also been used for the analysis in the case.

Questions

As the VCC and Ford case shows, introducing new technological systems is a complex process—in what ways does it transform social life in an organization?

When introducing new technology (in this case a new e-Business system) an important question is—how can the organizational structure be designed to provide the best use of the new technology?

Important questions based on the case are also how the new technology is constructed by its users, how it affects various processes of organizing, and other dimensions of the interplay between the social and the technological.

Introduction

The case on e-Business at VCC lays the background for this chapter that discusses organizing and technology. Technology is a central part of organizing, affecting everything from production to administration, and in ways that go beyond the mere use of machines for these purposes. In this chapter we explore a number of aspects of technology and how they are interlinked with organizational structures, processes, and boundaries. Technology in organizations is a rich field in itself and it is way beyond the scope of the chapter to cover all aspects of it. As information technology (IT) is a central part of today's technology, we use it to exemplify the role of the broader concept of technology in organizations.

The chapter focuses on the following topics:

- Definitions of technology and organizing, highlighting how the relation between technology and organizing can be understood from different perspectives.
- An overview of technology's role in industrialization until the 1940s as background.
- The **sociotechnical** movement which had its major influence during the 1950s.
- The 1960s focus on technology's role in relation to the organization's structure and success, developed within contingency theory.
- Various forms of IT and information technology as a social construction.

Organizing and technology

Because of the **Enlightenment philosophers'** idea that society can be designed rationally, technological inventions and rationalizations have played central roles in Western society. The Enlightenment philosophers strived for a modern society that should grow when the wild and uncultured are refined. Using reason, and especially the achievements that result from scientific reasoning, society can be directed and controlled (Bauman, 1991). This idea has been the impetus for extensive technological rationalizations (here including the use of technology to simplify production processes in order to reach higher productivity at less cost), and changes in work and in organizations, leading in turn to changes in many of society's structures. The case of e-business in the Ford case above is one of these extensive technological rationalizations, based on the idea that a better system will provide better productivity within the Ford Company. As it is a recent change, the subsequent societal changes are still not known. Yet, at the same time that technological development has increased productivity, new risks have emerged. For example, the sociologist Ulrich Beck (1986) believed that the possibility in the modern era of creating infinite prosperity also created the risk of causing infinite devastation. Uncontrolled actions in power plants or chemical productions are examples of events which may lead to extreme disasters in contemporary society. In the age of ICT the constant threat of viruses and computer breakdowns illustrates the organizational vulnerability connected with technology. The sociologist, Anthony Giddens (1999), pointed out that human's progress in science and technology has led to uncontrollable forces. For example, the phenomenon of global climate change is by now known to be the result of human's interference with the environment.

As a consequence of their progressive ideas about the human condition, Enlightenment philosophers had a large measure of confidence in the possibilities of technological inventions. They believed the very nature of technological inventions promised to make life simpler and better, at least for some of humanity (Czarniawska-Joerges, 1993). From an organization's perspective, such assertions are required to justify the effort and cost of introducing such technology. Because it is often very costly and time consuming to implement new technology in an organization, the decision to make such an implementation requires that the new technology present almost limitless possibilities. Although e-Business technology raises these possibilities, it is still necessary to convince even the users, who have always been positive toward e-Business solutions, as well as the more hesitant and sceptical users about making large investments and large changes (Latour, 1993). Some of the challenges in introducing new technology in a large company are elaborated upon in the link box below.

LINK BOX

The introduction of new technology at Ford and Volvo Car Company

Organizations introduce new technologies on a continuous basis, and often the changes are small and not far reaching. In other cases, more far reaching changes are introduced and they have the potential of radically redefining the mission and structure of the organization. The e-business example from Ford is a good example of the second type of technological change. It radically redefined how business operations were organized and it had far reaching consequences for the employees. The case clearly shows how problematic major technological changes can be, and especially when they transcend cultural and national boundaries. Technological change is seldom neutral—it is embedded in already existing cultural and social patterns that influence the implementation process and that also influence how new technologies are perceived. In the case of Ford and VCC, there were clearly cultural issues when the matters of currency, sales tax, and value-added tax surfaced as unanticipated obstacles to be solved. In addition, the e-business solution was based on the American method of procurement which differs from the Swedish one. For example, while procurement assistants would be found in America, a procurer in Sweden would have a more extended responsibility, with a budget of his/her own. Having more extended responsibility and freedom of making decisions, a Swedish procurer would handle some of the tasks corresponding to procurement assistants. In order to implement the American software system, the Swedish professional roles had to be changed, resulting in a situation where highly skilled and educated engineers spent their days entering product code and prices.

Reflection point: The Ford and Volvo Car Company example suggests that technological changes in organizations involve both cultural and social changes. How can an organization take care of the cultural and social aspects of change when introducing new technologies?

Definitions of technology

There are several definitions of technology to be found within the field of organizational studies. In the book *Technology and Organizations* from 1990, a group of well-known American researchers set out to explore the emerging field of new technologies and organizations. In this, three different definitions of technology are provided. The first was found in an edited book *Organizational Behaviour.* In this book Hulin and Roznowski presented their definition:

> 'We define technology as the physical combined with the intellectual or knowledge processes by which materials in some form are transformed into outputs used by another organization or subsystem within the same organization.'
>
> (Hulin and Roznowski, 1985: 47 quoted by Weick 1990: 3)

It should be noted in this definition that technology is not static but rather a set of processes that transform material to output. Skills, tools, and knowledge are parts of technology, and more implicitly, they are parts of technology that can be considered raw materials subject to transformation processes. Emphasizing what happens within the organization, the perspective is in accordance with that of contingency theory.

The second definition related to the upcoming tradition of Actor Network Theory (ANT) in which the social construction of technology was focused. According to Weick, this definition emphasized 'the contentious, adversarial environment of multiple constituencies that have a stake in the design and operation of technology' (1990: p. 3). Based upon the work of John Law the definition was:

> Technology is 'a family of methods for associating and channeling other entities and forces, both human and nonhuman. It is a method, one method, for the conduct of heterogeneous engineering, for the construction of a relatively stable system of related bits and pieces with emergent properties in a hostile or indifferent environment'.
>
> (Law, 1987, p. 115, quoted in Weick, 1990: 3)

According to this definition an implemented technology includes both the nonhuman material (what can be seen as the machine) but also humans who believe and support the new technology. This definition points to 'technology as a partially fortuitous emergent outcome of a relatively stable network among quite diverse elements' (Weick, 1990: 4). The definition thus offers an alternative to those definitions which see technology as a rationally planned and anticipated process, to be followed by an intentional, rational, homogenous, planned, and systematized implementation and production process. Weick foresaw the advantages of the definition informed by Law (1987) when Weick stated that this 'allows us to describe technology in a way more compatible with this quality in organizations' (ibid).

The third definition has bearing on situations where technical systems are described as a specific combination of machines, equipment, and methods used to produce some kind of valuable outcome:

> 'Technology refers to a body of knowledge about the means by which we work on the world, our arts and our methods. Essentially, it is knowledge about the cause and effect relations of our actions ... Technology is knowledge that can be studied, codified, and taught to others.'
> (Berniker, 1987, p 10, quoted by Weick, 1990: 3)

Emphasizing technical system leads to a situation when, for instance, the design of technology does not become an issue assigned to technicians only, but rather a process in which many take part. A shortcoming is that technology is first of all an outcome of technological systems, rather than being something that precedes the systems as such. A crucial point is the overlap between a certain technology and the technological system. Here Weick stressed new technologies, as these often became as extended as the technical system of which they were a part. A good example of this link between a specific technology and a broader technological system is the laptop and internet—this is described in the minicase below.

MINICASE

New technologies and organizing

The content in new techologies is, for obvious reasons, always changing, and does so in ways that are not always visible to the general public. At present, the Internet provides very extended technological systems in which routers, servers, technical solutions, and various organizational operations systems are hidden from most employees. The new technology represented by a powerful laptop becomes the tool for accessing almost any digitally based information in the world. In order to function as such, the new technology of the laptop has to be applicable to, or compatible with, the technical system of the Internet and its resources. As a result, technological systems based on new technologies have become even more central to organizations and the infrastructure of organizing. Members of organizations may only notice the laptop they use, and sometimes the wireless network, but otherwise the assemblage that makes up computerization in organizing is hidden from most of them. The modern information technology is permeating organizations in ways that few could have imagined just 20 years ago when the Internet was just about to be launched on a grand scale. When the laptop computer is connected to the wireless revolution and when mobile phones, notepads, and numerous embedded IT applications are dominating work spaces, the link between the visible computer artefacts (such as a laptop or an iPad) and the underlying systems is becoming even more hidden from the ordinary user. This raises both interesting and challenging questions when thinking about how to organize a company using modern information technology.

As indicated in all three definitions above, technology in general refers to the tangible features that exist beside the cultural, institutional, and situated aspects of the organization (Orlikowski, 2007). A problem in organization theory is that its primary focus on the symbolic and political dimensions means that the tangible and practical dimensions of organizing are seldom examined (Joerges and Czarniawska, 1998). As Joerges and Czarniawska state, 'all organizing, in its symbolical, political and practical aspects, needs to be inscribed into the matter in order to make organizations durable (indeed, possible)' (1998: 37). Contemporary organizations inscribe institutional order—the taken for granted way of doing things, which also includes a normative explanation—into their product. That is, assumptions of organizations, organizing, decision-making, division of labour and so on, will be inscribed into the machines. In other words, the symbolic, political, and practical aspects of organizing (the institutional order) are not only present in the organization as such, but also in the applied machines serving organizational production and administration. Inscribed in the machines, the institutional order becomes more or less concealed for the members using them.

Technology and practice

As a consequence of this reasoning, implementation of technology also means implementing new practices in an organization—new ways of working. For example, the introduction of the Spinning Jenny in eighteenth century England dramatically changed the home production practice of spinning thread. In a similar way, organizations have been greatly changed by the introduction of the conveyor belt, computing, and so forth. The introduction of cordless telephones to the workplace is another such example. As employees no longer needed to be at the workplace to make telephone calls, their ways of working changed. As e-mailing and Internet telephoning grew, the practice of traditional telephoning itself decreased. Similarly, the introduction of a new purchasing system at VCC, which we will return to, changed the various ways of making purchases at the company.

This is a relatively new way to look at technology's role in organizations. In a criticism of the minor place of technology in organizational theory, Wanda Orlikowski stated:

'Consider any organizational practice, and then consider what role, if any, materiality may play in it. It should be quickly evident that a considerable amount of materiality is entailed in every aspect of organizing, from the visible forms—such as bodies, clothes, rooms, desks, chairs, tables, buildings, vehicles, phones, computers, books, documents, pens, and utensils—to the less visible flows—such as data and voice networks, water and sewage infrastructures, electricity, and air systems.'
(Orlikowski, 2007: 1436)

There are, of course, studies in the area of technology adoption, diffusion, and use in and between organizations. One problem with this research is that these studies do not examine technology's influence over longer time periods, but rather only during special circumstances, for example, when new inventions are introduced. Technology as a tangible dimension of organizing is forgotten, first and foremost because organization practices are always integrated with materiality of other, everyday work, that is, with other forms of technology.

Furthermore, there are differences not only between definitions of technology as such, but also on how to understand the very technologies. These can be sorted into three groups.

Technical determinism: Orlikowski (2007) calls this the 'techno-centric perspective' where technology is seen as a lever for human action. On the whole, in this perspective, technology is viewed as exogenous, homogeneous, predictable, stable, and independent of time and place. A problem with technical determinism is that it ignores the economic, legal, social, cultural, political, and institutional conditions in its studies of how technology changes organizations. Despite the technical determinists' belief in technology as a uniform and external power, industrialization differed, for example, in England, France, and Germany, depending on the different political, social, and institutional assumptions of each country (Dillard, 1966; Winter and Taylor, 2001). Technological determinists advocate that machinery or technology can themselves change the organizing. In their accounts, technological determinists always emphasize the new machine or the new technology and the changes each brings, but they do not recognize the forces that lead to such inventions (Winter and Taylor, 2001).

The human-centred perspective: An alternative way of looking at technology is to begin with people and the ways they understand technology and make it comprehensible in various contexts. According to the **human-centred perspective**, technology is said to have different meanings in different contexts since people engage with it in different ways.

In the setting of e-business at VCC, research applying this perspective would start with asking employees how they understand the new technology and how they comprehended it in contexts such as working with suppliers, production, logistics, or reporting administrative issues to management. A weakness with this perspective is that its focus on sociocultural and historiccontexts tends to de-emphasize technology itself. Instead, the social is emphasized (Orlikowski, 2007).

Sociomaterial practices: Orlikowski offers a third perspective on technology and organizations that she calls '**sociomaterial practices**'. She wrote:

> '. . . seeing organizational practices as "sociomaterial" . . . allows us to explicitly signify through our language, the constitutive entanglement of the social and the material in everyday organizational life.'
> (Orlikowski, 2007: 1438)

These sociomaterial practices deal with 'the recursive intertwining of humans and technology in practice' (Orlikowski, 2007: 1437). The social and the material worlds are not separate; they should be examined and described simultaneously. Studies that take this perspective are presented in the chapter's conclusion.

The Industrial Era to the twentieth century

In the previous section, the concept of technology was introduced and some recent perspectives on the links between technology and organization were presented. In this section, we trace the modern perspectives back to the Industrial Revolution. We also introduce the reader to the so called **sociotechnical** perspective—the first major school that explicitly tried to link technology and organization. As the sociotechnical perspective is still the foundation for technological implementation, early findings within this tradition still provide crucial learning for students of organization and technology. In the Industrial Revolution, scientific inventions began to be employed on a large scale. One invention that contributed to the changed ways of organizing work in the eighteenth and nineteenth centuries in the Western world was the multi-spool spinning machine, the Spinning Jenny, that made it possible to spin more than one thread at a time. Because the Spinning Jenny was cheap and easy to use, spinners could use it at home. The spinning and weaving machines that followed, using the basic technology of the Spinning Jenny, were large, heavy, and expensive, requiring both investment capital and space. The result in England was the construction of the first factories. A second invention that caused great organizational change was the steam engine, patented by James Watts in 1774, that was first used in mining and as a source of power in factories before its use in steam boats and steam locomotives.

While the technological determinists, introduced in the previous section, stress that the inventions themselves contributed to the growth of factories, other researchers point to economic and political conditions as influential factors. Two examples of such changed conditions in particular are significant. When the Christian Church dropped the requirement of 'the fair price' and allowed interest to be charged, it became profitable to accumulate investment capital. The land enclosure movement in England, combined with new farming innovations, resulted in more food and thereby an increase in population and in the workforce (Dillard, 1966). Contributing to the change in social conditions was the disappearance of the guild system (Winter and Taylor, 2001). As wealth, more than tradition, began to determine social position (Polanyi, 1944), it became socially acceptable to earn money and accumulate capital.

To use the new technological solutions, more factories were built at the end of the nineteenth century and the beginning of the twentieth century in industrialized countries. With industrialization, new ways to organize appeared. Gradually, organizations began to integrate new elements into the production process vertically by buying competitors and suppliers. In this way, organizations could control their own distribution systems as well as increase their size (Perrow, 1986). In order to use the new technology to manufacture as productively as possible, a new system of work management was proposed by Frederick Taylor, 'the Father of **Scientific Management**'. According to Taylorism, workers would no longer work by their own rules of thumb (the Taylorist system is discussed in detail in Chapter 4). Instead, with the help of scientifically developed techniques, their work would be divided into smaller, discrete tasks. Every worker would be trained to perform only one task, and, in that way, production would increase. The advantage for the workers, Taylor claimed, was that through the increased productivity, their piece rate compensation would rise, leading to increased wages. However, the workers and their representatives were apprehensive and sceptical. They predicted that the division of work would lead to a decrease in their skills (deskilling) and less influence over their work processes as a whole.

During the first part of the twentieth century, organization researchers continued to develop and perform motion studies. As indicated previously, the central question at the time was how workers could perform their tasks as efficiently as possible. This concern, among other things, resulted in the Hawthorne Studies, an experiment on factory workers' productivity conducted between 1924 and 1932 (for further details see Chapter 5). In these studies, the factory's technology (originally, in the pre-studies a change in illumination levels) was veiled in order to advance the discovery of people's role and situation in the organization.

The sociotechnical movement

Studies of the Hawthorne effect laid the groundwork for the work at the Tavistock Institute in England where the sociotechnical movement developed. The idea behind this movement was that the social system and the technical system are integrated and should be understood as a whole.

DEFINITION BOX

Sociotechnical system

The guiding principle of social technology is a systems perspective which consists of:

- The social system, consisting of people, communication, and knowledge.
- The technical system, consisting of machines, equipment, tools, and other artefacts.

In 1949, a group of psychiatrists, clinical psychologists, social psychologists, and anthropologists opened the Tavistock Institute (Trist and Murray, 1990). Their goal was to connect the technical and social systems that anthropologists had developed in the 1930s. They thought that the connections between the two systems were interwoven and interdependent. This idea was advanced by Eric Trist who became one of the central advocates of the sociotechnical movement. A guiding principle of the Institute was that knowledge in the social sciences should be turned into practical knowledge. Specifically, this meant that theoretical inventions should be used to actively intervene in organizations and society (Miller, 1992). An example of this idea in action came from the Indian textile industry where, at the beginning of the 1950s, technical inventions led to rationalization (downsizing) of the labour force. With the help of the results from the Tavistock Institute and its researchers, the technical rationalizations were carried out concurrently as the work groups changed (Rice, 1951/1990).

In the sociotechnical movement, the perception is that the technological choices people make are also critical reflections of society's worldview. When new technologies are developed, people can choose to seize them and their associated possibilities, although the use of the technology may have unexpected consequences, as discussed below. First, we introduce some examples of studies in the sociotechnical movement.

Studies of sociotechnical systems

One area of the sociotechnical movement grew out of research on the military in Great Britain. The development of military technology during the Second World War led to greater interest by researchers in small groups (Miller, 1992). It was shown that small groups, described as self-regulating by the researchers, were flexible in making decisions and in continuing as a group even when the world around them changed quickly. As found out later by the sociotechnical researchers, this indicated that the groups were following the basic conditions of the systems theoretical perspective on organizations. Additionally, the military was having recruitment problems. It was revealed that up to thirty per cent (30%) of the future officers failed in their training, which made it difficult to find people who would eventually take leadership positions.

To solve this leadership problem, the British military began to focus on the younger officers, which raised the issue of the professional relationships of these officers with their subordinates. Compared to the older officers, the younger officers showed themselves to be more open and more democratic in such relationships. With this knowledge as a point of departure, the people in the War Office Selections Boards began to look for future officers in this group. Using a method that was developed by R.W. Bion, leaderless groups were organized where the military could identify the leaders who grew from within the groups and where it could see that the leadership role could be rotated as needed. As a result, the future officers could be selected from these group exercises (Murray, 1990). This research, together with Kurt Lewin's work on group dynamics and decision-making in groups, was another piece in the puzzle researchers at the Tavistock Institute were trying to solve (Trist, 1981). Today, we find results from these studies having influence on group processes, assessment centres and leadership programs. In the minicase below one of the many different studies in the sociotechnical tradition is described.

Jute weaving industry

MINICASE

The sociotechnical perspective has been very influential in defining how factories and other working spaces should be organized and there are numerous examples of successful implementations of the basic ideas. One study that laid the groundwork for the sociotechnical movement came from Eric Trist's experiences in the jute weaving industry in Scotland. Although the spinning operations in the Scottish mills were rationalized, the employees were not given notice of dismissals. Instead, their work assignments were greatly simplified at the same time that the supervision of their work intensified. The result was that the employees felt alienated to such a degree that they claimed they would gladly have lost their jobs. The union was also critical of the people performing time studies who were trying to rationalize the work still further. In this situation, the researchers could see how the changes in the spinning operations led to the growth of a new system. Previously, the jute weavers had worked together on multiple work tasks, but in the new system, they worked alone with simplified tasks. As a consequence, they felt socially alienated and depressed even though the new technology simplified their work (Trist, 1981). Even if being a great source for rationalizations, implementing new technology will not solely lead to high productivity. In order to function, the social system has to be adjusted in ways still permitting workers to use various skills and work in a setting with regular social encounters.

More information on the Jute weaving industry in Scotland is available in Trist (1981).

The concept of sociotechnology was first used by Eric Trist and Ken Bamforth in their work on English coal miners. Their studies exemplified the Tavistock Institute's goal of finding the intersection between research and practice. Whereas Trist had a research background, Bamforth had worked for eighteen years in the coalmines before he began his higher education. They decided to study coal mining because researchers had found that the mechanization of the work—the introduction of new technology—caused psychosomatic illnesses of nearly epidemic proportions among miners (Herbst, 1974). Despite the technologically improved mining equipment, productivity sank and personnel turnover and absence due to sickness increased. Productivity declined even when wages were raised.

In order to understand the situation, Trist and Bamforth (1951) studied twenty miners, as well as some management people, for two years. Their study showed that before the introduction of the new technology, the miners had worked in groups with responsibility for the entire process of coal mining operations. The groups consisted of at most eight miners, which meant all of them had an overview of the mining operations. In addition, each miner could work at many different tasks, using various skills. The group itself chose its members and functioned fairly autonomously. In the technological changes when the work was rationalized, among other things, a mechanical conveyor belt for moving coal was introduced. Previously, the miners themselves had operated the mine vehicles that moved the coal. With this new technology, the groups were also broken up and each miner could now perform only one task. Despite all the technical improvements, the research concluded it was the new technology that led to the worsening productivity. The results of Trist and Bamforth's coal mine studies showed that the technical system, that is, the recently introduced technology, and the social system with its social norms and appraisals that established what was considered reasonable work performance, reduced the miners' productivity.

The results from the studies of the sociotechnical system

Studies of the sociotechnical system show that it is complex and dynamic. It is partly an open system, which means it is influenced by its environment and must adapt both to local conditions and to changed circumstances. Furthermore, the sociotechnical system is characterized by joint optimization because the social and technical aspects support each other and thus create the best conditions for productive work (Brown, 1992: 65). By emphasizing the perspective of each member's role and function, social technology strives to find optimal solutions between the social and technical components of work.

In their focus on how the technical and social systems join together, the researchers from the Tavistock Institute could see how effective organizations could be formed. In contrast to the bureaucratic perspective (see Chapter 2) and Taylorism (see Chapter 4) that had claimed that the separation of work tasks was fundamental, the Tavistock studies pointed to the fact that the work system was an extensive collection of activities that in combination formed a functioning unit. While the bureaucratic and Tayloristic principles looked at people as an extension of the machinery, the sociotechnical design meant that people were seen as complementary to the machinery. Another result from these studies concerns variation. In bureaucracy and Taylorism, the goal was to reduce variation, while the ambition in social technology was to increase variation as much as possible, both for employees and for organizations (Trist, 1981). The strong links between the social and the technical systems are clearly visible in the Ford/VCC case. This is described in depth in the link box below.

LINK BOX

The Ford/VCC case from a sociotechnical perspective

Various consequences for the VCC purchasing agents resulted when Ford purchased VCC. For many years, the VCC people in purchasing were used to working with certain product groups, for example, the exhaust system group, and were used to visiting suppliers to learn about their production and to negotiate deals with them. They were also used to being the link between the design/production of the cars and the suppliers. Suppliers and VCC therefore came to depend upon the purchasing agents' long-term relationships with the suppliers. Ford worked with purchasing in a different way. Ford gave its purchasing agents responsibility for a production area for a maximum of only eighteen months, after which they were replaced. There were also several hierarchies in the Ford purchasing area, consisting of the purchasing assistants, the purchasing agents, and their managers. The managers negotiated contracts and the others checked that the facts and numbers were correct.

To prepare for the introduction of the new technology, the purchasing function at VCC changed to resemble that used by Ford. As the information on the suppliers was now available on the Internet, long trips to check on production and other conditions were no longer necessary. As part of these cost efficiency measures, the VCC purchasing agents' expense accounts were also cut back, which meant they could not invite suppliers to lunch or to some other event, as was the custom.

Dissatisfaction among the VCC purchasing agents spread. Among the people who had diminished work assignments, it was revealed that they spent less time at work.

Even if the changes in the social and technological systems in the Ford/VCC case were not completely connected to each other, VCC employees linked the two in their practices. Given the lessons of the sociotechnical perspective, however, there could have been less negative fallout from the case if managers had considered how the situation had changed for the employees. In addition, the managers would have to make efforts to let the involved purchasers regain influence over their situation.

Reflection point: What special challenges arise when two companies implement new technology?

Technology transforms the organization's structure

The sociotechnical perspective, described in the previous section, emphasizes the strong links between technology and social system. We now turn to a second major theoretical perspective on technology and organizations—contingency theory. This perspective was thoroughly introduced in Chapter 2 and we now present how it links technology and organization. The fundamental principle of this theory is that if an organization is to be successful, then all its structures must be designed to adapt to the situational demands that come from its technology, its market position, its product diversity, its rate of change, and its size. Here, technology refers to the 'generic sense of the study of techniques or tasks' (Perrow, 1986: 141). Taken together, these contingent factors—the situational demands—create various degrees of uncertainty and complexity. To develop a suitable structure so that management and employees will develop the right attitude and ways of doing business, these different contingent factors must be managed.

The organization sociologist, Joan Woodward, was a pioneer in this area. In her search for the best organizational form, she studied 100 English manufacturing companies (each employing 100 people or more) during the 1950s. The questions Woodward posed were: 'How and why do industrial organizations vary in structure, and why do some structures appear to be associated with greater success for the organization than others?' (Dawson and Wedderburn, 1980: xiv). By grouping the companies according to their degree of technical complexity—that is, by the technologies they used in production—Woodward found a pattern. The technical variables she researched were:

- the density of production,
- the flexibility of production facilities,
- the diversity of products, the time span of operations,
- the way in which production programmes were initiated and controlled.

In addition, 'note was made of recent technological developments, particularly those involving automation' (Woodward, 1965: 11–12). Woodward discovered that the different technologies that the companies used and their structures (control span, number of administrative levels, and degree of centralization in decision-making and management styles) correlated with their performance levels.

 DEFINITION BOX

Organizational characteristics relating to technology

Woodward presented the relation between organizational characteristics and technology as:

'Among the organizational characteristics showing a direct relationship with technical advances were:

- The length of the line of command,
- The span of control of the chief executive,

- The percentage of total turnover allocated to the payment of wages and salaries,
- The ratios of managers to total personnel, of clerical and administrative staff to manual workers, of direct to indirect labour, and of graduate to non-graduate supervision in production departments.'

(Woodward, 1965/1980: 51).

Woodward also found that there was not an optimal organization form as claimed by classic management theory. Woodward asserted the best organizational form depended on which technology the organization used. Because different technologies create different demands on people as well as on organizations, different structures are required to meet these demands.

Woodward (1965: 128) differentiated between three groups of production systems that all increase the technical complexity, although in different ways:

1. Unit and small batch (production by hand), for example, tailor-made clothes, artwork, machine prototypes). In this type of production, a few products are made from beginning to end by the same employees who are involved in the whole production process and understand the technology in use rather well. These organizations are characterized by minimum control span, few management levels and decentralized leadership. All in all, this type of technology and structure makes the organization successful, according to Woodward (i.e., organic organization form).

2. Large batch and mass (e.g., the conveyor belt in the car industry). Here, identical products are manufactured in large quantities. The methods used are routine and highly mechanized. The production processes can be broken down into many different steps, which can be performed by either machines or people. The employees work repetitively, each with a small part of the production. They are also sequentially linked to their co-workers who perform an activity before or after their own, in assembly line fashion. If these organizations are to be successful, management must have greater control and decision-making must be centralized (i.e., mechanical organization form).

3. Process (e.g., oil refineries or research laboratories). Here, a series of transformations take place in a certain continuous sequence. The raw materials enter at one end of the process and emerge refined at the end. The employees control their technical equipment that transforms the product. As in Group 1, the success of an organization is less dependent on control span and decentralized decision-making. Such organizations also have more administrative levels than in either Group 1 or Group 2 (i.e., organic organization form).

Woodward's results made clear that people must plan for organizational changes at the same time that they make changes in technologies, for example, when new technical solutions are introduced. A problem with Woodward's study was that she only studied small and medium-sized organizations, and her connection between technology and structure does not adequately explain the success of larger and more complex organizations. In addition, she focused only on manufacturing companies. Unfortunately, researchers after Woodward could not repeat her studies. Such a repetition would have confirmed her theory that technology, structure, and performance are related to each other. Furthermore, researchers have had problems with the ambiguous nature of her profitability idea. One of the many questions that has been asked is, how can profitability be related to efficiency? Finally, contingency theory is also criticized as deterministic (Dawson and Wedderburn, 1980).

Technology and open systems

One of Woodward's followers was James Thompson (1967) who began with the premise that the organization is an open system. This means that the organization is vulnerable to the influence of its surroundings and therefore lives with uncertainty. At the same time, the organization needs to reach its goals and to function rationally. Seen from this perspective, technology and the environment of the organization are the greatest sources of an organization's uncertainty.

Even if complex organizations are knowledgeable about working with highly developed technologies, they are still imperfect. To understand complex organizations, their technology must be understood. Thompson categorized three types of technology:

1. *Long-linked technology:* This technology refers to actions that are sequentially dependent, for example, Z can only be performed after Y has been performed, which in turn is dependent upon the performance of X, and so on (Thompson, 1967). The conveyor belt is an example of such sequentially linked technology. The advantage of this technology is that because of its instrumentalism, maintenance can be planned, and because of the repetitive nature of the tasks in the sequence, people can be studied and trained to reduce energy loss and mistakes.

2. *Mediating technology:* This technology refers to the actions taken to bring together (possibly independent) clients or customers, without their necessarily meeting. Commercial banks that match lenders (depositors) with borrowers, insurance companies that spread the risk among their clients, and telephone companies that link callers are example organizations in this technology category. A similarity among these organizations is that their complex operations require standardized processes. In order to work properly, middlemen are required for the transactions. Therefore, it is important that the different parts of the organization fit well together. As a result, such organizations are strongly characterized by the presence of bureaucratic principles.

3. *Intensive technology:* This technology refers to the multitude of different technologies used to make a change in a particular object. The object may be a bridge under construction or a patient in hospital. For example, X-ray machines, a laboratory, and medical specialists, in coordination, may be required to cure a seriously ill patient. In such a situation, specialist knowledge must be developed and applied to the new problems or situations requiring change.

While Categories 1 and 2 require far-reaching standardizations of their technologies, the opposite requirement applies to Category 3. However, given the logic of open systems, all three categories are vulnerable to the influence of their surroundings. To deal with such vulnerability, Thompson suggested that organizations should try to shield their best technology from such influences by creating buffers or by anticipating changes in their environments.

Organizations with several technologies

A third researcher in this tradition is Charles Perrow (1986) who observed that Woodward and Thompson had started with the idea that organizations have only one dominant technology. Perrow focused on the multitude of technologies in an organization. Among his questions, he asked if technology includes only the proportion of single-purpose machines or if it also includes sales, personnel, accounting, industrial organizations, and so forth. Taking this perspective, looking at the extent to which different organizational units use the technologies, it is clear that there are large differences in organizations.

To examine organizations' different technologies, Perrow classified organizations into two typologies: 'raw materials (things, symbols, or people), which are transformed into output through the application of energy, and tasks, or techniques of effecting the transformation' (1986: 14). He further divided the technologies he studied according to 'the degree of variability' and 'the degree of uncertainty'. The use of different technologies in one organization is evident in the Ford/VCC case and this is described in the link box below.

LINK BOX

Technology and complexity in car production

The introduction of new technology in an organization by necessity relates to already existing technologies and practices in the organization. The situation in many companies is that numerous technologies exist side by side, and they are intertwined in ways that make the introduction of new technologies a highly complex process. The e-Business case of the VCC car manufacturer is an example of a company that uses a series of different technologies. These include not only different technologies to design and manufacture cars, but also the old purchasing system that consists of a series of different subsystems based on different programming technologies. To say a company uses only one technology is a questionable assertion, given the recent development of the information community. In fact, at VCC, the several versions of subsystems would cause major problems as they were to be found as sediments within newer systems. These would have influence over the routines and tasks of lower-management, middle-management, and top-management. A problem, however, was encountered when trying to understand the various programmes. As the former programmers either had retired or were about to, a crucial part of the information on how the technology was developed was about to vanish. There are often positive aspects in already existing systems and technologies that need to be acknowledged when contemplating the need for new technologies. Systems that have developed over time in a specific organization are often tailormade for the needs of the users, and they have proven to be working. Replacing them for new ones might cause disturbances, and it is not necessarily the case that they are perceived to work better than the old ones.

Reflection point: Considering the complexities involved in launching new technologies in already existing organizations, how can these complexities be planned for in the introduction process?

Information technology

In the previous sections we have presented two major perspectives on technology—the socio-technical perspective and contingency theory. In this section we turn back to the introductory case and the role of information technology as an important driving force in organizations. The section also introduces a new perspective on technology that addresses some of the shortcomings of the earlier perspectives.

DEFINITION BOX

IT

IT has been defined as 'those mechanisms used to organize, store, manipulate, present, send, and review information' (Yates and Van Maanen, 2001: xxi). Today, IT also refers to computers, photocopiers, mobile telephones, computer-aided design (CAD), and computer-aided manufacturing (CAM) equipment. In a broader perspective, IT is everything from the library to blackboards to calculators and computers.

At a quick glance, information technology may appear to be a new phenomenon. There is a similarity between IT and the broader technology, however, with both being part of the organizational processes where 'patterns of organizing are inscribed in technology and the ways in which organizations inscribe the technical worlds they produce' (Joerges and Czarniawska, 1998: 364). However, IT has rather a long history. During the first half of the nineteenth century, Charles Babbage, the mathematician and all-around genius, with Ada Lovelace, 'the first programmer', developed the first mechanical computer that was based on a binary one-zero system (Spufford and Uglow, 1996; Plant 1997). Babbage also recommended the use of his machine in manufacturing because of his belief that inventions should help people achieve their goals (Babbage, 1833). In what today is referred to as the Babbage Principle, Babbage recommended a division of labour where work should either be divided into its various processes that require skills and strength, or alternatively all the work should be performed by one sufficiently skilful person who can perform all the most complicated tasks in the operations (for further details see Chapter 4).

The modern national census registration in England during the Victorian Era grew with the help of data processing, and Campbell-Kelly (2001) argued that the increasing scientific interest in statistics was an important reason behind this technology being used at all.

Although there was no direct connection between the English Census Office and the Babbage Principle, people in this office were employed precisely because they were skilful enough for the assignments. In the 1940s, scientists who were inspired by Charles Babbage's work began to develop prototypes for electronic and electromechanical automatic digital calculators (Iacono and Kling, 2001). In the 1950s, the insurance industry began to use IT for probability calculations following their development during the Second World War. Thus, it is a mistaken claim that the Information Age arose and developed only in the late twentieth century.

At the end of the 1950s, people assumed that the increase in data processing would result in better information for decision-making in organizations, a belief that resulted in the rise of the academic discipline of management information systems. In the 1960s, IT use spread to banks, public authorities, and manufacturers. The greatest expectations concerning the use of IT by organizations were that the investments in new technology would increase productivity and would permit substitution of machines for people in the workforce. Another less radical assumption was the expectation that less skilled, lower paid workers who used the technology could do more complex work. According to one calculation, one person using a word processor was estimated to do the work of up to five typists, and robots in car manufacturing were estimated to replace two workers (Iacono and Kling, 2001). In the middle of the 1980s, personal computers and various software applications became popular among professional employees. Today, the use of computers at work, the adoption of computers at home, and the ready access to the Internet has transformed work practices in many regions of the world.

Zara goes online

MINICASE

Using information technology to redesign organizational processes, and to find new ways of meeting customers is rapidly becoming a natural part of the strategy work in most industries. As the opening case of Volvo Car Company has shown e-business is one important means of meeting customers on the web. Many companies have understood the potential in selling and distributing goods and services using the Internet, but not all are successful. There are more and more companies that have realized that a successful e-strategy often requires a fundamental redesign of business operations. Launching an online store requires careful planning and a dedicated approach. A lot of people have been surprised that the highly successful chain store Zara was so late in opening an online store. It was not until 2009 that they announced that they were about to launch such an effort. The online store, due to be started 2 September 2010, was being advertised on the company's webpage during the spring of 2010. The company realized that launching an online store required much more than designing a fancy webpage. In fact, the company built quite a following on the Internet using social networks, and they urged all the company's retailers to raise their presence online. These, and many other measures, were important preparations for the 2010 launch of the official online store. The importance of opening operations on the Internet is underscored in the following quotation from the Chairman of Inditex (the owner of Zara): 'This vehicle for growth, set to launch in the second half of 2010, will complement the international expansion strategy the Group continues to roll out on all fronts.'

(Inditex Annual Report 2009).

Deskilling or upskilling

The computerization of organizations brought forward the question of whether this technology would lead to deskilling or **upskilling** of workers. Research results became contradictory. It was shown that specific changes in computerization led to upskilling for workers in production work (when they learn to handle operation processes using new system tools) even when their autonomy was not increased (Zuboff, 1988). Even professional workers were often expected to benefit from computerization since they were used to working with computers (Burris, 1998). However, this expectation of upskilling for professional employees may be doubtful when their tasks became highly computerized. Adler (1986) provided an example of professional analysts for insurance claims who were responsible for the more complex cases that required their expertise in complicated procedures and decision parameters. In the automation process, this expertise was programmed into a computer system, leading to a situation where clerical workers could process most cases. As Adler (1986) noted, this change, which resulted in the deskilling of the professional analysts, facilitated and upgraded the work of the clerks. As a result it is difficult to draw a general conclusion about the upskilling/deskilling effects of technological changes in organizations (Burris, 1998). In a similar vein, Bertolotti, Macrì, and Tagliaventi (2004) state that it is still unclear if the introduction of Computer Aided Design (CAD) leads to the enhancement or erosion of operators' skills.

In the debate on deskilling vs. upskilling, feminist inspired studies have focused especially on the phenomena of computerization and the changing work situation for women. Cynthia Cockburn (1983: 116) claimed: 'Skill is, however, not only a class political weapon. It is also a sex/gender weapon.' In her book, *Brothers: Male Dominance and Technological Change* (1983), Cockburn analysed changes in the typesetting technology in Great Britain. Where once typesetting was a highly skilled occupation in which most tasks were performed manually, from 1950 to 1980 the typesetting process was gradually computerized. Typesetters took early retirement, joined the dole queue, started their own businesses, or trained as computer operators, typists, data processors, or even graphics personnel. A few former typesetters became self-employed and began 'setting girls to work on *their* keyboards' (Cockburn, 1983: 193). For these girls, and the other women proficient in typing and secretarial tasks, word processors were the next threat. Wajcman (2004: 25) described how the introduction of word processors reduced the need for secretaries, while for those still employed, their work tasks 'would be increasingly deskilled, fragmented into routine, standardized tasks, and subject to the control of the machine.' When offices were rationalized, such white-collar workers were 'proletarianized' as their work became more like factory work (Wajcman, 2004).

There are various ways to measure the changing state of work viewed from the employee perspective. As possible measurements, Cockburn listed earnings, working hours and other working conditions, the degree of division of labour, and professional/social status. In the typesetter case, people were deskilled although simultaneously some saw their earnings increase, their working hours shorten, and their level of work pressure decrease. As far as the division of labour, there were no further subdivisions except for 'some cases of reintegrated detailed tasks' (Cockburn, 1983: 117). The actual effect of the degradation of the typesetters' work was largely experienced in their changed professional/social status. As their specialized work became more generalized and easier, the typesetters felt more like unskilled general labourers than skilled professional employees. This deskilling of women is, however, not a deterministic process as the minicase below shows.

MINICASE

Women and deskilling in clerical work

An example of deskilling of women comes from a study of clerical work in Canada. During the late nineteenth century and the first decades of the twentieth century, more women became clerical workers. (Altman and Lamontagne, 2003). Such feminization of an occupation is often associated with deskilling, particularly in social status (degradation of the occupation), and economic status (decreased wages). However, in Canada, this was not the result. Clerical work allowed women to work for comparatively good wages, and, unlike teachers who had to remain single, clerical workers could marry without fear of losing their positions. Clerical work also had managerial tasks as well as repetitive and relatively unskilled tasks. When managerial tasks were separated from less skilled clerical work in the IT-based administrative revolution, white-collar workers could do administrative work and thus deskilling did not result. 'Rather, it created new job opportunities for both women and men at lower levels of skill and responsibility compared with what was required of the manager-supervisor-clerk' (Altman and Lamontagne, 2003: 1057). A highly relevant and intriguing question is how the experiences from this historical example can be used in similar processes of change today. In order to avoid such, unintended, results it is very important to understand why deskilling occurs in the first place, and why it seems to hit women harder than men. The underlying processes are often subtle which further underscores the need to be aware of and understand them in order to avoid deskilling.

During the 1990s, the Internet, e-mail, and mobile telephones became key components in the world of information technology, generally replacing, for example, such communication tools as the fax machine (Coopersmith, 2001). In 2001, 122 million people in the world had access to the Internet at home, at work, at the library, or at school (Iacono and Kling, 2001). Today computers are found everywhere, from desks where primary school children play educational games to desks where farmers manage fodder systems for dairy cows.

A new perspective on technology

Research commenced by sociologists of science in the area of Studies of Science and Technology (SST) has shown how technology and science are socially constructed (Latour and Woolgar, 1979; Woolgar, 1991). There are also examples in this area of how the users' constructions of technological inventions are uncontrollable, often leading to unintended consequences (Bijker et al., 1987/1989; Lohan, 2000; Orlikowski, 2007). When a certain technology reaches consumers, they may interpret and use it in a way that differs from what the inventors intended. One example is the microwave oven that was developed to be used as a quick way to heat food on caravan holiday trips. The main users were men. As more microwave ovens were sold, it became clear that gradually they had become popular as a complementary accessory in daily food preparation (Cockburn and Ormrod, 1993). Thus, microwave ovens were used primarily by the person who prepared food at home. In cultures where housewives are common, this person was a woman. As a consequence of users' interpretation of the technology and its use in ways inconsistent with the inventors' intentions, technological inventions began to promise what were previously unimaginable possibilities. In the same way, when technological inventions come to the workplace in organizations, the consequences of their use are unpredictable.

A direction in SST research is Actor Network Theory (ANT) which becomes gradually more popular. In this tradition, they look at technology as socially constructed and the social as technologically constructed—something that the professor in sociology of science, John Law, calls 'the seamless web' of sociotechnology (1991). Science and technology are better seen as socially constructed sources of power that are part of, and dependent upon, relationships among people (Latour, 1993, 1998). An example of this idea is how myths and other social dimensions create our need for new technology. This is evident in the minicase on Apple and the iPad below.

MINICASE

Apple and the introduction of the iPad

In April 2010 Apple finally released the hyped iPad, a lightweight device, focused on social media consumption. Being something in between a large iPhone and a more regular laptop, however without phone, camera (which would be expected on any cell phone by this time), or office applications and USB port (to be expected on regular laptops), the question was who would use it, and for what? Even though it may be too early to say what will happen to this product, some forecasts can be made. According to the magazine Newsweek, April 5, 2010 (p. 47); 'The iPad will change the way you use computers, read books, and watch TV—as long as you're willing to do it the Steve Jobs way.' As the interface is user friendly, the iPad had after three weeks been reported to appeal to older consumers who were not too keen on using regular computers, as well as young consumers who quickly find their way through the apps, games, movies, and YouTube. For business, the usage could be expected to be anything from a meeting device—in which Internet resources are easily brought into meetings, for reading documents during travelling, for providing maps etc. If only applied to the Internet the product bears the promise of replacing GPS and might thereby become a new tool for logistics of trucks etc. The backdrop of the iPad might be the renewal of the vertical-integration model, as Apple includes both a microprocessor of their own with their own operating system. By this integration, rivals will not be able to readily compete. Customers have to use Safari as the Web browser, and will face various software being glitchy or blocked.

Myths about information technology

The use of technology is surrounded by myth. One reason is the technical deterministic prediction that the introduction of a new technology will change the way of organizing work.

Thus, there is a popular myth—similar to the predictions that technological inventions caused at the beginning of the age of industrialization—that information technology will fundamentally change work organizations. A very common argument in this vein is that IT leads to:

- efficiency and effectiveness,
- higher quality,
- faster market rollouts of products,
- lower overhead costs,
- increased customer orientation.

The introduction of IT therefore makes companies more competitive (Winter and Taylor, 2001). Furthermore, there are researchers who claim that IT, the defining technology of our time, will change people's relationship to nature in the same way that the mechanical clock and the steam engine did in earlier times. Bolter (1984), as reported by Winter and Taylor (2001), thought that we would become different people precisely because we lived with computers.

There are more predictions that arise as the result of the introduction of IT. For example, a reduced need for mid-level managers is predicted because the production functions and many personnel functions that previously were performed by such managers in large organizations can now be contracted out to smaller, more specialized companies. The result of such downsizing, among other things, may be that many non-productive, white-collar workers will lose their jobs. Mid-level managers may become even more unnecessary as IT produces information that is very accessible and transferable. While mid-level managers earlier functioned as the link in the chain of communication, the new form of information dissemination may now make them superfluous.

From a historical viewpoint it is questionable whether these changes will result in major differences. Winter and Taylor explained:

> 'IT seems to be restructuring the economy into a more flexible, dynamic network of organizations, with many smaller, leaner firms narrowly focused on their areas of competence and engaged in temporary partnerships with other firms in order to produce a product or provide a service in response to fluctuating demand. Interestingly, this scenario shares many characteristics of the flexible specialization form of industrial organization found in some manufacturing districts of the nineteenth century and currently seen in such areas as the textile district of Prato [in Italy] and the computer industry in the Silicon Valley of California.'
>
> (Winter and Taylor, 2001: 22)

It is also argued that IT creates more flexible organizations because the new technology makes it is easier for employees to work from home and for organizations to set up satellite offices. In addition, it is claimed that IT in the age of globalization makes it easier for small companies to compete in larger markets, allowing them to spread their fixed costs over more customers. Taylor and Winter saw this assumption as more of a myth than a conclusion supported by research. Even if advanced IT systems are introduced, such as, for example, computer-aided design and computer-integrated manufacturing, studies show that the most advanced parts of these systems are never used. Similarly, the large, established companies who gain the most from globalization can reach even larger markets. More detailed and empirical research is needed to examine these changes resulting from IT innovations.

It should be emphasized that there are also myths around technology that are not new. Researchers in the area of symbolism and technology have long observed that technology and myth are nearly interwoven. Cohen (1969) listed some purposes of myths:

- to explain, express, and maintain solidarity and cohesion,
- to mediate contradictions,
- to provide a narrative, anchoring the present to the past.

Relating this idea to technology Koprowksi (1983) claimed that even in modern societies where logic and rationality are highly valued and where technological inventions and science are emphasized, myths still play the special role that they have had earlier in our history—the role of providing people with meaning: 'For the more we master and are mastered by science and technology, the more we yearn for escape and meaning' (1983: 40). This yearning can be related to the fictitious content in technological projects. As Latour explained, 'by definition, a technological project is a fiction, since at the outset it does not exist, and there is no way it can exist yet because it is in the project phase' (1993: 23). A way to give technological projects meaning, despite their fictitious nature, is thus to ascribe mystical qualities to them.

Computerization movements

In the latter part of the 1990s, it became more or less obligatory for companies to be on the Internet. Claiming a presence on the Internet is somewhat ambiguous, however, because such a claim can mean anything from having an employee e-mail system to having a simple website to having an interactive website. The researchers Suzanne Iacono and Rob Kling (2001) suggested that the organizational changes that follow the introduction of 'Internet-working technologies' are as momentous as the labour movement and the women's movement.

In the general discussion on the Internet, it is claimed that organizations that use the Internet have faster communications and closer relationships to their customers. Consumers benefit from this technology because it is easier for them to look for alternative products, which means there is greater price competition in the market, even lower prices. On the Internet, consumers also have access to new markets at closer locations. Even companies who use the Internet are expected to have greater access to information on their competitors and possible partners. It is also claimed that the Internet offers more efficient and effective purchasing venues compared to the traditional ways of working with suppliers. This is, of course, the same argument that Ford used when it adopted e-Business. This is thoroughly discussed in the link box below.

But are these changes really valuable to companies? Iacono and Kling (2001) suggested that there are macro-social and cultural dimensions that people often ignore when companies implement new technologies. They summarized this conclusion:

> '... participants in computerization movements build up frames in their public discourses that indicate favourable links between internetworking and a new preferred social order. These frames help to legitimate relatively high levels of investment for many potential adopters and package expectations about how they should use internetworking in their daily routines and about how they should envision a future based on internetworking. Within organizations, meaning-making processes are ongoing as members attempt to restructure themselves around these new technologies. The symbolic struggle over these new technologies socially constructs the organizations that adopt them. Organizational change, then, is determined neither by the imperatives of the technology nor by the planned changes of organizational management.'
> (Iacono and Kling, 2001: 97–98)

LINK BOX

Back to the Ford/VCC case

The introduction of e-Business at Ford/VCC is an example of how macro-social and cultural dimensions influence decisions to accept new technology. In their report to Ford on the new economy and the possibilities of e-Business, McKinsey stated that Ford and VCC would enter a 'preferred social order' in the emerging business world where IT offered a number of possibilities. This vision of e-Business was presented in a very positive light. The Swedish purchasing agents immediately saw their chance to break away from their old and unwieldy purchasing system. Thus, they could designate themselves as positive supporters of e-Business. Among certain IT strategists, however, there was still some hesitancy toward the new technology:

> 'There are some presentations of eVEREST and what is good about this is that all purchasers are initially positive. The reason for this positive attitude is that everybody curses our old system, and they are happy a new system is about to be implemented. This happiness might be limited when they realise that this will affect our way of working. But initially, they are positive. If we told them that this would affect our way of working, however, they would turn sharply' (Interview, Feb 2002).

It was apparent that the Ford managers were strongly positive about the advantages of the new purchasing system that they thought would lead to changed and improved purchasing routines. However, they were also aware that the VCC purchasing agents perhaps did not agree with them. Yet instead of promoting these advantages among the purchasing agents, the Ford managers talked more about what would happen if the VCC people did not adopt the new system. Given the macro-social message—everyone must use the Internet in the purchasing activities—people were at risk if they opposed the emerging system and the company. Quite simply, their work opportunities would disappear.

Reflection point: The Ford/VCC case has illustrated the complexities involved in the introduction of new technology in an organization. How would you describe the introduction of a new e-business system?

Summary and conclusions

The opening case of this chapter showed the important, but at the same time problematic, role that information technology plays in today's corporations. Classic organization theory assigned technology a somewhat hidden role in organizing. With the sociotechnical perspective, the interplay between the social and the technical system came into focus. For its followers, the sociotechnical perspective dealt with planned rationalizations and with changes to the social system that enabled people to be productive despite the technological changes. As a consequence, rationalizations due to technology changes had to be followed by carefully prepared changes in the organization. Contingency theory emphasized that technology is an important element in relationship to the structure of organizations. If organizational technology and organizational structure were matched in the best way, organizations would be successful and productive, this perspective suggested.

Since the 1960s, information technology has played an ever-larger role in our organizations. IT contributes to change in various ways. Even though IT was expected, in concurrence with other technologies, to lead to deskilling of the workers, it has turned out to lead to upskilling as well as deskilling depending on the organizational settings. New research perspectives of STS and ANT show how some people invent technology with ideas of how it will be used, but in the hand of the users the technology will be constructed in unpredictable ways. Technology in its turn contributes to the construction of society in organizations.

 ## Questions

1. How can the relation between technology and organizing be understood from different perspectives?
2. What role did technology have in the early industrialization period?
3. How are the social and the technical systems connected?
4. Can the implementation of an e-business system be expected to affect the social system?
5. How is the relation between technology and organization understood within contingency theory?
6. How do new technologies affect processes of organizing?

 ## Literature recommendations and further readings

A good introduction to the sociotechnical school: *The Social Engagement of Social Science* (1990) by Eric Trist and Hugh Murray (Eds.) *Technology and organizing: Industrial Organization: Theory and Practice* (1965/1980) by Joan Woodward provides a good overview of technology in relation to practical organizing and also to classic organization theory. An excellent, up-to-date presentation on information technology in contemporary organizations is *Information, Technology and Organizational Transformation: History, Rhetoric*

and Practice (2001) by Joanne Yates and John Van Maanen. Readers interested in social construction of technology may find *The Social Construction of Technological Systems* (1987/1989) by Wiebe Bijker, Thomas Hughes, and Trevor Pinch (Eds.) to be a good introduction.

Take your learning further

online resource centre

http://www.oxfordtextbooks.co.uk/orc/erikssonzetterquist/

Visit the Online Resource Centre which accompanies this book to enrich your understanding of this chapter.

Students: explore web links and further reading suggestions. Keep up to date with the latest developments via 'What happened next' updates to appropriate cases from within the book.

Lecturers: you will find seminar exercises and teaching notes, for use in class or assessment.

CHAPTER 4
Operations management in day-to-day work

Toyota revolutionizes operations management through small means

In 1979, a group of executives from General Motors visited Japan. They were in Japan to learn more about the Japanese manufacturing industry, an industry offering more intense competition for American companies. What the General Motors executives saw was a radical reorganization and transformation of the manufacturing activities.

While the North American and European automotive industry had developed and remained truthful to what has been called the Fordist production system, a system based on extensive division of labour, assembly line production, and a hierarchical organization wherein the planning and development work were located in specific departments dominated by specialists such as engineers, the Japanese manufacturing industry had taken another approach. The single most important company in the reorganization of the operations management was Toyota, today the world's most well-known automotive company. What practical changes of the manufacturing work had been developed by the Japanese?

Firstly, the Japanese manufacturing industry had changed the organization of work. Rather than using individual work assignments and individually defined piece-rate payment systems, the Japanese practised team based work where job assignments were rotating and where the work team was responsible for what the Japanese called *kaizen*, continuous improvements of the operations. Kaizen was a method aimed at eliminating unnecessary movements and conceiving of better ways to arrange the work. In addition, kaizen was undertaken on the level of the work team and all members of the group contributed to the work.

Secondly, the Japanese had implemented more flexible machinery that was less complicated to use and therefore better able to change between batches. Thirdly, they had implemented so-called Total Quality Management (TQM) methods, a set of practices and procedures to safeguard the quality level of the output at a high stable rate. While North American and European producers invested significant resources to correct faults produced further upstream in the production process, the Japanese had worked hard to eliminate the quality problems at their sources. The Japanese also used a number of rather elementary tools and techniques for determining the quality of the goods delivered from the suppliers and the output from the production facilities.

Finally, the Japanese manufacturing companies had developed close-knit relationships with their suppliers with whom the end-producers (e.g., Toyota) collaborated. Using what became known as *just-in-time logistics*, the end-producers managed to lower the amount of capital bound up in components. In the just-in-time logistics regime, components were delivered to the end-producers when needed, that is, in small and timely batches.

Japanese manufacturing had adopted Fordist manufacturing practices but had gradually examined all aspects of this system and eliminated some of the quality concerns, work organization challenges (including monotony and the sense of alienation), and some of the logistics problems associated with large batch deliveries. Taken together, all these small changes and improvements resulted in a manufacturing industry that, in many ways, became more effective and demonstrated higher productivity figures than their Western equivalents. 'Learning from Japan' consequently became a central topic on the managerial agenda in a range of industries.

During World War II, the Japanese sided with Nazi-Germany against the allies. Japanese troops were also responsible for significant atrocities during the war. The bombing of Hiroshima and Nagasaki in August 1945 ended the war and left Japan to deal with substantial historical luggage. As part of the post World War II rehabilitation of (Western) Germany and Japan, the USA supported the reconstruction of industry. As part of this reconstruction work, American manufacturing engineers, such as W. Edward Deming, were brought to Japan to train the Japanese engineers to use statistical methods in the production planning. The Japanese were thus indebted to the Americans for helping them, not only financially, but also intellectually, to develop an advanced manufacturing industry.

In the beginning of the period preceding the war, in the 1950s and 1960s, Japanese products were regarded as being of inferior quality in comparison to European and North American products. However, in the 1970s, the emerging oil crises brought new attention to the automotive industry and the Japanese companies demonstrated remarkable productivity figures. 'Between 1970 and 1987, productivity in Japanese industry increased twice as fast as in France, the Federal Republic of Germany and the United States (5.9 per cent a year against about 3 per cent)' (Watanabe, 1991: 58). Moreover, Japanese products proved to be of high quality and began to sell well in the US. For instance, Honda motorcycles became a qualified competitor, especially in the North-American market, challenging companies such as Harley Davidson and other well known American motorcycle brands.

By the second oil crisis (in 1978), and until the early 1990s and the so-called Heisei recession (Lillrank, 1995: 972), the genre of 'learning from Japan' became a major industry:

> Pilgrimages were made to Tokyo, hundreds of books were written, and a consulting industry segment was created.

> The Japanese demonstrated an ability to take market share, establish technology leadership, and amass trade surpluses. They provided tools, management models and case material which stimulated copying as well as new thinking and experimentation
> (Lillrank, 1995: 972).

In fact, the entire interest for corporate culture in the 1980s was more or less derived from the success of the Japanese manufacturing industry.

Major sources of information for the case are: Lillrank, 1995 and Watanabe, 1991. A thorough description of the Toyota production system is also given by Ohno, 1988.

Questions

When examined individually these innovations do not appear to be very spectacular. So why then do you think they received a high level of attention from top management communities?

Why do you think these practices have featured highly in business school research?

What difficulties do you think may accompany the Japanese system of organizing work?

Introduction

It is clear from the case description above that the so-called Toyota model has changed production practices in many industries. In this chapter, theories about operations management will be examined in detail and we address theories that can shed light on the quality movement described in the Toyota case. Operations management is a field within organization theory that addresses issues such as work organization, the physical outline of the workspace, the logistics of the work-in-progress in the factory or office, leadership work, and other issues pertaining to the day-to-day production of goods and services. Traditionally, operations management has been associated with manufacturing industry, but since the contemporary economy employs more people in the so-called knowledge-intensive firms and in the service sector, new theories regarding the organization of such industries and activities have been developed in the field of operations management. It is important to emphasize that this chapter presents a view of operations management influenced by organization theory rather than the engineering sciences. In many cases, the term operations management denotes a set of instrumental and functionalist methods and managerial principles that can be applied to cases to increase the effectiveness of the operations including optimization methods, workflow analyses, and various problem-solving techniques. In contrast to such instrumental perspectives, this chapter discusses a range of studies in the field of management studies, organization theory, and industry sociology.

When presenting operations management theory, the discussion begins with perhaps one of the most widely known and debated management methods, that of Frederick W. Taylor's scientific management. Thereafter, various studies of operations management practices, in many cases developed in direct confrontation with the scientific management practices, are accounted for.

This chapter provides a comprehensive overview of the field of operations management and studies of shop floor behaviour and addresses the following topics:

- The emergence of scientific management as a systematic management method,
- The tradition of labour process theory and industrial sociology and studies of workplace behaviour,
- Work organization including the movement towards flexibility, the use of total quality management practices, business process re-engineering, forms of management control, and the use of various organization **routines**, rules, and practices.

The engineering revolution: Scientific management and Taylorism

Theories about division of labour

One of the axial principles in modern society and in contemporary organizations is the value of division of labour. The need for specialization and the social benefits from this procedure have been well known and debated since at least ancient Greece. 'It is impossible for a single person to practice many crafts or professions well', Plato emphasized in *Republic* (p. 49).

More than twenty centuries later, Adam Smith, the great British economist, made the division of labour a central principle in his seminal work *The Wealth of Nations* (1776), both in terms of individual specialization in the local community and in the global economy, increasingly characterized by protectionism and mercantilist ideologies in Smith's life time. In the nineteenth century, Charles Babbage (1833: 170–172) identified five sources of efficiency gains derived from the division of labour:

(1) Shorter time for learning a skill,

(2) Less waste in materials,

(3) Lower transaction costs,

(4) Less change of tools,

(5) Skills acquired by repetition.

The value of division of labour was then well known and debated both in the practical work and as a theoretical topic of interest. However, it was not until the modern age and the latter decades of the nineteenth century that the full potential of division of labour was more systematically examined and restructured.

Taylorist ideas and practices

The period 1880–1920 was when the Industrial Revolution swept over Europe and North America. This was characterized by the emergence of a new professional and social class: the engineer. After the Napoleonic Wars in Europe, where engineering expertise was used to construct bridges and in other ways supported the war efforts, polytechnic schools were started all over Europe in order to make use of engineering skills in the civil society. In the US, the engineering profession grew from about 7,000 engineers in 1880 to about 135,000 in 1920 (Jacoby, 1985: 41). The training of these engineers in using rational methods and scientific procedures enabled a wider reception of such approaches in industry and administrative pursuits. The engineers gradually became an influential professional class shaping the modern corporation and the public administration. The most widely known contributor to these engineering-based management methods was an American, Frederick Winslow Taylor.

Already from his early days, the young Taylor was interested in contriving innovations such as mechanical brakes on his sledge. After being trained as an engineer, Taylor was hired by Midvale Steel Company where he noticed the unstructured and haphazard procedures and practices, both in terms of work procedures and in the distribution of wages and benefits among the workers. Ineffective piece-rate systems and inherited 'rules of thumb' among the workers effectively inhibited more 'rational methods' being used. Taylor decided to develop more systematic methods for the day-to-day management work in organizations.

In his two major works *Shop management* (1903) and *Principles of Scientific Management* (1911), Taylor advocated what he named 'scientific management principles', that is, managerial practices grounded in the rational (i.e., 'scientific') analyses of work procedures and a reorganization of work in accordance with these analyses. The first principle is that it is the managers and specialist engineers that should examine and evaluate all the co-existing practices in the workshop and reformulate the 'rules' of the work procedures. In other words, Taylor did not approve the old regime of work where principles learned by doing things and 'rules of thumb' served a useful role. Instead, he advocated the use of scientific methods to identify the 'one best way of doing things'. The second principle prescribed that intellectual labour and manual work should be carefully separated:

'All possible brain work should be removed from the shop and centered in the planning and laying-out department, leaving for the foreman and gang bosses work strictly executive in nature.'
(Taylor, 1903: 36)

Again, an effective production facility is not accomplished through relying on traditional ways of organizing the activities, but Taylor had a strong belief in the value of the production engineer's analysis of the work procedures. As a consequence, 'brain work' should not be mixed up with manual labour. The third and perhaps central argument for making the scientific principles work properly is to reward the application of the scientific management principles through higher pay. Taylor strongly stressed this point:

'This task specified not only what is to be done, but how it is to be done and the exact time allowed for doing it. And, whenever the workman succeeds in doing his task right, and within the time limit specified, he receives an addition from 30 per cent to 100 per cent, to his ordinary wages.'
(Taylor, 1911: 39)

For Taylor, the use of his scientific management principles was a win-win situation where the employee is making more money when being more effective at work, and where the employer is capable of raising the effectiveness of the firm when eliminating old and irrational ways of structuring the work. Perhaps the most well known of Taylor's principles is the separating of manual and intellectual work. He believed that workers on the shop floor should not engage in intellectual work including decision-making but that all such more complicated work should be located in departments dominated by engineers and other professional groups who were better equipped to handle such assignments. In addition, Taylor did not regard manual labourers in terms of a source of human capital that could be trained and educated. Instead, he thought that companies should sort out intellectually inferior individuals—in many cases including recently arrived immigrants from southern and eastern European not capable of speaking proper English—to handle the more monotonous and repetitive tasks.

Taylor was not overtly concerned about humanist virtues. Needless to say, Taylor's scientific principles were immediately criticized for deskilling workers and for treating workers as cogs in a machine. Not only were the labour unions and the community of workers critical, but also, employers thought Taylor's principles were too far-fetched. To date, labour and capital (to use a Marxist phrase) had collaborated closely. Taylorist ideas undermined the temporal harmony between the interests of workers and employers. In intellectual circles, sceptics were questioning whether Taylor's principles would work in practice. For instance, Hugo Münsterberg, one of the first organization psychologists, criticized Taylorism in his *Psychology and industrial efficiency*:

> 'Those followers of Frederick W. Taylor who have made almost a religion out of his ideas have certainly often exaggerated the practical applicability of the new theories, and their actual reforms in the mills have not seldom shown that the system is still too top heavy; that is, there are too many higher employees necessary in order to keep the works running on principles of scientific management.'
> (Münsterberg, 1913: 49)

Taylor's critics either rejected his view of human beings as essentially prone to 'soldiering' and shirking, or thought his ideas were too complicated to use in practice. In order to bypass this critique, many employers used other management systems that were less burdened by negative connotations than Taylor's scientific management. For instance, the successful Bedaux system advocated by Charles Eugène Bedaux in his book, *The Bedaux Efficiency Course for Industrial Application*, first published in 1917, was one such management system. Guillén (1994: 56–57) writes: 'While avoiding the negative stigma attached to anything represented under the name of Taylorism, many employees and managers used the Bedaux System to introduce scientific management through the back door. Unlike Taylor's, the Bedaux System could be implemented without revamping the entire management practices of the firm, a feature that employers welcomed'.

Taylor's followers

After Taylor's death, some of his most prominent disciples such as Henry Gantt—today most widely known for the Gantt chart used in project management planning work—and Frank and Lilian Gilbreth continued to develop methods and procedures for implementing scientific principles. Gantt introduced time and motion studies (Iedema, 2003: 99) and thought of a well-designed 'management system' as a significant resource for the corporation. Such a system was defined accordingly:

> 'A system of management may be defined as a means of causing men to co-operate with each other for a common end.'
> (Gantt, 1919: 111)

Moreover, Gantt shared with Taylor the belief that workers were not to be trusted in terms of performing their work effectively. Instead, it is the trained engineer that should carefully examine the work procedure and propose an alternative procedure.

Gantt (1919: 258) suggested, 'The ordinary man, whether mechanic or labourer, seldom performs any operation in the manner most economical either of time or labour'. What Gantt suggested is that even a life-long experience from a trade or a work assignment does not qualify as a legitimate ground for how the work is structured. Instead, Gantt demonstrated a firm belief in the benefits of formal analysis of work. Consequently, Gantt followed Taylor closely in separating *expert work* from what he called *standard work*:

> 'All work, and all knowledge, for that matter, may be divided into two classes: *Expert* and *Standard*. Expert knowledge may be described as that which has not been reduced to writing in such a manner as to be generally available, or exist only in the minds of a few'
> (Gantt, 1919: 161)

Given this distinction, it is the manager that is solely responsible for the efficiency of the operations, not the workers. The minicase below shows how heated the debate between different categories of employees can be.

General practitioners and nurses struggle over professional authority and jurisdiction

MINICASE

Taylor's insistence on separating manual labour and the more intellectually demanding work is representative of a longstanding controversy in the contemporary society of relevance for a variety of professional groups and industries. For instance, in the health care sector, there is a perennial and ongoing discussion on how to distinguish between the medical expertise offered by medical doctors and the 'bedside care' offered by general practitioners and nurses. While medical doctors have staunchly resisted attempts at transferring some of the decision-making authority, nurses on their part have sought to upgrade their expertise and authority.

The Taylorist split between manual labour and intellectual work is therefore a contested line of demarcation in, for instance, the debate between obstetricians and midwives, both claiming their jurisdiction in the actual work in obstetrics. There have been many attempts at changing these institutionalized patterns, for instance, by promoting nurses to managerial positions in clinical departments and, in this way, reserving a 'sphere' of influence for nurses outside the actual medical work. Recent research suggests that these and similar changes are necessary, but that it takes a lot of dedicated managerial attention and support to change old habits and behavioural patterns. When it comes to changing patterns that are more central to the identity of physicians, changes are much harder to make. Relevant and important questions can be raised concerning the importance of breaking with these kind of institutionalized patterns, and not least if the patients' perspective is put at the forefront.

By and large, Gantt primarily refined Taylor's ideas, adding more sophisticated methods. Gantt's key focus was still the manufacturing industry and its demands for more systematic methods. Frank and Lillian Gilbreth were comparatively more innovative than Gantt in terms of applying the scientific principles in new settings, including the arts and using new media such as photography in their motion studies.

The Gilbreths lived as they preached and the couple had no less than twelve children whom they reared on the basis of scientific management principles. Both Frank and Lillian Gilbreth engaged in a wide range of social experiments and participated in many settings to implement and use the models. Unlike Taylor and Gantt, Frank Gilbreth was less negative regarding the qualities and potentials of the workers and he, in fact, anticipated some of the changes in perspectives brought by the so-called Human Relations School under the directions of Elton Mayo at Harvard University (discussed in detail in Chapter 5). One of the substantial contributions to scientific management is the development of more sophisticated motion studies procedures. Gilbreth (1911: 2) claimed, 'There is no waste of any kind in the world that equals the waste from needless, ill-directed, and ineffective motions'.

In the analysis, Gilbreth separated between (1) *variables of the workers*, including anatomy, health, and other personal and embodied capacities, (2) *variables of the surroundings, equipment, and tools*, including work clothes, monetary and symbolic rewards, tools, ventilation, and lighting, and (3) *variables of the motion*, i.e., all the motions and shifts in position the worker undertakes in his or her work. By carefully examining the interaction of the three variables, the efficiency of the workers may be increased substantially, yet again producing the win-win situation advocated by Taylor and Gantt.

While the work of Taylor and his disciples was not immediately received or implemented, the ideas proposed by the Gilbreths were, in the last decades of the nineteenth century and the first decades of the twentieth century, translated and transformed into complementary or competing methods and systems of management. The newly established engineering unions and societies published journals providing the latest news from the experimental work that was undertaken in both European and American industry. However, by the end of the 1920s, there was a general sense in the broader public that the engineers had taken their belief in 'rational methods' a bit too far.

Shenhav (1999: 46) wrote:

> 'Engineers were criticized for having created a 'machine civilization': a hyper-mechanized society characterized by monotonous jobs, alienated workers, lack of spirit, lack of aesthestic, and dehumanization ... The general feeling was that mechanization and systematization had gone too far.'

In Charlie Chaplin's praised film *Modern times* (1936), this efficiency craze is parodied as what is not leaving any human activity—including eating one's lunch, in Chaplin's film supported by advanced but not very sophisticated robots—without examination. The 'machine civilization' has also been subjected to numerous critical cinematic accounts, ranging from Jacques Tati's comedy *Mon oncle* (1958) where the everyday living in technically advanced houses is becoming overtly complicated, to more dystopic films such as Fritz Lang's *Metropolis* (1927).

The legacy of Taylor and scientific management

While scientific management and Taylorism without doubt are major components in contemporary day-to-day work in organizations and companies, the criticisms of Taylor and his followers has been high. For instance, in the mid 1950s, Peter Drucker (1955) pondered over the potential limits of Taylorism:

> 'Scientific Management ... has become stagnant for a long time. It is the oldest of our three approaches to the manager of worker and work ... From 1890 to 1920 Scientific Management produced one brilliant new insight after the other and one creative thinker after the other—Taylor, Fayol, Gantt, and the Gilbreths. During the last thirty years, it has given us little but pedestrian and wearisome tomes on the techniques, if not on the gadgets, of narrower and narrower specialities.'
> (Drucker, 1955: 248)

For writers more explicitly defending the community of workers against attempts at deskilling work, for example, the Marxist scholar, Dan Clawson (1980), Taylor is, at the end of the day, a villain in terms of serving in a war against workers' autonomy and craft production:

> 'Frederick Taylor was the Napoleon of the war against craft production, directing some battles himself and acting through lieutenants in other cases, but he was more than that. He was also the theoretician who comprehended the situation and explained the solution to the problems that had baffled so many before him. Taylor represented the unification of theory and practice in the cause of the capitalist class.'
> (Clawson, 1980: 202)

Gergen and Thatchenkery (1996: 358) credit Taylorism for establishing the concept of management in its contemporary meaning:

> 'Although shorn of the dehumanizing qualities of early Taylorism, the general orientation gave rise to contemporary beliefs that management is a process of planning, organizing and coordinating, and controlling. Such belief continued to pervade organization science theories and practice.'

Other commentators emphasize in a similar manner Taylor's vision and his anticipation of new ways of thinking emerging in the nineteenth century. Wagner-Tsukamoto (2007: 111) claimed:

> 'Like a behavioural scientist, Taylor ... focused in the human condition, drawing on behavioural intervention with social predispositions. In this respect, he interpreted institutions and institutional regulations in a way that anticipated later advances in organizational psychology, organizational sociology and behavioural economics.'

Still, Taylor and his scientific principles remain a contested figure in the history of management. The stress on scientific procedures and rational analysis in his thinking has been widely recognized, but what is perhaps detering wider reception of his contribution to modern management is his overtly negative view of the potentials of human beings; for Taylor, a 'stupid' worker is predestined to remain stupid and must therefore be used in the 'one and best way'. This naïve (at best) or cynical perspective on fellow human beings has undermined the credibility of Taylor in the field of organization theory. However, Taylor's legacy is present in a number of respects:

- An emphasis on the implications for managerial practice and the design of the organization to strongly determine the efficiency of the organization.

- Distinguishing the difference between 'manual work' and 'brain work'. Although the very formulation of this dichotomy is largely antiquated, the division of labour remains a central concern in organization design and Taylor was among the first to separate the execution from the planning of the work.

- Emphasizing the influence of motivation. Taylor conceived of motivation rather crudely in pecuniary terms, and only later were a broader set of human needs and demands brought into discussion by the human relations school. Still, Taylor formulated a 'win-win theory' of motivation that today is still influential in managerial practice and in the relationship between employer and employees.

As a consequence, Taylor may appear inextricably bound to his times and its views of human beings, but some of his master ideas remain a viable source of debate and discussions within organizations. Even though Taylor is generally used as a straw man in organization theory literature—he is put up only to be brought down by criticism—a fair account of his contribution is that he remains very influential in the history of organization theory. In the link box below we now return to the Toyota case to discuss the Taylorist view.

LINK BOX

Taylor and Toyota

The scientific management views are often treated as historical 'curiosities' in textbooks, and the assumption is that modern day companies have, a long time ago, changed their managerial practices. Taylor and his followers are often described in a negative way and we tend to forget the historical legacy of his ideas. The opening case suggests that rather than displacing Taylor and his ideas, the Japanese manufacturing system carefully used the best ideas regarding systematic evaluations and scientific or methodological procedures when revising the work process, but without assuming that the shop floor should be exclusively managed on the basis of principles developed by experts located in specialist departments. A major idea in the Toyota model is the empowerment of workers to use their expertise to solve problems, innovate and take local initiative to develop quality. This is in stark contrast to Taylor's idea that the power to do so resides in the managers rather than the workers. As we will see in the next section, work is not strictly a matter of adhering to a set of work procedures, but is a social practice embedded in sense-making and the collective production of meaning. An important learning from the Toyota case is that it is perfectly possible to develop a managerial system that leaves a lot of freedom and responsibility to workers, at the same time as managerial control is secured. The Toyota example shows that even though work is structured into procedures and routines, there is a need for involving co-workers in the development of the work procedures and for providing opportunities for creating a sense of belongingness and *esprit de corps* among co-workers. Seen from this view, the Japanese manufacturing system is a fruitful synthesis of the more instrumental orientation of the Taylorist tradition of thinking and the more socio-cultural understanding of the work in the labour process theory tradition.

Reflection point: How can a company take the best parts of Taylor's ideas and combine them with modern management thinking?

Labour process theory and industrial sociology: Studies of work

The scientific study of work

The engineering revolution ended in an efficiency craze in the 1930s that gradually lost its impetus as the marginal utility of rationalization diminished and humanist perspectives on production were gradually established. At the same time, not only was the structure of work process being emphasized, but the attitudes, interests, beliefs, and general psychological constitution of the workers were also discovered to be relevant aspects of the work organization. The Human Relations School (discussed in Chapter 5) in many respects replaced the scientific management tradition as the dominant management paradigm in the interwar period. In the war economies of the first years of the 1940s, a wide range of organizational and managerial experiments and developments were conducted and produced. The entrance of female co-workers on the labour market and in organizations represented a significant change. While organization theory and management practice remained essentially gender-blind until at least the 1970s, the use of female operators and co-workers impacted organizations in various ways. An early example of the introduction of more humanist values is shown in the minicase below.

MINICASE

Singing to prevent strain

Many companies realized early that the Taylorist ideas could have negative consequences on employee morale, wellbeing, and productivity, and over the years many experiments with more humanistic tools have been carried out. At the English confectionary company, Cadbury (now fully owned by Kraft Foods), founded by Quakers, the repetitive work was regarded by the company board as a potential threat to the health of the co-workers many of whom were young girls and women (Robertson, Korczynski, and Pickering, 2007: 217). To reduce the strain of the monotonous work, Cadbury advocated singing as a form of 'psychical exercise'. Rowntree, another English confectionary producer used singing in a similar manner. The Rowntree company magazine reported in 1922:

> 'The half-hour singing … is looked forward to and enjoyed by all concerned … By general consent … the half-hour is a pleasant one, according to more than one of the girls, it's the shortest in the day'.
> (cited in Robertson, Korczynski, and Pickering, 2007: 218)

However, the use of music should be monitored and managed in a rational manner; not all music was allowed. The report *Fatigue and Boredom in Repetitive Work* published in (1937) found that many of the workers favoured waltzes, but waltzes were never played in the factories since waltzes were 'found to be one of the types of music least conducive to increased output' (Korczynski and Jones, 2006: 155). In the Cadbury and Rowntree experiments, humanist objectives and managerial goals were brought together.

The period after World War II until the mid 1960s was a period of political stability and economic growth in both Europe and North America. This was also a period where industrial sociology flourished. While sociologists had previously neglected the study of work, in this period everyday work was increasingly subject to study, especially among the more empirically oriented scholars influenced by the Chicago sociology school (a group of sociologists working at the University of Chicago, examining aspects of the emerging urban modernity).

In the mid-nineteenth century Karl Marx suggested that the capitalist economic system had not only economic consequences but also sociological implications, such as, the risk of the workers suffering from 'alienation', i.e., a form of defamiliarization from one's 'essence' as human being, when engaging in repetitive and monotonous work.

Émile Durkheim, one of the 'founding fathers' of sociology besides Marx and Max Weber, predicted that division of labour would enhance what he called the 'organic solidarity' of the modern society. Weber, finally, had written extensively about the growth of the modern bureaucracy and its both positive and negative effects on modern society. Weber, arguably representing a middle position between Marx's critical perspectives and Durkheim's consensus theory sociology, had famously discussed modern life metaphorically as being an iron cage. A new generation of sociologists were interested in studying the nature of everyday work.

In the 1950s and 1960s, sociologists such as Charles Wright Mills, Robert Merton, and William H. Whyte published research on work in organizations and firms that served as the starting point for much sociological research. Mills and Whyte had published books with titles such as *White Collars: The American Middle Class* (1951) and *The Organization Man* (1956) respectively, examining the role, function, and cultural consequences of the emerging white-collar worker class in American society. As opposed to previous generations of Americans, the white-collar workers, a social group composed of administrators and professionals, were not entrepreneurs running their own small businesses but were primarily hired professional employees populating the increasingly large organizations in the American economy. For Mills and Whyte, this new social class represented a new social group produced by the advanced and regulated capitalist economy.

Shop floor studies

Propelled by theoretical contributions from the Human Relations School, industrial psychology research, and the empirically oriented sociology tradition, industrial sociologists aimed at understanding behaviour on the shop floor. For instance, one major concern for employers and a source of debate among employees was why piece-rate systems do not work as intended. Carefully designed to optimize output and to provide a win-win situation for both employee and employer, anecdotal evidence suggested that piece-rate systems did not in fact serve to promote efficiency. Donald Roy (1952) worked for several months on the shop floor to learn how the co-workers were conceiving of the piece-rate work. Roy learned that what was called 'soldiering', i.e., systematic deliberate underperformance among the co-workers, was to be examined as a 'group activity' (Roy, 1952: 427). That is, instituted norms and values in the community of workers regulated how hard one should work to accomplish the piece-rate.

Since some operations were regarded as being unfair, in terms of demanding more work to achieve the highest pay provided by other operations, the workers did not invest as much effort in these operations. The community of workers distinguished between what they called 'gravy jobs' and 'stinkers':

> 'On "gravy jobs" the operators earned a quote, then knocked off. On 'stinkers' they put forth only minimal effort; either they did not try to achieve a turn-in equal to the base wage rate or they deliberately slowed down. Jobs were defined as 'good' and 'bad' jobs, not only in terms of the effort or skill necessary to making out at a bare base-rate level, but of the felt attainability of a substantial premium.'
> (Roy, 1952: 436)

In the best of possible worlds, the workers would not have been capable of identifying the 'gravy jobs' and the 'stinkers', but for various reasons the engineers of the factory had failed to establish a reward system that was regarded as being fair. Roy accounts for extensive calculations on how much work time he and his colleagues were wasting, suggesting that he was himself working at an eighty-three per cent (83%) level due to systematic soldiering. In addition, Roy calculated that a thirty-three per cent (33%) increase in production was possible if the piece-rate systems would be designed differently (Roy, 1952: 441–442). A similar study is reported by Lupton (1963) in an English factory. Lupton suggests, just like Roy (1952), that the piece-rate system is to be conceived of as a social agreement embedded in predominant norms and values in the workplace.

Contrary to Roy (1952), who sought to, on the basis of mathematical calculations, point out that the piece-rate system is sub-optimizing and therefore should be abandoned altogether or restructured, Lupton (1963) does not see the value in seeking to optimize output as long as the various interests of workers and employer are capable of co-existing in harmony within the existing system. Lupton (1963) here speaks of 'the fiddle' of the workers rather than 'soldiering'.

Both Roy (1952) and Lupton (1963) suggested that the activities taking place on the factory shop floor are by no means regulated solely on the basis of 'rational principles' and economic incentives. Instead, the community of workers established certain values, norms, and beliefs that regulate day-to-day work. The shop floor work is therefore not managed by individual incentives, but through influencing the communal order guiding and structuring daily work. A more recent account of the central importance of values, norms, and culture is the study of Alvesson and Svenningsson (2008) suggesting that in order to change organizations, managers and leaders need to target the very culture of the corporation. **Resistance** to organization change is deeply rooted not only among individuals but also in the instituted routines and practices of the organization and in its very culture. This theme is further discussed in Chapter 9 on change in organizations.

Lupton (1963) also strongly emphasized the importance of maintaining harmony between a set of opposing norms, values, and objectives and that stability implies sacrificing some of the efficiency of the operations. Seen in this way, organizations are to some extent irrational in terms of highlighting some objectives (i.e., full efficiency serving as a formal goal) while in fact giving priority to other goals (i.e., the co-existence of norms and values). Other industry sociology studies have emphasized this difference between the formal and the informal organization.

In Dalton's (1959) *Men Who Manage*, the concept of *informal rewards* is introduced as the factor that mediates the difference between formal policies and actual behaviour. The co-workers at the company studied rewarded themselves by bringing product or other commodities home even though this was both against the company regulations and illegal. Top management were aware of this procedure, essentially making the boundary between theft and rewards blurred, but did not intervene as this socially enacted procedure did not lead to any formal demands for rewards. The use of informal rewards was the unofficial procedure for rewarding certain individuals who were generally seen as being unfavoured by the formal reward system. In a classic study of a gypsum plant in the mid-west, Alvin Gouldner (1954) examined what he called a 'mock-bureaucracy', the use of bureaucratic procedures to establish rules and regulations that few co-workers or managers cared to follow. For example, the rule that prohibited smoking in the production facilities was paid little attention. Dalton's (1959) examination of the use of informal rewards is representative of such mock-bureaucratic procedures; formal and informal procedures were blended and used inconsistently to handle various and at times incompatible demands and expectations.

Other industrial sociology studies have been more explicitly aimed at examining specific concerns. For instance, Robert Blauner's *Alienation and Freedom* (1964) examined whether individuals working in assembly line, batch, or process production settings were most likely to experience a sense of alienation or other psychological illnesses. Blauner (1964) found that individuals working in assembly-line work settings were more exposed to factors, such as stress, than workers engaged in batch or process production. Studies such as Blauner's have, since the 1960s, been part of the policy making procedures in Europe and North America, suggesting the occupational health regulations that are needed. In the link box below we describe how industrial sociology provided useful information on how the Japanese management models could be implemented in European and North American companies.

LINK BOX

Facing new management principles

In the general wake of interest for the Japanese manufacturing industry and the exportation of the Japanese management concept (just-in-time logistics, team-based work, joint decision-making on the shop floor, egalitarian corporate values etc.) there were a number of shop-floor studies conducted in both European and North American so-called 'transplants.' These studies, part of the industry sociology tradition from the 1950s and 1960s, showed that the Japanese companies were facing a challenge in implementing the new management principles in an alien setting. Many of the joint procedures and routines were met with cynicism, or were even ridiculed, as European and North American operators felt they were manipulated to provide all their expertise when using continuous improvement activities. More than one researcher warned against an uncritical adoptation of the Japanese production ideas, and over the years there has been a growing awareness that cultural differences between different countries and regions, and also between different companies, make it difficult to simply adopt ideas and transfer them to new contexts. This is also an experience many companies have made in mergers and acquisitions, when they realize that it takes a lot of energy to merge routines, standards, and systems. It is also clear that the Toyota ideas are seldom implemented in a consistent manner, and with the long-term perspective, as we have seen in Toyota.

Reflection point: Compelling as the production ideals of Toyota and other Japanese companies are, there are still a number of hurdles that needs to be overcome when implementing the ideas in new contexts. Think of a company or organization that you are familiar with—how could the production and quality ideas from the opening case be transferred to this company?

After the 1960s, industrial sociology has been a less influential field of research in organization theory but there are still several studies and ethnographies being published. Today, the theoretical perspectives enacted in the studies are more diverse and, for example, feminist theory (Pollert, 1981; Cavendish, 1982) or theories of subjectification (Collinson, 1992) have been used to show how individual identities are constituted through work.

Some studies have also successfully developed and re-articulated classic industry sociology studies, for instance, Michael Burawoy's (1979) study examining why factory workers do in fact work as hard as they do, a study indebted to Donald Roy's work in the 1950s. In Burawoy's Marxist analysis, the shop floor is a social domain regulated by norms and values and in order to avoid boredom and fatigue, the operators are competing with one another to accomplish their piece-rate as fast as possible. The operators cannot both 'play the game and question its rules,' Burawoy suggests, and therefore, they comply with the management system when participating in what Burawoy calls 'the game of making out'. In Burawoy's study, the operators are very well aware of the intricacies of the elaborated piece-rate system and they are by no means a gullible community, but they weigh the risk of boredom and fatigue against the value of competing with one another. In other words, workers work as hard as they do because there is something in it for them, and that something is not primarily better pay but the ability to join an 'output game' with one's peers.

While industrial sociology is no longer a driving force in organization theory, the concepts of the labour process and labour process theory have been vigorously debated in the UK over the last decade. On the one hand, more conventional sociologists claim that research should continue to emphasize the relationship between labour and capital as a principal binary category still influencing day-to-day work in organizations, while on the other hand, a group of researchers more inclined to recognize recent theoretical developments in, for instance, so-called post-structuralist organization theory render such traditional binary categories, if not obsolete, at least less central to the analysis of the labour process (Parker, 1999; Thompson, Smith, and Ackroyd, 2000; O'Doherty and Willmott, 2001; Friedman, 2004). If nothing else, this animated debate suggests that there may be a future for both industrial sociology and labour process theory, at least in the UK.

Work organization

The concept of work organization is a broad term including all practices, mechanisms, tools, procedures, and routines used in the day-to-day work in organizations. Work organization is used to denote the organization of a variety of industries and activities including manufacturing work, service work, and more so-called creative work, such as, artistic work and design work. However, the concept of work organization originally means the organization of factory work. In this section, the concepts of flexible specialization, total quality management (TQM), business process re-engineering, management control, work routines, and work roles are addressed. Taken together, these various concepts shape and form the work organization in contemporary organizations.

Flexible specialization

The field of operations management includes theories about work organization and the management control of operations. In the early 1980s, a series of changes in the world economy brought new attention to the field of operations management. First, as shown in the opening case, the advancement of new managerial innovation in the Japanese manufacturing industry created a new interest for work organization, new logistics solutions, and the use of more easily managed technologies in the production process. In addition, there was a substantial debate about what is called 'flexible specialization', a concept dubbed by Michael Piore and Charles Sabel in their book, *The Second Industrial Divide* (1984). Piore and Sabel argue that the mass-production regime that dominated the post-World War II economy was running out of steam and that new forms of production were gradually replacing the large-scale so-called Fordist production systems. Piore and Sabel (1984) discuss the case of north-eastern Italy, at times called the 'third Italy', dominated by small and medium-scale, family owned companies that were specialized in flexible manufacturing, that is, the ability to produce small and customized batches. For Piore and Sabel, large-scale production systems were too inflexible to fully adapt to more fragmented markets but the flexible specialization model proposed by Piore and Sabel represents a new viable model for manufacturing companies. *The Second Industrial Divide* brought a long-lasting debate on the concept of flexibility that included a number of positions and assumptions. The concept of *flexibility* was highlighted as the single most important issue for companies in the so-called post-fordist regime of production (Hyman, 1988; Smith, 1989; Blyton and Morris, 1991; Hirst and Zeitlin, 1991; Rowley, 1995). Flexibility in the operations was accomplished through various changes in the work organization, in the production technology, and in the way co-workers were contracted. In the 1980s, for example, temporarily employed workers—at times called 'temps'—were used to mediate the differences between the ebb and the flow of the market economy (Garsten, 1999).

Total quality management, business process re-engineering and other 'management fads'

While flexible specialization emerged more or less as a buzzword, it represented an underlying change in industry away from a large-scale mass-manufacturing regime to a more flexible and adaptable regime of production. In the large-scale production that existed in for example the automotive industry, the manufacturing system was made more flexible through the use of technologies that could be easily modified to produce shorter series and batches and through forging closer collaborative relationships with suppliers. In addition, the concept of continuous improvements, in Japan called *kaizen*, was used to accomplish small-scale improvements of the activities. In Toyota, an entire manufacturing philosophy based on joint decision-making, continuous improvement work, just-in-time logistics, and strong corporate cultures and identities served as a role model for Western companies well into the 1990s. The Japanese management innovations were translated into a set of managerial procedures and practices that were collected under the heading Total Quality Management (TQM), a concept that was heavily debated and researched in the 1980s and 1990s. TQM included a number of practices, norms, and values described in the definition box below.

DEFINITION BOX   ✓

TQM

- The products (or services) delivered should have a 'zero degree' defect rate. Rather than accepting, say, a 98% quality level one must always strive to further enhance the quality level.
- In order to accomplish this zero degree defect rate, the entire work organization needs to be involved and at times re-organized. Such changes include:
  (1) 'fool-proof' machinery and tools that are easily used and modified to new work assignments,
  (2) a team-based work organization actively involved in improving the work procedures through continuous improvements,
  (3) suppliers who are closely involved in the new product development process and the production planning and production activities. In the case of Toyota, long-term relationships with geographically closely located suppliers were developed.
- To lower cost and to reduce the number of components stored in the production facilities, components are delivered 'just-in-time' to the factory. American researchers eventually named this just-in-time production 'lean production', a term that since then has been used to denote the entire Japanese manufacturing philosophy and its reliance on close-knit relations with suppliers.

Although there are significant gains from using these managerial practices, much of the academic literature is explicitly critical of TQM, regarding it as another new form of management control capable of exploiting workers (see for example Tuckman, 1994; Wilkinson, Godfrey, and Marchington, 1997; McCabe *et al.*, 1998; Knights and McCabe, 1999; Townley *et al.*, 2003; Mueller and Carter, 2005). Delbridge, Turnbull, and Wilkinson (1992), for example, argue that TQM's more specific procedures such as just-in-time logistics leads to self-surveillance and peer pressure in work teams and that such management models impose additional work load and render work visible for inspection more easily. Wilkinson, Godfrey, and Marchington's (1997) study of eight companies implementing TQM shows that the use of TQM practices is contingent on local conditions. In some of the eight firms, employees reported that they had to work harder but they were also given more substantial decision-making authority, which increased their commitment to the work. In other companies, the use of TQM led to less positive effects. Wilkinson, Godfrey, and Marchington (1997: 816) thus conclude that rather than celebrating or vilifying TQM, it can be 'implemented in a variety of versions', displaying several faces, and that employee involvement under TQM is multi-dimensional with reality 'often obscured by rhetoric and jargon'. A similar contingency-based view is advocated by De Cock and Hipkin (1997). Edwards, Collinson, and Rees, (1998), also critical of the gap between praises and the overt critique of TQM, studied six organizations in the UK and found that even though the quality management principles were widely accepted among the employees, there was little evidence of 'substantial empowerment' of the workers in the organizations. Nevertheless, TQM is rapidly growing and gaining ground in many different lines of business. This rapid growth is discussed in the minicase below.

MINICASE

TQM outside of the manufacturing industry

While TQM has been traditionally associated with the manufacturing industry, the new ways of thinking brought by the Japanese managerial system has penetrated other domains of society. The very ideas of continuously improving the operations and measuring the outcomes derive from the TQM practice.

Today, customer or client evaluation forms are available in all sorts of domains, for instance, in hotel services. When spending a night at a hotel, there are in many cases small questionnaires for the guests to fill in some of which are open questions on how to improve the service or the comfort of the stay. In the category of luxury hotels, the satisfaction of guests is crucial to reputation and long-term survival, and hotels are using numerous tools to make sure they get feedback from customers. Consider the example of Burj Al Arab, one of the world's premier hotels, which promotes itself as a 7 star hotel. Great care is taken to make the guests' visit at the hotel a true experience. The guest can choose to arrive at the hotel driven in a Rolls-Royce. The hotel operates one of the world's largest chauffeur-driven fleets of Rolls-Royce's. On this level, customer feedback is essential to make sure that the hotel maintains an exceptional level of customer satisfaction.

TQM is therefore a managerial system—contrary to that of Taylorism for instance—that seeks to actively integrate and exploit the insights and know-how of all sorts of organizational stakeholders including customers and clients as well as all co-workers.

In their careful review of the TQM concept, Hackman and Wageman (1995) argued that TQM leads to a series of new challenges in terms of maintaining innovation, organization learning, and human resource management practices. Even though Hackman and Wageman (1995) call for more research on which form of TQM materializes in Western workplaces, they still point at the problem when 'rhetoric is winning over substance', that is, the official praises for TQM look rather different from the actual procedures and routines implemented. A similar conclusion is articulated by Zbaracki (1999), suggesting that the rhetoric advancing TQM deviates from the actual experiences with working to implement TQM. In the five organizations studied, Zbaracki (1999: 611) found that 'all sites were frustrated with the problem of integrating TQM into their daily routines' and that 'informants felt a tension between the demands of their work and the structured, rational problem-solving methods of TQM'. Zbaracki (1998) suggests that rhetoric is a managerial tool capable of mediating expectations and actual implementations.

In addition to the more 'pure' studies of TQM', there is also a quite substantial litera-ture examining the work in so-called Japanese 'transplants', factories in Europe, North-America, and elsewhere run by Japanese management and using Japanese manufacturing practices (Fucini and Fucini, 1990; Graham, 1995; Abdulah and Keenoy, 1995; Wilkinson, Morris and Munday, 1995). In most such studies, there is an emphasis on the cultural differ-ences between a Japanese corporate culture, embedded in a shared sense of belonging to the firm, arguably based on a Confucian ethics, and the Western co-workers' scepticism towards company songs and the symbolic management of the Japanese employers. In addition, some ethnographies of Japanese transplants suggest that the co-workers do not experience more freedom to act and think in their day-to-day work than in the Fordist regime of production. Instead, the co-workers find themselves under the pressure to participate in a series of com-pulsory activities. For instance, Delbridge (1998), reporting a study of a British transplant, examines his empirical material in the following terms:

> 'The Japanese transplants have been at least partially successful in establishing the technical systems of JIT and TQM, and, in appearance, its work organization and HR practices closely match the best practices identified by Womack *et al.*, (1990) and MacDuffie (1995). However, as we have seen, the effect of these is not to encourage mutual responsibility and high commitment but to extend management's control and to restrict worker opportunity for autonomy. As a result workers have very little involve-ment beyond the routine of their job tasks and are active in distancing themselves from management and in refusing to contribute discretionary effort.'
> (Delbridge, 1998: 178)

In summary, there is little empirical evidence of TQM being beneficial for employees in terms of empowerment, increased jurisdiction, or broader decision-making mandate. Instead, studies of TQM in practice suggest that TQM implementation is easily accompanied by jargon and rhetoric that promises more than can be delivered. A number of authors (Wilkinson *et al.*, 1997; De Cock and Hipkin, 1997; Edwards *et al.*, 1998) also emphasize the contingent nature of TQM, rendering it a managerial practice embedded in local conditions. TQM and similar quality development models are also discussed in Chapter 9 on change in organizations.

TQM as a business strategy in Nissan

Many companies have taken on the challenge of Toyota to make quality and quality improvement an integrated part of the company operations. The impressive results of Toyota were certainly noticed by the competitors in the automobile industry, and many companies, in Asia as well as in Europe and the US, made more or less serious attempts to adopt the Toyota ideas. There is also clear evidence that the ideas have also been spread to other sectors. A company that has attempted to develop a serious TQM strategy is Nissan, the Japanese car producer. Nissan is perhaps most well known for its cars, but they are also active in producing industrial machinery and marine equipment. Nissan recently launched an ambitious programme called Quality Leadership. An important part in this programme

MINICASE

is setting ambitious goals, a concept stressed in the literature on TQM. The goals are formulated in four areas:

- Perceived quality and attractiveness,
- Product quality,
- Sales and service quality,
- Quality of management.

The goals are set in relation to competitors to give a point of comparison. The goal for sales and service quality, for instance, is to reach 'top level customer satisfaction in Japan, US, Europe and 4 main regions' (www.nissan-global.com). Considering the research result that suggest that many TQM programmes do not deliver on the promises a relevant question when looking at Nissan's newly implemented quality initiative is how they can sustain and further develop a consistent quality programme.

Business process re-engineering

In addition to TQM, other competing or complementary concepts such as business process re-engineering (BPR) were advocated by so-called management guru writers (Hammer and Champy, 1993; Hammer, 2001) in the 1990s.

DEFINITION BOX

BPR

BPR was based on the idea that the entire corporation could be restructured ('re-engineered') and substantial efficiency gains could be accomplished when eliminating 'non-value adding activities'. That is, rather than being organized in a bureaucratic form or in a department or division form, all of which is based on functional departments, the BPR approach emphasizes the need for thinking in terms of processes.

Taking the idea of BPR as a starting point, Hammer and Champy (1993) provide a number of recommendations on how to render organizations process-oriented. For example health care organizations, traditionally hierarchical and organized into functional departments (e.g., cardiology, dermatology, geriatrics, etc.), and professional communities (e.g., GPs, nurses, technicians, laboratory personnel), have tried to develop what has been called 'clinical pathways', that is, work processes and procedures based on the need of the incoming patient rather than on the internal functional organizations. While clinical pathways is a fruitful idea that makes sense to most co-workers in health care organizations, studies show that implementing clinical pathways remains problematic (Iedema, 2000), especially when it comes to breaking down the line of demarcations between professional groups. For example, the individual and often mutually exclusive responsibilities of medical doctors and midwives embedded in a long-time historical struggle over jurisdiction in the work process, is not always of necessity the optimal one from the perspective of the woman giving birth. As a consequence, the process-based model advocated by BPR protagonists is not always easily implemented.

While TQM was based on a comprehensive and intricate number of activities and procedures developed in the Japanese manufacturing industry during the post-World War II decades, BPR was more of a theoretical model that Hammer and Champy (1993) formulated on the basis of their consulting experiences. Consequently, while TQM is today widely institutionalized in a variety of industries and activities, BPR appears as a curiosity in the history of management ideas. While it was heavily debated, discussed, and researched in the 1990s, it is today at times portrayed as a typical 'management fad', a management fashion that is introduced, becomes widely popular, and finally fades away, not too seldom, leaving a number of disgruntled managers, who thought that particular management practice would solve their concerns, behind. While proponents of BPR pointed at significant effects of BPR, studies of BPR practices did not support that the idea that BPR activities were capable of producing the desirable result (Case, 1999; Grint and Case, 1999; Knights and Willmott, 2000). In the link box below, the Toyota model, and the more generic term *lean*, are discussed from the perspective of fashion and fads.

LINK BOX

Management operations as fashion and fads

Like in most domains of life, management is also subject to fashions and fads. While the entire so-called Toyota manufacturing system was highly fashionable in the 1980s and early 1990s, and then gradually waned as the Japanese industry was facing new challenges in the 1990s, it has now been reintroduced under the general label *lean*, including lean production, lean product development, lean innovation, and so forth. Lean is used as an umbrella term for the ambition to use less resources, and especially, to keep less stock in place and rely on just-in-time logistics and forms of concurrent engineering. For instance, in the construction industry, operating on the basis of large fixed costs and major capital investments, the design and the construction phases overlap to some extent. This helps to cut down on the production times but also demands significant coordination activities between e.g., the architect and the construction engineers working in the design phase and the site managers responsible for the production. There is often a sound rationale in new production systems such as TQM and lean production. When the ideas of the originators start to gain a larger following, processes of imitation start to occur, this creates problems in implementing the ideas. To work, models such as TQM require a lot of managerial attention and energy. To implement the ideas because 'everyone else' is doing it, to jump on the bandwagon, is seldom a good starting point for a seriously attempted change effort!

Reflection point: The Toyota manufacturing system has been subject to processes of fads and fashion. What are the risks that can occur when ideas get popular and are rapidly spread over the world?

Management control and resistance

One topic of discussion in the organization theory literature is the concept of management control, that is, how managers optimize control of the work process. From the outset, organizations were directly managed by the owners of the production facilities. When corporations grew and the juridical form of the stock company was enacted, ownership and leadership was separated in time and space; those owning the company were no longer the ones managing the day-to-day work. In an agency theory perspective, the owner is then serving as the principal that gives the manager—the agent—the formal assignment to protect and support the principal's interests. While this arrangement is today very common, in the nineteenth century and in the early decades of the twentieth century this separation between ownership and management was a major concern for economists and social theorists (Berle and Means, 1934). In order to handle this separation, new procedures and practices for controlling the organization were developed.

The management control literature can be separated into mainstream or instrumental view of control and more critical perspectives on control. In the mainstream view, management control is a mechanism coordinating and aligning social action in an organizational setting. In the critical perspective, management control is a means for influential social actors to safeguard their long terms interests. Management control is in this perspective not a value-neutral mechanism in service of the interests of all organization members, but is always already embedded in social relations characterized by uneven distribution of power and influence. Tannenbaum (1968: 5), representing the mainstream view, defined management control as:

> 'Any process in which a person, or group of persons, or organization of persons, determines, that is, institutionally affects, the behaviour of another person, group, or organization'.

He (1968: 3) continues:

> 'It is the function of control to bring about conformance to the organizational requirement of the ultimate purposes of the organization. The coordination and order created out of the diverse interests and potentially diffuse behaviour of members is largely a function of control.'

Feldman (1989: 86) defined management control in a similar manner, 'Control is defined as the exercise of authority through a hierarchical structure that limits or channels behaviour'. Both Tannenbaum (1968) and Feldman (1989) speak of control as what is influencing and determining behaviour and what is essentially unproblematic or uncontested. Kärreman and Alvesson (2004), representing a more critical view of management control, speak of control in less functionalist terms:

> 'Management control typically includes an apparatus for specifying, monitoring, and evaluating individual and collective action. Management control is predominantly an activity carried out by a powerful social group that orchestrates and exercises definitional and executive authority over other social groups within an organization.'
> (Kärreman and Alvesson, 2004: 152)

In this perspective, specific social interests are mirrored in the means of management control in use; there are no disinterested means of control but management control is always shaped by inequality and uneven distribution of decision-making authority and power.

DEFINITION BOX

Forms of control

In the literature, there is a distinction between *direct control* (i.e., direct inspection and surveillance of the work), *technical control*, determined by machinery such as assembly lines or other forms of advanced machinery, and *bureaucratic control*, the 'internalization of rational rules and routines by organizational selves' (Kilduff and Kelemen, 2001: 2). In addition to these more conventional forms of control, there are more subtle and sophisticated forms of control that focus on discipline, identities, and self-surveillance as the principal means of management control.

Rather than imposing forms of direct or indirect control, these forms of control train and socialize co-workers into conceiving of themselves as enterprising and autonomous subjects that are responsible for producing value for the corporation or organization. This more advanced form of control has been referred to with a number of labels such as post-bureaucratic control, socio-ideological control, ideological control, or professional or cultural forms of control. Kärreman and Alvesson (2004: 152) prefer the concept of *socio-ideological control*, a concept they define as 'attempts to control worker beliefs'. For instance, when being trained as a financial analyst at a business school and when practicing the trade, one socio-ideological form of control may be the belief that one needs to work long hours (at times more than 60, 70, or even 80 hours per week) to justify the high pay, or subscribing to the belief that financial markets are in essence rational, fair, and in general the only way financial services could possibly be arranged. Such forms of socio-ideological control are of central importance for the individual to inculcate and maintain a professional identity and persona. As Debra Schleef (2006: 5), in her study of 'managing elites', based on students in a law school and a business school in an American elite university, underlined, 'the most important audience for professional ideology . . . is the professionals themselves—they need to believe in the higher mandate that the professionals are alleged to embody'. One is not born a professional, one is made one and becoming one includes the submission to a variety of socio-ideological controls.

While various forms of *socio-ideological control* are employed in knowledge and professional intensive work, more conventional technocratic forms of control are used in manufacturing industry and less specialized work. For instance, in call centres, many operators are monitored in terms of the number of incoming calls handled per time unit (Knights and McCabe, 1998; Kinnie, Hutchinson and Purcell, 2000; Taylor *et al.*, 2002). In some professions and occupations, such measuring of output is rarely applicable and socio-ideological control is playing a more central role in the work. In a study of a number of so-called knowledge-intensive work in the UK, Robertson and Swan (2004: 128) found that '90% of the firms relied on either cultural or professional forms of control, rather than bureaucratic forms of control'.

Another form of control discussed in the literature is the use of peer pressure or, team-based control. When team-based work organization became fashionable in the 1980s, the decision-making authority and some administrative assignments were decentralized to the work teams. Members of the work teams were therefore collectively responsible for the output and implicitly for the control of the work of the colleagues. Barker refers to this specific form of peer-based control as *concertive control*: 'Under bureaucratic control, employees might ensure that they come to work on time because the employee handbook prescribed it and the supervisor had the legal right to demand it, but in the concertive system, employees might come to work on time because their peers now have the authority to demand the workers' willing compliance', Barker (1993: 412) suggests. While much of the team-based work organization has been received positively in industry and among the co-workers, essentially enriching the work through broadening and deepening the work assignment, concertive control and peer-based control are complicated to manage because it easily makes the co-workers police their colleagues, thereby risking a higher degree of conflicts and controversies. For instance, when team performance determines the individual bonus—as may be the case in some manufacturing companies—there is a direct interest in the team to ensure that all team members make an adequate contribution to the team. The issue of control at the workplace is discussed in the minicase below.

MINICASE

Actual control in everyday work

In most everyday work, there are a variety of forms of control co-existing at work and it is not always easy to decode the forms of control that are part of everyday work. For instance, while technical control may be part of the infrastructure of the work activities (e.g., bank clerks may have restricted access to certain services offered to the clients on basis of rank or seniority) and is therefore not always conceived of as a proper form of control, other more direct forms of control (e.g., strict no smoking policies inside an office building, forcing smokers to, like in many American cities, stand outside of the office buildings on the pavement) are more visible and immediately 'lived'. Therefore, management control ranges from relatively insignificant and requiring little attention, to highly controversial topics engendering animated discussions and debates in organizations.

The forms of socio-ideological control are perhaps the most complicated to critically examine since they are part of a sociocultural and cognitive framework that are not always consciously addressed. These forms of control operate with more subtle means that are less visible to the employees. They can nevertheless be highly effective in controlling behaviour. Since socio-ideological control operates with ideas, attitudes, and cultural patterns, it is harder for the organization to manage, and the outcome is harder to predict. The role and importance of these 'softer' forms of control are very much in line with the dominant paradigm of charismatic/transformational leadership, which is further discussed in Chapter 6.

While the general tendency in industry—at least in Western Europe and North America—to make use of more subtle means of management control and to abandon more technocratic and bureaucratic forms of control, there is a growing literature on *surveillance* in the workplace. While surveillance—technically-mediated direct control (Lyon, 1994; Bogard, 1996)—may be justified in some setting (in e.g., public transportation during the night), the increased use of surveillance in all domains of public and organizational spheres has been debated among social scientists and management writers (Sewell and Barker, 2006;

Mason *et al.*, 2002; Sewell, 1998). Ball (2005: 90) pointed at the wide use of surveillance technologies in contemporary society:

> Surveillance is the practice of gathering and sorting data with the explicit purpose of influencing and managing the data target. This is characterized in many modern organizational processes and the networks of actors and institutions involved by:
>
> - Consumer monitoring through loyalty cards,
> - Credit scoring and geo-demographic profiling,
> - Workforce monitoring through various recruitment practices,
> - Email and internet usage,
> - Keystroke monitoring,
> - Access control,
> - Performance management.

(Ball, 2005: 90)

Technology plays a central role in surveillance systems and, in many cases, everyday office technologies such as computers may contain opportunities for monitoring the work of the employees. In many respects, the concept of surveillance and its everyday practice raises many interesting concerns regarding personal integrity, business ethics, and juridical matters. For instance, should employers be given the right to monitor the internet homepages an employee visits during work hours or track to whom e-mails are sent? Should this be regarded as a threat to the personal integrity rights enacted by most Western countries? Without doubt, contemporary society is a society whose degree of surveillance is unprecedented.

The literature on forms of organization control is accompanied (and at times overlapping with) the literature on organization resistance (Mumby, 2005; Roscigo and Hodson, 2004; Young, 2000; Jermier, Knights and Nord, 1994). Resistance is a broad term denoting a variety of practices aimed at undermining managerial objectives. Resistance can appear in many forms, ranging from outright protests and quarrels between managers and co-workers to more subtle forms including forms of sabotage and ignorance of enacted rules (Brown and Coupland, 2005). In labour process theory and industry sociology literature, the concept of resistance has played a central role. However, as forms of managerial control (e.g., direct control) are becoming substituted for more 'unobtrusive forms of control' (Perrow, 1986), the forms of resistance have also changed. In the new regime of socio-ideological control, control that emphasizes the worker as being entrepreneurial and enterprising, capable of monitoring his or her own work, and in the best of cases, generating his/her own income for the organization indicates that mangerial control is becoming more complicated.

One interesting form of resistance is discussed by Fleming and Sewell (2002) speaking of the concept of Švejkism after the Czeck author Jaromir Hašek's novel, *The Good Soldier Švejk*. *The Good Soldier* Švejk is set during the First World War and the soldier Švejk is a not too intellectually gifted soldier of a lower rank that is driving his superiors to the verge of insanity through following all procedures and instructions in great detail, to the point of undermining the intentions of the orders. In the Švejk mode of resistance, every rule counts as much as any, and following them all is what is expected from the employee. The Švejk mode of resistance is a form of 'fundamentalism' following of rules to the extent that their implications serve as a form of resistance towards managerial control systems that threaten the autonomy and the jurisdiction of the employee.

By and large, resistance in organizations is a perennial issue, and as long as there are management control systems there also will be forms of resistance. The study of management control must also take into account the forms of resistance that the use of the management control provokes and produces.

Organization routines, rules, practices

Another domain of research pertaining to work organization and operations management is the concept of routines, rules, and practices. Weber (1978) defined the bureaucratic organization form as an organization form based on the use of predefined and clearly demarcated work assignments, accounted for in written manuals. The bureaucratic organization is a routine-based organization. Traditionally, the concept of routines has been largely taken for granted as formally or informally enacted scripts for social action, and it has been assumed that routines are more or less fixed. In the evolutionary theory of organizations (Nelson and Winter, 1982), routines are more than such scripts; instead, routines are the bearers of organizational experiences and knowledge, accumulated over time and in numerous efforts.

More recently, Feldman and Pentland (2003, 2005) and colleagues have carefully examined organizational routines as actions that are, in fact, more flexible than historically suggested in the organization theory literature. They define a routine as 'repetitive, recognizable patterns of interdependent actions, carried out by multiple actors' (Feldman and Pentland, 2005). For Feldman and Pentland (2003: 95) a routine consists of two parts: one part is 'an abstract idea of the routine', i.e., the 'structure', and the other part is the 'actual performance of the routine'. The actual performance is always situated and embedded in specific time and place. Feldman and Pentland (2003) argue that the two parts are always interrelated, and that the one would not subsist without the other. As the performance of the routine is modified over time, the formal description of the routine will change. Rather than being fixed or semi-fixed, routines are instead highly flexible and malleable social institutions; they are, according to Pentland and Rueter (1994), 'the grammars of action'.

Studies of rules—for instance, in industry sociology or labour process theory literature (e.g., Leidner, 1993)—show that the skilled co-worker is capable of adjusting the routine to suit the specific situation: 'Members do not slavishly follow simple norms that are somehow fixed over time, but rather, they (re)produce the routine or normative character of activities for the first time again. The routine is an achievement,' suggest Hindmarsh and Pilnick (2007: 1413). Seen from this viewpoint, a social practice is not only guided by instituted routines; the social practice is what, de facto, constitutes the routine through repeating certain procedures over time. In addition, no routines can contain all the information required to accomplish the work intended. Rather than providing a full manual, there is always a certain tacit component (or residual) that must be taught in order to master the work. The experienced social actor is capable of following a routine procedure quite freely, while the neophyte has to be mindful of whether the routine is being followed to the letter.

The sociologist Harold Garfinkel (1968) speaks of the 'et cetera clause' in all social practice, denoting the residual knowledge that needs to be acquired before a script can be followed. The et cetera clause suggests that between the scripted routine and the masterful performance of the routine lies a certain amount of experience and acquired know-how that cannot be taught offhand. For instance, any recipe assumes that there are certain things to be known when cooking; recipes merely provide a few instructions, and what lies between the various steps in the recipe is not accounted for in detail, but must be known from previous experience. In summary, organizational routines are some 'elementary entity' of the organization, but by their very nature are more flexible and malleable than is often suggested. Skilled co-workers are capable of adjusting routine procedures to accomplish desired outcomes. On the other hand, routines may be invoked when shielding off demands from, for example, clients (Briscoe, 2007: Leidner, 1993). Seen in this way, routines are effective tools in the hands of experienced co-workers in organizations. They are part of what one may call the infrastructure of the organization, and this is indicated in the link box below.

LINK BOX

Continuously seeking effectiveness

Many authors have tried to understand the success of the Japanese production ideas, and numerous explanations have been offered. However, the answer is not in single details of a complex system, but rather in the combined effects of a number of interrelated aspects. The case of the Japanese manufacturing system shows that not only were the Japanese capable of bridging instrumental and sociocultural aspects of work, the Japanese were also capable of establishing a range of work procedures, routines, practices, and control mechanisms that taken together constituted a set of operation management practices that effectively balanced various interests, goals, and objectives. Therefore, if there is a 'secret' in the Japanese manufacturing system, it is the ability to bridge and combine seemingly heterogeneous components and processes. The Japanese manufacturing system adheres to past accomplishments while continuously seeking to establish new and more effective practices. A holistic view seems to encompass the success factors in the system and the ability to learn from previous accomplishments, while at the same time exploring the future. The Toyota example also suggests that an organization needs to learn how processes and practices fit together and how they, together, can be made to work in more effective ways. This can also be linked back to the discussions on new and innovative forms of organization, from Chapter 2, that highlighted the organizational ability to combine different strengths and forms of organizing in order to increase organizational flexibility.

Reflection point: As suggested above, in this link box, an important reason for the success of the Japanese production system is the organization's ability to connect different parts and take a holistic view. How can such a holistic view be implemented and what are the challenges involved in doing so?

Summary and conclusions

The opening case suggested that the Japanese manufacturing industry brought a whole new set of ideas and ways of thinking into contemporary management thinking. However, historical studies of how operations management have evolved suggest that the Japanese contributions were essentially a reformulation of a variety of ideas and practices developed and used in the West. From Taylorism and scientific management, we may learn to approach work in an analytic manner, carefully dissecting the work procedures in order to optimize their effectiveness. From labour process studies, we learn that work is always inherently social and that human beings interpret and negotiate how work should be accomplished. From work organization theories on managerial practices, routines, and management control, we learn that making organizations run smoothly is a matter of assessing different objectives and goals, and striking a balance between control, incentives, and motivational factors. The Japanese manufacturing system became influential by carefully adhering to a variety of existing practices and balancing these different needs and demands to the benefit of both employer and employees.

In this chapter we have explored operations management, outlining this is a term denoting all the day-to-day organizational practices and managerial activities that shape and influence the production of goods, services, and administrative work in organizations. The principal focus has been on manufacturing work, simply because that has historically been the largest sector of the economy. However today, this is no longer necessarily the case in Western Europe and in North America. Still, the principles and procedures developed by Taylor and his various followers including the Japanese manufacturing industry are still relevant for service work and administrative work. Rather than representing a change in perspective, administrative work is formed by the same principles of division of labour, managerial control, and routines as any manufacturing work. The analysis of administrative or service work is therefore more of a translation and adoption of conventional managerial principles, than the implementation of radically new procedures. As a consequence, what could be said of operations management in the manufacturing industry is *mutatis mutandis*, also relevant for other sectors of the economy.

 ## Study questions

1. What is the rationale for the division of labour?
2. How did Taylor's followers and co-workers further develop Taylor's scientific management concept?
3. In what ways did industry sociology research contribute to the understanding of the management of operations?
4. What are the principal forms of control in organizations?
5. What function have rules and routines played when managing organizations?

Literature recommendations and further readings

The standard reference for understanding the Japanese manufacturing industry in general and the automotive industry more specifically is Michael Cusumano's (1985) *The Japanese Automobile Industry*. More recently, a more popular argument in favour of the 'Toyota way' is offered by Jeffrey Liker (2004). The perhaps most intriguing introduction to scientific management and Taylorism is by Guillén (1994). A number of studies of Japanese transplants in the West are available, and Fucini and Fucini's (1990) *Working for the Japanese* gives some insight into the differences between north-American and Japanese management traditions. In the industry sociology and labour process theory literature, Dalton (1959), and Burawoy (1979), are classic studies frequently referenced in the literature. Sewell's (1998) paper in *Administrative Science Quarterly* remains a good read when it comes to management control, and a more recent theoretical contribution worth the effort is Kärreman and Alvesson (2004). Martha S. Feldman has published a series of excellent papers wherein she is discussing the concept of routine and the 2003 collaboration with Brian Pentland summarizes the basic arguments.

Take your learning further

online resource centre

http://www.oxfordtextbooks.co.uk/orc/erikssonzetterquist/

Visit the Online Resource Centre which accompanies this book to enrich your understanding of this chapter.

Students: explore web links and further reading suggestions. Keep up to date with the latest developments via 'What happened next' updates to appropriate cases from within the book.

Lecturers: you will find seminar exercises and teaching notes, for use in class or assessment.

PART II
MANAGING PEOPLE

CHAPTER 5   Finding people and motivating
             them to make the best of their
             potential   107

CHAPTER 6   How to lead in an organization   135

CHAPTER 7   Coping with external influences
             in organizations   165

CHAPTER 5
Finding people and motivating them to make the best of their potential

Recruiting and training future managers

Since the beginning of the 1950s, the multinational company, Primo, operating in the area of fast moving consumer goods, has recruited future executives by inviting them to participate in its 'apprenticeship programme'. The company invites recent business and engineering graduates to participate in a two-year programme focused on 'on-the-job-training'. In the programme, the recruits can train for positions in four different areas, for example, sales, marketing, economy, and finance. They can also participate in two introductory courses in the company's management programme. There are two apprenticeship meetings per year. After completing the programme, the apprentices take positions in the company as brand managers or something similar. The company expects that eight to ten years after they complete the programme, all apprentices will be in a company management group.

The programme is very popular among students. In the beginning of the 1990s approximately one in four students in Swedish university business programmes – some 2000 students annually – applied for the six to eight places in the programme. How did the company handle this many applicants?

The **recruitment** process took place twice a year and required the applicants to complete an application form detailing their grades, language skills, and leadership experience. They were also asked to answer the question, 'Why do you want to be an apprentice at Primo?' Based on an initial review of the applicants' grades, language skills, etc., the company first narrowed the applications down to two hundred from a thousand, and thereafter to eighty applicants who were invited to the first interview. In this interview, the applicants met for an hour with a group consisting of a personnel representative, an operations manager and a trainee who asked questions such as 'Assuming we had not seen your application, how would you describe yourself?', 'What are your career goals?', 'Why do you want to work for Primo?', and 'How do you balance your career and family?'

Following these interviews, about twenty applicants were invited to a second interview where they took a psychological test. These applicants also participated in an exercise at the company's Assessment Centre where they were given a group task to solve during the course of one morning (two groups of ten applicants each). Five managers from the company's leadership group and the personnel manager observed the groups. After lunch with the managers, the applicants were interviewed by the five managers and the personnel manager who asked them about their thoughts on the problem-solving exercise of the morning and about their perception of their futures at Primo. At the end of the day, the managers discussed each applicant and then decided which applicants would be offered positions. Two days later, at the latest, the successful applicants were offered positions. For this time, Primo's three-month recruitment process was over.

One idea behind the apprentice programme is the recognition that the new hires are highly visible in their prominent positions in the company. At the same time that each new hire is showing what he or she can do, the managers can decide what work the new hire is suitable for in the future and thus can direct each new hire's career. A position in an apprentice programme leading to a career involves visibility and direct encouragement. Therefore, the apprentices are prepared from the first day to work hard and to show what they can do. However, as in all everyday work life, there can be problems. The newly hired apprentices sometimes are a little too casual about revealing their ambitions, and fellow employees can sigh a bit over their insensitivity to established company standards.

The plan for the apprentices' career is very specific. At the same time, the apprentices are encouraged to set ambitious goals. During the training period and the management courses, they meet managers from the entire company who describe their careers in the company where most have spent the greater part of their working lives. These managers set the model for how the apprentices can think about their own career goals. In the recruitment process and training meetings, an ideal career model is presented as including, after six to eight years' employment, the possibility of working abroad for two years. A study of the apprentices showed that after six months' employment they shared one particular goal: they said that before taking up their expected positions in the management group, they wanted to work abroad. Thus, the managers' accounts and other narratives about career possibilities gave the apprentices an idea of how they could plan their careers, as well as the motivation to work directly toward the future they desired.

In addition to becoming the market leader in its own area, thus securing the company's future, Primo's goal is to promote its managers internally in the various levels of the company. This promotion practice is also considered a motivational factor for the newly hired apprentices. Because of the company's values and standards, presented in its motto 'This is how we are and this is how we work', and because a long-term future in the company is constantly presented as a possibility, for many years Primo has had very low personnel turnover among its managers who were once apprentices. In fact, after ten years, seventy per cent of such managers are still with the company.

Source: Information for the Primo case was mainly compiled through original research by Ulla Eriksson-Zetterquist. Deeper descriptions of the case are published in Eriksson-Zetterquist (2002); Eriksson-Zetterquist (2008); and Eriksson (2000).

Questions

Recruitment processes are aimed at finding the right person to employ, but can also affect the organization as well as the individual. What are these recruitment processes?

A central question in organizational practice is why people work? What motivates people and how can productivity be sustained?

HRM has come to be a common practice in many organizations. How can this be used as a part of the management strategies for controlling employees?

Introduction

In this chapter, the discussion is focused on how companies can recruit suitable personnel and motivate them to perform above expectations. The Primo case above describes in depth how a company can design a recruitment process to secure a steady supply of talent for important managerial positions. Recruitment is without doubt a strategic activity in most companies, but it is also important to understand the continuous work of keeping personnel once they have been recruited. The latter aspect is often referred to as a motivational challenge. The chapter provides a comprehensive overview over the field of recruitment, human relations, motivation, and human resource management. The following topics are addressed:

- Recruitment processes to find the best people for a work assignment,
- The Hawthorne Study exploring why people work and what makes them productive,
- Motivation theories and reformulation of these in terms of empowerment,
- Human Relations Management (HRM) that today is a catch-all term for employee management and control. Diversity issues are presented as an example.

Recruitment

Recruitment of new hires is in many ways a critical process for both the individual and the organization. The importance of recruitment is indicated in the link box below.

LINK BOX

Recruitment at Primo

Finding the right people and making the best of their skills is crucial for the long term survival of any organization, and especially so in highly competitive industries. Recruiting is both a costly and time-consuming process and it is important to try to do it right from the beginning. The apprenticeship programme in Primo described above is an ambitious, two-year programme that aims at finding the right people for demanding managerial positions. In most cases the recruitment process is less ambitious, but the example clearly shows how important recruitment is and how a well designed process can boost motivation internally, as well as keep turnover figures at very low levels. Many companies have developed formal programmes to ensure that the right people are hired, and that they get a proper introduction to the company, be it in the form of trainee programmes, apprenticeship programmes, or on-the-job-training. The purpose of these programmes is not only to make sure the individual is properly trained. The programmes fulfil important purposes in making sure that the company has made a good choice, and that the candidate is socialized into the culture of the company. In the case of Primo an important purpose was to recruit people for future managerial positions, and giving them a broad view of the company was a view to create a thorough understanding of the company and the different parts of the operations.

Reflection point: Many companies invest a lot of time and money in recruitment processes and they hope to get their money back by making good recruitment decisions based on ambitious screening and testing processes. The apprenticeship programme at Primo is a good example of the high level of importance given to the recruitment process. How can a company make sure that they have selected the right person for the job?

The first encounter between a future new hire and an organization typically occurs by some form of written advertisement. It is suggested that this advertisement should be inviting, but at the same time should describe the work requirements as closely as possible in order to attract, as well as prepare, suitable applicants (Mathews and Redman, 1996; Feldman, Bearden and Hardesty, 2006). For organizations, it is important to show as realistic a picture of the future workplace as possible. It will be a shocking experience for the applicant if, after having been presented an unrealistic picture of the organization as a recruit, he or she finds a different reality as an employee (see Feldman, 1994). A calm and relaxed interview situation can be a good way to prepare applicants for their future working conditions (Feldman, 1994; Wanous, 1992).

One purpose of the interview in the recruitment process is to test applicants' reactions in various situations. For the applicants, while the interview gives them the opportunity to respond in the right way, it also means that they can confirm their initial expectations about how they will gradually adapt to the organization (Van Maanen, 1976). By answering character questions, such as 'Are you willing to make sacrifices in this position?' the applicants experience a sense of commitment when they acknowledge that their employment is an exchange for the fulfilment of certain obligations. Thus is laid the foundation of what later becomes the '**psychological contract**' (Schein, 1965; Van Maanen and Katz, 1976) that describes the individual's and the organization's reciprocal commitments and expectations. These concern the nature and quantity of the work and the monetary compensation, as well as the rights, privileges, and duties of both the employee and the organization.

Various types of psychological or personality tests are often used in recruitment. One rationale for using such tests is that they provide an assessment that seems objective and can complement the subjectivity inherent in every recruiter's evaluation. It is important to remember, however, that these tests only seem objective. Because they have been created by people in a certain connection and particular context, they are always going to show a somewhat biased picture of the applicant and his or her abilities (Bergström, 1998).

From the individual's perspective, the recruitment process marks the separation between student life at university and work life (Schein, 1978). The transition from university student to organization manager is a special situation:

> 'In effect, the unlearning involves leave-taking from the well-organized, highly structured, well-understood role of being a student to a much more less structured and equivocal role. New managers are apt to find that matters move more slowly and less rationally than they expect, and that it may be necessary to participate in carving out their own job. Furthermore, having an immediate boss contrasts sharply with the autonomy of student life.'
> (Trice and Beyer, 1993: 140)

Successful recruitment means that the organization has acquired a new member who is well-prepared for his or her future working conditions. Less successful recruitment means that the new hire will not thrive in the new workplace or will not live up to the organization's expectations. As a result, the employee may quit or be fired, and then the organization must begin the costly recruiting process anew. Recruitment processes are, however, not unbiased. It is tempting to base the recruitment on other selection criteria than actual competence, for instance, gender, race, and friendship.

The term '**homosocial reproduction**' has been used where mainly men get recruited to organizational top positions. Homosocial reproduction derives from the male preference for identifying and socializing with other men. Because it is difficult to predict their future success and competence, management candidates are classified according to the similarity of their work habits, social background, education, and general behaviour to those of the current managers. It is assumed that those candidates with backgrounds similar to that of top-level managers will be trustworthy, loyal, and achievement-oriented, while those with different backgrounds are unsuitable for employment. The system is circular and self-fulfilling: men in management positions feel they are successful when they employ people who are like themselves (Kanter, 1977).

The Hawthorne Study

One of the most extensive empirical studies undertaken in organization theory was the Hawthorne Study that was carried out between 1926 and 1932. The primary purpose was to determine the best conditions for worker productivity in the Western Electric Company, a U.S. company that operated the Hawthorne Electrical Works. As the study ran and new findings were made, the purpose would change. The Hawthorne Study was preceded by a well-known pre-study, the lighting studies, in which the researchers tried to determine what level of light would produce the best effect as far as employee productivity was concerned. In part one of the pre-study, they began by selecting three departments where they could measure productivity under existing light conditions. Thereafter, they gradually increased the light at various strengths in these departments. As a result, the productivity increased in all three departments, but it was difficult to identify a pattern. In two departments, the productivity increase showed no regularity in relationship to the increased lighting, and in the third department, productivity went up and down without any evident relationship to the quantity of light. The researchers then decided to extend the experiment. In part two of the pre-study, employees of similar ages and with similar experience were selected from one department and were divided into two groups: a 'test group' and a 'control group'. In the test group, the employees worked under various levels of light, while in the control group, the light level was held constant. As both groups showed similar increased productivity, it was again not possible to determine the effect of the improved lighting levels (Gillespie, 1991).

Before beginning part three of the pre-study, the researchers asked themselves if it was a combination of natural light and artificial light that made it impossible to determine the optimal light level. Therefore, they used only artificial light in the third part of the study, gradually reducing the light levels in the test group. Even in this study the productivity proved stable in both groups. Finally, it was so dark in the test group that the assembly workers complained that they couldn't see anything. The researchers began to suspect there was a psychological effect that influenced the studies' results. They then conducted several informal experiments. Two clever and interested young women were put to work in a room with a light level corresponding to moonlight, but even here the women succeeded in maintaining the productivity level. In yet another experiment, an electrician exchanged the light bulbs with those of the same strength while the employees watched. These employees, who were told that the light level increased or decreased with each exchange, were asked what they thought. They responded in each instance that the light level had increased or decreased, depending on what the researchers had told them. Again, the productivity level remained at the same level (Roethlisberger and Dickson, 1939).

MINICASE

The legacy of the Hawthorne Study at ADM

The Hawthorne Study, and the lessons learned from the unintended effects of the experiments described in this section of the chapter, have inspired and informed managers in revitalizing their HRM practices in many companies. It is not an exaggeration to say that the Human Relations perspective that originated very much from the Hawthorne Study has built the foundation for a much more employee centered view on the managing of companies. Consider the example of Archer Daniels Midland Company (ADM), one of the world's leading agricultural processors. The company produces food ingredients, animal feeds and feed ingredients, biofuels, and other products that manufacturers around the world use to produce food (www.adm.com). Led by Particia A. Woertz (Chairman and CEO), the company has developed a consistent process to recruit and develop individuals. Career planning is a key priority and the company offers tailormade career paths in different areas of the company. An important tool that puts the individual in focus is internships that are frequently used in the company and give the individual the opportunity, not only to get to know the company from within, but also to work alongside experienced senior managers. The company offers a variety of different internship programmes, ranging from the intensive

MINICASE

eleven-week ADM Summer Internship Program to more extended programmes in selected areas of the company. For a company such as ADM, it is crucial for long-term survival to recruit and train highly qualified personnel, and people expect to be offered exciting working tasks and a lot of responsibility as well as to meet nice and interesting people. The Hawthorne Study was clearly a forerunner in pointing out a broader set of motivational factors, and pleading for a more humanistic view on managerial issues.

Part 1 of the Hawthorne Study: The Relay Assembly Room

As a result of the puzzling pre-study, researchers set up a new research program. The first aim was to control outside variables while examining the relation between productivity and physical aspects of work. To establish this control, six women were isolated in a workroom. In this they would not be influenced by newcomers, expectations about the work completion, and other changes in the work tasks. Using a small group, the researchers could observe both individual and group behaviour. They could also build a rapport with the employees so that the experiment was not adversely affected by attitudes of mistrust. The questions posed by this experiment included the following (Roethlisberger and Dickson, 1939):

- Were the employees really exhausted?
- Were the rest breaks worthwhile, or was the productivity higher with a shorter workday?
- How did the employees feel about their work and the company?
- What effect did the change in the work tools have?
- Why did productivity decline in the afternoon?

In the first part of the experiment, the women, without their knowledge, were observed and documented in their usual workplace for two weeks. They were given basic medical check-ups and were found to be healthy (Roethlisberger and Dickson, 1939). The experiment, which was conducted between 1926 and 1928, was divided into thirteen periods where the researchers tested different productivity variables. During the first period, no changes were made; instead, the possible effects of the move to the Relay Assembly Room were measured. In the subsequent periods, changes were made, for example, in the payment system (group piecework instead of department piecework), various forms of rest breaks (sometimes combined with snacks), shortened workdays, no work on Saturdays, and so on. The women were also interviewed on their home conditions.

The result—an increase in productivity

During the first two years of the experiment, the assemblers' productivity increased almost constantly. The research manager thought the explanation was the changed working conditions. Yet, that change could not explain the improvement in the women's morale, evidenced by how they helped each other when someone had a bad day, or that work absenteeism had decreased.

Gradually, the research leader began to relate the productivity investigation to the changed management conditions. The changes in the management system consisted of a series of events. The assemblers in the Relay Assembly Room were always convinced that their jobs and bonuses were secure. Because they were the only participants in an experiment that constantly changed, their social situation also changed completely. As the experiment proceeded, more and more people moved about the room. The original Relay Assembly Test Room observer, who had become a department manager, remained but was now joined by a young woman who handled the research statistics. In addition, visitors frequently visited the room, including company executives, experts on industrial relations, industrial psychologists, and university professors. Nevertheless, the changed management system offered no explanation of the increased productivity other than the fact that the researchers thought that it depended upon the women's working environments and attitudes.

Part 2 of the Hawthorne Study: The Interview Study

Against the background of this finding from the Relay Assembly Room, the research manager wanted to conduct a systematic study of the employees' attitudes toward their work environment and the company in order to learn more about the influence these attitudes had on productivity. Between 1928 and 1930, 21,000 employees were interviewed by thirty trained interviewers (Roethlisberger and Dickson, 1934).

In a preliminary analysis, the frequency with which different subjects were mentioned in the interviews was investigated (for example, absenteeism, ventilation, careers, the employees' lockers, and job monotony). Here, the researchers found that the male employees were more interested in economic matters and family security, such as pensions and job protection, while the women employees were more concerned with working conditions, such as overtime, fatigue, and social contacts. Roethlisberger and Dickson (1939) attributed this difference to the fact that traditionally men are the main family breadwinners, while women are less financially dependent on their work and want easier work in pleasant surroundings. This was, however, a contested conclusion.

Another conclusion was that the researchers realized that more must be learned about interpersonal relationships in the workplace. In the summer of 1931, during the Great Depression, the Hawthorne Electrical Works had to reduce working hours and dismiss workers. The researchers then began to interview managers at different levels to hear their opinions on the situation. The further down the management hierarchy, the more comments there were about reduced working hours and dismissals that directly affected the managers' own living standards. Many managers with years of experience also thought that married women should be fired before single women because a married woman who worked was thought to have too high a living standard. A single woman, on the other hand, was at risk of having to live homeless on the street if she didn't have the means to support herself. Above all, these comments came from the foremen who had daughters who worked at the company.

Results

The results from the interview programme were difficult to analyse, however they showed that certain working conditions could be improved. This realization created a basis for the education of managers and also provided material for researchers. Roethlisberger and Dickson (1934) reported that when management listened to their employees' complaints, they heard the creaking and groaning of their own social structure. Besides the insight that employees appreciated being interviewed, the researchers saw that the interviewees' comments had to be related both to the personal situations of those concerned and to their position and status in the factory.

Another conclusion was that the researchers found groups in the company who expressed themselves in similar ways as far as their attitudes toward each other, the management leadership, and the company's policies. With that conclusion as background, Part 3 of the study began.

Part 3 of the Hawthorne Study: The Bank Wiring Observation Room

The interview study revealed that there was an informally controlled arrangement among the employees that seemed to affect their productivity. It seemed to be a spontaneous, social arrangement that functioned in parallel with the formal organization of the company. The employees also seemed to form social groups that had very strong control over how their members worked. The foremen could not interfere with these groups because of the risk of being disliked. Furthermore, there were informal leaders who made each group's external contacts with the foremen, the engineers, and the inspectors. These leaders even taught new hires the acceptable norms at the factory. Thus, it became important to study these small groups. The Hawthorne Study took up this research as the last part of its work that was conducted from November 1931 until May 1932 when the lack of work at the company ended the research.

In this part of the study, the researchers used a new research method consisting of direct observation combined with interviews. Because they wanted to observe the social behaviour of an existing group in a changed environment, they tried to find people who had previously worked together as a group and who could participate without changing their group relationship. Therefore, the researchers selected a group of fourteen male assemblers who were moved to an observation room. Their work task was to assemble telephone exchanges for large office exchanges. The group consisted of nine men who worked with telephone couplings, three solderers, and two inspectors who checked the finished exchanges. In addition, hidden from the assemblers as an uninvolved spectator, was an observer to take notes along with the foreman. In contrast with the women in the Relay Assembly Room, these men were given very little information about the study's purpose. The idea was, in direct contrast with the study with the women, that the researchers did not want the men to have any reluctance about participating in the study. All the men were given a medical examination and were found to be healthy. They were also given an intelligence test—that showed that the most efficient employees were not the most intelligent—and a finger dexterity test. Finally, the men were interviewed before the study began and thereafter at least twice more during the study.

Results

It was soon evident that the men did not understand how the compensation system worked. They thought a day's work consisted of each man producing two telephone exchanges, a goal that was significantly lower than management wanted. For that reason, management designed a compensation system where the group's total proceeds would be divided among everyone in the group, with a per-hour rate determined by how much each man had produced divided by his work hours. If the group produced more, the individual thus earned more, but the men did not understand the system.

Another finding was that the men knew precisely how much they produced. They even used nicknames for each other that reflected each person's performance. For example, they called the man who was quick to take the lead 'Speed King' and the man, who, unlike the others, worked right up to the day's end, the '4.15 Special'. Those men who worked more than normal were physically punished by 'binging', which meant that someone in the group would hit the norm-breaker as hard as possible on the upper arm.

The observations showed that the group's managers were seldom there, and when they were there, the group concealed its work norms. Management thus never knew how the group worked. Additionally, it was shown that twelve of the fourteen group members divided themselves into two sub-groups. In these sub-groups, the men formed friendships and animosities and engaged in sports, job rotations, and discussions about opening/shutting the windows. The two men who were not in either sub-group produced more than the average and had good relationships with everyone in the whole group, including the foremen. In short, these two men showed the least adaptation to the group's norms.

In the group there were special rules that the members should follow:

- You should not turn out too much work. If you do, you are a 'rate buster'.
- You should not turn out too little work. If you do, you are a 'chiseller'.
- You should not tell a supervisor anything that will be to the detriment of an associate. If you do, you are a 'squealer'.
- You should not attempt to maintain social distance or act officious. If you are an inspector, for example, you should not act like one. (Roethlisberger and Dickson, 1939: 522).

These rules protected the group from outside intervention as well as from any incautious actions by group members.

The results from this study showed that there were two organizations that functioned in parallel, the formal and the informal (Roethlisberger and Dickson, 1939). This finding called into question the assumption that the employees were primarily motivated by economic interests where their work behaviour was logical and rational.

Results and criticism of the Hawthorne Study

In the previous sections, the Hawthorne Study was described in depth. The sociologist, Gilson (1940), immediately criticized the study for its poor insights into women's situations in working life. Gilson maintained it was also naïve to think that all variables could be controlled as was attempted in the Relay Assembly Room. In view of that, she pointed out that the Hawthorne Study researchers were not trained or experienced in previous, similar work. She also argued that Taylor had already warned that people should delay time studies until management had done everything possible to improve working conditions. The criticism is summarized in the definition box below.

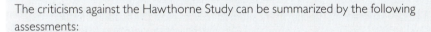

DEFINITION BOX

Criticisms against the Hawthorne Study

The criticisms against the Hawthorne Study can be summarized by the following assessments:

- Superficial theory construction and naïve methodology.
- Disregard of industry's overall problems and favouritism toward management.
- Indifference to the influence of the Great Depression.
- Indifference to the significance of gender differences.

In 1974, the sociologists, Joan Acker and Donald Van Houten, published a pioneering re-evaluation of the Hawthorne Study. They argued that the researchers at the Hawthorne factory treated the women and men research subjects quite differently. As is evident from the descriptions above, the women were treated as research objects while the men who were recruited as a group were treated as autonomous persons. Acker and van Houten (1974) illustrated how this difference in treatment influenced later researchers' understanding of the Hawthorne Study results. This difference also offered a partial explanation of why productivity increased in the study's first part (the women in the Relay Assembly Room) but diminished in the study's final part (the men in the Bank Wiring Observation Room). Gillespie (1991) also showed how the women in the first part of the study were openly encouraged to increase their productivity. The young women, who in large part were the main breadwinners in their immigrant families, needed to keep their jobs. Indirectly, the women's family situation may have caused the increased productivity and their willingness to cooperate (Acker and Van Houten, 1974). The study's generally agreed-upon conclusion that claims employees work more efficiently under benevolent management (the women in the Relay Assembly Room) and under increased work autonomy (the men in the Bank Wiring

Observation Room) should, in other words, be related to how the research subjects are treated. In the link box below some of the results from the Hawthorne Study are discussed in the context of Primo.

LINK BOX

Hawthorne studies in the year 2000

Like the researchers in the third part of the Hawthorne Study, the Primo managers who recruited applicants to their apprenticeship programme knew they needed to find people who were 'right' in various respects. An apprentice applicant who spoke good Arabic, or who had philosophical interests, might be rejected because he or she was too intelligent to fit into the organization. 'We prefer people just a step under the most intelligent people,' explained an experienced manager when it was time to make the final selection of the year's trainees. Similarly, there were few openings for people who had double degrees, such as business and engineering, because they seemed too goal-oriented and ambitious to be satisfied with the more reasonably paced career path the company offered.

Another similarity between the results of the Hawthorne Study and the Primo apprenticeship programme concerns the importance of being noticed by management. The apprentices were 'automatically noticed', a situation they experienced as particularly inclusive. Similarly, the women in part one of the Hawthorne Study seemed to thrive on the special attention they received. At the same time, however, many newly hired Primo apprentices expressed their frustration at not being able to show their full productive capabilities—when would they be able to take on important assignments and put in long workweeks? This attitude clashed with the local working norms in the temporary group they worked in where people had their own strategies for handling both the long-term work and the recurrent work stoppages.

Reflection point: Even though the original Hawthorne studies were conducted more than 80 years ago, the major findings and ideas of the studies are still highly relevant to understanding modern day organizations. What are the major learning experiences from the Hawthorne studies and how can they advise us in developing people in organizations?

Motivation in work life

As an extension of the Hawthorne Study, in the 1950s researchers continued to investigate how to motivate employees to work more efficiently and, as a result, more productively. The research area of motivation in work life became part of the research in Human Relations at the Harvard Business School after 1951 (Zaleznik *et al.*, 1958). The essential element of this research area is that *people's actions and behaviour in organizations are influenced by the motivation and satisfaction they derive from their work* (Büssing, 2002). Even if this assertion cannot be demonstrated in research, it is assumed that employee motivation and satisfaction are critical to the proper functioning of the organization. It is assumed also that employee motivation and satisfaction influence the organization's culture, its identity, the quality of its results, and the effectiveness of its leadership. The major streams of research on motivation are summarized in the definition box below.

DEFINITION BOX ✓

Motivation theory

There are two identified streams in an overall classification of motivation theory:

- Content-oriented: These theories examine the fundamentals of human needs. In this category, for example, are Maslow's Hierarchy of Needs, McGregor's Theory X and Theory Y, Herzberg's Two-Factor Theory and Hackman and Oldham's Job Characteristics Model.
- Process-oriented: These theories look at the different outside variables from which employees are assumed to choose their behaviour. In this category, for example, are McClelland's Achievement Motivation Theory, Vroom's Expectancy Theory, Adams' Equity Theory, and Porter and Lawler's dynamic Expectancy Theory.

Content-oriented motivation theories

In this section the **content-oriented motivation theories** are presented in the following order:

- Maslow's Hierarchy of Needs,
- McGregor's Theory X and Theory Y,
- Herzberg's Two-Factor Theory,
- Hackman and Oldham's Job Characteristics Model.

Maslow's Hierarchy of Needs

Abraham Maslow (1954) is often credited with laying the groundwork of motivation theory. Since he was trying to establish his distance from behavioural psychology, he wanted to use other scientific ideas than those that came from the natural sciences (that dominated in behavioural psychology). Maslow's other ambition was to differentiate himself from Sigmund Freud, who studied neurotic patients, by instead studying healthy people. A fundamental principle held by Maslow was that human beings by nature are fundamentally good.

Maslow's Hierarchy of Needs divides people's needs, in ascending order, into five stages:

- Physical needs,
- Safety needs,
- Social needs,

- Status and prestige needs,
- Self-realization needs.

According to Maslow, these needs are congenital, similar to instincts. When a person has satisfied a lower need and finds him/herself in a favourable environment, he or she begins to strive to fill the next higher need. Everyone, according to Maslow, strives to reach the highest level. When a need at a lower level is satisfied, a person in a work situation can, for example, be motivated to work harder if he or she wishes to satisfy the next higher need.

How can we use this theory in work life? Maslow's suggestion is that people establish social institutions that create the environment where the employee can develop. His Hierarchy of Needs is based on the idea that each person chooses his or her own path, and yet he also believes that a team, a group or a company can contribute to such individual development. In these types of social institutions, employees can be encouraged to work cooperatively, and thereby the individual's goals can gradually fuse with the company's goals. In order for the ideal work situation to arise and for the individual to become a better person, the employee and the organization must be integrated. The ideal work situation arises when every employee completely identifies with the company's mission.

Theory X and Theory Y

The theory of Hierarchy of Needs was further developed by Douglas McGregor, (1957, 1966). According to McGregor, many conventional organization theories were distinguished by questions of organization structure and goal-setting for management, and by practices and programmes with a view of humanity in which the average person was seen as naturally lazy, lacking in ambition, unwilling to take responsibility, and preferring to be controlled by others. The average person was self-centred and unconcerned with the needs of the organization. These theories assumed furthermore that the average person was opposed to change, and, because of his or her naïvety and mediocre intelligence, it would be easy to take advantage of them. Management may therefore need to use coercion, threats, and direct control over such individuals. Barnard (1938), alternatively, recommended the use of both the carrot and the whip on employees in organizations.

The alternative viewpoint that McGregor proposed was that people could be motivated to work, first, if the organization recognized the employee's basic humanity, and, second, if it satisfied his or her various needs. The idea was that the organization should strive to satisfy the individual's needs that lay higher up in Maslow's Hierarchy of Needs. McGregor used 'Theory X' to identify the attitude that organizations should only satisfy a person's physiological and safety needs. According to this model, people are lazy, passive, and make unreasonable demands about the compensation that they should receive for their work.

McGregor preferred instead 'Theory Y' that presented a different picture of people. According to this model, it is not an innate tendency that makes people passive or antagonistic to the organization's needs. Rather, their experiences at the organization create these attitudes. Theory Y proposes that all people have the capacity and the potential to develop consistent with the organization's goals. The task for management is to design the organization so that people can reach their own goals by synchronizing these goals with those of the organization.

MINICASE

HRM practices at Rolls-Royce Motor Cars

Being able to recruit the right personnel and develop them to attain a high level of performance is crucial for any line of business, and the HRM practices in successful companies can tell us a lot about their view of people. This is especially important in companies and industries with exceptionally high demands on quality. The market for luxury cars is a good example of this, and Rolls-Royce is probably the most prestigious brand in this small market. If economies of scale are highly important in the mass market for ordinary cars, quality and personal attention are the key features in the small, but highly competitive, market for super luxury cars. In 2009, Rolls-Royce delivered no more than 1002 cars and they still managed to make a healthy profit on those sales figures. Being able to recruit top talent and train them for a long career at Rolls-Royce is a top priority for the company. The company, which was acquired by BMW in 1999, is using a variety of tools to increase the competencies of its employees. The company takes great care in recruiting the right personnel, but its career development programmes constitute the distinguishing feature of Rolls-Royce Motor Cars. In the different business areas of the company the employees are offered a variety of courses, team activities, coaching, on-the-job training, and e-learning to permit continuous development. A number of programmes are also run to offer possibilities for apprenticeships, industrial placement, and a two-year programme for graduates. All these different activities are clearly centred on the individual and are very much in line with the Theory Y view.

The Two-Factor Theory

Maslow's theory was further developed in the Two-Factor Theory on satisfaction and motivation (Herzberg, 1966). The two sets of workplace factors are distinguished as follows:

- *Motivation Factors* consist of performance, recognition, the work itself, responsibility and career advancement. These factors vary with each person and are influenced by each person's particular goals. They also determine to what extent a person experiences work fulfilment. Employees are motivated to achieve these factors, but actual work conditions set limits on the extent to which there is scope to satisfy them.

- *Hygiene Factors* consist of company policies and administration, management control, compensation, human relations, and working conditions. These factors, along with various others, exist in people's surroundings and therefore lie outside their work requirements.

Hygiene factors can cause people to feel dissatisfied at work but cannot motivate them. As an example, when work conditions at a workplace change, the employees do not experience a sense of self-growth. Instead, motivational factors are the causes of worker motivation (Herzberg, 1966). Using the Two-Factor Theory, company management can easily find strategies to change employees' motivation. By offering career opportunities or greater responsibility, management can increase employees' motivation. Like Maslow, Herzberg considered compensation a less significant motivating factor. Of course, an employee may be dissatisfied with his or her compensation, but even if he or she thinks it is reasonable, this satisfaction doesn't create positive work motivation (Scheuer, 2000).

LINK BOX

Motivational factors in Primo

When designing both recruitment programmes, as well as career development and incentive programmes, companies often display their view on human nature in the very design of the programmes. And even though the glossy descriptions of the programmes pay homage to Theory Y and to Herzberg's motivational factors, the reality is often that these factors are forgotten. It takes a lot of effort and a change of mindset to realize the ideals of Theory Y. In realizing the Theory Y ideals, it is important to take the perspective of the employee, rather than just view the employee as a resource that should be utilized in the company. In the recruitment process described in the Primo case it seems like the company has a more traditional view of the employee, where the purpose is to select the people that fit the requirements of the company. But, when the apprentices have been selected, the perspective shifts and much more emphasis is put on the individuals' growth and development. The apprentices get a lot of support during the training period, for instance, through meeting other managers from the company that describe their careers in the company. The individual apprentice is encouraged to set up ambitious career goals and is given a lot of support in realizing these goals. Studies show that the support activities offered by the company have been instrumental in helping the apprentices to structure their careers and provide motivation to realize their goals.

Reflection point: The different motivational theories discussed in this section of the chapter all point out the importance of taking a people-centred view of the employees. This, however, takes a lot of time and energy to realize. Why is it important to emphasize the perspective of the individual in creating motivational structures in organizations?

Two weaknesses have been identified with Herzberg's Two-Factor Theory (Hackman and Oldham, 1980). First, it can be difficult to distinguish motivation factors from hygiene factors, and second, it is unclear how different people react to the different factors.

Job Characteristics Model

As an alternative to the Hierarchy of Needs Theory, to Theory X and Theory Y, and to the Two-Factor Theory, Hackman and Oldham (1980) developed the *complete job characteristics model*. In this model Hackman and Oldman tried to integrate three separate factors that, together, explain employee motivation:

- Internal work motivation,
- Job characteristics,
- Various motivations and outcomes.

Internal work motivation occurs when a person has knowledge of the results that his or her work have produced, and when he or she has responsibility for the work and finds the work meaningful.

Job characteristics influence internal work motivation. Meaningful work characteristics depend on how varied the tasks are, the knowledge required of those who perform the tasks, whether the tasks are perceived in their entirety and whether the tasks influence other people's lives. If tasks allow for freedom and independence, an employee's sense of responsibility will increase.

Various motivations and outcomes explain that different people are differently motivated toward different results. Here Hackman and Oldman identified three different employee groups:

a. People who have knowledge and competence and are productive in work with high motivation potential (compared to people with little knowledge who find work frustrating).

b. People who have a strong need to grow at work, for example, through education.

c. People who depend on work having a good context.

When the three factors (internal work motivation, job characteristics, and varied motivations and outcomes) are well integrated, employees are motivated. In these circumstances, employees grow as people and are generally content. Their work is characterized by high efficiency.

Process-oriented motivation theories

In this section, the **process-oriented motivation theories** are presented in the following order:

McClelland's Achievement Motivation Theory,

Vroom's Expectancy Theory,

Adams' Equity Theory,

Lawler's development of Expectancy theory.

Achievement Motivation Theory

In another way of looking at motivation, David McClelland (1962, 1965, 1985) argued that people have three basic needs. These are the need for *achievement*, the need for *power,* and the need for *contact and affiliation*. McClelland studied and tested his theory in various countries, labelling the needs as:

- NAch (Need for Achievement),

- NPow (Need for Power),

- NAff (Need for Affiliation).

In his research, McClelland concluded that people with a strong Need for Achievement will excel at tasks and will perform them differently than others. This capability differentiates them from results-directed and creative people. NAch people set demanding and well-thought out goals for themselves, and gladly welcome quick feedback to see how close they are to these goals. An example of this human type is the businessperson who seeks achievement through earning money. McClelland (1962) applied his Need for Achievement theory to countries as well. He showed that nations generally have a high achievement orientation for about fifty years after peaking in a business cycle, after which the need begins to decrease. This insight on human achievement needs has been taught in Indian management programmes, among others, as a way to contribute to the growth of undeveloped countries (McClelland, 1965).

People in the second group have a strong Need for Power. NPow people want control, are able to influence others, and aim therefore for positions that give them status and prestige. Since they are differentiated by their skill in communications, they like to talk in large groups. Company executives, for example, are in this group (McClelland and Burnham, 1976).

People in the third group have a strong Need for Affiliation. NAff people want to be with other people since they need friendship and others' approval. Thus, they also try to avoid conflict and criticism.

According to McClelland (1965), basic needs are learned and can quickly change through training. The result is that these needs may partially change as people try to satisfy them, to the extent that the needs can increase or decrease. Thus economic growth in a country will increase with the higher achievement needs of the population since the country benefits from their creativity and entrepreneurship.

Achievement Motivation Theory has been criticized for being an individualistic and competitive version of motivation theory. It is claimed that Achievement Motivation Theory places great weight on inner human factors but completely ignores exterior factors such as the work environment, for example. As is clear from the examples of various countries McClelland uses, he does not take cultural differences into consideration. As Maehr (1974) charged, what is valued as achievement is directly dependent on a country's cultural values.

Expectancy Theory

In the Expectancy Theory—the VIE model—Victor Vroom (1964) proposed that the probability that a person will work harder is a direct result of his or her expectations about what will happen combined with the perceived value of this outcome. Accordingly, the VIE model deals with what each person expects in relation to the value that person places on the results of that expectation. Because Expectation Theory concerns how individuals value the results of their work efforts, the theory has been criticized when a manager has difficulty using it to motivate employees.

Equity Theory

According to the Equity Theory, employees invest their skills, efforts, education, training, and experience in their work and this investment is also affected by their sex, age, and ethnic background (Adams, 1965). Employees want as much in return as they think they have invested, otherwise they think the exchange is unequal. What the employee expects in return can be higher compensation, higher status, more responsibility, or certain status symbols (for example, a larger office in connection with a promotion). Dissatisfied employees who believe their return is not equal to their investment may try to establish equality by:

- Decreasing their work commitment,
- Decreasing the quality of their work,
- Working less,
- Trying to change their status,
- Giving notice,
- Requesting a transfer,
- Being absent,
- Influencing their colleagues to leave their jobs.

As suggested by Adams (1968), both Expectation Theory and Equity Theory can be used to explain motivation under different conditions.

Expectancy Theory and Equity Theory in combination

In order to develop a compensation theory the Expectation Theory and Equity Theory (Lawler, 1968) have been combined. According to Equity Theory, a piece-work rate that is set too high leads to low productivity but high quality, while a too high hourly rate leads to both high productivity and high quality. Simply stated, compensation should be at the level where people feel obligated to be effective. As claimed by Lawler, however, the differences in compensation systems relate to other factors, for example, employee exhaustion. Employees are not motivated by higher pay if there are negative consequences associated with working harder. High productivity, they argue, is dependent on feelings other than the perception of being overpaid. Nevertheless, compensation may act as one important motivating factor when it is directly connected to productivity, that is, when employees receive more pay as they produce more. Moreover, Porter and Lawler (1968), posit that a person's abilities and traits, as well as the persons perception of his/her role, will have an effect on performance. The fit between subjective perceptions and the objective requirements of the role affects performance.

Motivation in movies

Popular culture is a contemporary and important source, as well as a reflection, of the norms we follow in different situations. In this respect, feature movies may have a special role. For example, company leaders who are frequent travellers may spend hotel time looking at movies and possibly being influenced by the morals and values presented in such films. In stylized and dramatized ways, movies show typical human situations and they can teach

MINICASE

us a lot about human interaction and motivation. Björn Rombach and Rolf Solli (2006) have developed this theory based on the sports movie, *Any Given Sunday*, in which a 55-year-old coach is the manager of an American professional football team. The coach's goal is to develop team spirit by motivating the team to play together. In various ways, including convincing players of the will to win, the film shows how the coach uses different methods to motivate his players to win games. He enthusiastically gives pep talks to the whole team, provoking feelings of both shame and camaraderie in the players. He also speaks quietly and intimately with individual players, encouraging them to play football differently. Of course, in his position as coach, he has the power to decide who plays, which is another way of motivating through control. The tools and techniques being applied by the coach in the movie are very much in line with contemporary HRM practices, and even though the film is not 'for real', it still shows what motivational processes can look like, and as indicated above learning can occur by watching the movie.

Challenging motivation theories

Motivation as a research area had its high point in the 1970s. Yet the research area had limitations, both regarding the questions posed and the methods used to seek answers. An early example of such methodology was used by Herzberg *et al.* (1959) who believed motivation theory's essential question was: What does an employee want from work? According to these researchers, management could answer the question through clues discovered by measuring employee attitudes in three ways:

1. Asking employees to indicate the importance to them of various work factors, such as compensation, supervision, company and management policies, and communications.

2. Asking employees to rank, most to least important, what they did, or did not, value in their work.

3. Asking employees multiple forms of questions that could be statistically analysed, allowing researchers to find relationships between the different factors.

By using these measurements, a company could learn what employees thought was important at work and how likely they would remain at a company. The attitude measurements approach, similar to the methodologically multifaceted Hawthorne Study, was clearly only one of many possible ways to research organizational phenomena, including employee motivation.

During the 1940s, the 1950s, and the 1960s, it was popular to research content-oriented theories and motivation theories. The aim of these studies was to find a universal pattern for how people were motivated at work, and to determine which actions followed different efforts (Scheuer, 2000). Subsequently, these studies were criticized for not showing how particular needs led to particular behaviours. Even the general claim by researchers, in the area of content-oriented theories and motivation theories, that their theories and assumptions are important for and applicable to all people, regardless of time and space, has been criticized (Spector et al., 2002).

It seems that models that integrate both process and content are better at predicting when employees will be satisfied with their work and when employees will fail to perform as expected. A common theme in such motivation research is that researchers continue to claim motivation in work leads to work satisfaction. Spector et al. (2002), however, found that these studies are often uncritical, lack theoretical basis, and have an artificial character.

New ways of understanding work motivation

During the 1970s, new ideas were advanced as a way to understand work motivation. One idea was **job enlargement**, which means that the employees' normal work tasks are increased in scope; another idea was **job enrichment**, which means that the employees' work tasks are expanded to include planning and control. Another idea was *life quality*, where a person's entire life situation, including family life, free time, and living arrangements, is used as the starting point for studying his or her attitude toward work (Stjernberg, 1977). Yet another idea is **commitment**, where it is believed that employees' dedication to work is built-in as a fundamental part of the work structure. In a factory with direct supervision, simplified work tasks, and specific work instructions, there is very little possibility of engaging employees' *commitment* and therefore very low likelihood that they will make suggestions for innovation. In work structures where the employees can both influence their work and involve themselves in it, there is, by contrast, room for change, innovation, and improved efficiency (Walton, 1980).

Empowerment was introduced in the United States as a work concept at the end of the 1980s (Conger and Kanungo, 1988). The idea means that the work group or the individual employee at lower levels in the hierarchy is given increased responsibility for administrative tasks and for planning in a process of 'directed authority'. Empowerment assumes that the Taylor idea of work, where intellectual work tasks are separated from manual work tasks, is no longer valid (Mills and Ungson, 2003). Soon the idea was much discussed among researchers. However, one problem was that the idea of empowerment was not based in practice but rather on an abstract conception dreamed up by researchers. It was also unclear if empowerment really created opportunities for new, interesting work tasks for employees, or if it mainly made them think they were more involved in the decision-making (Argyris, 1998; Sewell, 2001). Another question was whether empowerment agreed with the basic need in organizations for goal congruence (Mills and Ungson, 2003).

Parallel with empowerment, there were other popular organization changes in the late twentieth century workplace. These changes included **downsizing**, which deals with reducing the number of workers, **outsourcing** which means that certain functions or activities are moved from the company to its suppliers, and *lean production*, which is described as a process where the company's inventory is held to a minimum level through timely delivery of materials. The commonality among these business practices is that all are intended to increase the company's productivity. In light of these changes, one can see that the practice of empowerment, and its various offshoots, was a way to manage the company's demand for cost savings and greater efficiency rather than a way to make conditions better for employees. When empowerment was put into practice, it was shown to be, if anything, an extensive decentral-ization of certain administrative tasks and a broadening of work positions. In most instances, the proposed decrease in work tasks failed to materialize. Some of the challenges involved in developing HR standards in companies are described in the minicase below.

HR practices in networked organizations—the case of IKEA

Many companies have developed rigorous codes of conduct for treating employees fairly and to make sure that working conditions are up to standard. Companies that rely heavily on subcontractors and external suppliers are faced with special dilemmas in implementing high ethical standards in the HR area. IKEA, the Swedish home product retailer, is a familiar sight in many large cities around the world, with its characteristic yellow and blue stores. The IKEA production model builds on a large number of suppliers providing goods to the company. To make sure that working conditions are acceptable among the suppliers, IKEA has issued a list of minimum requirements for the suppliers. This list, called The IKEA Way of Purchasing Products, Materials and Services (IWAY), provides the supplier with clear guidelines concerning issues like child labour, wages, discrimination, and harassment. Issuing these ethical rules is the easy part of the process—the problem starts when implementing them. IKEA is faced with many challenges. Since their suppliers are spread all over the world, it is hard to keep tight control over all of them, and often, this is not possible or even advisable. One way of ensuring that the suppliers comply with the standards is to have IKEA personnel not only visiting, but actively working at the supplier's sites. It is a common practice at IKEA to have employees from product development, design, and purchasing work at the factories both to get to know them better, and to assist in improving processes and working conditions.

Human Resource Management (HRM)

As an outgrowth of the Hawthorne Study, research extended into Human Relations and partly into motivation theory. These two areas, together with the criticism against earlier theories on Personnel Management, gave rise to the area of Human Resource Management. Gradually, rather than researching motivation, researchers began to study HRM questions. In HRM research the ambition is to encourage employees to see their work as a challenge so that they will be motivated to work enthusiastically toward the company's goals. Like the area of Human Relations, HRM has an interest in communication between individuals, between individuals and groups, and between groups under various circumstances (Roethlisberger, 1968).

The term 'Human Resource' was coined by Peter Drucker (1955) in his book, *The Practice of Management*, in which he criticized the term's predecessor, 'Personnel Management'. Legge (1995) even argued that two incompatible functions are combined in the idea of Personnel Management: *personnel*, which implies employee welfare, and *management*, which implies control. For Drucker, the basic principle of Personnel Management is that firm control is necessary to keep uncommitted or lazy employees from cheating or slacking. Drucker maintained that Personnel Management should not be a specialist function in the Personnel Department but rather should be part of the work responsibility of all managers with people reporting to them. Another idea that Drucker promoted, popularized by his term 'management by objectives', was that managers, as well as rank-and-file employees, should be controlled. At the time Drucker was advancing these ideas, employees were mainly regarded as costs by US companies. However, Drucker encouraged companies to look at employees as resources. If every job had challenges, the employees in these jobs could be motivated to work toward the company's goals.

During the 1960s, Human Resource Management became a separate concept in the research literature. In the 1970s HRM was synonymous with Personnel Management, but during the 1980s, HRM became the more popular term as distinguished from Personnel Management. One reason was that HRM was now viewed as a strategic issue. Good personnel management was considered a prerequisite if an organization's strategies were to be executed. HRM therefore, had become a catch-all term for various personnel management practices as well as for more strategic practices (Tengblad, 2000).

The strategic element is central to the HRM area because of the importance of personnel questions in an organization. Yet, personnel administrators often hold marginal positions in companies (Guest, 1987), causing researchers to point out that questions concerning personnel are much too important to be handled so casually by people with little power. HRM questions should be separated from routine personnel questions since HRM focuses much more on maximizing the integration of employee and organization goals, increasing the employees' work involvement and defining the nature and flexibility of the work. Recognizing the truth of this reality, companies began to include HRM among the main management activities at the same time as HRM took over certain personnel functions. Moreover, because of the strategic perspective in HRM, personnel questions began to receive similar status as company business strategies and other important issues. In this way, companies could encourage employees' involvement in the organization and motivate them in a more sweeping way. Even the unions' influence on the company's efficiency could be reduced (Guest, 1987).

HRM consists of two different control philosophies that are described in the definition box below.

DEFINITION BOX

Hard and Soft HRM

- *Hard HRM:* This philosophy refers to strategic HRM. For an organization to achieve higher efficiency, personnel management should function in line with the overall goals and strategies of the organization.
- *Soft HRM:* This philosophy refers to the issue of the responsibility for HRM—either by a generalist manager or a personnel manager. The basic idea is that employees are a critical resource who should be involved in and motivated by various normative control measures in order to create an efficient organization that is profitable because its employees are motivated, enthusiastic and satisfied (Legge, 1995).

This is also described in the link box below.

LINK BOX

Hard and soft human resource management at Primo

Human resource management (HRM) has gained a lot of attention in the last decades and the positive connotations in the words human resources seem to make them more attractive than terms like personnel management or personnel administration. In spite of the positive association, it is not always the case that HRM practice takes the single employee as the natural focus. Companies can take different perspectives in working with developing employees and often the perspective is rather centred on the needs of the organization rather than the individual. There are, however, many examples of companies that have managed to find a good balance between the needs of the organization and the needs of the individual. The notion of hard and soft HRM captures the crucial difference between organizational and individual goals. Hard HRM refers to how the personnel management function is organized to achieve the goals of the organization, whereas soft HRM refers to the attempts at creating normative control mechanisms and to foster the needs of the individual employee. When designing the apprenticeship programme at Primo great care was taken to balance between the needs of the organization, for instance, in ensuring that the best suited individuals were selected in the recruitment process and the needs of the individual. For the later part, the apprenticeship programme was clearly tailor-made to enable individuals to develop ambitious personal goals and the company offered a lot of support in realizing those goals. The results from Primo also show that it is perfectly possible to strike such a balance.

Reflection point: The perspectives of hard and soft HRM indicate that companies need to focus both on the organization's needs as well as the individual's. How should companies find a good balance between the two perspectives?

HRM and the organization

One issue in HRM concerns its influence on the organization's activities in other respects. HRM's roots in the Human Relations Movement have been problematic since this linkage has caused people to use sensitivity training as a way to take a more human perspective on personnel matters in organizations. The result, according to Kanter (1977), has contributed to making Personnel Management an employment area primarily for women since they are assumed to have more emotional sensitivity. By contrast, men are assumed to be more qualified for decision-making positions. Consequently, women have tended to be distanced from the organization's main managerial positions while personnel managerial issues have been relegated to a lower status than issues related to the organization's economy, technology, finance, etc. Because of this view of personnel work as something soft and suitable for women, when HRM developed as a strategic and central management function, it was more or less implicitly accepted that the area should be managed by men (Townley, 1994).

The fundamental principle of the contemporary HRM tradition is that management and employees should have good relationships with each other in harmonious interaction at all levels of the organization. Harmony is essential for individual prosperity, organizational efficiency, and societal well-being, a conclusion reached by Mayo (1933) in the Hawthorne Study. If there are conflicts among the employees, it is the manager's job to resolve them. Thus, it is the manager who makes a better person of the employee (O'Connor, 1999).

Another principle of contemporary HRM is that the organization functions best when its members identify with the organization's goals. This situation occurs when the employees relate closely to the organization, mentally, psychologically, and morally. People in the focus of HRM develop collective motives. Townley (1994) stated that this collectivism is HRM's objective, that is to say, people must adapt to the organization and management's conditions. If the employees' motivations and morale are shaped in the right way, harmony will arise between them and their managers, and the company will increase its productivity (O'Connor, 1999).

Diversity

During the 1990s, diversity became an issue of interest that was raised partly by researchers and partly by consultants wishing to stake a claim to a new area (Litvin, 2002). For the consultants, diversity often means that in employing people with different backgrounds, a company can take advantage of their knowledge and so become more profitable. Diversity is concerned with the individual's gender, ethnicity, age, personal history, education, personality, lifestyle, sexual preferences, geographic origins, and organizational position, as well as the company's history and operations. All members in an organization thus belong to diversity groups and therefore diversity as an idea does not exclude certain minorities (Nkomo and Cox, 1996).

Diversity issues quickly resulted in the creation of management diversity programmes that aimed at promoting diversity in organizations (Nkomo and Cox, 1996; Litvin, 2002). Foldy (2002) identifies four main types of diversity programmes:

- *Diversity initiatives*: In these programmes, under-represented groups learn 'to play the game' in organizations so that they have better access to decision-making. The result is that marginalized groups adapt to the rules of the game. Thus, these programmes reinforce existing power relationships.

- *Diversity training*: In these programmes, courses on diversity allow organization members to describe their stereotypes and biases as well as learn more about other groups' cultures. Here, the aim is to change the employees rather than to change the organization.

- *Solidarity groups*: In these programmes, special groups in the organization are recognized. Members in the groups try to develop social and professional contacts. The idea is that a group makes people more visible in the organization and can therefore lead to career advancement. Because these groups must follow management strategies, they have no impact on changing the organization.

- *Mentoring programmes*: In these programmes, senior men and women in the organization are matched with employees at lower levels and with different backgrounds. Marginalized employees thus have greater access to people in decision-making positions. Because of the influence of these personal contacts that inspire careerism, the expectation is that the employees will abandon attempts to change the organization.

On the whole, managing diversity programmes has been criticised for not leading to changes in organizations. Another criticism of the diversity movement concerns what happens to people with different experiences and different backgrounds who are no longer viewed as contributing to the company's profitable operations—will they be dismissed? A company that is committed to diversity also risks creating large business projects instead of projects that integrate different groups into the organization (Omanovic, 2003; 2004). Another interesting finding in the study of diversity programmes is the revelation that male executives would rather talk about diversity issues than issues involving gender discrimination. An explanation may be that issues about gender are threatening to both women and men (Martin, 2003).

MINICASE

Diversity management at McKinsey & Company

More and more companies are realizing the positive effects of having a diverse work force, but as the discussion above shows it takes more than glossy words to make diversity programmes really work. In the end it comes down to questions about how seriously managers on different levels take the slogans of diversity, for example, in recruitment and promotion decisions. Serious questions can also be raised if companies take diversity issues seriously when selecting people to important decision-making bodies, such as boards and management teams. A company that has taken diversity issues seriously is the world leading management consultancy firm, McKinsey & Company. Through supporting a number of dedicated networks the company signals its support for diversity issues. One example of this is the network Gay, Lesbian, Bisexual, and Transgender consultants at McKinsey (GLAM). The stated purpose of the network is 'to cultivate and recruit gay, lesbian, bisexual, and transgender professionals to McKinsey and to meet, support one another, share ideas, and work on issues of importance to them as a community' (**www.mckinsey. com**). The members of the network have been engaged in a wide variety of activities, including organizing conferences to discuss professional development and organizing mentoring and coaching programmes. Why is a company like McKinsey so interested in supporting this kind of network? One important reason is that the consultants need to be prepared for meeting a wide variety of different customers and face complex situations. With a more diverse work force, a company like McKinsey can be better prepared to tackle complex problems and situations.

Summary and conclusions

This chapter describes different ways of looking at people in the organization. The chapter begins with the description of a recruiting case for the selection of the most suitable people for a training programme. The case shows the insights required for attracting and judging people in the recruitment situation and argues that good recruitment practices lead to hiring employees who will work well in the organization. Next, the summary and analysis of the Hawthorne Study references earlier research results on people's productivity, showing that workers react positively to benevolent management and that productivity standards are even set by informal groups. The chapter argues that these results should be considered in conjunction with the revelation that women and men are sometimes treated differently by researchers who perform experiments and interpret their results (Acker and Van Houten, 1974).

The area of motivation research was partly an extension of the Hawthorne Study's results. Such research had its high point in the 1950s to the 1970s when researchers performed attitude measurements to learn what motivates people to work, concluding that work satisfaction is the main motivator of employees. Later the area was criticized for its overly simplified view of people. Since the end of the 1980s, the question of motivation has been discussed within the framework of issues around empowerment of employees.

Another extension of the Hawthorne Study and motivation research is the area of HRM that examines the different ways employees and the organization can cooperate effectively. HRM is differentiated from Personnel Management by its emphasis on personnel issues that are strategic in nature and that require company attention as much as financial, economic, and technical issues. As an example of HRM strategies diversity issues has been presented.

Study questions

1. What effects do recruitment processes have on the individual?
2. What effects do recruitment processes have on the organization?
3. How can productivity be sustained in organizational practice?
4. What motivates people in work?
5. How is motivation challenged by more recent theoretical schools?
6. How can HRM strategies be used as a management tool to control employees?
7. What are the organizational effects of diversity management?

Literature recommendations and further readings

Interested readers can read more about the Hawthorne Study in Gillespie (1991) and in Acker and Van Houten's pioneering article (1974). In the area of motivation, Scheuer (2000) provides a good overview. For an introduction to and reflections on HRM, see, for example, Townley's (1994) Reframing Human Resource Management and Legge's (1995) Human Resource Management: Rhetorics and Realities.

**online
resource
centre**

Take your learning further

http://www.oxfordtextbooks.co.uk/orc/erikssonzetterquist/

Visit the Online Resource Centre which accompanies this book to enrich your understanding of this chapter.

Students: explore web links and further reading suggestions. Keep up to date with the latest developments via 'What happened next' updates to appropriate cases from within the book.

Lecturers: you will find seminar exercises and teaching notes, for use in class or assessment.

CHAPTER 6
How to lead in an organization

Ericsson—a meeting between different leadership philosophies

Ericsson, the big telecom company, was the pride of the Swedish business community. Students from the big universities and business schools in Sweden unanimously voted Ericsson as the best employer in the country and the stock price was sky-rocketing in the late 1990s. On both NASDAQ and the Swedish stock exchange the stock price had gone up by more than 1,600% in just a few years from the mid- to late 1990s (the stock exchange rate was down to 50 SEK in the beginning of 1995 and topped at more than 800 SEK in March 2000). Even though a number of analysts and journalists raised serious doubts concerning the valuation of the company on the stock market in 1998 and 1999, no one seemed to pay any serious attention. That is, until March 2000, when the whole IT/Telecom bubble suddenly burst, and Ericsson was severely hit by the crisis. Ericsson was losing a lot of money on producing and selling mobile phones (even though the consumer market was still booming), but what was worse was the deep cut in sales of their core product, telecom systems. When telephone operators all over the globe suddenly stopped investing, in the year 2000, this hit Ericsson more than competitors such as Nokia, due to their strong reliance on systems. Ironically, Nokia, who was much less dependent on systems and the undisputed leader (number 1) in the mobile phone market, was making huge profits on their phones, while Ericsson was selling every phone they produced at a loss.

Many observers wanted to attribute this to the prevailing leadership and management culture in the company, with a strong and partly elitist and inward-looking engineering culture. People in the company took pride in inventing new and technologically sophisticated phones, aimed at advanced end-users, primarily business people, that they thought preferred function over form. The customers, however, started to view mobile phones as more than just a technological device, and no company understood needs and wants better than Nokia, with well designed and easy-to-use phones that appealed to a young audience. The look of a mobile phone mattered, but the people at Ericsson were slow to realize this.

The severe crisis was met by a new top management team led by Mr Kurt Hellström, a gentleman in his 50s who had spent a major part of his working life at Ericsson—he knew the culture. He initiated and carried through three waves of cost-cutting programs. From the beginning of 2000, to the middle of 2003, Ericsson shrunk from 107,000 to around 50,000 employees. Mr Hellström symbolized, in his public appearances, the engineering-driven and inward-looking organization. The press conferences, from early 2000 to the beginning of 2003, and presentations of the quarterly and full year results took place in a large auditorium with Mr Hellström and his (male) companions, in dark grey suits, seated above the audience on a podium showing only their faces and shoulders. It soon became a standing joke among analysts and journalists whether Hellström would start his presentation with the now familiar phrase—there is no light in the tunnel!

Despite Mr Hellström's less than charismatic stage appearances during press conferences and other public occasions, the cost-cutting programs produced good results, even though the market still viewed Ericsson as a company in deep crisis. To a large extent the feeling of crisis and hopelessness was reflected in body language and formulations of Kurt Hellström and his associates. A number of his presentations signalled a deep lack of self-confidence, which was a new thing for a company used to being viewed as number one.

In the beginning of 2003, it was announced that a new CEO was being recruited, and this time it was an 'outsider'—Mr Carl-Henric Svanberg. Svanberg was a popular choice and he had a strong track-record from previous positions, the latest as CEO for one of the largest companies in the Swedish security industry. Far from telecom! In his first public appearances, Mr Svanberg met the mass media standing around a small round table. Gone was the distance to the audience, replaced by a much more relaxed communicative style, and a willingness to talk to the media. The leadership style exhibited by Svanberg signalled strength, and above all, self-confidence. After the third quarter of 2003, he could proudly present the first quarter with a profit in more than three years. Even though this was largely due to the successful cost-cutting programs of his predecessor, the whole attitude towards Ericsson was 'smitten' by the enthusiasm and confidence of Svanberg, and Ericsson continued to show healthy profits for more than four years after that. Through a combination of internal growth and strategic acquisitions the company managed to grow, and by the end of 2008, the number of employees was 78,740. At the end of 2007, however, the confidence in Svanberg (and Ericsson) was shaken by a sudden and unexpected halt in the growth figures, due to high market turbulence. The figures for Q2 of 2008 showed a decrease in the operating profit of close to fifty per cent (50%), down from 9.3 to 4.7 billion SEK, and the verdict from the stock market was immediate and strong.

The first four years of his tenure at Ericsson had been marked by rapid growth and positive market outlooks, effective operations, and positive relations to the mass media and analysts. At the end of 2007 and beginning of 2008 the market growth halted and the relations to media worsened. By the end of 2008, the financial crisis hit the world market and Ericsson got its fair share with a downturn in sales, even though the company seems to have managed the crisis better than most of its competitors. Finally, in 2009, it was announced that Mr Svanberg would leave the company and the work to recruit a new CEO started.

General information for this case was compiled from articles in daily newspapers in Sweden. Company figures were retrieved from www.ericsson.se. The analysis of Mr Svanberg's public appearances is based on television broadcasts, and a thorough analysis is available in Müllern and Elofsson (2006). A description of the change processes described above can also be found in Narayandas *et al*, (2007).

Questions

Is the difference between the public appearances of the two CEOs in Ericsson indicative of a deeper change in how leadership is exercised today?

If so, what are the basics of the new, emerging approach to leadership?

What are the practical challenges in mastering leadership in modern organizations, and how do rapid market changes, new values, information technology, and organizational innovations and changes join together to create new challenges and opportunities for managers at all levels?

Introduction

This chapter introduces the reader to the role of leadership in managing organizations and captures the major changes in how leadership is described and carried out in different organizational contexts. The presentation of Ericsson and the changes in leadership exercised by the two recent CEOs in the case introduction above might seem like a straightforward story about a successful turnaround of a company in crisis and the pivotal role of the CEO in leading the change effort. It can also be read as a shift from a traditional view on leadership, towards a new, more change-oriented view. The theoretical shift from an autocratic and leader-centred view on leadership to a charismatic/transformational view, based on a more democratic and vision-based relation between manager and co-workers, is a theme that will be thoroughly discussed in this chapter.

This story can, however, be questioned and a very different tale can be told. The story is focused on a group of main actors that fit with the common stereotype of a successful CEO in a European/American company—male, white, and in his mid 40s or 50s. This stereotype is not consistent with the population statistics in companies. Male, white, and middle-aged CEOs are over represented in top management positions, and they are leading in companies with a much more varied composition of employees. Issues of gender differences, ethnicity, religious tolerance and pluralism, and various forms of expressing sexuality are more and more on the corporate and general agenda. A chapter on leadership would not be complete without also covering these issues, and how they mix together to form, what we will call *intersectionality*.

Irene Rosenfeld of Kraft Foods

MINICASE

In the 2010 Fortune 500 ranking of the worlds largest companies only 12 (!) companies were led by a woman (Fortune, July 26, 2010). This was even a decrease from the previous year when 13 women acted as CEOs of companies on Fortune 500. Depressing as these figures are, there are some great examples in this small but exclusive group of female top

MINICASE

managers. Irene Rosenfeld is, since 2006, CEO of Kraft Foods, the world's second largest food company, and currently placed at 179 on the Fortune 500. Kraft Foods owns a number of the world's most well known consumer goods brands, such as Cadbury, Maxwell house, LU, Philadelphia, Kool-Aid, and numerous others. Irene Rosenfeld has become known as a change-oriented leader, and she has led major restructuring efforts in the company. Her accomplishment as CEO of Kraft Foods has not gone unnoticed and she is often featured in rankings of the most powerful women in business. One of the success stories accredited to Rosenfeld is the acquisition of Cadbury in early 2010. The acquisition was highly controversial, not least in Cadbury, and it was considered to be an important victory for the company and for Irene Rosenfeld, when the board of Cadbury said yes to the offer from Kraft Foods. But with all processes of mergers and acquisitions, the hard work starts after the decision is taken, and much work remains to integrate Cadbury in the Kraft Foods organization. Many challenges, however, remain in securing the commitment and enthusiasm of the employees.

But, the story is also misleading for a second reason. As Henry Mintzberg (1973) showed in his study of CEOs they play important roles as symbols of their companies. They act as **figure-heads** and undertake important communicative roles externally and internally. However, it has also been noted that their capacity and possibility to actually influence all parts of a big organization are limited. The decision-making power of CEOs is usually high, but strategic decisions have to be followed by action, and in this sphere the influence of CEOs is more limited. They rely, to a large extent, on managers in lower positions to carry out decisions and to realize the strategic intent of top management. The roles of *middle managers*, *project managers*, and many others that take on leadership tasks, cannot be overemphasized.

The theories on leadership covered in this chapter therefore need to be set in a context, not only of change and renewal, but also of middle and project management. The organizational context of leadership is rapidly changing and an important part of this chapter introduces a number of factors that influence and change the conditions for leadership at all levels. The important role of *charismatic* and *transformational* leadership in modern management is not the sole responsibility of top management.

To summarize, the chapter addresses the following issues:

- Leadership put in an organizational context and how it reflects changes in the ways present day companies are organized,
- Contemporary theories of leadership,
- Gender, intersectionality, and the challenges for modern leadership,
- Leading in the middle.

Leadership in its organizational context

Leadership is one of the more important groups of activities carried out in an organization, and it is intimately linked to the formal aspects of organizing. The formal structure is part of the context in which leadership is realized—it is always situated in a certain organization with individuals having certain predefined positions in a formal structure and with systems and routines in place. When managers try to make things happen, they are constrained by the formal patterns in the company. Leadership is also one of the activities where the formal structure is created and made to work.

Context is a broad concept and it covers a wide range of aspects that can shape the conditions for leadership—formal structures, people, relations, culture, legislation, and technology are a few examples. In this section we will highlight two important contextual factors that show how intimately leadership and organizations are connected. The first factor, *organizational structures*, makes the point that leadership is mostly (but certainly not always) carried out by people set in formal positions in a formal structure—what we usually refer to as *managers*. Depending on the 'shape' of the formal structure different conditions for leadership are created. The second factor, *values*, deals with broader societal trends that directly and indirectly influence both the way leadership is exercised and how it is accepted/met by people who are subject to it—what we here refer to as *followership*.

Organizational structures and leadership

As indicated above, a number of structural features can, potentially, influence how leadership is affected. The idea of a link between contextual factors and aspects of leadership is not new. Beginning in the late 1960s, leadership theory was inspired by the ideas of general system theory, and a number of theories were proposed that highlighted certain relations between context and leadership. Two of the most popular are summarized in the definition boxes below.

DEFINITION BOX

Situational leadership

Situational leadership. This theory was formulated by Hersey and Blanchard in 1969. Their basic idea was that managers differ in terms of the leadership behaviour they exhibit. Based on previous research they proposed two general styles of leadership—task behaviour and relationship behaviour. The specific relations between these two styles are formed in interaction with the employees, and are determined to a large extent by the maturity of the followers. Depending on the level of maturity of the follower, different combinations of task and relationship behaviour by the manager may be appropriate. With low levels of maturity they suggested that a task oriented style be used. As subordinate maturity increases, a less task-oriented style and a more relations-oriented style was suggested. With highly mature subordinates they suggested low levels of both task and relations-orientation. The motive for this was that the very mature subordinate is less dependent on the leader and can do the work without much direction and monitoring. The model by Hersey and Blanchard has been heavily criticized (Aldag and Brief, 1981; Haley, 1983; York and Hastings, 1985) but is still very popular among practitioners and is often used in leadership training.

Contingency theory

Contingency theory. The contingency theory of leadership formulated by Fred Fiedler (1967) builds on the idea that leadership is exercised in a relation between the manager and the concrete situation. Fiedler uses three situational factors – the relation between manager and follower, the nature of the task to be carried out, and the positional power of the manager, to describe the situation. He also suggests a psychological measure of leadership behaviour, the so called LPC-score (Least Preferred Coworker), in which the manager is asked to describe his/her relation with the person he/she has the most problems cooperating with. A high score indicates, according to Fiedler, a more relationship-motivated person, whereas a low score indicates a task-motivated person. Compared to Hersey and Blanchard's model of Situational leadership, the Contingency theory is more elaborate and theoretically more sophisticated. The model, however, never did reach a wider audience and it is seldom used for leadership training nowadays.

We will, in this section, discuss four aspects of organizational structures and how they shape the conditions for leadership.

Decentralization: Probably the clearest difference between a present-day company and its counterpart in the 1960s is the increase in local authority, or to use a more theoretical term, the increase in *operative decentralization*. In Chapter 2, we presented the INNFORM study, and one result from that study was that forty-seven per cent (47%) of the companies had increased the operative decentralization from 1992 to 1997. Operative decentralization means that people with operative tasks take on decision-making authority concerning their specific tasks. The rationale behind operative decentralization is two-fold. First, it reduces the need for control on the shop-floor level, and one consequence has been a rapid reduction of the foreman function. Secondly, the increased responsibility acts as a motivator and creates more stimulating tasks for the individual. This fundamental change was clearly already visible in the late 1960s, and it gained momentum in the 1970s with a broad introduction of tools such as management-by-objectives (MBO) and performance-based measurement. This gave personnel on operational levels more freedom to decide *how* to carry out work.

A more empowered workforce creates, in itself, a new and more challenging situation for managers on different levels. A leadership based primarily on the manager's position in the formal hierarchy, and with an authoritarian leadership style, proved to be a poor match with the new demands from more empowered co-workers. The increase in operative decentralization has clearly changed the landscape for managers to exercise leadership. But there is also a second form of decentralization that has the potential to transform the corporate landscape even more—*strategic decentralization*. This form of decentralization encourages personnel on different levels and positions to participate in strategic decision-making processes. The rationale for this form of decentralization is to absorb and make use of the competencies people have, and to incorporate their knowledge and skills, from the beginning, in strategic processes. This reflects a growing awareness of the need for having people on more levels than top management involved in important strategic processes. The results from different studies show an increase in strategic decentralization, even though small (Pettigrew and Massini, 2003). Strategic decentralization, when implemented, gives a new meaning to the word *empowerment*.

Projects and other temporary forms of organizing: The basic assumption in most books on organizations (and this was evident also in Chapter 2) is that the formal structure is designed for *permanent* use. This assumption does not imply that formal structures are not subject to change. On the contrary, as Chapter 9 will show, change is part of the daily routine in any organization. Permanency means rather, that the organization (or a part of it) is not dissolved once it has accomplished an assigned task or mission. With *projects*, and other temporary forms, the situation is different. Projects, by definition, are temporary—when a project mission is accomplished the project organization is terminated and the participants either go back to their permanent position or continue working on other projects.

What, then, is the significance of this from a leadership perspective? Recent studies show that companies, to a growing extent, are using projects to organize and carry out important tasks, and that this reflects new challenges for companies, such as shortened product life cycles, narrow product launch windows, increasingly complex and technical products, and the emergence of global markets (Morris and Pinto, 2007). This does not automatically mean that companies get rid of the permanent formal structure. The situation for many companies is that they operate with dual structures—projects alongside the permanent structure. This poses many challenges for leadership. The most obvious challenge is that more and more leadership is exercised in projects, with the temporary nature of projects creating a different situation for the project manager. For the line-level manager in departments, and other units in the permanent structure, a situation arises where they have to lead with personnel that sometimes partly work under their control and sometimes are 'lent' to projects. Tensions and conflicts between the line and the projects are legion in many companies, and the leadership vested in both project managers and line-level managers (middle managers) has to deal with this.

Information technology: The decentralization and project trends are easy to pinpoint and the leadership consequences are clear cut. With the third factor, *information technology*, the situation is more complex. Information technology has, without doubt, transformed the ways work is carried out, and it is often the single most important instrument or technology used to perform daily work tasks. Many occupations and companies are nowadays unthinkable without computers, software, systems, and other related IT-technology and applications. Think of a travel agency, a stock broker, a bank, or an insurance company without integrated information systems. As was shown in Chapter 3, IT is much more than just the use of computers and IT-systems to organize and carry out work. IT also creates opportunities for, and demands new patterns of communication and socializing, and here lies an important transforming effect for workplace relations and leadership.

The advance of information technology has called into question the very idea of the organization as a meeting of people at a predefined location (an office, a factory, a shop, or any other physical meeting place). With information technology work can be carried out in a much more distributed fashion, and numerous studies show that information technology is rapidly transforming work places, which in turn creates new challenges for managers. For instance, so-called virtual organizations or virtual project development teams may be distributed over large geographical distances and over time zones, creating new types of leadership challenges (Krikman *et al.*, 2004; Markus *et al.*, 2000; Maznevsky and Chudoba, 2000).

While many proponents of information technology conceive of computer-based media as being a value-neutral tool in the hands of organization members, much research demonstrates that information technology:

(1) Changes the organization and the work fundamentally (Zammuto *et al.* 2007; Heracleous and Barrett, 2001; Pinsonneault and Kraemer, 1997),

(2) Embodies various assumptions, beliefs, and ideologies, regarding the nature of work and how knowledge and information may be coded into documents and databases (Bloomfield, 1991; Bloomfield and Hayes, 2009).

Adressing the former issue, Pinsonneault and Kraemer (1997) demonstrated that implementation of information technologies is often accompanied by a cutting down on middle management, thereby relying less on 'face-to-face leadership' and more on what Bloomfield and Hayes (2009) call 'electric governance'. Such a shift from leadership practice to technologically mediated forms of control is indicative of what Bloomfield and Hayes (2009) critically refer to, which brings us to the latter issue, that of ideology, as *technocratic utopianism*, the belief that all kinds of information management problems are capable of being solved through 'technical means' (e.g., IT). For its proponents, information technology is effectively substituting for traditional leadership work. For others, such as Bloomfield and Hayes (2009), leadership is at best, accompanied by computer-based media, enabling a faster and more efficient handling of information but never fully taking the role of actual leadership work.

Fuzzy boundaries: We concluded Chapter 2 with a number of observations on the Intel case. It was noted that Intel, to a growing extent, is dependent on external relations. Intel is in no way alone in this trend. Ericsson, the case study at the beginning of this chapter, is more and more dependent on cooperating with different actors to keep track of, and utilize technological trends and breakthroughs, as well as market related changes. This is described in the link box below.

LINK BOX

Sony Ericsson—boundary crossing in practice

Traditional wisdom suggests that the organization should be protected against forces in its environment and that strong measures should be taken to manage the boundaries so that the inner core of the organization is not exposed to the environment. The boundaries are there to protect and buffer the organization from the organization. This view is more and more giving way to a view that organizations should open their boundaries and work to make the environment a much more integrated part of the organization. There are many ways to do this and some were used in Ericsson. One of the most important measures taken by Ericsson to deal with the crisis in the year 2000 was to enter into a joint venture with Sony corporation to harbour the former's mobile phone division. Five years later, Sony Ericsson, as the new company was named, was established as a successful player with a market share of around nine per cent (9%) in this highly competitive market, even though the market share has shrunk since then. Ericsson owns fifty per cent (50%) and Sony the remaining fifty per cent (50%) of this company. Sony Ericsson is also dependent on relations with other companies, for instance, for producing mobile phones. This creates many challenges for managers on different levels in Sony Ericsson to deal with projects, and other tasks, that cross the boundaries of the company. The outsourcing of production of low cost mobile phones was clearly a useful strategy in the early years of Sony Ericsson. With the strategic move towards more expensive, computer-like phones by the end of the decade, production was moving back to the company.

Reflection point: The careful managing of organizational boundaries in an open world is more and more becoming a crucial part of the top management agenda. How does this influence and change the managerial work in a company like Sony Ericsson?

There is a growing amount of research that describes how companies rely on external relations and partnerships to organize and carry out important tasks. This has been noted for a long time in the strategic management literature, and influential authors such as Ghoshal and Bartlett (1997), Nohria and Goshal (1997), and Pettigrew *et al.,* (2003) argued for a new focus on value-creation in interorganizational relations. Leadership is more and more affected in relationships with individuals and groups that may be within, or outside of the boundaries of the focal company. The leadership strategies to master this situation of boundary crossing are different compared to a situation with strong internal control, and managers need to find ways of constantly monitoring boundaries. It is also important to realize that the influence tactics used by managers in leading people outside the formal control of the organization need to be different. In collaborative settings, such as interorganizational projects, leadership is much more based on mutual understanding and shared visions and goals.

Post-materialist values and leadership

An important conclusion from the discussion above is that there is a direct link between organizational practices and leadership, where organizational structures, processes, and boundaries create the local conditions for managers and co-workers alike. But the relations between managers and co-workers are also influenced by broader, and indirect, patterns. In the new leadership paradigm that will be described below the concept of *values* is important. There are a number of aspects of this.

- In modern leadership, ethical considerations are more important and managers need to integrate ethical considerations, for instance in formulating and communicating visions.
- A second aspect is that aesthetic considerations grow in importance. This is evident in the strong emphasis on branding and the need for creating appealing images of the company, its products, and guiding values.
- A third aspect has to do with the importance of creating a sense of belonging among employees, customers, and other stakeholders. Strong values are a means of achieving a corporate identity or self-concept.
- In a more general way it can also be argued that managers and co-workers act upon values they hold and that these are often shaped and changed as part of larger societal changes.

In this section, we focus primarily on the fourth aspect in the list above—the values and value-systems that shape managers/co-workers both as individuals and as part of broader groups in society. An important starting point for a discussion on values that shape leadership is the observation that values change over time, and reflect the society in which you live.

'The people of different societies are characterized by enduring differences in basic attitudes, values and skills: in other words, they have different cultures. During the past few decades, economic, technological, and socio-political changes have been transforming the cultures of advanced industrial societies in profoundly important ways.'

(Inglehart, 1990: 3)

In the global study, *World Values Survey* (WVS), attitudes and values were studied in more than 80 countries, on five different occasions (1981, 1990, 1995, 2000, and 2005). In the large battery of questions, many different aspects of human life are covered, and a number of the areas are of interest to us in this chapter. The data from the survey are publicly available for analysis on their website and, in Table 6.1 below, we discuss some of the data. We will focus primarily on the questions that relate to how people value work and how they view democracy. The overall hypothesis in the WVS program is that there are strong mutual relations between belief systems on the one hand, and economical, political, and social conditions on the other hand (Inglehart, 1997). The emergence and growth of, the so-called, post-materialist or life-style values follows a curvilinear pattern, where societies with a high growth rate (usually measured in gross national product per capita) are characterized by strong life-style related values.

There is a clear pattern in the questions in the survey where countries with a high GNP consistently score high on life style related questions and low on questions expressing traditional, materialist values. To value friends highly is a good example of a life style oriented value and countries such as Sweden and the United States accordingly score high on this question. In a life style oriented society you would also expect work to be less important, and this is validated in the following question—how important is work in your life—where countries from northern Europe score low.

The emergence of life style oriented values clearly influence how people value work, how they are motivated, how they will view their relationship to managers, and also how they will view leadership. The research on leadership has started to approach and make use of this type of values study, and to understand the relationship between value systems (and changes in them) and leadership. Later in this chapter, we will present the outline of the new leadership paradigm *charismatic/transformational* leadership, and how it has started to describe how people, in many countries, are driven by the motivation to express themselves, to identify with valued role-models, and to enjoy life beyond a stable 9-5-type of job.

Leadership theory—contemporary approaches

In the preceding section, a number of trends that shape the conditions for leadership were introduced and discussed. In the following, three of the more important advances in leadership

Table 6.1 Data from world values survey

How important are friends in your life (% very important)?		How important is work in your life (% very important)?	
Lithuania	17	Tanzania	96
Pakistan	20	El Salvador	95
China	20	Switzerland	47
United States	64	Germany	45
Northern Ireland	65	Great Britain	42
Sweden	71	Denmark	40

How important is leisure time in your life (% very important)?		How important is religion in your life (% very important)?	
Sweden	55	Indonesia	98
Netherlands	53	Egypt	97
Great Britain	51	Jordan	96
Egypt	9	Denmark	8
Vietnam	7	Japan	7
Pakistan	5	China	3

Which aspects are important in work: Good pay (%)?		Which aspects are important in work: Security (%)?	
Morocco	98	Morocco	98
Jordan	98	Turkey	98
Nigeria	97	Bangladesh	97
Sweden	58	Belgium	47
Norway	58	France	46
Denmark	54	Netherlands	29

Which aspects are important in work: People to work with (%)?		Which aspects are important in work: Job respected (%)?	
Netherlands	89	Turkey	94
Sweden	84	Jordan	94
Iceland	83	Morocco	92
Russia	55	Sweden	29
Slovakia	51	Norway	23
Latvia	32	Denmark	11

Free access data from the world values survey (from the 1999–2001 survey) available for analysis at **www.world valuessurvey.org** thinking are presented. The overview starts with a brief presentation of traditional views on leadership. Before leadership was formalized as a theoretical field in itself, much emphasis was placed on the manager and his/her personality traits, and the top management function (including top business managers, political leaders, and militaries) was at the forefront. This, so called, **trait approach**, was followed by the **style approach to leadership**. In the middle of the 1940s, a very influential programme referred to as the *Ohio State Leadership Studies*, started at Ohio State University. This programme started out as a critique of the trait approach described above, and the research group wanted to study what managers were doing—their *behaviour*. Two strong factors emerged from the studies: *consideration* and *initiating of structure*. Consideration is similar to relationship orientation, and it describes a leadership style centred on building good relations with the subordinates, caring about people, and emphasizing the well-being of others. Initiating structure, on the other hand, describes a leadership style that focuses on carrying out tasks, achieving results, and emphasizing production. The Ohio studies have inspired a lot of research, and a number of similar dichotomies were studied in the 1950s and 1960s, such as task versus relations-orientation (Bass, 1967; Blake and Mouton, 1964), goal achievement versus group maintenance (Cartwright and Zander, 1960), and directive versus non-directive (Burke, 1966). The dichotomies of task versus relations-orientation, and goal achievement versus group maintenance, are all variations of the same basic idea—leadership is either focused on people (relations, people, group maintenance, consideration) or tasks (goal achievement, tasks, initiating structure, production).

The style approach evolved during the 1960s and a major step was the introduction of the idea of leadership style being *contingent* upon situational factors. Two of the more famous contingency theories were briefly described in definition boxes 1 and 2 above. The idea that different leadership styles match/should match different contextual conditions has been very popular and is still often used in leadership training, even though the scientific support for the theories is inconsistent. A variety of different contingency factors have been suggested, but it has proven difficult to study the links between leadership and situational factors. How the different contextual factors specifically influence leadership is a big and complex question, and research has failed to come up with consistent results. This does not, however, discredit the basic idea that leadership (needs to) differs in different situations and contexts.

The activity approach to leadership

The style approach is based on the view that leadership is exercised directly and aimed at managing human *behaviour*—simply put, to get people to do things. Even though that approach allegedly had a focus on the behaviour of leaders, actual leadership behaviour was seldom studied. Beginning with the Swedish researcher Sune Carlson (1951), a tradition emerged based on observational studies of actual managerial behaviour. Carlson asked a selection of CEOs in Swedish companies to keep a journal of their daily activities (this journal was in most cases maintained by a secretary or an assistant). This study inspired a series of studies in the 1970s and onwards (Kotter, 1978; Mintzberg, 1973), and it is nowadays referred to as the *activity school*.

John Kotter, in an influential study published 1978, introduced a more cognitive view of the studies of leadership activities. He studied the work of 15 general managers in

American organizations (in both the private and public sector). The basic question for Kotter was to identify the specific managerial behaviours that contributed to effective leadership. What are the factors that enable some managers to get much more out of the co-workers, and to inspire them to carry out more and better work? He identified two factors that seemed to explain the difference between more and less successful managers. The first factor had to do with the *network* the single manager was building. The successful managers had much more extensive networks of people that they befriended and could draw upon when they needed something done. The second factor was the *strategic agenda* the more successful managers developed and used to guide their work as managers. This agenda could be viewed as a mental map that provided the manager with a clear image of what needed to be done.

The charismatic/transformational approach to leadership

The different approaches to leadership that were proposed during the 1960s and 1970s were, in most cases, firmly rooted in the style approach presented above. The theories, to varying degrees, shared a number of features that were becoming more and more criticized, both from practitioners and academics. The most important implicit assumptions were:

- There is a unidirectional relation between manager and co-workers, with the focus on getting the co-worker to do things. The responsibility to achieve this is vested in the manager. Obedience is thus an important goal in exercising leadership.

- There is a strong focus on external motivators such as financial incentives, promotion, attention, and the like (firmly rooted in the motivation theories presented in Chapter 5) and the relation between manager and co-worker being shaped by the manager, rather than a more mutual relationship.

In the 1980s, a number of influential writers started to question the assumptions above, and the basis of a new leadership paradigm was gradually emerging. One of the earliest attempts to formulate a new credo for leadership was the book, *Leaders*, by Warren Bennis and Burt Nanus (1985). Bennis and Nanus launched the idea that a primary role of leadership is to create *meaning* for the co-workers. The quotation below is typical of their arguments.

'Leaders have failed to instil vision, meaning and trust in their followers.'
(Bennis and Nanus, 1997: 31)

A primary task of managers, according to Bennis and Nanus, is to both create and communicate a shared vision. The vision is a tool used very effectively by managers, it is communicated and the purpose is to create a shared way of looking at the company and its future direction. They point at a new set of tools and techniques that managers needed to master to be successful. In the minicase below the role of a compelling vision is described.

'Leaders articulate and define what has previously remained implicit or unsaid; then they invent images, metaphors, and models that provide focus for new attention.'
(Bennis and Nanus, 1997: 37).

Lou Gerstner and the promise of the new economy

One of the key features of the charismatic/transformational theory is the role of a vision to provide a direction for the employees. It seems like an attractive vision has important motivational effects on the employees, and can contribute to creating a sense of purpose for the employees. Following is a quotation from Lou Gerstner, former CEO and chairman of IBM. This was in the heyday of the so-called New Economy in the late 1990s, and it is very interesting to compare the prophetic tone in Gerstner's speech with the networked world as it looks today. What seemed like a noble dream in 1999 is now common practice in most industries and something most consumers view as the basic infrastructure of society. Speeches like this inspired employees, in companies like IBM, to work relentlessly to make the new economy happen, and figure-heads like Gerstner were highly instrumental in making the IT-revolution pick up speed in the late 1990s.

'We had a pretty good crystal ball when we first saw this world of e-business. Today, when we look into that crystal ball again, we see some very exciting extensions of the e-business world. We see that computing is going to touch every aspect of our lives. Computing will be everywhere—pervasive—because the basic elements of technology—chips and storage devices and networking—are getting ever smaller, more powerful and less expensive.'

(Lou Gerstner, then Chairman and CEO, IBM. Annual Meeting of Stockholders, 27 April 1999)

The relation between manager and co-workers is described as a more democratic relationship, thus challenging the first assumption above. The focus on obedience gives way to a focus on engagement and acceptance for the vision. The goal of getting people to do things, or to exceed expectations as Bennis and Nanus would phrase it, is a result of the strong engagement of the co-workers. Strong visions also imply a focus on creating shared values with which people, internally and externally, could identify. A good example of the role of strong values is given in the minicase below.

Anita Roddick and Body Shop

Leading by values and strong assumptions are keywords in modern leadership philosophy, and the ability to create a following by relating to strong values and ideals is crucial here. It appears that people are attracted to organizations with which they share values, and this can be used to nurture a culture in the organization and to recruit employees with similar values. This is, however, easier said than done, and it takes a lot of sincerity and hard work for a top manager to create and communicate a set of values that are perceived as honest and inspiring. There are a number of good examples of this. One very good example of a top manager who embodied the ideas of values based leadership was Anita Roddick (1942–2007), the founder of Body Shop. In many ways Roddick put strong values at the forefront of her business and she relentlessly struggled for good causes. She always promoted the products of Body Shop in a context of justice, green business, and truth telling. She took fight with big companies, such as Coca-Cola, to fight against injustice and exploitation, and the brand name of Body Shop is now synonymous with the fight for animal rights and environmental friendly products. These values are also strongly held among the employees and the franchise owners running their own Body Shop stores.

The story of Anita Roddick and Body Shop is well described in the literature and the interested reader is referred to Anita's own book, *Business as Unusual*.

Beginning in the late 1970s, a number of authors, from different perspectives, were trying to launch a new paradigm for leadership that became known as the *charismatic/ transformational perspective*. The concept of charisma in a leadership context was derived from the studies of Max Weber (1978) and his notion of charisma as a source of authority. Weber differentiated between three forms of authority—legal, traditional, and charismatic. Charismatic leadership, according to Weber, grew out of a situation of crisis where the charismatic manager lifted the organization out of the crisis. Weber also noticed that this is a temporary state and that charisma tended to be *routinized*. Although Weber was criticized by many authors in the 1980s, his influential work has made the concept of charisma known and widespread. Weber is a continuing source of inspiration and in his work he points towards a number of important themes in the charismatic/transformational view, and not least in his persistent claim that it is the follower who 'lifts' the leader to his/her state of charisma.

'If those to whom he feels sent do not recognize him, his claim collapses; if they recognize it, he is their master as long as he 'proves' himself.'
(Weber, 1978: 1111)

The concept of transformational leadership was coined by James Burns (1978) in his book *Leadership*. Burns noticed that traditional theories on leadership started from a simplified view on human motivation and interaction, what he described as transactional leadership. Transactional leadership is based on the idea that leadership is an *exchange* relation, where the manager uses different incentives in exchange for the effort of the co-worker. The type of motivation process described here is called *extrinsic* since it makes use of an external motivator (money, working conditions, praise, and similar tools) that is introduced to arouse the energy of the individual.

'Such leadership occurs when one person takes the initiative in making contact with others for the purpose of an exchange of valued things.'
(Burns, 1978: 19)

In contrast, Burns saw the need for another form of leadership that he called *transforming* leadership. Transforming leadership is described as a mutual effort of manager and co-worker to go beyond the realm of self-interest, to work for a common cause or value. This is done by explicitly addressing the co-workers' (or 'followers' as Burns calls them) needs, wants, and other motivations. Transforming leadership is a direct response to the second assumption in earlier theories that we presented above, and he points at the need for also focusing on *intrinsic* motivation. The idea that the inner motives of people are important drivers for human effort has been acknowledged by a lot of current research in the leadership field. An interesting and important question in this respect is whether co-workers' inner motivation can be altered or if it must be viewed as something given? Shamir, House, and Arthur (1993) have launched the idea of individuals' *self-concept*, and they describe how successful charismatic managers can activate the self-concept of individuals by different tactics. They argued that since individuals strive for consistency between their self-concept and behaviour, managers can try to influence the self-concept, and thus indirectly the behaviour.

> 'More specifically, we have argued that such leaders increase the intrinsic value of efforts and goals by linking them to valued aspects of the follower's self-concept, thus harnessing the motivational forces of self-expression, self-consistency, self-esteem and self-worth.'
>
> (Shamir, House, and Arthur, 1993: 584)

Since the groundbreaking work of Burns (1978) and others in the late 1970s and early 1980s, the charismatic/transformational paradigm has gained widespread attention, and today it totally dominates the research field. Many attempts have been made to summarize the basics tenets of this rapidly growing paradigm, and in the following we try to capture some of the more important features. We are, in particular, interested in the specific leadership behaviours that create a relation between manager and co-workers that is in line with Burns' vision presented above. Numerous attempts have been made to pinpoint the successful types of leadership behaviour, and the research on charismatic/transformational leadership can point at a few clear patterns. Nadler and Tushman (1990) present three components of charismatic leadership:

- *Envisioning:* Describes the need for managers to be active in formulating an appealing vision for the future that enables co-workers to identify with the manager and the company. This component points at the need for strong communicative skills in managers and the growing realization that leadership is a democratic rather than autocratic relation.
- *Energizing:* Covers the important aspect of motivation—how to engage individuals to realize the vision in a way that goes beyond the simplistic motivation theories based on the contribution/inducement model of Chester Barnard described in Chapter 5. Nadler and Tushman point at the need for managers to create meaning and to engage the employees in the continuous work of understanding and developing the vision.
- *Enabling:* Indicates that charismatic/transformational leadership also relies on managers supporting employees and contributing with the resources to carry out tasks. Enabling also includes emotional support by creating dialogue—listening to and understanding the worries and questions of employees.

Conger, in an attempt to summarize the research on charismatic/transformational leadership described the following three principal leadership processes where leaders may:

(1) Heighten followers' awareness about the importance and value of designated goals and the means to achieve them,

(2) Induce followers to transcend their self-interests for the good of the collective and its goals,

(3) Stimulate and meet their followers' higher order needs through the leadership process and the mission.

(Conger, 1999: 151)

The perhaps most well known model of charismatic/transformational leadership is the *Full Range of Leadership Model*, which is based on the Multifactor Leadership Questionnaire (MLQ). This model was developed by Bass and Avolio (1994) as an attempt to create a bridge between transactional leadership and transformational leadership. The model measures four transformational behaviours of managers.

- Idealized influence—behaviour that arouses strong follower emotions and identification with the leader.

- Individualized consideration—includes providing support, encouragement, and coaching to followers.

- Intellectual stimulation—behaviour that increases follower awareness of problems and influences followers to view problems from a new perspective.

- Inspirational motivation—communicating an appealing vision, using symbols to focus subordinate effort, and modelling appropriate behaviours.

The MLQ instrument is well tested and it is frequently used in leadership training. Even though the model can be criticized for putting a lot of focus on the leader, rather than the relation between leader and followers, it nevertheless captures important elements of the charismatic/transformational paradigm. It points at the important role of communicating a vision for the future (inspirational motivation), and also emphasizes identification with the company, stimulation, and consideration as strong motivators. The mini case below shows how a well-known CEO can exhibit many of the behaviours in the Full Range of Leadership Model.

Steve Jobs at Apple

MINICASE

The ability to communicate an appealing vision and to arouse commitment and motivation among followers is an important part of charismatic leadership. There is a growing realization that the communicative skills of managers are crucial to the success of the leadership. Few, if any, top managers understand and master this better than Steve Jobs, founder, and since 1997, also CEO of Apple Inc. In his public appearances Steve Jobs not only symbolizes, he in fact embodies the core of the Apple culture—innovative technical solutions, attractive design, and devotion to the company and the brand. Jobs and Apple have, since Jobs' return to Apple in 1997, succeeded in launching a series of innovative products/services (such as the iTunes store, iPod, iPhone, App store, and most recently the iPad), and creating a rapidly growing and at the same time very loyal customer base. Job's key note speeches, where he often launches new products, are legendary and when he, rhetorically, asks 'what else' everyone knows a new, exciting product is about to be launched. The appearances are carefully staged and well performed with a delicate balance between stage presence by Jobs and the use of multimedia.

The story of Apple has been told in numerous books and articles. In Alan Deutschman's book, *The second coming of Steve Jobs*, his return to the company in 1997 is analysed in depth. Gallo's book, *The presentation secrets of Steve Jobs* analyzes some of the tricks of his presentation skills.

Contextual factors that contribute to charismatic/transformational relations

The charismatic/transformational leadership research emphasizes the context of leadership, and different contextual factors have been suggested that, potentially, contribute to effective leadership. Max Weber pointed at the crucial role of a crisis for the emergence and acceptance of charisma. Weber (1978) argued that people facing a situation of crisis, what he referred to as moments of distress, were drawn to a charismatic person that could give them a sense of direction in meeting the crisis. When the crisis was successfully met the charisma tended to be routinized.

More recent research has confirmed some of Webers' ideas. Beyer (1999), for instance, argues for a strong link between a crisis and an appealing vision:

'Without a crisis, the radical vision is unlikely to be attractive to followers. Without a radical vision, a person of exceptional qualities may be an inspirational leader who attracts people, but is unlikely to achieve the kinds of dramatic social change that charisma can produce.'

A number of additional contextual factors have been suggested in reasearch. Shamir and Howell (1999) show that charismatic leadership emerges in dynamic situations that demand the introduction of new strategies, products, and technologies. This is well in line with the important role a clear vision would have as guidance for organizational work. Pillai (1995) also suggested that charismatic/transformational leadership is associated with more flexible organizational structures. A high degree of operational and strategic decentralization, delayering and frequent use of projects, is thus expected to drive the need for more charismatic/transformational leadership. A final factor suggested in the literature is the distance between the manager and her/his co-workers. Yagil (1998) showed in a study that close relations to the co-workers shape their attribution of charisma to the manager in a positive way. The role of a crisis to drive the charismatic/transformational leadership is described in the link box below.

LINK BOX

The role of a crisis in Ericsson

The charismatic/transformational leadership theory has gained a lot of attention the last 30 years and it is clear that it has become the common view on leadership today. As discussed above, there are different ideas on what contributes to charismatic/transformational relations, and one of the most frequently mentioned factors, is crisis. As Max Weber suggested, in situations of crisis the followers are more prone to accept a charismatic manager who can give them a sense of direction. In more modern terms, it makes sense to assume that a compelling vision, that points a way out of a crisis, can create a feeling of relief, and thus reduce the uncertainty and anxiety inherent in a crisis situation. It is clear from the Ericsson case, presented in the beginning of the chapter, that the company was facing a severe crisis in the first few years of the new millennium. By the end of 2002, the company was on the verge of bankruptcy. When the new CEO entered the company in 2003, he was able to tap in on the feeling of crisis and to use this in presenting a 'fresh start' for the company. The role of the crisis to 'support' the entrance of the new CEO should, however, not be exaggerated. When he entered the company much effort had been put in to manage the crisis by his predecessor, and the immediate financial crisis had been resolved. Mr Svanberg also exhibited a number of the behaviours associated with charismatic and transformational leadership, for instance, by communicating an appealing vision and by increasing the followers' awareness of problems.

Reflection point: This link box has discussed the role of a crisis in charismatic leadership. What roles do you think a crisis can have in leadership?

Gender, intersectionality, and leadership

In the previous section, contemporary theories of leadership have been presented. The presentation can rightfully be accused of neglecting the important role of gender in understanding leadership. In this section we introduce the reader to an important stream of research that tries to understand how gender interacts with leadership. Here, we describe and discuss the following topics:

- Women and leadership in the 1970s,
- The criticism against Women in Management (WIM), a focus popular in the 1980s,
- Gender and leadership in the 1990s and the early twenty-first century,
- Recent perspectives on gender and leadership: intersectionality,

Women and leadership in the 1970s

In the 1970s, research studies reported on women's positions in work life and their career opportunities (Epstein, 1970). Acker and Van Houten (1974) showed that earlier organizational research on female and male work life was gender-blind; these researchers concluded that the organization's structures and processes are indeed influenced by gender. In 1977, Rosabeth Moss Kanter published her landmark study, *Men and Women of the Corporation*, where she researched the career possibilities for men and women in organizations.

Kanter worked for five years as an ethnography-inspired researcher and consultant in a company, labelled Indsco, in the study. The company employed 50,000 people, of whom sixteen per cent (16%) were women and nine per cent (9%) were racial or ethnic minorities. This distribution of employees was typical of American companies at the time. In reporting the results of the research, Kanter described people's roles and positions in organizations, focusing in part on why women and men seemed to act differently, and on the difficulties involved in making any changes to that perception.

The fundamental premise in this study is that work makes the person. Kanter therefore resisted the often-promoted idea claiming that, because women and men are different, women cannot handle certain work assignments, for example, those associated with management positions. In support of her argument, Kanter stated that if women really were different, then they would humanize society when they become company and organization leaders. However, women in management positions were found to act no differently from men. The problem was rather, that as long as entities are organized in the same way, it does not matter if women assume men's leadership roles because, in such an exchange, one dominant group has simply been substituted for another. A second, widespread assumption is that the differences between women and men derive from their biological and social differences. Kanter disagreed with this assumption as well. She found that the organizations and the way they worked, explained why women do not have the same career possibilities as men. To equalize such possibilities, she argued, the work organization itself must be changed.

Kanter described three interrelated structures in organizations that explain why only certain men reach the highest management levels:

The opportunity structure: According to Kanter, a person's work performance depended on the opportunities she/he had in a given position. If people found themselves in positions with good opportunities for promotion, they would develop policies and attitudes toward work that were conducive to advancement. They would set high career goals and would actively work toward achieving them. On the other hand, if their positions offered little potential for advancement, they would lose interest and may even give up hope of advancement. Women—*and men*—who were unmotivated at work had realized that there were few career opportunities in their current positions. Women, in such situations, seemed to devote more effort to personal relationships, while men seemed to commit themselves more to free time activities outside work. In effect, the limited expectations about career advancement had become self-fulfilling prophecies. As there were few women with positions within the organizational centre, the majority of the women at Indsco were not given opportunities to commit to work. The role of opportunity structures is illustrated in the link box below.

LINK BOX

Gender issues at Ericsson

There is a lot of evidence that women are under-represented in managerial positions, and the process to change this is slow. One of the explanations that has been suggested is that women are presented with fewer opportunities than men to enter senior positions in companies, what Kanter refers to as opportunity structures. The lack of opportunities becomes easily a self-fulfilling prophecy—with little opportunities they become less willing and motivated to work for advancement in the company. In the case of Ericsson it is clear that women are under-represented in the management team, with only one woman out of twelve members. In the board of directors six out of sixteen members are female. Ericsson is a high-tech company with a strong engineering culture, and the workforce is dominated by men. Out of the 78,740 employees (Dec 2008) only twenty-two per cent (22%) were female. The representation on the board shows that it is certainly possible to find qualified women for a professional board. The opportunity structure, alone, could however not explain the lack of women in the management team. Other factors that are frequently discussed is lack of role models, lack of support and mentoring, resistance to let women in, and most probably, all these factors contribute to the lack of women in the top management team in Ericsson.

Reflection point: Interesting and intriguing questions arise around the consequences of an uneven gender balance in an organization, and whether a better balance can be beneficial for the organization. What are the negative consequences of one group (in this case, women) being under represented in important decision-making bodies? What can be done to change such a situation?

The power structure: Power, according to Kanter, is the possibility to do things, to mobilize resources and to acquire and use whatever means are necessary to reach goals. New managers, seen from this perspective, are often powerless. They often seem authoritarian, overbearing and critical, while obsessing on details and slaving under the bureaucratic system. This is true for both women and men in new leadership positions who still haven't seized the opportunity to use their power in a different way. Because most people would rather work for winners than for losers, this preference has consequences for those with power (the winners). A woman in a powerful position will no longer be seen as a woman, but instead, as a winner with power, and the people around her will want to work with her, regardless of the fact that she is a woman.

The frequency structure: The composition of groups is also an important factor in explaining why women and men succeed in organizations. According to Kanter, Indsco's male dominance at the various managerial levels was the result of the rarity or even lack of qualified women for managerial positions, rather than because of their intrinsic female characteristics. Kanter used the expression '*token*' to describe the representative of a group of people (e.g., 'a typical woman') where the person is viewed as a symbol rather than as an individual person. The consequence of such tokenism in work life is that people are identified and categorized as members of a group, rather than for the work of the positions they hold. When a category of people represents something less than fifteen per cent (15%) of the entire group, according to Kanter, the token situation is likely to arise. As women were rare at Indsco, they became token with limited opportunities to continue their career. The major traits of tokenism are summarized in the definitional box below.

DEFINITION BOX

Three important observations related to tokenism

Visibility: A token representative stands out and therefore is noticed. Normally, visibility is good for one's career, but when tokenism is involved, it means that a person is visible as a stereotype rather than as an individual.

Contrast: When a token representative comes into a group, other group members try to preserve their commonality by excluding this token person. Thus the group tries to appear more similar than they really are.

Assimilation: A token representative's individual abilities are not recognized: instead, individual abilities are stereotyped and generalized. In the token role, the individual loses her or his own identity.

Patterns and actions which appear to be a typically feminine characteristic or action are rather a reflection or consequence of the organization's structures and processes, Kanter concluded. Of course, discrimination against women can result from individual biases, but such discrimination may also be part of the organizational establishment.

Researchers after Kanter found similar results among other occupations, for example, police patrols, academics, doctors, and the military (Yoder, 1991). Kanter has, however, been criticized because her theory on tokenism disregarded gender discrimination, for example, in the form of sexual harassment and pay inequalities. It has also been suggested that she is too optimistic about the resolution of the problems she identified (Yoder, 1991; 1994). Nor does she indicate how gender and the organization structure interact (Acker, 1990). There have also been studies that applied her theories to men in minority situations where it was shown, despite their token status, that these subjects quickly took advantage of their positions and advanced in their careers (Lindgren, 1985; Acker, 1990).

Women-in-Management (WIM)

In the 1980s, some researchers adopted the feminist viewpoint in which it was assumed that women have certain essential and universal characteristics. Women's experiences in bearing and raising children as well as their hormonal activities were assumed to have implications for women in organizations. In the framework for Women-in-Management (WIM) literature, the assumption is that women, who are claimed to have a different management style than men, perform differently as managers. In this perspective, the management style of women is characterized as democratic, inclusive, and cooperative while men's management style is characterized as competitive, controlling, and insensitive, with an emphasis on analysis and hierarchical thinking (Colwill, 1995). This point of view is often advocated in the popular scientific literature that argues that women managers complement men managers. The criticism of this idea, however, is that while women are seeking leadership positions, their leadership characteristics may be the very reason they may not become executives (Alvesson and Billing, 1997).

Soon studies appeared that showed other difficulties with this point of view. For example, one study, which tried to explain the differences between women and men leaders, concluded that no differences could be identified (Marshall, 1984). Later studies similarly showed no differences between women and men as entrepreneurs (Ahl, 2004). Instead, more nuanced comparative studies of women and men in executive positions showed that both groups have similar expectations, values, personalities, abilities, and action patterns (Alvesson and Billing, 1997).

Recent ideas on gender and leadership

In the beginning of the 1990s, researchers began to emphasize that ideas surrounding gender differences were socially constructed, a conclusion that had implications for research on leadership and gender. This research argued that ideas about women and leadership are socially, historically, and culturally constructed rather than developed from innate female characteristics. This understanding of gender as a social construction permeates, for example,

Table 6.2 Feminine expressions and their interpretations

Implicitly feminine expressions	Interpretation
Soft	Not tough
Connected to	Not independent
Helping others	Not achieving individually
Surrendering	Not heroic

leadership theory (Calás and Smircich, 1991) where in various ways it was assumed that a 'leader' is implicitly understood to mean a 'man'. The language used by management authors supports this conclusion, such that, men in executive positions will not, or cannot, use certain expressions that are conceived of as feminine. Fondas (1997) gave several examples of such expressions that are *interpreted* as implicitly feminine and subordinate in the context of leadership:

In this area, studies of masculinity and leadership have had widespread impact. It has been shown that the society's stereotypical image of masculinity is that of white, heterosexual, middle-aged, upper-class men. According to Connell (1995), masculinity is also understood as hegemonic, which causes differences in masculinity to be ignored. Kerfoot and Knights (1996) claimed that masculinity in organizing reflects and reproduces instrumental rationality, and thus becomes oppressive for both men and women. The benefit of raising the issue of masculinity in organizing and leadership is that it becomes clear that both men and women have bodies (Gherardi, 2003). By extension, this benefit allows us to view the prioritizing of 'the manly body' in leadership positions in a new light.

Recent perspectives on gender and diversity: intersectionality

In recent years, the issue of intersectionality has become more popular among researchers (Crenshaw, 1989; Crenshaw 1994; Eriksson-Zetterquist and Styhre, 2007; Styhre and Eriksson-Zetterquist, 2008). An 'intersection' is the crossroads where roads meet and intersect. Thus, in social science research, intersectionality refers to the *simultaneous* intersection of ethnicity, gender, social class, sexuality, religion, age, and similar categories. Therefore, intersectionality deals with these different categories that, together, influence one another. One research application of the intersectionality viewpoint, for example, is the study of why certain men become executives; the intersectionality perspective looks at men as members of a certain ethnicity, social class, gender, and age rather than simply as managers who are male.

It is argued, in the intersectionality literature, that a person's superior or subordinate position in an organization depends on factors like ethnicity, skin colour, social class, culture, nationality, age, sexuality, physical function, normality, and reproductive powers (Hutchinson and Mann, 2004). An individual's opportunities in an organization depend on the various categories to which she or he belongs. These categorizations are thoroughly described in the minicase below.

MINICASE

The lemon-yellow dress

An example of how people in organizations handle this kind of identity categorization comes from a study of an Irish woman's identity when establishing a career in the British Labour Party. In the study, Christina Hughes (2004) showed how the woman acted when confronted with various career impediments facing her. Wishing to pursue a career at the organization, she presented herself in a certain acceptable way that involved her clothing, her speech, her dialect, and her body language. For example, to advance her career, she carefully applied her make-up: if she wore too much make-up, she would reveal her class background, but if she wore too little make-up, she risked being labelled a feminist or a lesbian. By carefully selecting her clothes as well, she signalled to others which categories she wanted to be associated with.

The style of clothing worn in a work place, it appears, can either attract or discourage people as they plan career paths. In one instance, the Irish woman did not accept a new position because it was offered by a woman whose clothes (a girlish, lemon-yellow dress), hairstyle (out-of-date), and clothes sense (too womanly) seemed old-fashioned and middle class. If the Irish woman had taken this position, against her inclination, she would have been forced to change, not only her appearance, but also her values and identity. Ultimately, clothes and general personal style can signal superior ambitions—to the extent superiority creates opportunities for subordinates outside and above a department (See Kanter earlier in this chapter). Additionally, a subordinate's adaptation—for example, in the choice of work clothes—signals to what extent she or he consents to authority.

By highlighting how different personal categories influence each other, it becomes clear that a person's situation in an organization cannot be understood solely in the context of her or his gender or her or his ethnicity. While gender perspectives and diversity perspectives (see Chapter 5) emphasize a person's inclusion in a particular category, new research shows, that in the area of intersectionality, the different categories are reasonably understood as related to one another.

Leadership in the middle

An important group of managers in companies are middle managers in different positions. They are subject to many different types of demands and expectations. They are expected to:

- Carry out decisions taken by senior managers,
- Give support to, and balance the needs of their co-workers,
- Have contacts with other departments and units in the company, as well as with external partners.

This is often done in a situation of downsizing and strong pressure to make operations more effective.

As argued in the beginning of the chapter, middle managers are important facilitators and 'doers' of change initiatives. They often find themselves in the midst of important, strategic processes in organizations, with expectations from both above and below to be active and support the different stakeholders. The notion of the middle manager as a person working under stable conditions—the archetypical bureaucrat—is not an accurate description of modern middle management.

The research on middle managers and middle management is vast and covers a number of important areas. A growing tradition of research is to try to understand the roles of middle managers in modern corporations, and how they cope with different organizational trends and situations, such as delayering, information technology, and strategic and organizational change.

Delayering. A dominant theme in the literature on middle managers in the 1980s was the effects of downsizing. Early research suggested that there were many negative effects of downsizing on the motivation and morale of middle managers. This was referred to as the *survivor syndrome*, the tendency of middle managers, and others, to exhibit a number of negative behaviours and attitudes which cancel out the assumed positive benefits of downsizing (Thomas and Dunkerley, 1999). Many of the problems of survivor syndrome come from the breaking of the traditional psychological contract where employees were promised job security and hierarchical advancement in return for their loyalty and commitment to organizational goals. When a middle manager sees his/her colleagues being fired, he/she might believe that he/she is 'on the waiting list' and could be the next one to be fired. This often affects them hard, psychologically, and many of the survivors display a state of emotions similar to those being made redundant.

Despite the generally pessimistic tone of much of the literature, there are also articles which suggest that many middle managers now feel 'empowered', with a greater strategic role which is more entrepreneurial, challenging, and fulfilling. The removal of layers has enabled these managers to have more freedom to make decisions and a more strategic role in the organization. The job was therefore enriched, rather than being made redundant. The increased empowerment, deliberate or not, is usually driven by the belief that no one knows a job better than the person who does it, and therefore, by allowing those who are most knowledgeable to make decisions on the day-to-day issues surrounding their jobs, the organization becomes more efficient (Denham *et al.*, 1997). A more drastic step than downsizing is the closedown of a factory, and in a series of articles Hansson and Wigblad (2006a; 2006b) showed that the threat of a closedown can give rise to increased productivity rather than a decrease, as hypothesized in the literature on the survivor syndrome.

Information technology. The common stereotype suggests that the need for middle managers decreases with the increased use of information technology. IT is believed to increase the capacity of higher managers to control employees without the direct help of middle managers, which should lead to a downsizing effect that severely impacts the middle management levels. Pinsonneault and Kraemer (1993) reviewed the previous literature and found a very mixed picture. Some studies showed empirical evidence for, and argued that, the number of middle managers will be reduced. Their prediction was that middle managers have often provided an informational link between top management and operations managers, a function which structured decision-making and IT would now perform. IT would permit top managers to bypass middle managers in both upward and downward communication and information would now be able to flow directly to executive management rather than through middle management.

Other empirical findings do not agree with this and subscribe to the totally opposite position. They argue that IT increases the number of middle managers and decentralizes decision authority. Middle managers, according to this view, are more than just information transmitters. They also perform interpersonal and decisional roles. Furthermore IT, overwhelms organizations with information that needs further processing by middle managers to become endowed with relevance and purpose. IT decreases the need for a small portion of managerial activity, the communication portion, rather than the need for their jobs as a whole. The richness of information allows middle managers to uncover details that were not previously known but are relevant for management decisions, and analyse more alternatives in greater depth than before. Thus, rather than decreasing the roles of middle managers IT enlarges and enriches their jobs.

A study indicating that other factors, rather than just the IT itself, affects the number of middle managers was done by Pinsonneault and Kraemer (1997). They set up 4 hypotheses, indicating what happens as IT penetration increases within an organization:

- In extensively centralized organizations, the higher the extent of IT penetration, the substantially lower the number of middle managers. This hypothesis was supported in their empirical study.

- In extensively decentralized organizations, the higher the extent of IT penetration, the substantially higher the number of middle managers. This hypothesis was supported in their empirical study.

- In partially centralized organizations, the higher the extent of IT penetration, the slightly lower the number of middle managers. This hypothesis was supported in their empirical study.

- In partially decentralized organizations, the higher the extent of IT penetration, the slightly higher the number of middle managers. This hypothesis was not supported in their empirical study.

Their study showed clearly a mixed picture when it comes to the effects of IT on middle managers.

Strategic and organizational change. Little research has examined the role middle managers play during change implementation, and what helps or hinders them in fulfilling this role. Middle managers are traditionally seen as linking pins between the strategic apex and the operating core, supplying information upwards and consuming strategic decisions passed down, therefore they play an important role in the change process (Thompson, 1967). They are part of the implementation chain and act as change implementers but can be both the target and agents of change. Balogun (2003) has explored the process of change implementation through the eyes of middle managers. A major task performed by middle managers was that of convincing their staff that there had been a change and that the change was required. Another task was keeping the business going alongside all the changes taking place.

The phrase 'business as usual' was used to explain to staff that they had to keep up their work as the organization changed. According to Balogun, with the change process happening very quickly, middle managers found it difficult to continue doing business as usual, forward plan, and also spend time with members of staff explaining what was expected of them as a result of the changes in the organization.

Balogun's findings showed that middle managers in change processes have a complex and demanding task that consists of four roles:

• They are simultaneously expected to undertake personal change,

• Help their staff through change,

• Implement changes in their part of the business,

• Keep the business running.

It is important to keep in mind that although middle managers execute what top management decide, the actual change outcome depends on how middle managers interpret what is required and what they can personally accomplish. Some of the consequences of radical change on middle managers are discussed in the link box below.

LINK BOX

Middle managers and downsizing in Ericsson

As discussed above, the role of middle managers in change processes is the subject of much debate among researchers, and it is more and more being suggested that they, in fact, play crucial roles in change processes. Recent research cast doubt on the view that middle managers are the ones the company should get rid of in downsizing, and it certainly casts doubt on the view that middle managers do not do a useful job in organizations. When Ericsson was facing their deep crisis in the beginning of 2000, they were met with a difficult dilemma related to the need for cost savings. As described in the beginning of the chapter severe measures were taken to lower the number of employees, and many middle managers had to leave the company. There is, however, little evidence that middle managers in Ericsson suffered harder from the downsizing activities than other personnel categories. It seems rather that cost cuts were evenly spread throughout the organization, and great care was also taken to minimize the harmful effects of downsizing. It was nevertheless clear that the remaining members of the staff were left with the challenging task of realizing an ambitious vision with less than half the workforce remaining in the company. This also made it clear that the remaining middle managers were key actors in the work of creating a 'new Ericsson'. It should also be clarified that the company started to grow again after the year of crisis and by the end of 2009, the company had grown to more than 82,000 employees.

Reflection point: In the process of downsizing, great care has to be taken in reducing the harmful consequences of getting rid of key personnel. How can an organization make sure that the negative consequences of downsizing do not outnumber the positive effects of cost savings?

Summary and conclusions

The theories of leadership have gone through a shift during the last decades, from the former autocratic and leader-centred view on leadership to the charismatic/transformational view, focusing the democratic and vision-based relation between manager and co-workers. A central theme in this chapter is that leadership is contextual, that is, it takes place in a spatial and temporal context, which it at the same time, co-constructs. The contemporary context of leadership is affected by the practical challenges from decentralization, projects and other forms of organizing, information technology, and the situation with fuzzy boundaries. In this chapter, this was exemplified by the change in leadership style at Ericsson. The cost-cutting, engineering-driven leader oriented towards the internal culture, was replaced with a charismatic and change-oriented leadership style represented by a new person who was relaxed in communicating with the media. These changes in context highlight changes both in leadership as figure-heads and decision-makers and the leaders in middle and temporary functions. The new role of leadership can be described as the task to create meaning for the co-workers and shared meaning through the organization. As organizations at the same time take part in constructing their context, the task to create meaning is not limited to the organizational boundaries, but as shown in the introductory case, extends nowadays to the media. Still, when applying a gender perspective, the term leader is often implicitly understood to mean a 'man', a situation which reveals the hegemonic masculinity within leadership theories and practices.

 ## Study questions

1. What are the major differences between the transactional perspective on leadership and the charismatic/transformational?
2. Which are the major assumptions in the charismatic/transformational leadership paradigm?
3. The new charismatic/transformational paradigm is driven by a number of changes in how companies are organized and in deeply held values. What are the major changes that drive the new paradigm?
4. What are the challenges in leading a diverse workforce, and how does gender pattern influence the leadership?
5. The challenges of middle managers differ in many ways from those of the top management. What are the major challenges middle managers face, and how does current research describe them?

 ## Literature recommendations and further readings

The literature on leadership is vast and rapidly growing, and it is way beyond the scope of this chapter to go into depth on it. There are, however, a number of excellent summaries of the field. For the reader who has a strong interest in the research on leadership, an in depth overview is given in *Bass and Stogdill's Handbook of leadership*. The charismatic/ transformational paradigm is presented in a number of introductory books. In the book *Transformational leadership*, Bass summarizes the research on transformational leadership, and his book gives a good introduction to the early research on transformational leadership. In a similar way, Conger and Kanungo summarize the research on charismatic leadership in the book *Charismatic leadership in organizations*.

Take your learning further

online resource centre

http://www.oxfordtextbooks.co.uk/orc/erikssonzetterquist/

Visit the Online Resource Centre which accompanies this book to enrich your understanding of this chapter.

Students: explore web links and further reading suggestions. Keep up to date with the latest developments via 'What happened next' updates to appropriate cases from within the book.

Lecturers: you will find seminar exercises and teaching notes, for use in class or assessment.

CHAPTER 7
Coping with external influences in organizations

Managing the portfolio of innovations in the pharmaceutical industry

In 2008, the British-Swedish AstraZeneca decided that the company would outsource the majority of the ongoing gastrointestinal drug projects to partnering organizations. Gastrointestinal medicine had been a flagship domain for the company since the 1980s when the Swedish company AstraHässle registered the ulcer medicine Losec, the best selling drug in the world for a period of time. However, the pharmaceutical industry underwent substantial changes in the 1990s and in the first decade of the new millennium. First, new regulatory demands were introduced by authorities in order to ensure that new registered drugs did not have any adverse effects, i.e., effects that could lead to injuries or death of patients. The new regulatory demands, which led to increased demands for documentation and more extensive clinical testing, were well received in the industry. Industry representatives and AstraZeneca workers thought the regulatory demands were reasonable, but also thought that it would limit the number of drugs that could be developed. Second, the scientific advancement of a number of new techniques, technologies, and procedures had fundamentally altered the drug development practice. The robotization of part of the laboratory work, the use of *in silico* testing (computer-based simulations) and the emergence of genomics, proteomics, pharmacogenomics, personalized medicine, scientific techniques derived from the human genome project, and scientific advancements in the life sciences, were all new scientific practices that influenced new drug development. For major pharmaceutical companies such as AstraZeneca, these new techniques demanded substantial investments not only in technology and laboratory equipment, but also in human capital in terms of training and education of the workforce. In addition, pharmaceutical companies, operating in an industry where product development times were substantial (approximately 10–15 years) and the costs of developing new drugs were enormous (hundreds of millions of dollars), increasingly came under pressure to deliver bottom line results and shareholder value to the financial markets and stockholders. While the pressure to deliver actual results posed specific problems and challenges, what was perhaps even more problematic for the pharmaceutical companies was that their ongoing work was being evaluated by financial experts who were not trained in the biosciences. Ramirez and Tylecote (2004: 109–111) point to this problem:

> 'Technologies, like genomics, high-throughput screening, and bio-informatics, have become buzzwords. Analysts ask companies whether they have invested in them, and as long as this is the case they are satisfied. However, the lack of scientific background among industry analysts is part of the problem. Even when this exists, the present rapid

pace of change of science means that it is not always easy for analysts to understand or fully appreciate the implications of the new technologies.'
(Ramirez and Tylecote, 2004: 109–111)

For the top executives in the pharmaceutical industry who, in most cases, themselves had a background in the biosciences coupled with extensive experience in the industry, this continuous evaluation of the market potential of scientific procedures presented a significant pedagogic challenge: How do you convince a non-scientific community that ongoing scientific work may pay off further down the road? The Head of Corporate Finance in AstraZeneca emphasized this challenge:

'If we go out to the market and say we've got these enormous opportunities to drive growth in 2003, but in order to get there, we are going to take a hit in our earnings growth in 2001 and 2002, then it's like a profit warning for those two years which may result in a decision to sell the stock.… The main problem is the mismatch between what is perceived to be of most value to shareholders in the short term versus the long term.'
(Head of Corporate Finance, AstraZeneca, cited in Ramirez and Tylecote, 2004: 109–114)

The pharmaceutical industry has traditionally been a mostly 'academic' industry, forging close-knit relationships with academic hospitals and universities, and essentially driven by 'scientific curiosity' and the will to contribute to society. However, the gradual 'automatization' of certain laboratory procedures and the increased pressure to deliver shareholder value has partially undermined the traditional pharmaceutical industry culture. The Head of Corporate Finance in AstraZeneca points to these changes:

'The room for blue sky stuff today is very limited; the question is whether this is good or bad? There is nothing wrong with suggesting that a very academic approach may be inappropriate for the industry. But equally, it would be wrong to say that it should not be so. I and some others think that the current environment is moving towards a situation that inhibits our ability to put resources into things that are high risk, high return long-term developments, because of the pressure to get results earlier.'
(Head of Corporate Finance, AstraZeneca, cited in Ramirez and Tylecote, 2004: 109, 115–116)

Top management in pharmaceutical companies therefore need to consider a range of options for the future. First, they have to decide which parts of the scientific portfolio should be prioritized and invested in. Such decisions are riddled by substantial uncertainties since only a handful out of thousands of promising so-called New Chemical Entities (NCEs) actually make it to market. This choice and selection is also a matter of choosing the drugs with the greatest market potential, determined by which illnesses the population in key markets are expected to suffer from in the next ten years and also the alternatives of complementary drugs on which competitors may be currently working. Second, the choice and selection of drugs needs to be based on available expertise and dominant traditions of thinking and working in the company or at the local site. If there is a path-dependency in the pharmaceutical industry, it takes a significant amount of time to develop world-class scientific expertise at a site. Another factor influencing the decision depends on the expertise available on the market. While some new drug development work demands specific advanced technologies and tools, other activities are less capital-intensive and therefore more easily outsourced.

The portfolio selection is therefore far from being trivial. It is a decision that includes substantial risks, but also opportunities for making substantial profits if the outsourcing and licensing work as intended.

In the day-to-day work in organizations, managers and co-workers on different levels are expected to make decisions on the basis of limited or unsatisfactory information. Decision-making is at the very heart of the organization's life and is determined by a long series of conditions, factors, and traditions of which some decision-makers may be only vaguely aware. In this chapter, a series of theoretical perspectives pertaining to such decision-making will be examined. First, decision-making theory, per se, will be examined, followed by institutional theory which explains how organizational activities are always, of necessity, dependent on social and material conditions in the organization's environment. Finally, organization culture is discussed as a theoretical framework that is capable of explaining certain organizational features and behaviours.

> The original research for this case was conducted by Alexander Styhre. Further information on the case can be found in Ingelgård *et al.*, 2002 and in Ramirez and Tylecote, 2004. An analysis of the general strategy of AstraZeneca can be found in Samad Sayed (2005).

Questions

How is it possible to align long-term objectives and short-term financial goals in industries like the pharmaceutical industry?

How can one take advantage of the 'academic tradition' and the commitment to producing new knowledge in the field of the life sciences in the pharmaceutical industry at the same time as it is adjusted to existing market goals regarding transparency and performance?

How can decision-making be conducted under genuine uncertainty?

Introduction

This chapter addresses how day-to-day work is managed in organizations under the conditions of uncertainty that most managers face. While short-term demands and technological changes are reasonably predictable and possible to anticipate, the long-term changes in consumer preferences and technological breakthroughs are more complicated to handle. For instance, in the pharmaceutical industry characterized by a fierce speed of development both in terms of technologies used in the laboratory work and the underlying theoretical understanding of the biological system (e.g., the human body), it is difficult to predict which technologies will play a key role in the future. This genuine uncertainty makes the pharmaceutical industry fertile ground for studying decision-making, and the procedures leading to the selection and choice of a number of alternatives. In this chapter, the concept of decision-making will be addressed. Decision-making theory is one of the most prestigious and oldest fields of research in organization and management studies and decision-making is one of the key processes in any organization. In some organizations such as political and juridical bodies, decision-making is the *only* outcome from the activities, and the decisions made are implemented, or acted upon, by other associated organizations. Even though decision-making is largely a matter of collecting and evaluating information, such procedures never take place in isolation from the broader social setting. Norms, values, beliefs, traditions, etc. strongly influence decision-making. Such socially enacted and shared beliefs are referred to as *institutions* in organization theory. Institutional theory is the second largest theoretical body examined in this chapter, very much complementing decision-making theory in terms of emphasizing that the capacity of making decisions is not only cognitive, but that all decision-making is also social in nature, embedded in a communal order of norms and beliefs. Institutions are contingent on local conditions, even while they extend over large geographical distances. Companies with operations in the US, Brazil, Germany, and Japan are run on basically the same global operative principles. However, there is still room for local variations. The third body of theory addressed in this chapter examines the influence of corporate culture and professional culture, that is, the totality of practices, procedures, symbols, and so forth that shape and form activities in organizations.

In this chapter, the following theoretical perspectives on day-to-day work in organizations will be introduced and discussed:

- Theories about how decisions are made in organizations,
- How so-called institutions are influencing both organizational form and structure and managerial practice, thereby setting the limits for which activities are socially legitimate to conduct,
- The influence and importance of organizational, national, or professional culture in the daily work in organizations.

Decision-making in organizations

Theories about decision-making is one of the oldest and most prestigious fields of organization theory. In fact, the only Nobel Prize in economics that primarily addresses organizational practices was won by Herbert Simon in 1976 for his work on decision-making. Everyday work life in organizations is pervaded by decision-making, more or less conscious, more or less dramatic, but always following certain procedures and mechanisms. Over the course of history, formal and rational procedures for decision-making have gradually been replaced by more behavioural theories of decision-making. Pettigrew (1973) is here distinguishing between mathematical-rational and behavioural theories of decision-making. While the former tradition of thinking has flourished in the micro-economics field of game theory, serving as one of the most prestigious and influential domains of economics, the main focus in this chapter is on the behavioural theories of decision-making. However, mathematical-rational procedures have also been widely used in organizations. In his intriguing study of strategic planning, *The Rise and Fall of Strategic Planning* (1994), Henry Mintzberg shows that the post World War II era was dominated by the belief in large-scale planning systems, including decision-making under various scenarios. Since such large-scale planning rarely if ever worked as intended—i.e., it was complicated to predict various outcomes given the complexity of the organization's environment—these planning procedures were gradually abandoned.

The starting point for a more behavioural science view of decision-making was the publication of Herbert Simon's *Administrative Behaviour* in 1945. Simon rejected the overtly abstract assumption—that humans are always capable of optimizing their interests in all transactions in which they participate (an assumption underlying to the so-called *rational choice theory*)—that dominated theories about decision-making at the time. Rational choice theory postulated that human beings, conceived of as the *homo economicus* ideal type, are capable of making rational decisions under determinate conditions. Simon thought that rationalist models of decision-making were useful as theoretical models but that the underlying assumption poorly corresponded to actual conditions including uncertainty and emerging properties facing the decision-maker. Rather than being able to make decisions under certainty, decision-making is, in practice, always embedded in significant sources of uncertainty and cognitive limitation on the part of the individual or the community of decision-makers.

DEFINITION BOX

Decision-making according to Herbert Simon

Simon was interested in understanding how decision-making takes place in the organization, and he was thus faced with the challenge of going from the individual to the organization. He acknowledged that administration was a group activity, and that it essentially was a decision process that consisted in establishing organizational procedures to select and determine elements in decisions by individuals (Simon, 1945/1976).

In his *Models of Man* (1957), Simon introduces the concept of **bounded rationality**, a master concept of the behavioural theory of decision-making. The concept of bounded rationality denotes that the individual seeks to act rationally when making decisions, but cognitive and practical limitations make him or her only 'limitedly rational'; decision-making is a social procedure under the influence of too many factors to be practically possible to accommodate for the individual. Simon also distinguishes between 'objective' and 'subjective' rationality: 'A decision may be called "objectively" rational if, in fact, it is the correct behaviour for maximizing given values in a given situation. It is 'subjectively' rational if it maximizes attainment relative to the actual knowledge of the subject' (Simon, 1976: 76). Given that most decision-making occurs under subjective rationality, most decisions are aimed at *satisficing* rather than *optimizing* the outcome; rather than making the best possible decision, decision-makers tend to take into account a range of possible outcomes and avoid the 'worst case scenarios'. In the classic text *Organizations*, first published in (1958), March and Simon emphasize this tendency in decision-making: 'Most human decision-making, whether individual or organizational, is concerned with the discovery and selection of satisfactory alternatives; only in exceptional cases is it concerned with the discovery and selection of optimal alternatives' (March and Simon, 1958: 162). Some of the complexities involved in decision-making in organizations are discussed in the link box below.

LINK BOX

Decision-making processes in AstraZeneca

Decision-making can involve a great deal of uncertainty and complexity, and traditional decision-making models are usually not sufficient to account for this complexity. Even though March and Simon pointed at the 'real-life' complexity involved in human decision-making, the challenges meeting decision-makers in companies today by far exceed the situations they where describing in the 1950s. In the opening case, executives in pharmaceutical companies have to take into account a great number of factors regarding the potential of a New Chemical Entity, the active substance of the drug. They have to consider the cost of clinically assessing the drug, the existing products in the market, the size of both the actual and future market, the regulatory demands of the authorities and so forth. There are in fact too many aspects and parameters involved in the decision—making process to account for. In such situations, executives can at best hope to accomplish bounded rationality in their decisions, i.e., they are capable of processing as much 'input material' as possible and then hope for the best possible outcome. This type of complex decision-making process is in no way unique to the pharmaceutical industry—decision-makers in a variety of industries would certainly recognize the dilemmas described above. This presents companies with difficult dilemmas—despite the fact that the consequences of wrong decisions are very high, they have to rely on incomplete information and bounded rationality in taking decisions. The recent advances in Information Technology have done a lot to provide decision-makers with technology to collect, structure, and analyse information, but we are still far from having good models for decision-making under uncertainty.

Reflection point: In facing a great deal of uncertainty, how can a company structure its decision-making processes to make sure that best possible decisions are taken?

The decision-making theory, developed by Herbert Simon and his followers James March and Richard Cyert in the 1950s and 1960s, was indebted to what has been referred to as 'the cognitive revolution' in both linguistics (represented by Noam Chomsky) and in academic psychology (Bruner, 1990). After the Freudian inception of psychology at the turn of the twentieth century, providing some of the basic terms and procedures for dealing with psychological processes and illnesses, the behaviourist school of thought dominated academic psychology for a long period of time. The behaviourist school conceived of the human psyche as machinery that could be fine-tuned and 'shaped' by using various techniques. The cognitive revolution of the 1950s represented a radical critique of this instrumental and positivist view of human beings, and cognitive mechanisms and procedures such as memory, associations, and creativity were emphasized as analytical categories. Above all, the cognitive view suggested that the world is not objectively given but is instead enacted by the individual; the world is as we see it, is our construction, based on our individual capacity to sense and perceive the shared social reality. Seen from this perspective, decision-making is embedded in processes of enactment, procedures where an image of the social reality is collectively constructed and acted upon. In practice, all decision-making is based on individual and collective constructs of perceived realities and as a consequence decision-making can be, at best, 'boundedly rational'. In addition, the behavioural theory of decision-making suggests that decision-making is always a social process wherein different objectives and interests are taken into account. To balance all these interests, decisions are not primarily optimizing but satisfying the interests of involved parts.

In the 1970s, the behavioural theory of decision-making was further developed by James March and Scandinavian researchers such as Johann P. Olsen. March and Olsen (1976) found that in practice, decision-making does not occur in one time and in one place. Instead, decision-making tends to be distributed over time and space and involves a community that may not be always present. Using the term garbage-can decision-making, March and Olsen (1976) showed that decisions may be initiated in one point in time, continue as an information collection process, and finish sometime later with some kind of decision. At the point of decision, individuals present in the initiation phase may no longer be present and the initial problem may have been rephrased or even displaced by some other problem. In addition, it is not always the case that all problems find a solution; instead, solutions may seek a problem to gain legitimacy within the organization. Seen from this viewpoint, decision-making is not a linear process, but is instead what is put into the garbage-can, and what demonstrates non-linear and complex patterns of arguments, information, decisions, and agency (March and Olsen, 1976; Cohen, March and Olsen, 1972).

What is of particular interest is that March and Olsen suggest that not only do problems look for solutions, but also that solutions at hand need to have a problem to remain on the agenda. For instance, the use of information and communication technology (ICT), such as computers, provide a set of technical 'solutions' that needs to be accompanied by some 'problem' to justify the investment. Studies show that investments in ICT rarely produce any increase in productivity in organizations (Orlikowski, 2007), yet the annual investments in ICT are astronomical. IT is apparently good to connect ICT with legitimate organizational problems. Management consultants are an example of a professional group that is skilled in narrating stories connecting their favoured solutions (be they technical or social) with actual or potential organizational problems. The garbage-can model of decision-making is a development of Simon's works in the 1940s and 1950s and is empirically grounded. It represents a fair account for how decision-making is emerging in practice.

Three decision-making models

The political scientist, Graham T. Allison, examined the Cuba crisis managed by the Kennedy administration in October 1962. American security agencies identified Soviet Union missiles in Cuba, potentially capable of destroying a number of American cities within minutes. The discovery brought the fragile US-Soviet relations to the verge of a full military confrontation, but at the last moment the Kennedy administration and the Soviet party secretary Nikita Khrushchev managed to avoid a potentially disastrous outcome. Allison (1971) examined the event from three complementary decision-making frameworks. Allison is, just like Herbert Simon, critical of the inherited view advocated by rational choice theorists, that of human beings being capable of making 'rational choices' between alternatives:

'We are assuming [that] governmental behaviour can be most satisfactorily understood by analogy with the purposive acts of individuals. In many cases this is a fruitful assumption. Treating national governments as if they were centrally coordinated,

purposive individuals provides useful shorthand for understanding problems of policy. But this simplification—like all simplifications—obscures, as well as reveals. In particular, it obscures the persistently neglected fact of bureaucracy: the 'maker' of government policy is not one calculating decision maker but is rather a conglomerate of large organizations and political actors.'
(Allison, 1971: 3)

Political decision-making is always already embedded in policies, bureaucratic procedures, and other forms of instituted and legitimate behaviour. Allison (1971) thus proposed three alternative models for understanding the decision-making under the Cuba crisis:

(1) The Rational Actor or 'Classical' Model (Allison, 1971: 4),

(2) The Organization Process Model,

(3) Governmental (Bureaucratic) Politics Model.

In the first model, the various desirable and potential outcomes must be carefully examined and ranked, and risks and opportunities must be weighted against each other. The 'classical model' is, therefore, an instrumental and rationalist model based on the assumption that at one single point in time, it is possible to fully overview and predict potential outcomes. Allison (1971) writes:

'The goals and the objectives of the agent are translated into a 'payoff' or 'utility' or 'preference' function, which represents the 'value' or 'utility' of alternative sets of consequences. At the outset of the decision problem the agent has a payoff function which ranks all positive sets of consequences in terms of his values and objectives. Each bundle of consequences will contain a number of side effects. Nevertheless, at a minimum, the agent must be able to rank in order of preference each possible set of consequences that might result from a particular action.'
(Allison, 1971: 29)

The event of the Cuba crisis contained too many unpredictable conditions and unknown factors to justify an analysis by the classic model. The Kennedy administration did not fully know, or understand, what the Soviet leader wanted to accomplish by his actions. From the American point of view, it was a most aggressive act. The political conditions and stability in the Kremlin were not fully known and the status of Khrushchev himself was a source of speculation in the Kennedy administration. In short, it was a most complex situation, and presented difficulties in acting 'rationally' on the basis of the paucity of available information.

The Organization Process model, the second model, instead emphasised the context of the decision-making, the particular organization within which the decision is being made. In the case of the Cuba crisis, there are a series of instituted procedures and channels guiding and limiting the decision-making activities, for instance, formal diplomatic communication and needs for following administrative and politically sanctioned procedures. The Kennedy administration therefore aimed at using the tools at hand when negotiating with the Soviet leaders. At one point in time, President Kennedy agreed to withdraw a number of missiles from Turkey, a substantial threat to a number of major cities in the Soviet Union. The Organization Process model is close to the decision-making theory of Simon, March, and

Olsen in terms of emphasizing organizational procedures and their effects on decision-making. Even if you are the president in the United States of America and expected to handle the most delicate political situations, you are expected to adhere to some of the routines and procedures instituted within the organization.

Finally, the Governmental (Bureaucratic) Politics model, which is closer to the political science framework and emphasized the political procedures of negotiations between various interests and actors. In managing the Cuba crisis, a number of secretaries representing different departments of the administration articulated their views on how to proceed in order to accomplish the best possible outcome for all parties, including the Soviet and Cuban leaders and the wider global community. While the military representatives argued for a straightforward military action to deter any further Soviet aggression, other participants weighted the possible military and diplomatic outcomes against each other. President John F. Kennedy has been acclaimed for his ability to navigate between the arguments of the 'hawks' and the 'doves' and to balance the various interests during the crisis. In fact, much of Kennedy's status as one of the most charismatic and qualified presidents in the twentieth century derives from his decision-making and authority during these dramatic days in October 1962. Allison argues that the second and the third models more adequately account for how decision-making happens in reality. Allison (1971: 246) concluded that 'many crucial details of implementation followed from organizational routines rather than from central choice'. No matter what analytical models you employ when examining decision-making, they offer complementary perspectives on how decision-making emerges. Even though Allison is sceptical of the rational choice theory model of decision-making, it offers some generic traits of how actors proceed when making decisions. The minicase below gives further input to the description of decision-making.

The Cuban crisis in movies

In trying to understand complex organizational phenomena, management research has turned to culture for inspiration. It is nowadays common practice to use literature, art, and movies as empirical illustrations of organizational phenomena. Movies can be especially illuminating in capturing organizational processes such as decision-making even though the movie itself is dramatized. The events described can tell us a lot about human interaction. The events accounted for in Allison's study have been the source for a number of movies. *Thirteen Days* (2000), directed by Roger Donaldson, is a drama showing how President John F. Kennedy and the members of his administration responded to the information about the Soviet missiles in Cuba and how this major political crisis evolved. The film effectively demonstrates that Kennedy had several choices on how to handle the situation and that his decision-making was affected by the various positions taken by the members of his administration and the US military. In the Oscar Award winning documentary *Fog of War* (2004), directed by Errol Morris, the former US Secretary of Defence, Robert S. McNamara, serving in both the Kennedy and the Johnson administrations, tells the story from his perspective. McNamara admits that, at times, it is very complicated to predict what outcomes specific decisions would lead to, and that security politics is a most delicate act of balancing various interests and concerns. The film offers an intriguing illustration of some of the issues addressed theoretically in this chapter.

MINICASE

Group thinking and decision-making

While Allison arguably examined a paradigmatic example of the triumphs of adequate decision–making procedures—the Cuban crisis was solved and the Soviet Union withdrew their missiles, World War III did not break out—Irving Janis (1982), conversely focused on the sources of various 'political fiascos' in American foreign policy decision-making, for instance, the notorious invasion at the Bay of Pigs in Cuba in 1961, decided by the Kennedy administration. Janis argues that close-knit groups, working together over a period of time, tend to overrate their own ability to handle practical problems and may produce a skewed image of reality.

DEFINITION BOX

Group thinking

Group thinking derives from three distinct sources:

1) An exaggerated belief in the group's competence and moral.
2) 'Close-mindedness', a tendency to think in too narrow terms, and the inability to perceive a problem from various angles and perspectives.
3) A proclivity to develop uniform beliefs and to eliminate alternative or complementary perspectives, so-called 'mind-guarding'.

A group that develops a firm belief that it is both highly competent and represents a morally correct stance has greater tendencies towards being close-minded, which in turn, further reduces the ability to 'think outside the box' that is being constructed. The close-minded thinking thus easily leads to 'mind-guarding' and moralist sentiments are easily brought into the discussion, i.e., alternative perspectives on a problem are framed as being morally questionable. In the case of the Bay of Pigs invasion, the highly skilled and very quali-fied group making the decision had a firm belief in both the American military apparatus and subscribed to the moral credo that the USA had a responsibility to act against the com-munist regime in Cuba. As a consequence, the group ignored all kinds of warning signals. The psychologist Leon Festinger (1957) proposed the term *cognitive dissonance* in cases where individuals or groups perceive the outside world as radically different from other social actors. For instance, individuals that are strongly emotionally involved in an activity may tend to overlook difficulties and 'weak signals' and interpret occurrences in positive terms, thereby further reinforcing the cognitive dissonance. An individual lacking this emotional commit-ment may regard events and occurrences somewhat differently. Janis (1982) proposed that all groups that collaborate over time are susceptible to group thinking; individual charismatic members of the group may convince the other members that certain views of a complex social reality are more accurate than others, or the group may collectively enact beliefs and assump-tions that are rarely if ever questioned. To handle group thinking, teams may establish pro-cedures for systematically questioning assumptions or new members may be introduced. In addition, an open discussion climate is important for avoiding too much yes-saying.

In terms of decision-making in organizations, group thinking is problematic in terms of limiting the process of information collection and thereby fewer choices are available in the end. Being aware of the social-psychological processes at work in group-based decision-making is perhaps the easiest way to avoid being stuck in group thinking. The link box below gives further evidence of the social-psychological processes involved in decision-making.

LINK BOX

Group thinking in the pharmaceutical industry

One of the standing critiques about the pharmaceutical industry over the last few years is the inability of the industry to produce genuinely innovative drugs. The so-called 'me-too-drugs', modifications of previous and financially successful drugs, constitute a substantial share of the new drugs being launched in the market. To some extent, this is indicative of the difficulties involved when developing new drugs and the demands for capital investment. In addition, it is, critics contend, also indicative of the inability of the leading pharmaceutical companies to think in new terms. What has been called the 'block-buster model' for new drug development will gradually be succeeded by new innovation models that seek to exploit opportunities for 'personalized medicine', one of the buzzwords and catch-phrases in the pharmaceutical industry in the new millennium. While the block-buster model is based on the 'one size fits all' perspective, personalized medicine is hoping to be able to produce therapies for more targeted groups such as ethnic groups, age-groups, or men or women. The term 'personalized' is then a misnomer because it is not, as the proponents of genomics medicine once hoped for, financially or practically possible to produce individually designed therapies on the basis of the human genome. Instead, proponents of personalized medicine today make references to the 'post-genome era,' and advance possibilities for developing therapies for larger groups. Using the group-think concept, the pharmaceutical industry is today struggling to move beyond the block-buster new drug development model to move into a new regime.

Reflection point: As described above, companies in the pharmaceutical industry are faced with different types of challenges in innovation processes. How can the phenomena of group-think be counter-acted?

Concluding remarks

Decision-making is one of the most central processes in organizations and the research on decision-making is substantial. While decision-making is a process wherein choices are made in order to advance the activities, it is also a social procedure that helps project collectively shared images of what the organization is, and what it seeks to accomplish. In a world characterized by uncertainty and extensive opportunities for choices, the event of decision-making is what brings an open-ended system to a closure. Robert Chia (1994) emphasizes this aspect of decision-making:

'Decision-making as an ontological act operates on a general principle of economy. It acts to reduce ambiguity and to punctuate our field of experience thereby helping to

configure a version of reality. Decision is not so much about 'choice' as about the prim-
ordial urge to order and control our human experiences. As such it embodies and
exemplifies the ongoing contestation between order and disorder, routine familiarity
and breakdown, organization and disorganization, chaos and cosmos.'
(Chia, 1994: 803)

Seen from this view, decision-making is a ritual, a collective act of deciding the outcomes that one prefers. According to March (1994), in a society like ours, a late-modern
society preoccupied with reason and rationality, decision-making becomes a 'sacred
activity':

'In a society based on reason, rationality, and a conception of intellectual human control over destiny, decision making is a sacred activity. The world is imagined to be
produced by deliberate human action and responsive to human intention.'
(March, 1994: 216)

The hope for rational decision-making is central to organizations. Operating under the
influence of uncertainty and complementary images of social reality, social actors can at best
hope to use bounded rationality to accomplish decisions that satisfy the greatest possible
number of individuals involved. In a behavioural theory of decision-making, the all-too-
human condition characterized by cognitive and emotional limitations strongly interferes
with the ideology of the perfectly rational decision.

Institutional theory: How organizations are determined by norms and practices in their environments

Another central theoretical field in the organization theory literature is *institutional theory*.
Institutional theory depicts the organization as an open system strongly influenced by the
organization's environment. Rather than being a closed system, capable of operating like a
machine and largely detached from broader social interests, beliefs, and occurrences, institutional theory points out that processes and activities inside the organization are strongly
determined by political decisions, consumer behaviour, economic conditions, and so forth,
which emerge in the organization's environment. Institutional theory thus shares its roots
with systems theory developed in the 1940s and 1950s by, for instance, the biologist Ludwig
von Bertalanffy (1968), and the cybernetic theory formulated by the mathematician Norbert
Wiener (1948, 1950), as a general theory of the regulation and control of complex technological or social systems. Systems theory conceived of any technological or social system as sharing a number of key characteristics and mechanisms, such as, information processes,
feedback loops, and self-regulating mechanisms, which stabilize a system and keep it in
equilibrium. The cybernetic programme has been remarkably influential in a range of disciplines including the emerging field of computer science. A more recent use of systems theory

in organization theory is the autopoiesis theory of social systems developed by the German sociologist Niklas Luhmann (2005). However, contrary to systems theory, institutional theory recognizes the influence of social actors in the system and conceives of institutions as being embedded in collectively shared norms, values, and beliefs that dominate in a certain social system such as a society, an industry, or an organization. Rather than being self-enclosed and sealed from external influences, organizations are, in the institutional theory perspective, open to external influences. In addition to institutional theory, this view of organizations as being both open to, and relying on external influences and resources is emphasized by the resource-dependency theory developed by Pfeffer and Salancik (1978), and so-called stake-holder theory (Hodgkinson, Herriot and Anderson, 2002; Key, 1999), which conceive of organizations as being in the position to balance the interests of a variety of stakeholders, including clients and customers, stockholders, authorities, suppliers, and partnering compan-ies. These theories share the view that organizations are open systems in constant interaction with the external environment and its various actors.

In the case of the management of AstraZeneca's research project portfolio, a number of factors, derived from the company's environment, affected the decision on what products to outsource and what to keep. For instance, the Food and Drug Administration's decision to demand larger and more detailed clinical studies limited the number of drugs selected on the basis of the costs to conduct such studies. The research portfolios of competitors also influenced the decisions. Finally, the rather short-term perspective of the financial markets put pressure on top management to cut costs, even though some of the gastrointestinal drugs had a very promising market potential. Institutional theory is an analytical framework capa-ble of explaining behaviour in organizations on the basis of processes and occurrences in the environment.

The concept of institutions

The concept of institutions is one of the more complicated concepts in the social science vocabulary. It is a concept used by a range of social science disciplines including sociology, economics, anthropology, and organization theory, but almost always, with slightly different meanings. The concept was used by Émile Durkheim (1995: 7) in his sociology of religion, suggesting that institutions are sets of beliefs or assumptions that guide and structure every-day life; for instance, religious beliefs impose meaning and direction for everyday living (for example, the ten commandments in the Bible, or the instructions on how often to pray or what food to avoid in the Qur'an). Durkheim was one of the founding fathers of modern sociology and his writing was enormously influential in the emerging anthropology litera-ture. The British anthropologist Radcliffe-Brown (1958: 174) defined an institution as 'an established or socially recognized system of norms or patterns of conduct referring to some aspect of social life'.

In the same vein, the social philosopher and critical theorist, Theodore W. Adorno (2000) speaks of institutions as 'congealed action', 'something which has become autono-mously detached from direct social action'. Institutions are then not the actions per se, but what strongly influences action in terms of offering guidelines for social action. The French philosopher, Georges Canguilhem (1989: 380) similarly spoke of institutions as the 'codification of a value, the embodiment of value as a set of rules' (Canguilhem, 1989: 380). Shared social values are instituted as a set of rules; rules are always, of necessity, normal in terms of prescribing which acts are legitimate and which are not. An institution is, in these three definitions, a highly abstract concept. It is not action per se, but it is a set of norms or rules that are collectively shared in a specific community. Institutions are not tangible, but are abstract principles that are manifested in social action. To further complicate things, institutions can at the same time be used to denote semi-material or tangible social arrangements, such as, 'the marriage' or 'parenthood', wherein actual practices and more abstract principles are combined. For instance, the institution of the marriage denotes the adherence to certain principles, such as, 'adultery is wrong', and 'husband and wife should be faithful to one another'. At the same time, a marriage is accomplished only after a set of rituals (e.g., a traditional 'church wedding' is arranged) and administrative procedures (e.g., the marriage is formally registered by the authorities, thereby producing certain juridical obligations).

Within organization theory, institutional theory has had a long and prestigious history as one of the most central theories capable of explaining or exploring organizational activities (Zucker, 1987; Tolbert and Zucker, 1996; Scott, 1995). In the 1950s, Talcott Parsons, one of the most influential sociologists of the twentieth century, emphasized the contribution of institutional theory: 'I conceive of the theory of institutions to be one of the principal branches of general sociological theory, hence the theory of all social life in one aspect, not the theory of one particular concretely separable department of social life' (Parsons, 1990: 320). In more specific terms, Barley and Tolbert (1997: 96; emphasis in the original) define institutions in an organization theory setting as *'shared rules and typifications that identify categories of social actors and their appropriate activities of relationships'*. The verb institutionalization is also used in the literature to denote the actual process wherein such 'rules and typifications' are established, i.e., are instituted. For instance, Pfeffer and Salancik (1978: 234), in examining how different divisions of an organization relate to one another, spoke of institutionalization as 'the establishment of relatively permanent structures and policies which favour one subunit's influence'. More recently, Lanzara and Patriotta (2007: 637) provided a similar definition: 'We conceive institutionalization as the phenomenological process by which a social order, a pattern, or a practice, comes to be taken for granted and is reproduced in structures that are to some extent self-sustaining'. The concept of institutionalization underlines that institutions are not a given from the outset, but instead emerge over time and become established. Occasionally, changes in the sociocultural or economic environment may undermine certain institutions. For instance, Jonathan Rutherford (cited in Bauman, 2000: 6) uses the term 'zombie institutions' to denote institutions 'which are 'dead and still alive'', that is, institutions that still play some role in society while at the same time are taken less seriously. For instance, in a secular society, many people still say they believe in God but fewer and fewer actually join the religious services. The Church is therefore tending towards a 'zombie institution', neither dead, nor alive, and largely maintained by a few dedicated individuals and traditions. As a consequence, even though the concept is used to represent something that is relatively stable over time, institutions are capable of changing when new sociocultural or economic conditions occur. The influence of institutions is clearly visible in the pharmaceutical industry, as described in the link box below.

LINK BOX

Institutional patterns in the pharmaceutical industry

Institutional theory has become a very influential theory within organization theory and offers a number of intriguing explanations to organizational phenomena. An interesting dilemma many companies face is when dealing with partly conflicting institutional demands, for instance, when operating in more than one institutional field. In the pharmaceutical industry, derived from the domain of academic medicine, there are two principal institutional fields that need to be aligned. On the one hand, the field of academic research, following its own rules and tradition, and essentially focused on providing credible scientific solutions to collectively defined problems. In this institutional field, it is basically the community of scientists that formulate legitimate research questions and then collectively work to address these research questions. On the other hand, pharmaceutical industry needs to relate to the pharmaceutical market, characterized by detailed control and monitoring practices of the authorities, strong competition, and demanding customers (i.e., medical doctors and other experts, patient groups, insurance companies and/or public health care organizations). This market functions essentially as any other market: costs and revenues need to be in balance, goods and services need to be marketed, the company needs to position itself in the market, and so forth. Being capable of aligning efficient in-house research work while, at the same time, operating well in the market is a key to competitive advantage in the pharmaceutical industry. Therefore, over the last 15 years, the pharmaceutical industry has undergone radical changes in terms of being less of a 'pseudo-academic' domain of research and has become more market-oriented.

Reflection point: The pharmaceutical industry operates in the midst of two different institutional fields which clearly influences their modes of operation. How can the companies within this industry find a proper balance between the two fields?

Old and new institutional theory

Perhaps the most classic study in the field of institutional theory is Philip Selznick's study of the Tennessee Valley Authority (TVA) set up by the Franklin D. Roosevelt Administration during the depression in the USA in the 1930s. Roosevelt's 'New Deal' programme, aimed at both helping the unemployed and the economically impoverished through the depression years and getting the American economy back on its feet after the great Wall Street crash in 1929, led to a number of local initiatives. One such initiative was the TVA organization, an organization with the assignment to produce both new jobs and new entrepreneurial activities in the South-Eastern region of the USA. The governmental TVA organization enacted a 'grass roots ideology' wherein local organizations and agencies collaborated with the local organizations. Two central terms of Selznick's study were 'infusion with values', denoting the process wherein the TVA organization was gradually adopting new norms for how the day-to-day work should be arranged, and 'co-optation', a term Selznick reserved for the adjustment to emerging objectives as the activities develop. Rather than sticking to its original objectives, the TVA organization wanted to grow and remain viable, and to accomplish this, new values and norms were co-opted. Selznick thus suggests that the TVA was responding to emerging social and economic changes by remaining open to new influences and recruiting new co-workers. The TVA organization was never a self-enclosed organization but maintained the ability to respond to changes in the environment.

The institutional theory of Selznick and Parsons is often referred to as early or even 'old' institutional theory', while more recent contributions to the field (i.e., from the 1970s) are commonly addressed as neoinstitutional theory (Selznick, 1996). For the layman, the distinction between the two schools is not self-explanatory, but Scott provides some guidance:

> 'Earlier theorists such as Selznick (1949) and Parsons (1960) stressed the regulative and normative aspects of institutionalized systems. Later neoinstitutionalists recognized these as significant factors, but they also called attention to the role of symbolic elements—schemas, typifications, and scripts that perform an important, independent role in shaping organization structure and behaviour.'
>
> (Scott, 2004: 7)

The neoinstitutional theory pays more attention to symbolic and cultural factors, but also addresses more cognitive aspects of institutions, such as, the schemas and scripts adhered to in day-to-day work. One of the most widely cited articles in the field of institutional theory is Meyer and Rowan's paper from 1977, which strongly emphasized the ritual and symbolic aspects of institutions. In Meyer and Rowan's (1977: 340) account, formal organizations are defined as 'systems of coordinated and controlled activities' that are 'embedded in complex networks of technical relations and boundary-spanning exchanges'. To fully understand organizations, such formal features are to be examined in tandem with the 'ceremonial conformity' to instituted rules that organizations demonstrate. Meyer and Rowan argue that all organizations are 'driven to incorporate' instituted rational concepts into their practices. That is, in order to reduce uncertainty, organizations seek to adopt standardized and legitimate solutions to organizational control problems. Expressed differently, organizations are always striving to adopt practices and procedures that make them look institutionally legitimate, that is, to conform to the action of other actors in the field. In practice, this conformity means that most firms have a similar human resource management system, they often employ quality management practices, and they demonstrate an awareness of what is recently being discussed in the organization's environment. Today, under the threat of global warming and environmental disasters, it is for instance *comme-il-faut* to announce environmental policies in all conceivable industries. Seen from this view, organizations to some extent cease to serve as enclosed entities but rather become open systems that are constantly adopting new procedures to stay institutionally legitimate. Meyer and Rowan write:

> 'According to the institutional conception developed here, organizations tend to disappear as distinct and bounded units. Quite beyond the environmental interrelations suggested in open-systems theories, institutional theories in their extreme forms define organizations as dramatic enactments of the rationalized myths pervading modern societies, rather than as units involved in exchange—no matter how complex— with their environments.'
>
> (Meyer and Rowan, 1977: 346)

In the minicase below the recent trend to develop policies for Corporate Social Responsibility is described.

Implementing a CSR strategy in Petrobras

Institutional theory has described and tried to explain how management concepts and models are spread between organizations, and the processes involved when companies, in a sense, imitate each other. Based on evidence from numerous studies in the field of institutional theory, it is clear that companies can 'benefit' from complying with institutional norms. This is done, for instance, by implementing programmes, routines, models, and the like, that are thought to be modern and that are used by valued organizations. This isopomorphism is clearly evident in the rapidly increasing use of corporate social responsibility concepts and models. Many companies have realized that having a CSR-strategy is expected from them and they try to comply with this institutional pressure by adopting policies to conform to the expectations from the general public, employees, and other groups, to be a socially responsible organization. A good example of a consistent CSR-strategy is provided by the Brazilian petrochemical giant Petrobras, the largest company in Brazil. The company is renowned for its investments in a number of programmes and initiatives to work with environmental issues and to take a social responsibility. In the Petrobras Development and Citizenship programme steps are taken to address poverty and social inequality in Brazil. The company is also active in a number of projects supporting culture and sports. According to company records more than 2,300 projects were carried out in these areas in 2008 alone.

Information on Petrobras and the company's CSR-strategy is retrieved from **www.petrobras.com**

MINICASE

The tendency to adopt the same procedures and practices as other companies and firms is referred to in the institutional theory as **isomorphism**, a concept derived from the Greek words *iso*, 'similar', 'same as', and *morphe*, 'form', 'shape'. Isomorphisms are observable in all sorts of industries and in some cases, specific practices are transferred from one industry to another. For instance, the Total Quality Management procedures first developed in the manufacturing and automotive industries are today applied in a range of industries and domains. Meyer and Rowan (1977) emphasized that the development of isomorphisms help organizations deal with a range of problems and challenges:

Isomorphisms with environmental institutions have some crucial contingencies for organizations:

(a) They incorporate elements which are legitimated externally, rather than in terms of efficiency.

(b) They employ external or ceremonial assessment criteria to define the value of structural elements.

(c) Dependence on externally fixed institutions reduces turbulence and maintains stability.

As a result ... institutional isomorphism promotes the success and survival of organizations.

(Meyer and Rowan, 1977: 349-349)

Meyer and Rowan suggested that by looking like all other organizations, organizations gain legitimacy in the field and thereby reduce uncertainty and promote the long-term survival of the organization. By and large, being 'dedicated followers of management fashions' is therefore a rational procedure for the organization. However, at times, Meyer and Rowan emphasized, the adherence to instituted procedures and rules may be in conflict with short-term goals in the organization. Meyer and Rowan (1977: 355) stated: 'Categorical rules conflict with the logic of efficiency. Organizations often face the dilemma that activities celebrating institutionalized rules, although they count as virtuous ceremonial expenditures, are pure costs from the point of view of efficiency'. For instance, when an organization is hiring a new manager, they may already have very qualified candidates within the firm, that could, if selecting the most practical solution, be given the job straight away. However, if the rule that all managerial positions should be announced in public to permit responses from external applicants has been instituted, the firm cannot simply ignore this rule without losing some of its acquired institutional credibility. Therefore, the management position has to be announced even though the costs of recruiting the new manager would be higher and more complicated than if the very qualified individual could have been given the position directly. In this case, there is a direct conflict between short-term gains and long-term institutional credibility. At times, firms may find loopholes and take shortcuts to avoid some of the instituted rules and regulations, but such activities always run the risk of compromising the company's institutional credibility. At the same time, some industries are more susceptible than others to different institutional rules. For instance, 'drinking at work is unethical' is a general institutional rule, but it would be far worse for a pilot or a nuclear plant control room supervisor to be caught drinking at work than it would be for a waitress or a restaurant chef, simply because the risks involved in the former occupations are larger than in the two latter. Skilled practice means navigating between the various instituted rules that influence everyday work without jeopardizing the firm's institutional credibility.

In a more recent article, another of the most widely referenced institutional theory papers, DiMaggio and Powell (1983) discussed three forms of isomorphism which influence the organization. First, *coercive isomorphism*, refers to instituted rules and procedures that are compulsory. In many cases, coercive isomorphisms are based on political decisions and are central to the legitimacy of the firm. For instance, pharmaceutical animal testing is regarded by some social groups as being unethical. Given the controversy of the practice, political and regulatory bodies have established firm procedures in this regard, and the pharmaceutical companies have little choice but to follow the rules and regulations. However, in practice, the coercive isomorphisms may offer some leeway since few procedures can be fully accounted for in detail. Second, DiMaggio and Powell (1983) spoke of *mimetic isomorphism* in cases where firms imitate one another or leading firms in order to gain institutional legitimacy. For DiMaggio and Powell (1983) mimetic isomorphism represents the firm's will to reduce uncertainty through taking on the same procedures and practices as relevant competitors. Third, *normative isomorphism* is based on professional identities and ideologies and derives from professional training. For instance, general practitioners, medical doctors with a broad expertise in general medicine, represent a category of 'knowledge workers' that wish to maintain their jurisdiction over a specific domain of work. In accomplishing this, it is important that general practitioner's maintain their authority over, for instance, decision-making. While nurses may be qualified and in many cases more suitable for making certain decisions in the health care work, general practitioners may want to keep that privilege for themselves. The relationship between general practitioners and nurses is therefore guided by strong normative isomorphisms; in all hospitals, the relationship between general practitioners and nurses looks similar, because the medical profession and training instituted normative isomorphisms. To put it differently, professional and occupational groups are competing over institutional legitimacy, and therefore their relationships are regulated by instituted norms and beliefs.

In summary, both Meyer and Rowan (1977) and DiMaggio and Powell (1983) strongly emphasized that institutions influence organizational activities and the organization's formal structure. By and large, the adherence to instituted rules and beliefs enables the organization to survive, but in some cases there is a direct conflict between long-term goals and short-term objectives. In addition, instituted norms and beliefs are not 'good or bad' per se; in many cases, for instance in the case of gendered or racial prejudices, instituted beliefs impose strong barriers that need to be overcome when promoting a more fair and just society, while in other cases, instituted beliefs help in maintaining organizational activities. Institutional theory is a theoretical framework capable of explaining similarities between organizations, industries, or clusters, but is less qualified for explaining differences. In addition, institutional theory primarily examines organizations on an aggregated level but is a more blunt tool when examining individual practice. As Meyer and Rowan (1977) emphasized, there is a loose coupling between, on the one hand, an organization's formal stance on a matter and the actual practices. Therefore, the values a firm claims to endorse may differ from what it actually practices. Brunsson (1985) even claimed that firms need to be hypocritical in order to accomplish their activities, that is, there is always, of necessity, a divergence between what firms can say and what they must do to survive in the long-term. No firm, Brunsson suggested, is capable of being perfectly institutionally legitimate and of acting in accordance with these various norms. The minicase below gives further empirical evidence of institutions at play.

Accounting procedures as institutions

Many of the managerial procedures and tools used today have a long history. The so-called double-entry bookkeeping that is one of the principal accounting procedures has its roots in medieval Northern Italy where the merchants were expected to keep account of all their financial activities. The double-entry bookkeeping was given its first formal introduction in Luca Pacioli's introductory text published in 1494 in Venice, one of the great trade centres in medieval Europe. By keeping accounts that could be inspected by business partners and others, merchants were able to establish themselves as credible and ethical members of the community. The church, drawing on the writings of Aristotle, was sceptical about the ability to make money based on transaction of goods, and usury. Money-lending, was generally disliked because it was based on interest and consequently time, and time, the clergy decided, belonged to God. As a consequence, the Jewish community were often in charge of the financial services (as in the case of William Shakespeare's *The Merchant in Venice*).

MINICASE

As a consequence, the merchants were put in the position where their work could be accounted for in more detail and clarity to avoid all speculations that their wealth was produced through unethical means. Over the centuries, the practice of double-entry bookkeeping further developed into a rich variety of procedures, financial derivative instruments, etc., all sharing the underlying instituted belief that transparency in financial activities is a virtue, and that numerical representation of economic activities are legitimate and valid indications of the financial activities. The case of double-entry book-keeping is a good example of how instituted beliefs led to social and material practices that after centuries of use are, more or less, taken for granted.

(Carruthers and Espeland, 1991).

The concepts of culture and organization culture

A third factor strongly influencing the day-to-day work in organizations and decision-making is various forms of culture, that is, organization culture, professional culture, and national culture. In AstraZeneca, just like in all industries and organizations where innovation is based on scientific expertise, there is a certain tension between, on the one hand, managerial objectives in terms of creating shareholder value and other short-term objectives and, on the other hand, the professional ideology of the trained scientist, always eager to explore the scientific possibilities within a specific domain of investigation. Researchers employed in the pharmaceutical industry have to learn to live with this tension. Using a more positive note, one may say that these researchers develop certain ambidextrous capacity (Tushman and O'Reilly, 1996); they can act on both short-term and long-term objectives.

Beginning in the late 1970s and early 1980s, propelled by the increased competition from the Japanese manufacturing industry, the concept of organization culture became in vogue. In addition to the new managerial practices and techniques developed by the Japanese, observers from the West noticed that the leading Japanese companies nourished organization culture that emphasized egalitarianism, collective decision-making, and continuous improvements of the operations. The challenge to compete with the Japanese companies then not only evolved around technical solutions and workplace organization, but also more intangible aspects of work. When Tom Peters and Robert Waterman published their best-selling *In Search of Excellence*, a book that was a directly concerned with 'learning from Japan' management genre and was an attempt at reinstituting the American management tradition as a source of pride in the US, the market for management guru books and accompanying research on organizational culture virtually exploded. If nothing else, in hindsight, 1980s was the 'decade of organization culture' (Barley and Kunda, 1992). Conferences, journals, and research monographs and anthologies addressing organization culture were started and published.

Culture is, just like notoriously complicated social science terms like power or gender, a most complicated concept. The literature offers a long series of introductions to the field of organization culture (Deal and Kennedy, 1982; Trice and Beyer, 1993). Rather than referring to all the various definitions of culture, we can return to perhaps the first study that actively used the concept of culture in an empirical study. Jaques (1951) studied an organization change project in a British factory. In this study, Jaques used the following definition of culture: 'The culture of the factory is its customary and traditional way of thinking and doing things, which is shared to a greater or lesser degree by all its members, and which new members must learn, and at least partially accept, in order to be accepted into service of the firm' (Jaques, 1951: 251). The culture is then operationalized by Jaques as a communal order regulating what behaviour and what activities are regarded as in the community of factory workers. In addition, culture is largely unreflected and taken for granted: 'Culture is part of second nature to those who have been with the firm for some time,' suggested Jaques (1951: 251). In Jaques' understanding, organization cultures are systemic in terms of structuring the behaviour of individuals; culture is something that is always present, but not always explicitly articulated.

This idea is shared by a number of other social theorists addressing the concept of culture. Franz Fanon (1986: 191), the French-Martinique post-colonial theorist and a trained psychiatrist, speaks of culture as a form of 'collective unconsciousness', a form of thinking that is largely unreflected. Tzvetan Todorov (1984: x), argues that culture 'consists in the discourses retained by collective memory ... discourses in relation to which every uttering subject must situate himself or herself'. That is, culture is what is entangled with the everyday use of language, and in the very stories being told in daily conversations. In organization theory, Smircich (1983) argued convincingly that organizations do not *have* culture, but instead, they *are* cultures. Just like we tend to speak of or instance the Hellenic period or Victorian England as distinct cultural periods or entire civilizations such as the Aztec Indians or the Inuit as cultures, so must we speak of Volkswagen or Wal-Mart not only as formal organizations but as cultures in their own right. A series of studies has also actively used this view of culture in ethnographies of organizations, for instance, Kunda's (1992) study of the culture of Tech, an engineering firm. Tech culture is based on engineering expertise and the entire corporation is shaped by the engineering culture. More recently, under the influence of new theoretical frameworks such as complexity theory, poststructuralist theory, and feminist theory, all being sceptical about an inclusive and all encompassing definition, culture has been conceived of as an assemblage of larger and smaller 'sub-cultures' coexisting and co-evolving in time and space. Parker (2000: 1) suggests that 'organization cultures should be seen as 'fragmented unities' in which members identify themselves as collectives at some times, and divided at others'. This image of culture underlines the fragmented and loosely coupled nature of organization culture. Rather than being unified and singular, culture is always of necessity manifold, always plural. This more complex image of culture is discussed by Bauman (1999):

> '"Culture" is as much about inventing as it is about preserving; about discontinuity as much as about continuation; about novelty as much as about tradition; about routine as much as about pattern-breaking; about norm-following as much as about the transcendence of norm; about the unique as much as about the regular; about change as much as about monotony of reproduction; about the unexpected as much as the predictable.'
> (Bauman, 1999)

In organizations, there is ample evidence of organizational, professional, national, and gendered cultures coexisting and intersecting along complex patterns. A feminist organization culture researcher, Gherardi (1995: 4) strongly emphasized that organization cultures are gendered; for instance, a female professional, e.g., a medical doctor, may prefer to think of herself in professional rather than gendered terms (Faulkner, 2007). At the same time, her role and status in the organization are determined by conditions that are gendered. In addition to the gendered identity of the medical doctor, studies of health care organizations point at the difference between managerial cultures and the medical culture. Medical doctors and other clinicians do not want to take up management positions because that would risk their status: 'Any clinician taking up a management position—even within the medical establishment— risks loss of respect and clinical visibility. Perceptions of the secondary status of managers are deep in a medical culture that have not esteemed management work,' wrote Llewellyn (2001: 604). A similar finding is reported by Parker (2000): 'Many medical staff still see ... management as threatening. I think many see it as being irrelevant to their day-to-day jobs, and I also see that a number of or them think that even if it's not threatening, it just isn't going to be of any help to them' (General manager, National Hospital Service (NHS), UK, cited by Parker, 2000: 116). For the medical doctor or clinician, meddling with managerial work is risking their status in their community. Not only does culture impose modes of thinking; it also imposes clear normative guidelines for how to perceive one's own role in a broader social setting.

A series of studies of organizations has suggested that rather than being the 'glue' that keeps the organization together, workers tend to take a cynical attitude towards corporate cultures and identities being imposed on them. In knowledge-intensive firms, especially, and firms where the output cannot be fully controlled, corporate cultures tend to play a role in encouraging workers to take on identities and subject-positions where they should 'have fun' and 'act professionally'. Fleming and Spicer (2007) report a study from a call centre where this 'culture of fun' is a good illustration of what Thomas Frank (1997) speaks of as the 'conquest of cool' in the world of business as being actively promoted by the management. The workers were encouraged to 'express themselves', recognize their personal qualities, and act as social beings. Management also explicitly recognized the role of homosexual co-workers because they wanted to portray the call centre as a 'liberal' and 'modern' workplace, but also because the gay culture is commonly associated with glamour, fun, and creativity. However, even though such cultural traits were in many ways liberating, some of the workers demonstrated a sceptical or even cynical attitude to such cultural manipulations, conceiving of these managerial activities as a charade to conceal the dull and repetitive nature of the work in the call centre. No matter how much 'fun' there is in the workplace, the call centre work was still heavily monitored and performances, in terms of incoming calls handled, were carefully reviewed. In this case, organization culture was envisaged as being a source of relief from the ordeal of everyday work, but the workers saw through this thinly veiled ideology of 'having fun' and thus refused to embrace the managerial initiatives wholeheartedly. The hugely influential British comedy TV series 'The Office' is a fine illustration of this delicate balance between promoting a 'culture of fun' and provoking cynicism on the part of the workers.

National, professional, and regional cultures

Few beliefs are so ingrained as is prejudice between different national cultures. In different parts of the world, people tell jokes about their neighbours. Swedes tell jokes about Norwegians, the French about the Belgians, the Americans about the Poles, and so forth. Whether these national stereotypes are based on a kernel of truth or not, does not make a major difference to the viability of these jokes; they are part of a standardized en-cultured repertoire of typifica-tions that helps individuals navigate through day-to-day life. The Dutch Business School professor Geert Hofstede published a book in 1980 that, to date, is the most widely-cited study of national cultural differences. Using a survey methodology in the computer company IBM's multinational organization, Hofstede structured the analysis of the data by speaking of low/high power distance and feminine/masculine values as the main analytical categories. Power distance denotes the degree of perceived hierarchical relations in the firm; low power distance means that communication and decision-making may occur informally, while high power distance suggests there are few opportunities for informal collaboration. The femi-nine/masculine values continuum suggests that cultures favouring more feminine values recognize open communication, joint decision-making, and a more nourishing corporate culture. The masculine orientation represents a stronger emphasis on individual activities and the capacity to demonstrate agency. Hofstede emphasized that none of the four positions (in the four-cell matrix developed from the two dimensions) are better than the other. Hofst-ede's analysis does show that there are some differences between nations and regions. While for instance, the Scandinavian workers demonstrated a preference for feminine values and low power-distance, many Latin countries in, for example, South America, had a preference for masculine values and high power distance. The role of different national cultures is dis-cussed in the link box below.

LINK BOX

Sub-cultures in the pharmaceutical industry

Studies in major international pharmaceutical companies suggest that there are a variety of sub-cultures that need to be managed. For instance, when studying AstraZeneca's Swedish operations, it is commonplace to come across differences between departments (most notably between the more laboratory-oriented work in the so-called discovery organization, and the clinical trials work in the so-called development organization), professional groups, (for instance, medical doctors and general practitioners being used to work in the rather hierarchical milieu of health care organizations bringing a certain attitude towards colleagues when working in clinical trial teams), and national cultures (for instance, the Swedes regard the British sites as being overtly hierarchical and formal, while the Brits tend to think of Swedish work procedures as being non-transparent and fuzzy). Working in a globalized corporation puts great pressure on the co-workers when dealing with such perceived differences and is thus a major challenge for leaders in globalized companies. In many cases the cultural differences between units in a global company such as AstraZeneca do not interfere with the operations in a negative way, and they can thus be easily managed. The problems start when units need to interact and when it becomes obvious that there are sub-cultures with expectations, attitudes, and norms that are not aligned with each other. Creating a global culture is indeed a challenge in AstraZeneca, and it can certainly be asked whether it is ever possible to achieve this.

Reflection point: In managing global companies, managers are often faced with different sub-cultures that make it harder to implement strategies in different parts of the company. How can these sub-cultures be understood and how can they be properly managed?

In addition to national culture, one may speak of professional or occupational cultures. The concepts of profession and occupations are central to the sociology of work and denote that specific groups of workers or specialists demonstrate a shared set of beliefs and assumptions on how their work is to be accomplished and what qualifications are needed to be fully recognized as a member of the professional or occupational community (Attewell, 1990; Abbott, 1988; Larson, 1977; Strauss, *et al.*, 1964). Studies of professional and occupational identities and professional and occupational cultures show that it is in the early phases of formal training that these beliefs and assumptions are acquired (Becker *et al.*, 1961). Debra Schleef's (2006) study of graduate students at a law school and a business school in an American elite university suggests that the process of acquiring these attitudes and identities means balancing a sceptical attitude towards the profession, while at the same time, recognizing the status of the profession and the social role and position one can expect to earn in the future when graduating from the university:

> 'Student contestation of dominant ideologies is integral to the transformation that occurs during elite professional socialization . . . the process of becoming professional includes learning to think critically and to question assumptions. Far from being unwilling dupes of ideological indoctrination, students are self-reflective, and they strategically accommodate and resist the ideologies of their education. During professional socialization, they must confront and rationalize their future status as a means of facilitating and thus legitimizing the reproduction of elite privilege.'
> (Schleef, 2006: 4)

Professional training is essentially about rendering things and conditions problematic and questioning social reality. At the same time professions are elite groups in society and hold a privileged position. To balance these incompatible components of training, the students develop what Schleef calls 'surface cynicism'. Students are critical about the education and the training in university (for instance the 'Socratic method' used in law school training), but they never question the education more profoundly. After a few years of training, students start to claim they 'think as a lawyer or a manager', testifying to the socialization into the profession. Schleef uses the example of Danielle, a law student who 'firmly believed during her first year of law school that most lawyers were overpaid and took advantage of their powerful position in society. Danielle now says without criticism, "Lawyers work really, really hard . . . the money is deserved. I think lawyers are really, really smart. I think they are very articulate and on top of things."' (Schleef, 2006: 2). Students tend to converge toward a position where they believe in their right to act as the professional they are trained to be. Schleef (2006: 5) concludes, 'The most important audience for professional ideology . . . , is the professionals themselves—they need to believe in the higher mandate that professionals are alleged to embody'.

In organizations, the differences between professional and occupational groups and their various beliefs and assumptions are standing sources of concern. Even within a specific professional group, for instance among engineers, there are significant differences in training that demand careful attention. Differences in status, vocabularies in use, the ability to decode quantitative information, and so forth, are some differences between professional and occupational groups that influence the day-to-day work in organizations. In some cases, for instance with medical doctors, the individual tends to identify more with the profession than with the organization. Strauss, *et al.*, (1964: 371) argued, 'Professionals follow careers and specific institutions are, more often than not, waystations'. Another form of professional culture, arguably substantially less common, is what may be called a 'cluster culture', a specific culture developed in a specific region dominated by one or a few related industries.

AnnaLee Saxenian's (1994) study of the San Francisco Bay Area's computer industry, the well-known Silicon Valley, a vast geographical area covering a number of cities between Stanford University in Palo Alto and San Jose in the southern part of the San Francisco Bay, suggests that there are substantial differences between, on the one hand, the California-based computer industry and, on the other hand, the East-coast competitor, the so-called Route 128 corridor in Massachusetts. Saxenian strongly emphasized the entrepreneurial spirit in Silicon Valley: 'Although many Silicon Valley entrepreneurs became millionaires, most appear to have been motivated less by money than by the challenge of independently pursuing a new technological opportunity. The culture of the Valley awarded the highest regard to those who started firms; status was defined less by economic success than by technological achievement' (Saxenian, 1994: 38). Many of the entrepreneurs in Silicon Valley had their roots in the midwest of the USA and were sceptical about the formal business culture in Eastern USA. Rather than wearing suit and tie, the computer industry entrepreneurs wore T-shirts and sneakers and the whole business culture was based on detailed expertise and a passion for computers rather than financial interests. Since the venture capital in Silicon Valley primarily derived from other successful computer industry entrepreneurs, there was a higher degree of expertise in evaluating and promoting new entrepreneurs in the industry; rather than negotiating with some middle-aged banker with limited insight into the industry as in the Route 128 region, the Silicon Valley entrepreneurs discussed their ideas with peers. One of the principal consequences was that while failure was stigmatizing in the East, in Silicon Valley failure was not considered a major problem: 'In Silicon Valley, failure is an accepted way of life, unlike the east where failure is viewed as a death-sentence ... If you bomb in Palo Alto, you blame the advertising agency and start another company' (Boston-based professional, cited in Saxenian, 1994: 68). One of the explanations for the long-term success of the Silicon Valley computer industry, Saxenian suggested, is that a true entrepreneurial ideology, tolerating failures and setbacks as an integral component of the entrepreneurial experience, was established and has been maintained over time, even in periods of crisis such as the mid 1980s. In addition to the national and professional cultures influencing organizations and firms, there are also examples of more cluster-based or regional cultures that affect the organization. The two minicases below further illustrate the cultural factors discussed in this section of the chapter.

Exporting the Japanese model to the West

When Japanese manufacturing started to compete fiercely with the American Automotive industry the more radical wings of the American Automotive Workers Unions regarded the Japanese car industry as a major threat to the work of thousands of car workers. In the early 1980s, Japanese cars in the streets were even smashed by furious car workers and it was in places even regarded as being unpatriotic to drive a non-American car, and especially, a Japanese car. The Japanese responded to these challenges by building car factories in the US thereby providing job opportunities in the states where the factories

MINICASE

were located. When these so-called transplants were started, one of the big questions for both the Japanese owners and managers, and the American workers, was how much of the idiosyncratic Japanese managerial system could be successfully brought into the American setting. Japanese companies are largely based on egalitarian and collective values and norms, and in the more individualized US, practices such as team based decision-making, company songs, and an extensive use of intricate symbolism in the reward system might not be successfully employed. The ethnographic work of Fucini and Fucini (1990), *Working for the Japanese* (see Chapter 4), is an intriguing account of how the two cultures had to mutually adjust to one another to make the activities run as smoothly as intended. The book, *Global Japanization*, edited by Terry Elger and Chris Smith (1994) showed how Japanese manufacturing practices spread across the globe.

Aligning business objectives and traditional family values in an Israeli textile factory

Israel Drori's ethnography of an Israeli textile factory located in the rural parts of the country, and hiring primarily Palestinian and Druse female textile workers, is another example of how different norms, values, and cultures have to be brought into harmony. In the factory, production of a series of garments for major European and North American clothing companies was managed by Jewish managers and the workers were younger, in most cases not yet married Palestinian and Druse women. The managers were concerned about the financial performance of the factory, and the ability to meet customers' expectations on timely delivery of ordered products. However, the patriarchal culture of the Palestine and Druse communities prescribed that the younger women should always take care of their families first if there were cases of illness in the family, and the managers had to live with periods of absence of workers when the younger women were helping their mothers with domestic work. 'Here the family is part of the plant', one manager said (cited in Drori, 2000: 85). In addition, when conflicts between managers and workers emerged, the parents of the female seamstresses arrived to resolve the conflict.

In order to make the textile factory run effectively, the Jewish managers needed to bring into harmony both the managerialist norms of predictability and sound financial performance, and the traditional, patriarchal culture of the surrounding society wherein younger women were first and foremost, accountable to their families. In order to accomplish such a balance, the company hired so-called supervisors, recruited from the community of workers. The supervisors were experienced workers capable of bridging these two cultural systems, i.e., could both inform the managers what actions would be received favourably, and discuss the importance of reaching organizational objectives and goals with the workers during periods of competing family matters. Local cultures and universalized norms of the capitalist economic regime are thus major issues influencing managerial practice.

Summary and conclusions

Decision-making in organizations, especially when it deals with important strategic issues, is a social process strongly determined by various institutional conditions and various cultural traits of the organization. In AstraZeneca, some of the historically most profitable research areas were decided to be outsourced to external clinical research companies. This decision is embedded in a large number of considerations regarding the firm's long-term strategies and objectives, but also in an analysis of how the pharmaceutical industry and the various competitors may evolve in the future. The decision to outsource some of the research projects also affected the corporate and professional culture, generated and accumulated over decades. Some of the researchers specializing in gastrointestinal medicine moved out of the company or had to direct their research interest elsewhere. The company's entire self-image or identity could be affected by the choice to abandon a domain of research. In the day-to-day work, managers and workers in organizations have to make important decisions that are always, of necessity, the behavioural theory of decision-making suggests, based on bounded rationality and satisficing. No decision-making is ever capable of embodying and weighting all the available information pertaining to a decision. Instead, decisions are made with the best possible intentions, but always under conditions of the human cognitive shortcomings.

Study questions

1. What are the principal components of garbage-can decision making processes?
2. When Herbert Simon says that humans make decisions under the influence of bounded rationality, what is he suggesting?
3. What are the three forms of institutional isomorphism, and how do they differ?
4. On what levels can one speak of cultures in organizations?
5. What are the two key parameters in Hofstede's culture model?

Literature recommendations and further readings

Decision-making theory is based on the foundational work of Herbert Simon and James March published in the period from the late 1940s to the early 1960s. March's *A Primer on Decision Making* (1994) is an excellent introduction to the field. March and Olsen's *Ambiguity and Choice in Organizations* introducing the very central term 'garbage-can decision-making' is a seminal work. Institutional theory has to a larger extent been advanced in the form of journal papers. Two very central papers are those of Meyer and Rowan (1977) and DiMaggio and Powell (1983). Richard Scott's (1995) introduction to institutional theory (available in many editions) is recommended for the newcomer and the more recent handbook on 'organizational institutionalism' (Greenwood et al., 2008) provides an authoritative overview of the field. The so-called 'old institutionalism' is best represented by Philip Selznick's classic *TWA and the grassroots*, a study of the Tennessee Valley Authority (TWA) which was part of Roosevelt's New Deal programme (1949). The literature on organization culture, rather limited until the end of the 1970s, but thereafter virtually exploding and engendering new journals, books series, and conferences is quite diverse. There are a number of introductory texts that give an accessible overview of the field (e.g., the work of Jane Dutton). When it comes to actual studies, the studies of Geert Hofstede (e.g., his 1980 research monograph) is a standard reference and perhaps the most cited book in the field and the most widely criticized.

**online
resource
centre**

Take your learning further

http://www.oxfordtextbooks.co.uk/orc/erikssonzetterquist/

Visit the Online Resource Centre which accompanies this book to enrich your understanding of this chapter.

Students: explore web links and further reading suggestions. Keep up to date with the latest developments via 'What happened next' updates to appropriate cases from within the book.

Lecturers: you will find seminar exercises and teaching notes, for use in class or assessment.

PART III
MANAGING CHANGE AND PROCESSES

CHAPTER 8   Managing innovation in and
             between organizations   195

CHAPTER 9   Balancing radical change
             and continuous improvement   217

CHAPTER 10   Managing learning and knowledge
             in and between organizations   241

CHAPTER 8
Managing innovation in and between organizations

Managing innovation work in industry–university collaboration

Chalmers University of Technology, a research university founded in 1829 and located in Gothenburg, Sweden, is ranked among the best technical universities in Europe. Chalmers includes a variety of departments in the engineering and natural sciences, a business school, and an architecture school. In addition to the regular department structure with departments in chemistry, physics, mechanical engineering, civil engineering, and so forth, Chalmers hosts a number of so-called research centres . A research centre is a platform for closer collaboration between industry and the university, in most cases financed by the three parts: the Swedish state, the university (Chalmers), and the participating companies. A research centre can conduct research in any domain of interest where both industry and academic researchers demonstrate a shared interest and a need for close collaboration. In 2008, some 30 research centres were running at Chalmers, including industry–university collaboration in, for instance, catalyst development and emission lowering technologies, high frequency mobile communication technologies, lower energy consumption technologies in architecture and constructions, and logistics and transportation research.

While the idea of a research centre is intuitively appealing—industry and university joining hands to explore their joint interests and collective know-how to advance technical solutions to perceived problems—in reality there are some issues that need to be addressed when collaborating over organizational boundaries. For example, many commentators suggest that even though industry research and university research tend to converge over time, there are still some cultural differences between industry and the university. For instance, Lam (2007: 997) reports 'industry–university collaboration has long been shown to be problematic because of the difficulties in reconciling the divergent work norms and reward structures governing the two different knowledge production systems'. Lam (2007) calls for more 'entrepreneurial professors' that are both capable of producing world-class research at the same time as they are capable of understanding the needs of industry and be able to communicate with industry representatives effectively. Markides (2007) talks about such professors as being 'ambidextrous', that is, having the ability to use 'both hands', a metaphor for mastering both basic research and development research. In general, if universities are committed to conducting 'upstream research', that is, basic research that precedes actual applications and thus represent the 'R' in the R&D concept, and industry is primarily concerned about how to make use of this know-how in 'downstream' applications, that is to conduct the 'D' in R&D, then there is a need for providing a platform where the two domains of expertise can meet. Such a 'trading zone' (to use Galison's 1997 apt phrase) is provided by the research centres. Much innovation research suggests that innovative industries or innovative industry clusters demonstrate close collaboration over industry–university boundaries. Universities here become nodes in networks of firms that, in intricate ways, both collaborate and compete over resources and attention. In many ways, many of the problems facing mankind in terms of, for instance, creating a sustainable economy, need to effectively combine long-term and short-term perspectives, basic research, and practical applications in technologies or practices. Balancing these various interests and competencies is the principal objective of the trading zones provided by the research centres at technical universities such as Chalmers. What are the challenges thus facing industry representatives collaborating in the research centres? While both groups (to simplify what is a much more heterogeneous group than this simple dichotomy suggests) appreciate the collaboration, the university professors tend to think of the research centres as being at times too focused on producing actual products and services, that is taking a too-short-a-time perspective on the topic of investigation. Industry representatives, on the other hand, may be impatient with the insistence on publishing research findings in academic journals, anchored in a time-consuming procedure that in many ways is out of joint with the industry's short production time cycles. However, in most cases the collaboration works smoothly and the two parties learn to tolerate the various idiosyncrasies. However, reaching such a point of mutual understanding may take some time. When interviewing on academic research engaged in a research centre dedicated to railway transportation research, Dierickx and Cool (1989) reported on what they called 'time-compression diseconomies':

> It takes ten years to create a research organization ... then you may of course close it down really quick if you want to .... That may be justified in some cases, but then you need to be aware that it takes ten years to create something similar. You may take a shortcut through hiring people, but I guess you can never make it in less than five years.
> (Associate professor)

The case of research centre based industry–university collaboration shows that in the new competitive landscape, there is a need for exploring and exploiting all intellectual resources and know-how at hand. Universities, on the one hand, need to become 'entrepreneurial' and hire 'ambidextrous professors' capable of not only conducting intramural research and lectures, but also to actively create meaningful relations with industry. Industry, on the other hand, needs to open up its boundaries and promote active collaboration, not only with suppliers and other firms in their close proximity, but with universities, research institutes, and non-governmental organizations that in various ways may provide useful know-how, further strengthening the innovation work process. In the new millennium, little innovation takes place in closed laboratories and R&D departments, but innovation activity is increasingly produced in open systems, in networks of alliances, joint ventures or collaborative associations. As the case of Chalmers University of Technology suggests, establishing the 'trading zones' between these different actors is a principal challenge for all organizations with a view to collaborating over organizational boundaries.

The original research for this case was conducted by Alexander Styhre. See also Lam (2008); Markides (2007); Galison's 1997; Dierickx and Cool (1989).

Questions

Can innovation activities be more effectively managed in collaboration between organizations, or would that allow that firm's specific competencies to be lost to competitors or collaborating firms and organizations?

How much time and effort should companies invest in collaborating with other firms? Isn't it safer to organize innovation work in-house since the pay-back time is shorter?

How are the trading zones between organizations managed and organized? In joint ventures, share laboratories, jointly owned subsidiaries, or in some other form?

Introduction

The Chalmers case above stresses the importance of industry–university collaboration, and the need for crossing existing boundaries between the traditional realm of academia (the R in R&D) and industry (the D in R&D). Innovation is, to a growing extent, managed in relations *between* organizations, and not only *within* the single organization. In this chapter we introduce the concept of innovation and try to give a balanced view of the challenges indicated in the Chalmers case above. More specifically the chapter addresses the following topics pertaining to innovation management research:

- The definition of innovation,
- A discussion of the various innovation phases,
- An analysis of the social nature of innovation,
- A systemic view of innovation,
- An analysis of the relationship between innovation and organization forms.

Defining innovation

In order to survive in the long-term, most companies need to be capable of providing new goods, services, or events, that is, what organization theorists and management researchers call *innovations*. The capitalist economic system is characterized by an intrinsic creativity and continuous change that strongly encourages, indeed demands, new goods and services to be produced. The Austrian-American economist Joseph Schumpeter spoke of the 'gale of creative destruction' in the capitalist economic system. By this poetic expression, Schumpeter meant that all new innovations are, of necessity, undermining the role of its predecessors. The printed book succeeded the hand-written scroll, the typewriter displaced hand writing, the computer word processing program took the place of the typewriter, and so forth. For Schumpeter, the capitalist economic system is characterized by restless movements and changes. Every innovation is therefore both creative and destructive—it creates new opportunities while simultaneously destroying the market for the preceding technology. As a consequence, there is a strong orientation in today's economy towards invention and innovation. In some cases, innovations are without doubt needed, for instance, in the transformation of society to a more sustainable *modus vivendi*, while in some cases innovation is driven by human curiosity and the demand for the new (as in the case of change in fashion in the garment and design industry). From the perspective of the individual firm, the capacity to either produce new innovations in-house, or outside the organization, is of central importance to long-term competitiveness and ultimately survival. In this chapter, the concept of innovation management will be examined. The literature is diverse and includes a variety of perspectives, theoretical orientations, methodological traditions, and epistemological and ontological assumptions. As Pavitt (2005: 87) summarized, 'A growing number of 'innovation studies' show little allegiance to any particular discipline, and widely disparate theories and methods coexist in relevant journals and handbooks'. However, this diversity of perspectives and definitions does not mean that the field of innovation management is fragmented or riddled by more controversies than other comparative fields in the organization theory literature. Instead, innovation management is a viable and dynamic field of research, enriched by the scope of the research and the variety of perspectives.

In the literature, there are a number of definitions of innovations provided. To start chronologically, Schumpeter defined innovation in the 1930s accordingly:

This seminal definition emphasizes the combinatory nature of innovation; innovations

DEFINITION BOX

Innovation according to Schumpeter

Schumpeter (1939) is renowned for his work on entrepreneurship and innovation and following is a quotation that indicates his view on innovation:

> We simply define innovation as the setting up of a new production function. This covers the case of a new commodity, as well as those of a new form of organization such as a merger, of the opening of new markets, and so on ... innovation combines factors in a new way ... it consists of carrying out New Combinations.
>
> (Schumpeter, 1939: 87–88)

are never completely 'new' but are rather to be conceived of as assemblages of previous know-how, technologies, or services. Innovation is then a bundle of pre-existing resources packaged in a new way. More recently, innovation has been defined by Thompson (1969):

DEFINITION BOX

Innovation according to Thompson

Thompson defined innovation as:

> The generation, acceptance, and implementation of new ideas, processes, and products or services. Innovation, therefore, implies the capacity to change and adapt.
> (Thompson, 1969: 5)

In this view, innovation includes the capacity of the organization and its employees to change its routines and to adapt to emerging demands and expectations in the market. To innovate is, in this perspective, what creates substantial demands on the organization to actively overturn its established procedures, and taken-for-granted beliefs, and to recognize new and emerging opportunities.

Innovation at Nokia—the case of Ovi store

MINICASE

The capacity of an organization to change is, according to Thompson, one important feature of innovation. He points to the need for an organization to be able to adjust routines and standards to adapt to changing demands on the market. An organization that has fully understood the role and importance of building change into the organization, and that has managed to organize an impressive row of innovations, is Nokia, the Finnish telecom giant. Nokia is the undisputed market leader in the mobile phone market and they have, in the Nokia-Siemens joint venture, a large stake in the mobile system market. The last few years have, however, seen a number of important changes in the market for mobile phones. The recent successes of Apple in launching iTunes store and App Store, the growing dominance of Google and the introduction of their Android operating system, to name a few changes, put increasing pressure on Nokia. In May 2009, Nokia launched their version of the App Store, called Ovi Store. The Ovi Store has a number of similarities with Apple's App Store. The Nokia people have obviously used App Store as an important source of reference. For Nokia, the work with Ovi Store has shown that the company has developed a strong capacity for innovation and that they master the ability to reorient the company in the face of new demands and expectations. Whether Nokia will be able to meet the challenges from Apple and Google only the future can tell.

Innovation is defined as:

'The development and implementation of new ideas by people who, over time, engage in transactions with others in an institutional context'.
Van de Ven (1986: 591)

Just like Thompson (1969), Van de Ven (1986) underlines the institutional context of innovation, thereby suggesting that the capacity to innovate is anchored in the joint ability to both preserve instituted beliefs and practices, while effectively putting them into question.

To innovate is then to stand with one foot in the past and one in the future. Dougherty, speaking about 'products' rather than services or events, provides perhaps the most comprehensive definition of innovation.

DEFINITION BOX

Innovation according to Dougherty

'Product innovation' is defined as the conceptualization, development, operationalization, manufacture, launch, and ongoing management of a new product or service ... 'New' means new to the organization, and can involve customers, new uses, new manufacturing, new distribution and/or logistics, new product technology, and any combinations of these'.
(Dougherty, 1999: 175)

While the other definitions have emphasized the *content* of innovation, that is, its inherent components and its relationships to organizational capacities, Dougherty (1999) took a temporal perspective. Here, innovation evolved through a series of activities and operations, beginning with the concept phases and ending with the launch of the new product in the market. Much innovation research has adhered to this temporal perspective and examined the various phases and their relationships towards the finalization of the new product. A similar perspective is provided by Slappendel (1996) who defined innovation accordingly:

'The term "innovation" is also used to refer to the process though which new ideas, objects and practices are created, developed, or reinvented. In its broadest conceptualization, the innovation process typically embraces periods of design and development, adoption, implementation, and diffusion.'
(Slappendel, 1996: 107–108)

Again, innovation is what is first initiated inside the firm, mobilizing available resources, and then gradually brought to the market. This change of perspective from the inside of the firm to the market is common trajectory for the innovation in the literature. Some of the complexities involved in defining innovation in relation to other concepts are discussed in the link box below.

LINK BOX

The differences between research and development

The concept of Research and Development (R&D) is a notoriously slippery term where the line of demarcation between what is 'proper research' and 'mere development' is difficult to define once and for all. While *research* tends to denote more generic, basic research, *development* is mostly used to refer to actual product or service development activities. Chalmers University, described in the introductory case, has made a point of participating in this melting pot of research and development. Boundary crossing, between academia and practice is being institutionalized, and collaboration between research groups at Chalmers and companies is abundant. However, critics claim that state-funded research in, for instance, the European automotive industry is primarily as a form of thinly veiled state support for nationally owned companies, such as, Renault in France or FIAT in Italy, or privately owned firms, such as, Volvo and SAAB in Sweden, that still rely on state-funding to finance more long-term research. For these critics, there is little research in R&D funding simply because there are few radical innovations provided on the basis of such activities. As a consequence, it is rather unfortunate that research and development activities have historically been bundled as if there were only marginal differences between these two terms. Chalmers, as well as most technical universities, has to understand the crucial differences between the two, and find ways of excelling in them both. Many companies are also struggling to make sense of the differences between the two, and they have found that research and development are different and that it takes different approaches to master both of them.

Reflection point: Research and development are important activities in many companies, and they require a lot of managerial attention. How can research and development activities be organized to optimize the success of each of them?

Perspectives on innovation

As was emphasized by Pavitt (2005), the field of innovation research is diverse and includes a variety of perspectives. In Wolf's (1994) review of the innovation literature, three distinct research questions are identified. First, a field of research explores how innovations are 'diffused' in society, that is, how innovations are distributed, adopted, and eventually modified to suit idiosyncratic needs and conditions. Second, a domain of research explores the factors that determine organizational innovativeness. This perspective takes a more intrinsic look at the individual firm, and identifies the assets and resources that are correlated with high innovativeness. Third, a specific school takes a process perspective on innovation activities and explores the various stages and phases through which an innovation is produced.

In Wolfe's (1994) view, the three perspectives are complementary although they take different approaches to innovations. The first view explores the patterns of diffusion, the mechanism and processes of the adoption of the new service or artefact. The second view examines the assets and resources *inside* the individual firm or a network of collaborating firms. This rather static view, conceiving of the relevant assets and resources as stationary entities under the control of clearly bounded organizational units, is complemented by the third perspective on innovation, which conceives of innovation as what is produced in a series of events and occurrences, that is, innovation is produced under the influence of temporality. Here, innovations are the outcome of the collaboration of a number of often heterogeneous actors, including for instance, various forms of engineers, designers, and marketers.

The innovation phases

As suggested by Dougherty (1999), the innovation work passes through a series of phases on its way to the market. Speaking about 'the conceptualization, development, operationalization, manufacture, launch, and ongoing management' of the innovation, Dougherty (1999) points to the various competencies and skills involved in the process. During the early phases—often referred to as the 'fuzzy front-end' of the innovation process—specific competencies are demanded, especially in terms of detecting and analyzing 'weak signals' from the market in terms of what goods or services the existing and potential customers might demand in the future. In the development and operationalization phases, engineering and design skills are needed to translate specifications into tangible artefacts. Most larger firms have R&D departments that specialize in working on innovation projects in the stages in-between the concept phases and the actual production of the new product. After the R&D department has managed to turn concepts into actual artefacts, the manufacturing department must have the competence to put the new product into production. With flexible production technologies and work organizations, new innovations can be introduced into the production schedules with lower costs and shorter time spans. Finally, once the new product is ready for its launch in the market, market departments must have strategies for how the new product will fit into the existing product portfolio and how it will be positioned in the market. The launching of a new product is a major event for many companies in many industries and it is accompanied by intensive collaboration with various organizations and stakeholders in the firm's environment including journalists and suppliers. Seen from this view, the innovation work is best conceived of as a process wherein a series of succeeding activities and events are organized and objectives and goals are accomplished. Pavitt (2005: 86) spoke of three distinct phases in the innovation work: 'The production of knowledge; the transformation of knowledge into artifacts—by which we mean products, systems, processes, and services; and the continuous matching of the latter to market need and demands'. To be capable of producing an innovation, the focal firm needs to develop or acquire the know-how demanded for this specific objective. Thereafter, this know-how or knowledge is transformed into an artefact (or service). Finally, the innovation is managed in the marketplace through various marketing activities. Pavitt (2005) emphasized the 'matching' of the innovation and 'market needs and demands'. This is a somewhat unorthodox view of innovation work that in most cases tends to emphasize the phases prior to the very launch of the product or service. However, whether an innovation will be regarded as successful or not, essentially depends on its success in the market. Therefore, arguably, Pavitt (2005) integrates the marketing phases into the innovation perspective.

Angle and Van de Ven (2000) spoke of three phases of the innovation work:

(1) The initiation period,

(2) The developmental period,

(3) The implementation/termination period.

This separation into phases is widely recognized in the innovation literature. In the more normative innovation literature, there is a strong emphasis on managing such *linear* innovation processes, providing a number of so-called stage-gate models and tools for structuring, organizing, and monitoring the innovation process. For instance, Gantt-charts are popular tools for creating an overview of increasingly complex innovation processes. However, research on innovation work suggests that innovation work rarely follows a linear pattern (Dodgson, Gann and Salter, 2005). Instead, innovation processes are non-linear or complex. Decisions are made in a garbage-can decision-making manner (i.e., solutions may precede the problem rather than the other way around) and events that should have been passed return to the agenda. In general, there tends to be strong path-dependencies and lock-in effects in innovation work, that is, historical decisions and choices strongly determine what leeway there may be in the emerging innovation work, and technology choices limit the possibilities. Altogether, the professional and seasoned innovation project leader uses linear models of the innovation process to enact and structure a complex social and material reality, but is in fact aware of the limitations with such a model. Rather than being able to plan the entire process, the innovation project leader has to muddle through a complex and non-linear process, rich with emerging properties and unknown conditions and factors. Innovation work is, by definition, characterized by factors not known from the outset, and therefore the innovation project leader needs to be capable of handling and responding to merging events and occurrences.

The social nature of innovation

While much innovation research emphasizes the activities in-house, i.e., inside the focal firm engaging in the innovation work, it is increasingly popular to conceive of innovation work in terms of being part of a broader social system wherein institutional factors and conditions strongly influence and determine the innovation work. Factors such as motivation, creativity, and playfulness have been more systematically addressed in the innovation literature. For instance, Angle and Van de Ven (2000: 669) emphasized that innovative capacity is largely a matter of leadership practice: 'People generally have the potential to be innovative. The actualization of this potential turns on whether management develops an organization context that not only enables, but also motivates individuals to innovate'. They continue: 'Innovators are often mavericks, fitting the classic description of the entrepreneur who is not comfortable with authority relationships. This type of personality has been termed 'counterdependent' by personality psychologists' (Angle and Van de Ven, 2000: 689–690). Innovation work is often initiated by individuals that are entrepreneurial in their orientation. In an organization or company pervaded by an innovation ethos, these 'mavericks' are not treated as sources of concern, but as important drivers for change and creativity. While many organized activities are established to create predictability and transparency, these entrepreneurial and creative individuals are often at odds with the prevailing innovation system, and new ideas are often quenched before they are further developed. In the history of technological innovation, there is ample evidence that there is a substantial educational challenge facing the innovator. New technologies have to be carefully grounded in pre-existing social institutions and practices to become viable. This is illustrated in the minicase below.

MINICASE

The challenge of establishing the idea in pre-existing social institutions and practices

Nye (2006) presented the following examples:

> At first, Samuel Morse had trouble convincing anyone to invest in his telegraph. He spent five years 'lecturing, lobbying, and negotiating' before he convinced the US Congress to pay for the construction of the first substantial telegraph line, which ran from Washington to Baltimore. Even after it was operating, he had difficulty findings customers interested in using it. Likewise, Alexander Graham Bell could not find an investor to buy his patents on the telephone, and so he reluctantly decided to market it himself. Thomas Alva Edison found few commercial applications for his phonograph, despite the sensational publicity surrounding his discovery … In the mid-1970s, a prototype of the personal computer, when first shown to a group of MIT professors, seemed rather uninteresting to them. They could think of few uses for it, and they suggested perhaps it would be most useful to shut-ins. In short, the telegraph, the telephone, and phonograph and the personal computer, surely four of the most important inventions in the history of communications, were initially understood as curiosities. (Nye, 2006: 41)

These historical examples show that innovations are not always embraced immediately, and that the advantages of new technologies are not obvious from the start. Numerous contemporary examples of this can be given, and it certainly shows that there are social and cultural dimensions of innovation that are important to acknowledge. Crucial questions thus arise concerning how to plan for these aspects of innovation.

Technologies that today serve as the bedrock for the contemporary society such as the telephone or the personal computer were, Nye (2006) suggests, 'understood as curiosities'. The innovator faces not only legitimate technological and economic questions regarding the viability of the technologies, but also something much worse: common sense thinking. In order to gain recognition for new technologies, innovators need to connect their innovation to pre-existing institutions. Hargadon and Douglas (2001: 476) suggested that 'One cultural determinant of an innovation's value is how well the public, as both individuals and organizations comprehend what the new idea is and how to respond to it'. They continued: 'When innovations meet institutions, two social forces collide, one accounting for the stability of social systems and the other for change'. Further evidence of the institutional complications involved in industry–university collaboration is given in the link box below.

LINK BOX

Innovation at the interface between industry and universities

The opening case suggests that systematic industry–university collaboration is difficult to accomplish because of differences between industry being primarily concerned about short-term goals and objectives (an effect of the 'quarter economy', governed by the financial markets), on the one hand, and the university system, focused on placing the emphasis on producing new scientific knowledge, on the other hand. As the innovators (Samuel More and others) suggest, there are significant hurdles that need to be overcome before new practices or new artefacts may be considered useful or interesting. Therefore, the emerging university–industry collaboration is still in its infancy. It is likely that in the future, industry–university collaboration will count for a much higher share of the innovation work than is the case today. Learning from history, new ways of working and new ways of thinking are likely to be recognized only after significant, so-called, 'incubation periods'. The increasingly intensive collaboration between industry and universities, and the Chalmers case is not unique in this respect, also suggests that collaboration between organizations is an important part of innovation processes. In many industries, research and development leading to innovation are carried out together between different parties in the forms of networks, joint ventures, inter-organizational projects, and the like. This is very much in line with the new forms of organizing, and the more open boundaries between the organization and its environment, that were discussed in Chapter 2.

Reflection point: As recent research suggests, collaboration between organizations is becoming a more and more common practice in innovation processes. How should innovation be organized when more than one organization is involved?

Innovations first demand change and thereafter create change. Institutions provide stability. In-between the two, the innovator needs to enrol as much political, technical, and financial support as possible. Akrich, Callon, and Latour (2002a,b) speak of the process of enrolling partners and spokesmen for the new innovation as, (with a French term) the *inter-essement*, the process of making individuals interested and involved in the new innovation. They emphasize the unknown and emerging factors which influence the innovation work:

> 'An innovation in the making reveals a multiplicity of heterogeneous and often confused decisions made by a large number of different and often conflicting groups, decisions which one is unable to decide a priori as to whether they will be crucial or not.'
> (Akrich, Callon, and Latour, 2002a: 191)

As a consequence, the innovator needs to gain legitimacy and political support from 'significant individuals' either within the firm or in the firm's environment:

> 'Since the outcome of a project depends on the alliances which it allows for and the interests which it mobilizes, no criteria, no algorithm, can ensure success a priori. Rather than speak of the rationality of decisions, we need to speak of the aggregation of interests which decisions are capable or incapable of producing. Innovation is the art of interesting an increasing number of allies who will make you stronger and stronger.'
> (Akrich, Callon, and Latour, 2002a: 205)

The innovator feeds on hope; he or she cannot promise anything, and therefore needs all the allies that may be enrolled. Success is never assured until the product or service has

been proven to be financially viable when launched on the market. Like the technology innovators examined by Nye (2006), the innovator needs to convince a sceptical public and targeted audiences (e.g., banks and politicians) that the new innovation is capable of changing
society for the better. Using the well-known (and on the border of being exploited) case of
Thomas Alva Edison, 'the Wizard of Menlo Park', one of the most emblematic innovators in
the modern times, Akrich, Callon, and Latour (2002b) locate Edison's genius in his very ability to enrol allies as partners in his innovation work:

> 'Edison is everything but a handyman of genius. He is an organizer, an entrepreneur,
> a strategist, a researcher, a public relations man and if there is any genius, it is in this
> ability to pass from one role to another and to play each of them with equal delight,
> that it must be situated.'
> (Akrich, Callon, and Latour, 2002b: 215)

As historical accounts of Edison's work suggest, Edison had a significant ability to
respond to public demands and political expectations in order to support his ideas and his
technological apparatuses. For instance, when America was electrified, Edison possessed the
ability to tell intriguing stories, characteristic of the popular press at the time (including sex-
ist remarks and mystical speculations), thereby positioning himself as a provider of technological wonders beneficial for mankind:

> 'Edison expressed utopian ideas about the uses that were characteristic of the popular
> press. He predicted that electrification would eliminate the distinction between night
> and day and the speed up of women's mental development, making them the intel-
> lectual equals of men. Constant light might lead to the elimination of sleep. In later
> years he even hinted that he was experimenting with electric ways to communicate
> with the dead.'
> (Nye, 1990: 147)

Edison knew instinctively that in order to make the broader public adopt his innovations, the technologies had to be accompanied by effective and intriguing storytelling. Akrich,
Callon, and Latour (2002b) strongly underline this aspect of innovation work: innovations
are of necessity a threat to an established social order and therefore 'resistance to change'
needs to be mediated by narratives of progress and bright futures:

> 'The innovator can only put himself in the hands of some (very) rare speakers, of whom
> he never completely knows who and what they are representing, and whether indeed they
> really are representing him. Doubt, trust, then gratitude and admiration, or on the con-
> trary, suspicion, defiance, and even hate, are at the heart of innovation. These passions do
> not come to interfere with the work of the engineer or researcher; they are the innermost
> and fundamental constitutive elements of their work. This is why it is pointless to try to
> separate the human factors and the technical factors, passions and reasons.'
> (Akrich, Callon, and Latour, 2002b: 222)

The same view is advocated by Doughtery and Heller (1994), speaking about innovations as factors that are 'violating' instituted practices:

> 'They (innovations) either violate prevailing practice, inside or outside of the firm, or
> require ways of thinking and acting that are 'undoable', or 'unthinkable', albeit in

intractable or opaque ways. The activities of product innovation, therefore, are illegitimate.'

(Dougherty and Heller, 1994: 202)

The world of the innovator is never solely technological. As soon as the technology leaves the workshop, the laboratory, or the R&D department, it becomes associated with other instituted beliefs and assumptions. The innovators thus need to forge alliances with various legitimate spokesmen and proponents of the technology to make the technology gain recognition and legitimacy in the broader public. This 'cultural' perspective on innovation is captured by Hung (2004):

'The power to innovate ... derives not so much from individual actors, but from their identification with, and appropriation of, the structural context. These distinctive notions in characterizing the structure are particularly identified: 'regime' as a knowledge base; 'paradigm' which embodies a model and a pattern of enquiry; and 'tradition', which is cognitively based. The spread of regime, paradigm or tradition comes partly through the emergence of dominant designs and partly through the prevalence of technological guideposts.'

(Hung, 2004: 1481–1482)

Expressed differently, innovation work is always a process strongly shaped and influenced by predominant social and cultural beliefs. No innovation can survive in a socially and culturally hostile milieu. In essence, technology is socially and culturally determined. A compelling illustration of the links between innovation and social and cultural beliefs are given in the minicase below.

Edison and recorded music

Numerous historical examples suggest that it is complicated to anticipate the full scope of a technical invention. One example is Edison's invention of the phonograph, whose patent application is dated 19 December 1877 (Gitelman, 1999). For Edison, the phonograph was regarded as an aid when taking notes, that is, it was conceived of as a recording machine and a device used in administrative and other serious matters. Notwithstanding Edison's alleged genius, he thought of his invention in terms of 'preservation' rather than 'mass replication' (Attali, 1985: 91). Neither Edison nor any others were capable of seeing the phonograph as a medium for recorded music and entertainment. Since there was an established industry for orchestras providing live music in music halls and other public venues, 'no one foresaw the mass production of music' (Attali, 1985: 92). Today, we are exposed to recorded music everyday, and it is getting increasingly problematic to escape music altogether. A study conducted by the BBC, where listeners were asked to keep diaries and carefully record all music, including bird song, ring tones, and radio jingles, that they listened to during a 24 hour cycle, found that on average, an individual listened to an average of 2 hours and 46 minutes of chosen music as against 1 hour and 16 minutes of unchosen (White, 2007). It is somewhat curious that Edison and others failed to see this market opportunity for the new apparatus. It was only in 1914 that the first symphony was

MINICASE

recorded for the phonograph. It took almost 37 years to finally conceive of the phonograph as a medium for 'mass replication'. Today, the phonograph is regarded primarily as a forerunner to the gramophone, the CD player, the mp3 player, and other media for recorded music. Other technological innovations suggest that innovators tend to reserve their technologies for high-brow matters and thereby underrate the social consequences of the innovation. For instance, the developers of the modern telephone were disappointed when they learned that the telephone lines were used by housewives to have a chat rather than being a communication system exclusively used for the sharing of important information. Innovations are rarely linear and users tend to influence and shape technologies through their use.

Systemic view of innovation

While some innovation management research schools emphasize the social and practice-based views of innovation, other researchers take a more systemic view of how innovations are produced in what has been called innovation systems, that is, interrelated fields of organizations that mutually support and help one another. An innovation system may, for instance, include end-producers, suppliers, universities, governmental institutes and organizations, and active consumer organizations. By collaborating over organizational boundaries, and with coordinated, yet not shared interests and objectives, such innovation systems may be effective arenas for new innovation work. Van de Ven and Poole (2000: 32) expressed such a systemic view of innovation:

> 'A theory of innovation is fundamentally a theory of change in a social system. While *innovation* is defined as the introduction of a new idea, the *process of innovation* refers to the temporal sequence of events that occur as people interact with others to develop and implement their innovation ideas within an institutional context. *Events* are instances when changes occur in the innovation ideas, peoples, transactions, contexts, or outcomes while an innovation develops over time. *Change* is an empirical observation of differences in time in one or more dimensions of an entity.'
>
> (Van de Ven and Poole, 2000: 32)

Distinguishing between the process of innovation and the actual event taking place, Van de Ven and Poole (2000) conceived of innovation work as a string or series of events that accumulated to produce the new innovation. At the same time, one must not reduce the innovation process to a linear flow of events. As many studies show, there is a strong tendency that the innovation process is non-linear and complex: 'The tendencies to reduce complex innovation processes to simply unitary stages and their lack of empirical substantiation suggest that many of the process models in the literature are suspected of being simply inadequate.' Schroeder, *et al.* (2000: 113) remarks.

The systemic view of innovation adequately represents the innovation process in specific industries. The construction industry, for instance, is characterized by loose organizational couplings, i.e., individual firms and organizations collaborate on the construction site but lack an integrated management, and tight technological couplings, i.e., technological changes in one part of the construction has implications for other parts. Since various organizations have to be strongly coordinated to accomplish a new technological innovation, the construction industry innovation system emerges as what Winch (1998) called a 'complex product system' demonstrating the following characteristics:

- Many interconnected and customized elements organized in a hierarchical way,
- Nonlinear and continuously emerging properties where small changes to one element of the system lead to larger changes elsewhere in the system,
- A high degree of user involvement in the innovation process.

(Winch, 1998: 269)

Innovations in complex product systems are inherently interactive and demand coordination between the micro and the macro levels of the system. 'Innovations on complex product systems are inherently interactive with the rest of the system—innovating within the parts, while losing sight of the whole is inherently dysfunctional' (Van de Ven, 1986: 598). In the case of the construction industry, the ability to coordinate complex innovation products is rather limited, and consequently, there is a continuous debate in the industry and in the construction management literature on how to promote innovations in the industry. One of the targeted explanations for this low innovation capacity is the project-based organization of the industry, promoting only the project goals (i.e., on the micro level), while 'losing sight' of the macro level, the construction industry system. 'Because every project is unique and there are few possibilities for repetition, there is little reason for a building contractor to invest in innovation beyond the optimization of his own processes, which means that economies of scale and learning effects are largely absent' (Drejer and Vinding, 2006: 922).

By and large, the systemic view of innovation work underlines the interrelationship between a number of organizations, conditions, and factors in an industry or a region. Rather than assuming that innovation management capabilities derive from individual accomplishments and skills, innovation is here treated as what emerges in the joint collaboration between various actors. Innovation management capabilities can therefore not easily be reduced to the level of the individual actors without losing the understanding of how the broader milieu is affecting the innovation work.

Innovation and organization forms

On the intermediate level, between that of social practice and the larger innovation system, a number of innovation management studies examine the role of the particular organization form and its ability to handle the complex and often non-linear innovation process. The assumption is that the size and the structure of the organization play a central role in influencing the innovation management capabilities of the individual firm. A starting point for this discussion is the assumption that organization size is negatively correlated with innovative capacity; the larger the organization the smaller the relative innovation output. Sharma (1999) claimed that bureaucratic organizations—here a synonym for a large organization—are relatively poorly equipped for promoting innovativeness and creativity. Sharma (1999: 146–147) argued:

> 'Many observers of innovation note that the bureaucracies that govern large firms suppress both the creativity necessary to generate radically new ideas and the initiative necessary to build them into businesses. The elaborate administrative systems and the accompanying risk-averse attitude burden entrepreneurial initiatives with seemingly mindless procedures that dampen flexibility and responsiveness. The mechanisms that facilitate predictability and order in existing operations smother the entrepreneurial flair necessary to deal with the unpredictable and disorderly innovation process.'

Bureaucratic organizations praise transparency and predictability in its operations. Work is regulated by relatively narrow standard operating procedures and new thinking and creativity are not prioritized in the bureaucratic organization form. In a study of innovation management work in 15 'very large firms', Dougherty and Hardy (1996: 1121) found that 'most of these firms were not organized to facilitate innovation: occasionally innovation did occur, but it occurred in spite of the system, not because of it'. That is, in comparison with smaller firms and organizations, large firms have a declining marginal cost for innovation. For every penny invested in innovation work, the less innovation is produced as the size of the organization grows. However, this criticism of large firms has not been uncontested. Craig (1995), presenting a study of innovation work in the Japanese brewery industry, suggests that the bureaucratic structure of Japanese breweries, structured around highly skilled and experienced experts, in fact promoted innovation. Since innovation work is, as Joseph Schumpeter (1942) suggested, a combination of pre-existing knowledge, the bureaucratic organization serves as an arena where such bits and pieces of know-how can be effectively brought together:

> 'Bureaucratic means are useful not only for overcoming specific organizational weaknesses, but also for providing stability and discipline to the product development process and the organization as a whole. While newness and raw creativity are often thought of as the key ingredients in new product development, as Von Hippel points out, 'most innovation projects in most firms do not involve great novelty'. As important as novelty is, the discipline provided by an organizational arrangements and procedures that guide and facilitate the efficient transformation of inputs and ideas into a marketed physical product ... product development is a purposeful, not a haphazard, activity.'
> (Craig, 1995: 33)

Given these features of the innovation process, Craig (1995: 32) is critical of the research suggesting that large-scale, bureaucratic organizations are incapable of hosting innovative work. His Japanese brewery case is one example of how large organizations are in fact capable of promoting new and innovative ideas:

> 'The bureaucratic machinery of an organization is not necessarily a blocker of innovation and change, but can be used effectively to promote it. Bureaucracy is one of the dirtiest words in business, signifying unresponsive, slow, and costly. Yet one of the

most striking aspects of Japan's beer companies in the 1980s is their use of bureau-cratic means such as formal working arrangements, systems, and procedures to achieve goals—innovation, responsiveness, and change—that are the exact opposite of what bureaucracy generally represents.'

(Craig, 1995: 32)

Rather than organizing the innovation work in a large-scale structure, large organiza-tions are capable of imitating the smaller companies and their short distances for communi-cation and their ability to handle creative thinking. In other words, large organizations often organize their innovation work into small departments or even specific divisions or inde-pendent institutes or companies. Damanpour (1992: 395) reported:

'A survey of 4,000 innovations and innovative firms in the UK over four decades has shown that the average size of innovative firms is increasing, but the average size of divisions within those firms is decreasing (Pavitt et al., 1989). Therefore, it appears that large innovative organizations are creating the required flexibility and autonomy needed for innovation by founding smaller (more specialized) divisions, while main-taining the advantages associated with large size.'

(Damanpour, 1992: 395)

A similar finding is reported by Argyres and Silverman (2004) who found that the location of the R&D department within the organization structure strongly affected the type of innovation promoted: 'We find that firms with centralized R&D organization structure (i.e., corporate-level R&D labs only) and centralized R&D budget authority (i.e., funds coming from corporate headquarters) generate innovations that are significantly different along sev-eral dimensions from those generated by firms with decentralized R&D organizations' (Argyres and Silverman, 2004: 930). In decentralized R&D departments, innovations were more specific while the innovations produced by centralized R&D departments were more general. The findings of Damanpour (1992) and Argyres and Silverman (2004) are thus consistent with Alfred Chandler's (1962) much-cited formula 'structure follows strategy': the strategy leads to certain decisions regarding organization structure. A well known example of innovation as a strategy is given in the minicase below.

Innovation at Google

There are many companies that have made a name for themselves as innovative, and there are a few companies that have managed, over a short time span, to grow at phenomenal speed thanks to a high rate of innovation. One of the best examples of rapid growth through innovation is Google. Employing approximately 20,000 people, Google can be characterized as an organization with bureaucratic elements. In spite of size and short time of existence, Google was, in 2010, reported to be the most valuable brand in the world. An explanation of the success is its general focus on innovation which, according to their web page, encourages every employee to share their ideas and opinions. To facilitate this, almost every employee is reported to have their lunch at the Google café where they sit wherever

MINICASE

MINICASE

there is an available place and talk with everyone. As part of the employment contract every employee has to spend twenty per cent (20%) of their working time working on innovations. This slot cannot be reserved for other working tasks. The search engine 'Google scholar' is a result of this twenty per cent (20%) innovation time. Hence, it took one employee who spent six months of his innovation slot developing this tool, which today enables students, researchers, and others all over the world to find current research results in various areas. There is of course much more to the story of innovation at Google than just making it a part of the employment contract, but the case clearly shows that it is perfectly possible to develop an organization where innovation is part of the daily work.

While much innovation management work is commonly located in either the regular organization, or in specific R&D divisions or R&D departments, the latest trend and topic of discussion in the popular and academic management literature is the emergence of network-based innovation work. Rather than being located in one or a few sites, innovation, in this view, emerges in the network of relations between firms and organizations in the form of alliances, joint ventures, collaboration, and so forth. This is further explored in the link box below.

LINK BOX

Innovation in networks

The idea of research and development being carried out in networks of organization, and also drawing upon the strengths of universities is not entirely new. Universities have been an important source of knowledge for companies, and contacts between the two have been taking place for a long time even though the intensity is much higher nowadays. At Chalmers, collaborating with industry partners is part of the daily life, and as argued in the case introduction, universities can provide effective trading zones for innovation. Chalmers has developed the idea of research centres that focus attention on specific areas of interest, and where companies are invited to participate. These centres are, however, far from easy to manage. There are constant problems with understanding between the different parties—the university professors complain that too much time is devoted to producing products and services, while industry representatives have a hard time understanding why so much attention is focused on writing and publishing articles and books. There are institutional differences between industry and universities, and these differences must be understood and addressed if collaboration is to be successful. The same issue with differences in culture, expectations, ambitions and attitudes can be found in virtually any type of collaboration between two or more organizations, and the differences between industry and universities are not unique. From the perspective of the actual work being carried out in innovation projects involving more than one party, these institutional differences can be difficult to handle, and they certainly have an impact on the results of innovation projects.

Reflection point: When engaging in collaboration with another organization—how can you make sure that there is a solid understanding between the two parties?

In the literature and in the popular press and media, there is a tendency to favour a one-best way solution to problems in the field of innovation management. For instance, the quest for the optimal firm size in terms of innovation is a discussion that tends to overlook the obvious differences between industries and firms. In general, there is a belief that small firms are better equipped to accomplish innovations, partially because of shorter communication paths, informal structures, and partially because of the mere pressure to produce innovations that can safeguard long-term survival. In reality, in many industries, there is a need for access to advanced technology and many domains of expertise to orchestrate innovations, and therefore much innovation work is primarily conducted in large-scale firms. For instance, in the pharmaceutical industry, the pressure to invest in new advanced laboratory technologies and equipment is great and favours the largest firms with the financial resources, the hubs of innovation networks. By and large, when taking into account the firm structure and the demands to have access to state-of-the art technology, small firms are generally overrated and large firms relatively underrated in terms of accomplishing innovations. This debate is however far from exhausted.

Innovation in networks

One of the major tendencies in the last decades with the emerging knowledge economy is for innovation work to be increasingly organized in the network form. That is, rather than being developed in closed R&D departments, new products are developed across organization boundaries. For instance, Powell, Koput, and Smith-Doerr (1996: 119) in studying the medical technology industry in the Boston region in Massachusetts, USA strongly emphasized the value of networks:

> 'We argue that when knowledge is broadly distributed and brings a competitive advantage, the locus of innovation is found in a network of inter-organizational relationships ... To stay current in a rapidly moving field requires that an organization have a hand in the research process. Passive recipients of new knowledge are less likely to appreciate its value or to be able to respond rapidly. In industries in which know-how is critical, companies must be expert at both in-house research and cooperative research with such external partners as university scientists, research hospitals, and skilled competitors.'
> (Powell, Koput, and Smith-Doerr, 1996: 119)

Since advanced, state-of-the-art knowledge is in essence specialized and broken down into components, it is difficult for one single firm to hire all the required expertise in-house. Instead, such knowledge may be distributed over a large number of firms and through collaboration new innovations are enabled. 'Established pharmaceutical firms', Powell, Koput, and Smith-Doerr (1996: 124) continued, 'have been unable to create internally the kind of research environment that fosters continuous innovation and discovery. So the various participants in biotech have turned to joint ventures, research agreements, minority equity investments, licensing, and various kinds of partnerships to address their lack of internal capabilities and resources'. While the medical technology cluster in the Boston region is arguably one of the most distinct and knowledge-intensive clusters in the world, one may wonder if these observations are of relevance for other regions and industries as well. Powell and Grodal (2005: 57) reported that an American Research Council assessment of 11 US-based industries found that in every sector there was 'increased reliance of external sources of R&D', such as, universities, consortia, and government labs, as well as domestic and foreign competitors. They concluded their analysis as follows:

> 'Complex networks of firms, universities, and government labs are critical features of many industries, especially so in fields with rapid technological progress, such as computers, semiconductors, pharmaceuticals, and biotechnology.'
> (Powell and Grodal, 2005: 58).

In a variety of industries, there is an increased emphasis on collaborating over organizational boundaries. Even though this tendency may be further accentuated in knowledge-intensive and research-intensive industries, the whole spectra of industries operate within a network form or structure to accomplish their innovation work. In the case of Chalmers University of Technology, there is a strong orientation towards tripartite collaboration between the state, the university, and partnering firms. However, issues of organization of the research centres within the conventional bureaucratic organization structure, and the right to the intellectual properties jointly produced, remain some of the concerns for researchers and industry participants. Despite these issues, there is a strong sense among the faculty that the university could make a worthwhile contribution to the community when collaborating more closely with industry.

Summary and conclusions

Not only does innovation work produce new goods, services, and events for the benefit of the broader community, innovation is also a source of renewal in organizations. Greve and Taylor (2000: 72) found that industries that engaged in innovation work demonstrated a higher degree of change than comparative industries with lower degrees of innovativeness. Innovation is in many ways the primus motor in the contemporary capitalist economic regime. However, innovation is by no means subject to the strict application of rational principles but is instead embedded in intricate social relations. All innovation is, in effect, an act of creation, and therefore one needs to understand the context of the innovation work to understand how innovations are produced. For some researchers, innovations are by definition always Trojan horses brought into a hostile world and therefore they have to be aligned with broader social interests. For other researchers, innovations are instead combinations of already existing materials and solutions. In other words, innovation work is a bundling of old goods or services into new assemblages. However, in both perspectives, innovation is always produced in open-ended processes, the end product of which cannot be fully anticipated, but is in a state of becoming or 'in-the-making'. As a consequence, the management and leadership work in innovation work needs to demonstrate appropriate sensitivity to new and intriguing ideas, even in cases when they may be premature and consequently, regarded as all-too-visionary or even absurd. Foresight and tolerance are two of the distinguishing marks of the skilled manager of innovation processes.

Study questions

- In what ways can innovation be defined?
- What are the phases in innovation work?
- What is the relation between the organization and the innovation?
- Would organizational bureaucracy hinder or enable innovation?
- What are the advantages and disadvantages of organizing innovation work in-house?

Literature recommendations and further readings

The literature on innovation is broad and diverse. Introductory texts such a Dodgson (2000) or so-called *handbooks* (e.g., Fagerberg *et al.,* 2005) are the best way to approach the field. The social nature of innovation is accounted for in an excellent way by Akrich, Callon, and Latour (2002,a,b), but can be complemented by a variety of more ethnographic or even journalistic studies of innovation (e.g., Werth's *The one billion molecule,* a study of a biotechnology start up in the Boston region). Powell, Koput, and Smith-Doerr's (1996) study of innovation in networks in the Boston region's biotechnology industry is a common reference supporting the argument that innovation is becoming distributed in networks of organizations. For readers more interested in innovation, there is a range of journals dedicated to the topic, for instance *Research Policy, R&D Management,* and *Creativity and Innovation Management.* The so-called 'general management journals' (e.g., *Academy of Management Journal* or *Journal of Management Studies*) also frequently published studies on innovation.

Take your learning further

http://www.oxfordtextbooks.co.uk/orc/erikssonzetterquist/

online resource centre

Visit the Online Resource Centre which accompanies this book to enrich your understanding of this chapter.

Students: explore web links and further reading suggestions. Keep up to date with the latest developments via 'What happened next' updates to appropriate cases from within the book.

Lecturers: you will find seminar exercises and teaching notes, for use in class or assessment.

CHAPTER 9
Balancing radical change and continuous improvement

Healthy Eyes for Life

The year 2008 had proven to be yet another profitable year for Ciba Vision, despite warnings about a world economic slowdown. The eye-care subsidiary of the Swiss pharmaceutical giant Novartis managed to spur growth by seventeen per cent (17%) for the first half of 2008, as well as having sales growth of 13% and net sales in Consumer Health of 12%. Ciba Vision was created in 1980 under a technology licensing agreement with Titmus Eurocon, a German contact lens manufacturer. Initially, its headquarters were in Bulach, Switzerland, but are now located in Atlanta, USA, along with its main R&D and manufacturing units. After Ciba Vision acquired Titmus in 1983, a second major manufacturing and R&D unit was set up in Grosswallstadt, Germany. Ciba Vision continued to expand its operations and presence around the world by further acquiring companies.

Ciba Vision has grown from a start up to a company selling more than $1 billion, but its growth path was not always carefree. Although at the beginning of the 1980s Ciba Vision was the pioneer of a few innovations, namely bifocal contact lenses and the first tinted contact lenses to be approved by the USA's FDA, the company became a distant second to one of its main competitors, Johnson & Johnson in 1987. It was in 1987 that J&J introduced the first disposable contact lenses (the 7-day disposable lens) after a technological breakthrough and completely dominated the market. Although Ciba Vision developed its own double-sided moulding process it did not manage to recapture large market shares because J&J had had a first mover's advantage.

At the beginning of the 1990s, it became clear to then President Glenn Bradley that if Ciba Vision wanted to maintain its top position in the eye-care market and regain its leading spot, it would have to continue making incremental changes and coming up with breakthrough products at the same time. This decision did not come lightly and not without trial and error. After all, the company had never been good at combining the two. Three years passed before Bradley took a final stand and only after a failed large enhancement programme initiated with the hope of improving business. The program was initiated in 1989 and aimed at cutting costs by enhancing automation, rationalizing process flows and improving process controls. Unfortunately, although it was supposed to make operations more efficient, the program only brought to light the deep-rooted challenges the company was facing. According to many, lack of communication, running too many projects at the same time, insufficient human resources for the projects, etc., were all part of the challenge.

Over the course of the enhancement program many meetings were held but nothing substantial was achieved. It was at that point that then CEO Walter Patton decided to open a new manufacturing facility in Indonesia as a cost-saving move, because Ciba Vision could take advantage of local low wages and tax concessions while producing the mature line of soft lenses that did not need much supervision or technical support.

In 1991 the executives of Ciba Vision met in the headquarters in Switzerland to discuss what could be done to get out of its precarious situation. It was clear that innovations were necessary, but Bradley believed that some restructuring was also needed. He proposed that Ciba Vision develop 2 new products—a daily disposable lens, the research for which would be carried out in Germany, and an extended-wear lens, the research for which would be in Atlanta, but would be organized as an autonomous unit from the one that already existed there.

It was not the potential technical difficulties of developing the novel products that brought about emotional outbursts at the conference table. It was true that no suitable material for extended wear had yet been developed which could allow for good oxygen permeability for the lens. There was also a concern that if daily disposable lenses would be developed, their rather low price (they had to be inexpensive enough for consumers to be willing to dispose of them everyday) would be associated with low quality. However, the main problem was that no one knew how such units would be able to function, how to manage them, and how to incorporate them in the existing organizational structure. The existing marketing division insisted on doing more research prior to allocating the whole budget to only a few projects. Furthermore, the Atlanta division was afraid that it was only getting the project leftovers by not working on either of the large projects. Not only that, but Ciba Vision would have to focus on both developing the new lens and achieving an enormous cost breakthrough—something that the company had not been good at before. Also, by locating one of the projects in Germany, should the R&D be successful, manufacturing would have to also be done there, which would incur higher production and wage costs. Last but not least, the executives felt that if these projects were successful they would cannibalize the existing lucrative business of soft contact lens production. These concerns pointed to high risks.

After the meeting Glenn Bradley launched six different projects and cancelled all small projects in the company to free both financial and human resources. The new projects consisted of four product development projects and two new manufacturing projects. As all of them required different technical skills, they were all organized as autonomous units, each with their own R&D, marketing, and finance divisions as well as project leaders. The project leaders were requested to report to the same executive and also to sit with Bradley at executive meetings. This allowed for separate cultures and processes to form, independent of the traditional business units' influence. At the same time, since all units shared the same executives, they could also take advantage of, and were encouraged to share the expertise of, the traditional business units. A new vision statement was created and although it was only a symbolic gesture it gave a common cause to all employees—'Healthy Eyes for Life'.

The results are staggering. More than 15 years later, Ciba Vision has managed to launch a new series of contact lens products and become either first or second in the contact lens market. Apart from being first in the market with daily disposable and extended-wear lenses, it has pioneered lenses for correcting astigmatism and was the first company to launch fashion coloured lenses. It also pioneered a new lens manufacturing process that allowed it to cut production costs and has managed to overtake J&J in various market segments as a result. Furthermore, the traditional business units have remained profitable and they supported the autonomous units at the beginning by generating the needed funds for some of the projects.

Ciba Vision is well documented in the literature and this case description uses information from a variety of sources, including information from **www.ciba.com** and from **www.optitianonline.net.** Garret (2004) also gives a detailed account of the strategic development of Ciba Vision.

Questions

The case of Ciba Vision shows the need for balancing radical change efforts with continuous improvement. What organizational arrangements need to be in place to find this balance?

What specific methods and techniques can be applied to carry out change in organizations?

Combining different approaches to change in an organization requires dedicated leaders. How can a company like Ciba Vision develop the leadership capacity on different managerial levels and functions?

Introduction

Few would question that organizations need to change. As Goshal and Bartlett, in their Managing Across Borders (1998), point out—'The world's largest companies are in flux'. The Ciba case shows how a determined and consistent approach to change can help an organization develop its position in a highly competitive market. There are many lessons to be learned from the case and this chapter aims at exploring a number of aspects of change in organizations. A major theme in the Ciba case is the ability to balance between different types of change, incremental as well as radical, through the creation of autonomous units.

Through a new organizational arrangement the company managed to create a change in focus in the organization. This should, however, not be taken as a simple recipe for change in any organization. In the Ciba case it worked to the benefit of the organization. This is partly due to a successful choice of structural changes (the introduction of autonomous units) and partly due to the skilful management of the change process.

Many textbooks on organization theory in general, and **organizational change** in particular, assume that change is a structured and planned process by which an organization moves from one steady state to another. It is tempting to view an organization as a stable entity that, sometimes, is subject to change. A typical textbook definition is given below:

> **Organizational change** is the process by which organizations move from their present state to some desired future state to increase their effectiveness.
>
> (Jones, 2010: 192)

This assumes that stability is the normal order of an organization and that change disrupts this stability. We are not challenging the view that people in organizations often initiate and carry through planned changes. As the case introduction shows top managers spend a lot of time contemplating the need for changes, and many middle managers participate in the implementation of change efforts. This, however, is not the full picture of change in organizations. A strong case can be made for viewing change as a normal part of the day-to-day management of organizations, and that it, in fact, is the normal order rather than the exception. Tony Watson (2002: 418) describes the area of **change management** in the following way:

> 'An integral part of all managerial work that (a) copes with the changing patterns of resource input and knowledge available to work organisations and the shifting demands

made upon them by the parties with which they deal, and (b) initiates changes that managers perceive to be in their interests or the interests of those who employ them.'

Mastering technology through continuous improvement at Shimano

Many companies claim to have understood how to be change oriented and to survive and prosper in the long run. The truth is, rather, that companies have problems achieving long term growth and being able to cope with the demands for change they face in different eras, and it is not always the high-profile companies that are most successful. A good example of successful change management is the Japanese company Shimano, well known for their high quality cycling and fishing equipment. The company started by producing cycling equipment in 1921 and has, over the years, proven that they can cope with changing circumstances and can draw upon the strengths of the organization to move into new directions. Some new inventions such as external and internal speed changers were put on the production line in the late 1950s. It came as a little bit of a surprise when the company announced that they would move into the fishing sector—at the outset it appeared to be quite a change of orientation. The fishing tackle division was established in 1970 and the fishing operations are now a world wide operation. As in the cycling sector, Shimano has established itself as a world leading innovator. The trademark of Shimano is highly ingenious technological solutions with an ability to produce high quality equipment with high tolerances. Innovation is built into the organization, but rather than making big jumps the company is proud of continuously improving the product line in small steps towards perfection.

In this chapter we will present a number of perspectives, approaches, and theories that can enhance the understanding of change in organizations, ranging from the view that change is a *planned process* of taking an organization from one stable stage to another, to the view that change is an *emergent process* that is part of the ongoing processes of managing organizations. The field of change in organizations is rich and rapidly growing, and it is way beyond the scope of this textbook to cover all different perspectives in depth.

Our major emphasis is on understanding the nature and driving forces of change in organizations, but we will also briefly introduce the methods and techniques for managing change efforts. The literature on change methods is usually covered in textbooks on organizational behaviour and organizational development. We, however, feel that a brief account of this stream of research is also relevant for a textbook on organization theory.

It is also important to acknowledge that change can take different forms in organizations. Organizations differ in how they approach change, both in terms of the scope and ambition of change efforts as well as the philosophies they build on. A major theme in the literature on change deals with the scope of change, and we present two basic perspectives here. The first perspective views change as a continuous process of improvement. By making a number of small, incremental changes the end result, viewed over a longer time period, can be a substantial change compared to the initial state of the organization. The second perspective argues that organizations need to make company-wide, radical changes to achieve necessary results, and many authors claim that this is one of the key factors in gaining competitive advantages and for long term survival (Volberda, 1998). The two perspectives are clearly indicated in the link box below.

LINK BOX

Balancing radical and continuous change in Ciba

When organizations are facing demands for change they can choose different strategies for mastering the change. Even though it is an oversimplification to say that there are only two perspectives available, they still point at two major directions in which change can come about in organizations. A major theme in this chapter is that the two perspectives are not mutually exclusive. In the Ciba case above, finding a balance between continuous improvement and more radical change efforts was a major priority for top management, and the case also shows some of the techniques for managing the two forms of change. The company was facing a severe threat and they needed to take decisive steps to catch up with the current market leader—this called for radical change. At that point in time, and considering the history of the company, there was probably no alternative to a radical change effort. At the same time top managers in the company realized that implementing a radical change effort would not be sufficient to create and uphold a position as market leader. In addition to the radical change efforts described in the case description above, the company also initiated the work to redesign the manufacturing process to enable the autonomous units to both excel in innovation and in keeping a strong cost-focus. There was a growing awareness in the management team that they could not rely solely on one-time change efforts.

Reflection point: Change in organizations is traditionally assumed to be a major effort that takes place infrequently. Together with this view the view that change is a continuous process is gaining ground. How do you think these two perspectives can be combined in an organization?

This chapter will:

- Present the development of the field of organizational change and describe the major theoretical perspectives on change,
- Introduce the reader to an institutional perspective on change in organizations,
- Describe two managerial approaches to change in organizations—continuous improvement and radical change,
- Discuss in depth the concept of resistance to change; its origin, processes and consequences.

Change as a planned process—traditional views

Above we presented an overview of the chapter and introduced some of the perspectives on change. We now move over to present the major theoretical perspectives on change. Reviewing the literature on change makes it clear that change can be described in numerous ways, and it is not obvious within the field of change in organizations how change should be conceptualized. The concept of change has a number of meanings and uses that are relevant for our understanding of organizations. In this chapter we are primarily interested in planned efforts to carry out change in organizations but also how change can come about in the absence of a completely planned and rational process. The concept of change carries a number of meanings that we don't explicitly cover in the chapter. We are not dealing with individual change and the multitude of perspectives in the field of individual psychology. Some of these perspectives are, however, presented in Chapter 10 on learning in organizations, where behavioural and cognitive perspectives on learning are discussed.

Planned organizational change—the early advocates

The idea that 'organizations' can be deliberately managed is not new. If we also consider nations, states, and other administrative groups of people to be organizations, the idea is indeed old. In his Republic, Plato described the principles of the ideal state and he laid out a number of principles for the governance of a society. Even though the modern student of Plato could find his ideas anti-democratic, the Republic still makes interesting reading for anyone interested in the management of organizations. A word of caution is however needed. Plato did not explicitly talk about organizations the way we know them. His focus was on society at large, and how a small number of 'guardians' could govern a larger group of people. The same goes for a number of influential writers during the history of Western thinking who gave important input to political theory as well as to the practical management of states, churches/congregations, businesses or armies (Plato, Paul, Machiavelli, Marx, and others). The idea that organizations, per se, exist and can be managed is, on the other hand, fairly new.

When, for instance, Henri Fayol (1916) defined the basic functions of administration (planning, organization, leading [from the French *commandement*] coordination and control) he assumed that any type of organization (he was mainly discussing industrial organizations) could be properly managed. From a more behavioural perspective Chester Barnard (1938) tried to create a complete theory of organizations as social systems and how they, once understood, could be managed. Neither Fayol nor Barnard was explicitly discussing change as a prioritized activity in organizations, and we had to wait another few decades for a more explicit focus on change in organizations.

In the 1950s a number of influential authors made important contributions to our understanding of change in organizations. Below we give a few examples of leading thinkers that, from different perspectives, defined organizational change as an important managerial activity. One of the early authors to address change in the context of organizations was Philip Selznick. In his book, *Leadership in Administration* (1957), he argued for a change of perspective, from organization to *institution*. Inherent in his definition of institutions was that they are subject to change.

> 'An "institution", on the other hand, is more clearly a natural product of social needs and pressures—a responsive, adaptive organism.'
> (Selznick, 1957: 5)

Selznick was neither describing the driving forces for change in and around organizations nor the principles by which change is carried out. His major contribution was rather to move from the more mechanistic view of organizations to a more social and adaptive view. In his classical case study of an industrial organization (*Patterns of Industrial Bureaucracy*), Alvin Gouldner (1954) described important processes of change. He was in particular interested in the processes of bureaucratization, and how managerial initiatives (changes implemented by a new plant manager) led to the growth of bureaucratic organization. Gouldner's use of a single case study has been a source of inspiration for the empirical study of organizations, and he gave clear evidence that organizations do change and provided a lot of observations on the driving forces of change as well as the process of change.

Perhaps the most influential writer on change in the 1940s and 1950s was the German/American psychologist Kurt Lewin. His work on group dynamics and organizational development and change is still a major source of inspiration. Lewin conceptualized change as a process emerging in what he called *force fields* (Lewin, 1951/1997). Any type of social event, for instance, the initiation of a change project, depends on the social field as a whole. This implies that there are many *interdependencies* that influence the outcome of change efforts. Periods of change in a social field are different from periods of relative stability, and Lewin was interested in describing and understanding the prerequisites for change, including both the motivations for and resistance to change. Depending on the structure of the social field different psychological forces characterize the direction and strength of change in the field. When the forces in the social field promoting change are stronger than the forces resisting it, change can occur.

Lewin saw change as a process in a social field (could be an organization or any type of social system) of moving from the present level to a desired one. This process, in order to be successful and lasting, should pass through three stages: *Unfreezing* the present level, *moving* to the new level, and *freezing* group life on the new level (Lewin, 1951/1997: 330). In processes of change Lewin noticed that there are forces that strive to keep the organization at the present level and change initiatives run the risk of being short lived, for instance when there is a conflict between driving and restraining forces. In the link box below the unfreezing phase is illustrated.

LINK BOX

Unfreezing Ciba for change

Kurt Lewin's model of change—unfreezing, change, and refreezing—is useful to understand the process of change in the Ciba case. The case description does not go into depth on the change process as such, and there are many more details that need to be added in order to understand all the complexities involved in a major change effort. It is still clear from the case description that the unfreezing phase was a bumpy ride, and it took a failed change initiative to bring about the necessary awareness of the need for change. The enhancement program that was initiated in 1989 made it perfectly clear to the management team that the company was facing substantial challenges, but it was not until 1991 that the CEO was able to launch a more consistent change effort (and thus move to Lewins second phase—change). A triggering event was the gathering of senior executives in the headquarters in Switzerland to discuss the challenges of the company. The meeting surfaced a number of tensions and made it clear to the

CEO that the current organizational structure was less then optimal for achieving the desired balance between incremental and radical change. The case shows that the unfreezing phase can take quite some time, and it also shows the importance of mental awareness of organizational change efforts. Preparing the organization for a change effort, including trying to make employees understand the rationale for change is very important, and it requires time and dedicated efforts from many managers in the organization.

Reflection point: A major point made in this link box is that the success of a change effort requires a carefully managed unfreezing phase. Why do you think that the unfreezing phase is so important in the process of change?

Planned organizational change—a systems view

In the open system view of organizations (see Chapter 2 for an introduction to open system theory) change is, by definition, an integrated component in organizations. In trying to keep the character of the organization in a stable state, the organization tries to adapt to its environment. In the open system view the assumption is still that stability is the preferred and natural state of an organization, and it borrows from Lewin the view that change is a planned process of transition from one steady state to another. The inclusion of the environment as a determining factor for how to organize a company makes it, however, necessary to develop Lewin's view on change. Even though he was emphasizing the driving forces he was mainly referring to the psychological determinants of change rather than the external factors that trigger change within organizations.

The open systems perspective on organizations was thoroughly summarized in Katz and Kahn's (1966) *The Social Psychology of Organizations*. They devoted two chapters of the book to describing the nature of change and different approaches to managing change. The open system view of change emphasizes the following aspects:

- Change in a system requires an understanding of the system as a whole and how different parts of the system influence each other.

- Change in a system requires an understanding of the environment and the adaptive processes needed to survive.

- Change in a system requires an understanding of organizations as basic feedback systems, where information is processed and used in managerial processes. Change should be viewed as a structured process where information is fed into the change processes from the beginning to the final evaluation of the change effort.

- Change in a system requires an understanding of the point of entry, that is, the origin of the change attempt (could be a managerial decision or any event that triggers a change effort).

The last point above indicates that change can be viewed as a strategic, decision-making problem of defining the need for change as well as staking out the content and direction of change. The open systems view on organizations, including the contingency theory that we described in Chapter 2, contains a rich variety of ideas and concepts that are useful for our understanding of change. Buckley (1967) uses the concept of *morphogenesis* to describe the processes in a system that changes the system, including learning, growth, and differentiation. A fundamental assumption in the systems view is also that the systems that are most alert to the demands from the external environment, and thus manage to change in reply to demands, are also most likely to survive.

Change as an emergent process—the view of institutional theory

In the previous section we presented the development of the field of organizational change, and we presented theories within the field viewing change as a planned process in organizations. Another perspective on continuous improvement and radical change by organizations comes from institutional theory. While the rational perspective of organizations views the organization as a tool where people, in choosing between different alternatives, decide on the most rational alternative and thereafter carry out this alternative, advocates of institutional theory believe that the management of change, for example, in organizations is rather the consequence of the organization's environment. Here it is assumed that organizations are influenced by (and influence) their environments that consist of other organizations. It is this environment that changes organizations, for example, as a response to the fad for change that is popular at the moment.

Institutional theory as it is used in organization theory has its roots in studies by Thorsten Veblen, Max Weber, Emile Durkheim, and Karl Polanyi, and also in phenomenology (DiMaggio and Powell, 1991). The fundamental idea is that institutions grow as people construct their social reality (Berger and Luckmann, 1966). Institutional theory in organization theory emphasizes that organizations are in institutional frameworks that form their goals and methods. Richard Scott has expressed this idea as follows:

> '... institutional theory reminds us that interests are institutionally defined and shaped ... Institutional frameworks define the ends and shape the means by which interests are determined and pursued. Institutional factors determine that actors in one type of setting, called firms, pursue profits; that actors in another setting, called agencies, seek larger budgets; that actors in a third setting, called political parties, seek votes; and that actors in an even stranger setting, research universities, pursue publications.'
> (Richard Scott, 1987: 508)

The concept of the institution has many different meanings and even in organization theory the concept has many different meanings, where those who have taken that perspective often have used only preliminary definitions (DiMaggio and Powell, 1991).

Ronald Jepperson (1991: 145) defined institutions and institutionalization as follows:

> 'Institution represents a social order or pattern that has attained a certain state or property; institutionalization denotes the process of such attainment. By order or

pattern, I refer, as is conventional, to standardized interaction sequences. An institution is then a social pattern that reveals a particular reproduction process. When departures from the pattern are counteracted in a regulated fashion, by repetitively activated, social constructed, controls—that is, by some set of rewards and sanctions—we refer to a pattern as institutionalized. Put another way: institutions are those social patterns that, when chronically reproduced, owe their survival to relatively self-activating social processes.'

Thus, one may assume that an institution points to an organized and established procedure that represents a social order. A later definition of the institution comes from 'The Sage Handbook of Organizational Institutionalism':

'... more-or-less taken-for-granted repetitive social behaviour that is underpinned by normative systems and cognitive understandings that give meaning to social exchange and thus enable self-reproducing social order.'
(Greenwood *et al.*, 2008: 4–5; italics in the original)

The emphasis thus is a taken-for-granted management pattern that has grown out of the interaction between different people who create the normative system that is transmitted down the generations.

The new institutional theory

There are two main ideas in institutional theory that explain the influence of the environment and therefore how organizations change to become more stable entities. These ideas are organizational fields and isomorphism (DiMaggio and Powell, 1983/1991).

Organizational fields shows how the environment is created by and shapes organizations. The organizational fields consist of, for example, companies in the same industry or companies that are linked in the supplier–producer–seller relationship. It is evident that even when organizations lack direct contact with each other, they nevertheless influence one another by cultural and normative processes. The fields thus include organizations that have an acknowledged role in the institutional lives of organizations so that even organizations that deliver raw materials create restrictions or possibilities (DiMaggio, 1983). Other such organizations include those that provide knowledge or professional valuations (DiMaggio and Powell, 1983/1991). As part of an organizational field, organizations achieve the legitimacy they require in order to obtain resources and competent staffing and whatever else they need for their survival (Meyer and Rowan, 1977).

Isomorphism explains how organizations tend to become more and more like each other in form. After a field has been established, the demand for homogenization arises—with isomophism as the result. DiMaggio and Powell (1983/1991: 66) define isomorphism as 'a constraining process that forces one unit in a population to resemble other units that face the same set of environmental conditions.' There are three forms of isomorphism: coercive, mimetic, and normative. *Coercive isomorphism* is the result of political pressure by government regulations and control (e.g., legislation), and of coercion from stronger organizations in the same field that force the weaker organizations to adapt to their formal and informal demands. *Mimetic isomorphism* arises when organizations find themselves in uncertain situations. In these circumstances, organizations may model themselves after other organizations they think successful; in this way, they avoid having to solve their own problems. The modelled organizations may not even realize that they serve as a handy source of practices for other organizations to imitate. *Normative isomorphism* comes from professional pressures and the influence of education on organizations. An example is when certain professional members try to define the methods and relationships applicable to their work and thereby characterize the nature of their professions.

The foremost change for organizations is that, in their attempts to survive, they become more like each other—that is, the influence they have on each other is greater than the inner dynamics of their organization. An example is given in the minicase below.

Changes related to environmental issues

Since the 1960s the chemical industry in the USA has undergone significant changes as a result of the renewed environmental movement. In 1962, Rachel Carlson's book, *Silent Spring*, with its study of the environmental effects of pesticides, had an enormous impact that meant sweeping changes for one organization field. In the beginning the chemical manufacturers tried to stay away from the controversy, but gradually they were forced into conversations with the field. The field consisted of the governmental authorities, scientific organizations and groups that opposed the use of environmental contaminants. Other significant events followed the publication of *Silent Spring*—the death of thousands of fish in the Mississippi River in 1964 in an area where pesticides were used, and the first Earth Day in 1970. Together, these events called much greater attention to the issue of environmental pollution. In December of 1970, the U.S. Environmental Protection Agency (EPA) was established in the presidency of Richard Nixon. The EPA became an organization with a formal structure that could act as the opposition party to the chemical industry in court cases. Thus the EPA assumed a more formal role than the loosely structured volunteer organizations that had brought the environmental issues to the attention of the general public.

As a result of these various events, the organization field grew as new institutions developed and the understanding of environmental issues increased. By the end of the 1980s, even companies in the chemical industry had begun publishing, in their annual reports, commentary on environmental issues and their programmes to reduce environmental pollution. They also began to employ environment managers to help them handle these issues (Hoffman, 1999).

Scandinavian institutionalism

While new institutional theory has focused on how organizations change by becoming more stable through homogenization, Scandinavian institutionalism emphasizes that stability and change exist in parallel. By studying practices, we can see, that organizing is oriented around management instead of decisions (Brunsson and Jönsson, 1979). A research area in Scandinavian institutionalism concerns changes that follow reforms. A study from 1990 questions whether the traditional conception of reforms, which seem rational and carefully evaluated, leads to the desired result (Brunsson and Olsen, 1990). One may ask: Why is it so difficult to carry out reforms according to the set goals? Why is it so difficult to achieve these goals? Why is it so difficult to learn from previous reforms? Brunsson and Olsen (1990) show that if organizations are understood as institutions, it is evident that it is difficult to make changes in an organization that is mature and relatively fixed in its routines.

If a reform is to succeed, it is fundamental that both the reformers and the organization members share actively in the work. Additionally, the organization's plan, key symbols, and ways of managing must change. Furthermore, reforms may fail when the reformers and members do not agree that a particular reform offers a successful solution. People may also oppose a reform as a problem solution, for example, when organization members either want better insights (or simply, already have better insights) on how the present organization operates.

These ideas have been developed further in the sociology of translation where people have asked why changes in many organizations occur simultaneously, why people follow the same change models and why previous ideas seem to be repeated. In other words, people study changes that depend on other ideas and fashions (Czarniawska and Sevón, 1996). The starting point is that an idea is transformed to a specific connection where it will be used. Translation is an analogy for the process by which such practices and structures are spread among organizations (Czarniawska and Joerges, 1996). Change ideas, then, are a mixture of intentions, chance incidents, and institutional norms that are adapted and transformed to ideas and material objects.

Czarniawska and Joerges (1996) deal with the question of where ideas originate and where they travel to, arguing that organizations imitate popular ideas about practices and solutions. The effect of an idea is strengthened by the isomorphic power that causes more and more organizations to follow fashionable ideas. However, when an idea becomes widespread, accepted by many organizations, it begins to lose its popularity. Then the organizations that originally had the idea look for a new fashion. In this way, change continues and the organizations that accept the ideas use them differently.

Types of change in organizations

We have so far presented a number of theoretical perspectives to capture and understand change, ranging from theories that directly address how to carry out change efforts (planned change), to theories that are more descriptive and try to depict how change is actually carried out (emergent change). We will now move over to discuss the scope of change efforts. It was evident in the Ciba case, that introduced the chapter, that they worked with two very different types of change efforts, one that emphasizes that change is best managed in small, incremental steps, and the second one arguing that change should be dealt with in a system-wide way (see the link box below).

In the literature on change in organizations, a number of ways of capturing different types of change have been proposed, and we have chosen to contrast two of them—*change*

LINK BOX

Continuous improvement in Ciba Vision

It is clearly a risky strategy to rely solely on radical change efforts. There is a growing consensus, among both researchers and practitioners, that change is a process that can come about in many small steps, and the combined effects of these small steps can lead to dramatic change. This, however, requires a change of mindset that needs a lot of managerial attention. Ciba Vision faced a lot of uncertainty in trying to catch up with Johnson & Johnson, the world leader at the time, and this caused a lot of concern in the management team. The development of a daily disposable lens raised questions about the customers' perception of the company—would they be associated with low quality? The strong emphasis on developing new products also raised questions about the organizational structure—was it really possible to incorporate the autonomous units in the existing structure? It was also clear that the company needed to cut costs while at the same time focusing on development of new products. The solution to the organizational problems was to make sure that the project organization reported back to the regular organization. The six autonomous units that were created reported to the same executives, and the project leaders also participated at executive meetings. The new organizational structure with the matrix between projects and the permanent organization has proven successful. The company has managed to both develop new products and to continuously cut production costs, and in this way find a good balance between more radical change efforts and continuous improvement. The case also shows that it takes decisive organizational measures to enhance the capacity for continuous improvement. In the Ciba case a new organizational structure was implemented to help in this.

Reflection point: Why do you think it is a risky strategy to rely solely on radical change efforts to develop and adapt an organization to changing demands?

as continuous improvement efforts and *change as radical, system-wide efforts.* In the definition box below we give examples of a number of dichotomies that have been suggested in the literature on change and strategic management. It is obvious from this list that there seems to be some agreement on the existence of two fundamentally different types of change efforts.

DEFINITION BOX

Types of change

Continuous improvement	Radical, system-wide
Organizational development	Organizational change (French *et al.*, 2005)
Incremental change	Revolutionary change (Hamel, 2000)
Incremental change	Discontinuous change (Handy, 1989)
Segmentalism	Integrated action (Moss Kanter, 1983)
Transactional leadership	Transforming leadership (Burns, 1978)

Many authors, for instance Hamel, Handy, and Moss Kanter in the definitional box above, have a more normative purpose and therefore promote one side of their dichotomy, and this masks the necessity for both types of change. Below we describe the two models of change, and the reader should bear in mind that they are not mutually exclusive.

Change as radical, system-wide efforts

There is no question that organizations often try to carry out change efforts that radically alter old ways of structuring and managing the organization. The more popular business press is filled with success stories of business turn-arounds, involving major changes in the internal operations. It is also assumed that organizations need this form of change to sustain competitiveness. Less is, however, known about the processes and results of radical change efforts.

The term radical change suggests that the change involved is deeper and more far-reaching than other types of change, and that it involves a higher degree of uncertainty than small scale change. Radical change is often described as jumping into the unknown that requires a different mindset in the organization. It is often events and activities in the external environment that force the organization to act. A basic assumption in the literature on change is that radical change requires a change in the underlying values and belief systems, and that it therefore has consequences for the whole organization. Failure to understand and deal with deeply held, and hard to change, values and attitudes is also an often attributed reason for failure in radical change efforts (Fiol and O'Connor, 2002; Huy, 1999). Jarvenpaa and Stoddard (1998: 16) describe radical change in the following way:

'Radical change changes the deep structure of the organization. Such a change unfolds rapidly and alters fundamentally the basic assumptions, business practices, culture, and organizational structure. High levels of identity crisis, disorder, and ambiguity are associated with radical change.'

A growing body of research describes the underlying processes of radical change and there is ample evidence of the complexity of change in organizations. Below we summarize some of the recent findings on the processes and outcomes of radical change under three headings.

Radical change involves fundamental changes in belief systems. With the so-called *interpretive turn* in the social sciences it became clear to many organization theorists that there are important cognitive aspects of change in organizations. Drawing upon the ground-breaking work of Berger and Luckmann (1967), a number of authors started to study the role of human enactment and social action in the context of change (Björkman, 1989). In a much cited article, Daft and Weick (1984) described organizations as interpretation systems, putting the effects of managerial cognition and cognitive processes at the forefront. With this emerging stream of research came a growing awareness that radical change is strongly linked to the belief systems in the organization. This link between change and belief systems has, at least, two important aspects. First of all, radical change often requires changes in the belief systems—the whole strategic intent with radical change is usually to move away from the current way of operating and the beliefs that guide that. Secondly, radical change would be hard to carry through without strong beliefs and values. These two aspects put managers in front of the challenge of *unfreezing* the current set of beliefs, at the same time as they contribute to *installing* a new set of beliefs. The vast and rapidly growing literature on organizational culture and organizational identity, has, however, cast doubt over the possibilities of managers to control the processes of change in belief systems. The role of culture in organizational change is thoroughly described in the minicase below.

Changing the culture in mergers and acquisitions

Cisco, the American producer of routers and other network equipment, has experienced rapid growth and change which is the very essence of Cisco's strategy. Cisco has made it an integrated part of their growth strategy to acquire companies and to rapidly integrate them into the Cisco organization. The company has understood that a successful integration involves a transformation of the culture. By 2010 Cisco had completed close to 140 mergers and acquisitions, and with this experience the company has learned how to master the integration process; cultural change is now an integrated part in the transformation process when a new company is bought. The company has a well developed technique for making the necessary 'cultural change' in the acquired company. When acquiring a company Cisco uses a generic integration strategy in three steps: Assessing the company, Integrating, and Monitoring. The integration phase is crucial and depending on the size of the acquired company different considerations have to be made. For Cisco it is very important to align the IT/network infrastructure and business processes to make sure that the new unit 'breathes and thinks' Cisco. For each acquisition Cisco put together an integration team that works intensively with the integration process, and usually the new unit is completely integrated into the Cisco structure. The team put special emphasis on the integration of people and they have a high rate of employee retention after acquisitions. Employees in the acquired companies are often surprised to find that they, within days, are provided with new business cards, titles, access to computer networks, incentive schemes, and new managers. It is widely acknowledged that speed and professionalism is of utmost importance in the integration process. An important part of the Cisco culture is the focus on community and collaboration, and newly acquired units are rapidly 'hooked up' to the rest of the organization and stimulated to collaborate within the Cisco network. Cisco also takes special care to communicate plans and timelines for the integration to avoid resistance and speculation.

Information on Cisco's acquisition strategy and processes is publicly available at **www.cisco.com**.

MINICASE

Radical change involves highly politicized processes. Radical change not only involves changes in beliefs and belief systems, it is obvious that it both threatens established political positions and interests as well as being driven by such interests. The idea that organizations can be described as systems of coalitions and comprised of groups of interests is old, and it was pointed out, for instance, by Chester Barnard (1938) that people in organizations act based on specific purposes and ends. A political perspective of organizations was launched by Simon (1948), March and Simon (1958), and in particular by Cyert and March (1963), in an attempt to understand the underlying processes of organizing. A more detailed and accurate picture of the processes of change was given by Pettigrew (1973; 1985) in his case studies of large British companies on change, for instance, the single case-study published in *The Politics of Organizational Decision-making*, as well as the in-depth study of change in Imperial Chemical Industries published in the book *The Awakening Giant*. From a political perspective, change is understood and explained by concentrating on the bases and uses of power in decision-making processes in organizations. In radical change processes different coalitions and interests collide and use different political tactics to influence the change process.

Radical change involves the work of managers on all levels. It is easy to get the perception that radical change is a process driven by top management. Numerous studies indicate, on the contrary, that transforming change processes needs to involve managers on all levels in the organization. It is certainly both a neglected and important aspect of the growing literature on middle managers to emphasize their roles in strategic change processes, and how they contribute to, but also resist change. Radical change processes also challenge established role perceptions and identities, and can thus be used as opportunities for personal development. The middle manager's identity is thus not set once and for all. Middle management reality is in flux, and it is acknowledged by many observers that change is a crucial element in the day-to-day activities of middle managers, and that this leads to new roles (Westley, 1990; Brubakk and Wilkinson, 1996; Jaeger and Pekruhl, 1998; Balogun, 2003). Many companies are characterized by frequent and often radical changes resulting from both competitive and technological pressures (Feldmann, 2003), and this calls for a constant reflection on your own identity as a middle manager, and how this identity reflects and contrasts with organizational changes.

Change as continuous improvement efforts

There is a growing awareness in the field of change in organizations that large-scale, organizational change efforts are hard to carry out successfully. Burke (2008) discusses a number of reasons why major change efforts often fail to meet specified goals. Beyond the fact that it is very difficult to change the deeper layers of an organization (be it the culture or inherent ways of working), he mentions two more reasons. Firstly, it is hard to motivate major change efforts when things seem to be working fine. He argues that it is at the peak of success that the organization should start to worry. Secondly, the knowledge of how to implement change is limited, and that makes most of us amateurs on change.

Many authors support the view that a low risk strategy in achieving long term change is to implement change in small, incremental steps. When change is taken in small steps, goes the argument, it is easier to control the process and outcome of the change effort, and taken together, a number of small steps can produce astonishing results. The idea of continuous improvement originates from Deming and his work on quality improvement. Deming was Professor of Statistics and consultant in the field of quality and quality improvement. He is most well known for helping Japanese companies to improve quality. After the Cold War

Deming was invited to Japan to transfer some of his ideas on quality improvement to companies. Firmly set in the theory of open systems, Deming developed a coherent set of tools for working with continuous improvement in any organizational setting. Using statistical tools, Deming showed that it is perfectly possible to increase quality and cut cost, while increasing customer satisfaction and loyalty.

Continuous improvement, in a strict sense, can be defined as the creation of a culture of sustained improvement aimed at reducing waste in all systems and processes of an organization (Bhuiyan and Baghel, 2005). In a broader sense, it has grown to be a model for any type of change, and it is often described as a different way of achieving large-scale change in a step-wise process, rather than as a one-time event. A consistent strategy of continuous improvement is described in the minicase below.

Using microsystems to foster a culture of improvement

MINICASE

Many organizations have tried to follow the example of Toyota in persistently working with continuous improvement, and sometimes in sectors where you would not expect to find ambitious change agendas. The health care sector in any part of the world consumes enormous resources. Therefore, a top priority among politicians and managers is improving quality and effectiveness to ensure the money that is put into the health care system is put to good use. The county council of Jönköping, Sweden, with its 10,000 employees (primarily in health care) is a very good proponent of the continuous improvement movement, and is internationally renowned for its strong improvement focus. The county council has developed a bottom-up strategy for improvement work, based on the notion of *micro systems* as the area for improvement. A micro system is defined as the arena for interaction with the customer/client and the place where customer value is ultimately created. Using a variety of tools, the organization supports the improvement work within a large number of such clinical micro systems. The commitment to local improvement work has led to some amazing results in terms of both clinical performance, cost reductions and improved customer satisfaction. As a by-product, employee morale, involvement, and enthusiasm, is also considerably higher. Many employees now view improvement as a natural part of the daily work.

The minicase is based on material from original research by Tomas Müllern.

A growing number of authors have begun to realize that the two types of changes described above are not mutually exclusive. Some authors, writing from the perspective of business process re-engineering, suggest that radical re-design of processes and structures can be combined with a more evolutionary process. By keeping the ideals of radical change in the analysis and decision-making phase, and using a more evolutionary perspective in the implementation, Jarvenpaa and Stoddard (1998) try to combine the two models within the overall model of radical change. Finding the balance between radical change and continuity is a challenging task, and the minicase below describes some of these challenges.

Rapid change and sustainability in the Emirates

Change can be far reaching and touch upon the very culture of an organization or a region. One of the best examples of radical change, that problematizes the balance between change and continuity, is the case of the emirate Dubai (one of the emirates in the federation of seven emirates called the United Arab Emirates (UAE)). Dubai's economy has traditionally been dominated by the oil industry, petroleum, and natural gas, but the last decades have seen a rapid change, and the oil industry now accounts for only six per cent (6%) of the gross national product of Dubai. The largest revenues, over the last years, have come from financial services, and property and tourism, but the dependence on finance and property has proven to be risky. UAE was severely hit by the financial crisis in 2008 and it was evident that the growing dependence on the financial sector and the boom in property was a big problem. A good example of a company operating in the midst of demands for change and continuity is the Emirates, the official airline of the United Arab Emirates. Since its inception in 1985 the company has evolved into a globally recognized player. The company is fully owned by the Government of Dubai, but operates under fully autonomous commercial conditions. There is a growing awareness that protectionism is not a good business strategy and that it is perfectly possible to develop a modern airline without sacrificing the unique Arabic culture.

Facts and figures for the case were retrieved from official statistics from UAE. A thorough introduction to Dubai and the other Gulf states is given by Rehman (2008).

Resistance to change—why change efforts often fail

Change in organizations is bound to stir up emotions among employees, and resistance to change is a common reaction that has spawned a lot of research. It is fair to say that resistance to change is one of the more researched areas of organizational change. We will cover some of the most important aspects of resistance and how it influences planned organizational change efforts. There is general agreement among researchers that resistance is something that affects and influences change efforts. Whether resistance has a purely negative impact on change efforts is the subject of much debate. Recent research suggests that the traditional wisdom of overcoming resistance might be misguided and that resistance can have a number of positive consequences (Pardo del Val and Fuentes, 2003). Since change is not necessarily good for organizations, resistance can be viewed as an important signal to change agents that change efforts might not be necessary or that they might even be harmful. Resistance can also point at forgotten, neglected, and important aspects of the change process that might otherwise not be considered. It has also been pointed out by critical theorists that the term, resistance to change, is only meaningful if considered from managers' points of view, and that the interests of managers are often given priority over the interests of the workers (see Jermier, Knights, and Nord, 1994) for a critical review of the literature on resistance and power in organizations). Some authors also challenge the very notion of people being against change as such. We will come back to some of the critical views below, but we will start with a presentation of the dominant view on resistance to change.

Lewin, presented earlier in the chapter, was one of the first authors to deal explicitly with resistance to change. In a force field, there are forces that try to counteract change initiatives as well as forces acting for change.

'The practical task of social management, as well as the scientific task of understanding the dynamics of group life, requires insight into the desire for and resistance to, specific change.'

(Lewin, 1951/1997: 309)

More specifically Lewin argued that the source of resistance lies in the relation between the individual and values held by the group (what he refers to as value of group standards). Factors acting against change include fear of change, complacency of workers, reliance on current skills, and the need to maintain current performance norms (Sherman and Garland, 2007). It is also important to notice that, for Lewin, the handling of resistance resided in the group and how it managed to change attitudes or conduct. Lewin's model is abstract and it does not give much guidance on how to understand and deal with resistance to change. Many authors, however, have picked up on Lewin's ideas and an emerging literature has tried to pinpoint both reasons for resistance as well as advising on how to deal with resistance. The link box below illustrates resistance to change.

LINK BOX

Resistance to change in Ciba

One of the reasons why radical change efforts are risky to carry out is that they are often met with considerable resistance. This is, however, not a necessary feature of radical change, and carefully managed radical change processes can be run in ways that avoid too much resistance. It rather reflects how the change is implemented—the actual change process. The case introduction clearly shows that radical change ideas can meet with considerable resistance, and the Ciba case is no different in this respect. Within the management team individual members raised serious concerns about the consequences of moving into the disposable lens market as well as the market for extended-wear lenses. There was a lot of uncertainty voiced at the management team meeting, and there were also concerns from different departments that they would be excluded from working on the major projects. Both uncertainty and fear of losing influence are reasons for resistance that fit well with the theoretical review in this section. The cognitive effects of uncertainty are clearly visible here—people in organizations know what they have but not what they will get. This makes it harder for people to embrace the need for change. There seemed, however, to be a thorough understanding of the need for change in the management team, and the continued change process was marked by very good results. As was discussed in chapter six on leadership, having a clear vision and being able to communicate this vision, is an important part of modern leadership. The CEO, Glenn Bradley, spent a lot of time communicating the rationale for change.

Reflection point: Resistance often occurs in change processes, and it is often perceived to be harmful. Why do you think resistance occurs, and do you think it is always negative?

In their classical article, *Choosing strategies for change*, Kotter and Schlesinger (1979) describe a number of reasons why people resist change. In their article they observe that most change efforts encounter problems of various sorts and that many of these problems can be traced back to resistance to change. They describe the following reasons for resistance:

Parochial self-interest—people resist change because they think they will loose something of value if the change is carried out.

Misunderstanding & lack of trust—people resist change because they simply don't understand the implications, which can occur when there is a lack of trust between the change agent and employees.

Different assessments—people assess situations in different ways than managers and therefore see more costs than benefits.

Low tolerance for change—people resist change because they have different abilities to change, and organizations sometimes require people to change too much and too quickly.

There are a number of ways to respond to people resisting change, and Lawrence (1954) identified four ways for managers to act:

- Broadening staff interests: The problem with self-preoccupation can be dealt with by encouraging a broadening of people's interest in other areas then their own.

- Using understandable terms: Lawrence pointed at a typical gap between male managers' way of expressing themselves and the staff's views and understanding of this, and Lawrence recommended the use of understandable terms to deal with this problem.

- New look at resistance: Lawrence had observed a tendency for managers to expect people to resist change, therefore producing a self-fulfilling prophecy. He suggested changing perspective from viewing resistance as something to be overcome, to viewing it as a warning signal, a red flag that signals that something is wrong. This shifts the focus away from the resistance to the root causes of it.

- New job definition: Lawrence's final advice to managers is to change their perception of their own role, to appreciate and understand that he/she is dependent on the contributions of others to produce change.

In an attempt to summarize the research on resistance Pardo del Val and Fuentes (2003) identified three generic groups of reasons for resistance:

- Wrong initial perception of the need for change: This would include both a failure of the company to look into the future, as well as denial of problems and a tendency to go on as before.

- Low motivation for change: The authors identified a number of sources of low motivation, including the direct costs of change, cannibalization costs, and past failures.

- Lack of creative response: This impedes fast and complex changes in the environment, slows reactive mind-sets and reflects inadequate strategic vision.

In the general Organizational Development (OD) literature there seems to be an agreement that change can be managed and that resistance is inevitable, and needs to be met. The rich literature on OD suggests a number of possible interventions to deal with resistance.

Intervention is a concept that is important to the OD perspective, and it builds on the assumption that it is possible to carefully manage change processes. Chris Argyris (1970: 15) defines an intervention in the following way:

> To intervene is to enter into an ongoing system of relationship, to come between or among persons, groups or objects for the purpose of helping them.

Interventions to deal with resistance can be made in different ways and on different levels. The OD literature suggests that interventions are typically made either on the individual, the team, and/or on the organizational level (Anderson, 2010). The intervention is usually described as a process of going through a number of steps that try to address the root cause of an organizational problem. A generic structure of an intervention process typically looks as follows:

1. Identify a problem or an issue that needs to be addressed in the organization,

2. Derive the consequences of the problem for the organization,

3. Find out possible causes of the problem,

4. Define possible interventions,

5. Implement change effort,

6. Follow up.

The research based literature on resistance to change has focused very much attention on understanding the nature of resistance and the reasons for it. Less emphasis has been placed on researching how to overcome and/or deal with resistance, even though the more popular press is full of good advice. It is, however, very hard to evaluate different techniques for dealing with resistance and the research based literature usually refrains from giving such advice. There are a multitude of specific techniques for addressing change and resistance on the individual, team, and organizational level. On the individual level typical techniques that are used are coaching and mentoring, individual change and assessment instruments, career planning, and the like. In the literature on social psychology a number of tools are suggested to address change on a group or team level, most of which focus on making teams function in an effective way by clarifying roles and expectations, dealing with conflicts, and structuring meetings. Large-scale, organizational interventions typically focus on understanding and changing culture, structural re-design, and strategy changes.

During the last two decades, the literature on resistance has exploded and we have today a much better understanding of how people react to change and the factors that spur resistance, as well as motivation to contribute to change. One stream of research has focused on the unconscious mechanisms that help people cope with change, what is referred to as *defence mechanisms*. Research shows that people try to maintain a level of comfort, and external input can disturb this stable state. Defence mechanisms are ways to protect the zone of comfort, and avoid the pains of going from the known to the unknown (Bovey and Hede, 2001). The notion of defence mechanisms indicates that parts of the resistance can be accounted for by processes that are involuntary and used by the individual to provide relief from anxiety. Bovey and Hede (2001) make a difference between adaptive and maladaptive defence mechanisms. Individuals with high adaptive defence mechanisms, such as humour and anticipation, are more prone to support change efforts, while individuals with high maladaptive mechanisms, such as denial, projection, and acting out, generally resist change. They, in particular, found support for the idea that individuals that use humour were less likely to resist change.

Other authors challenge the assumption that people resist change. Dent and Goldberg (1999) argue that both researchers and practitioners are stuck in a mental model where resistance is a taken-for-granted fact of change. Their basic argument is that people do not resist change as such. What people resist is rather, the consequences of change, such as loss of status, loss of pay, or loss of comfort, which is something different than resisting the change in itself. Based on a literature review on the early literature on resistance to change, they identify the following problems with our understanding of resistance to change:

- The phrase 'overcoming resistance to change' suggests that the root of the problem is mainly within the subordinates.

- The prescriptions offered focus mainly on things the supervisors can do, and not on the ones supposedly resisting change.

- The literature confuses preventing resistance from occurring, with the techniques for overcoming it once it surfaces.

- Resistance is assumed to be natural and something to be expected in change efforts.

The authors argue for restoring more of a holistic, systems view of resistance, where resistance is treated more as a symptom of underlying problems and issues, rather than a problem in itself.

Summary and conclusions

Organizational change is one of the principal issues for practicing managers in their day-to-day life. It is consequently a major field of research not only in the field of organizational theory but in many social and behavioural sciences. Learning how to change organizations and their workers' behaviours and preferences is thus a social issue that is constantly addressed in organizations. Some researchers even suggest that in the capitalist society, there is nothing but a continuous change and therefore the very idea of 'organization change' as a discrete event is a mistaken idea as there is continuous and ongoing change within organizations. However, the human mindset often takes comfort in thinking that some things in life are stable and consequently organizational change becomes the transition periods where certain organizational configurations and certain regimes of organizing daily work are transformed into new arrangements. Such transition periods often demand patience and emotional energy on the part of the organization's workers as the taken-for-granted world of work is overturned and changed into something new. The management of organizational change, preferably a balancing of radical change and continuous improvement, is thus basically very much a matter of handling people's expectations and fears regarding an uncertain future where familiar routines and procedures are put into question or even abandoned. As a consequence, so-called organization psychology or industry psychology has been an influential domain of research in the organizational change literature.

Study questions

1. What are the main differences between planned and emergent change?
2. Account for Kurt Lewin's theory of organizational change.
3. What does the concept isomorphism denote and what kind of organizational phenomena can it help to explain?
4. Why do employees often resist change?
5. How can resistance to change be handled by managers?

Literature recommendations and further readings

The literature on organizational change is diverse and includes a variety of perspectives. For an authoritative overview of the field, see Collins (1998). On the one hand, there are a variety of 'how to change organizations' books written to direct and help managers cope with organizational change initiatives. This body of texts often provides overviews of the field and seeks to provide a few theoretical explanations for why people tend to resist change, and how one can deal with intellectual and emotional responses to change. On the other hand, the organizational change literature includes more scholarly works wherein a variety of theoretical perspectives and methodological approaches are used. For instance, institutional theory or critical management studies provide complementary perspectives on organizational change, where institutional theory sees organizational change in more neutral terms as the continuous adaptation to external changes in the organization's environment (see Bennis's *Changing organizations* (1966)), and where critical management studies scholars think of organizational change as being inherently political, always including a struggle between various members of the organization and stakeholders over authority and resources (see e.g., Collins's *Organizational Change* (1998) and Alvesson and Svenningson's (2008) *Changing organizational culture*). In addition to the research monographs and textbooks, there is an extensive literature published in organizational theory and management studies journals addressing organizational change. Journals such as *Journal of Organization Change Management and Industrial* and *Corporate Change* target organizational change research.

Take your learning further

http://www.oxfordtextbooks.co.uk/orc/erikssonzetterquist/

Visit the Online Resource Centre which accompanies this book to enrich your understanding of this chapter.

Students: explore web links and further reading suggestions. Keep up to date with the latest developments via 'What happened next' updates to appropriate cases from within the book.

Lecturers: you will find seminar exercises and teaching notes, for use in class or assessment.

CHAPTER 10
Managing learning and knowledge in and between organizations

The Melfi Model—a learning factory

During the 1980s the automobile manufacturer Fiat experienced a major crisis that resulted in inferior product quality, low productivity, and conflicts between the union and the company's management. To deal with the crisis, Fiat management and the union cooperated on an experimental design project. A key group of 1000 knowledge workers received intensive training at Fiat's head office. Their task was then to travel to 'the greenfield site at Melfi' in southern Italy where they were to help build a new assembly plant.

Fiat's goal was to build a learning factory. Of the people chosen for the project, seventy per cent (70%) were controllers and accountants with higher education but little experience of factories. The intensive training for these people, which consisted of classroom lessons as well as practical exercises, had two goals: to form a socially homogeneous group of employees with a strong 'commitment' to both the project and to the company; and to develop highly educated knowledge workers who 'thoroughly understood production assembly in the overall system of industrial manufacturing' (Lanzara and Patriotta, 2007: 641). The idea was that these knowledge workers would develop a common understanding and culture of industrial values, as well as a common idea of how the integrated factory should be organized.

A group from Fiat consisting of top managers, consultants, and professional trainers decided on the organizational values that the group should acquire. These values consisted of identifying with the company, an acceptance of challenges, both personal and collective responsibility, pride in good work, and team spirit. The group of knowledge workers discussed these values and then gradually spread them throughout the whole factory workforce during the plant construction. Because the group lacked previous practical experience, company management instead developed a 'learning to do things' method where problems were disassembled and reassembled, and thereafter formalized. The result of this method was that the employees learned to diagnose, solve, and anticipate problems, and also to reform structures and processes as they worked with them and communicated them to others.

After these trained employees built the factory, they used the same method to build cars. They began by disassembling and reassembling manufactured cars from Fiat's factory in Turin. Based on their previous experiences, these exercises required the employees to think of ways to improve the production cycle. Thus, they built their learning and knowledge into the machines that produced the cars.

It was soon apparent that Fiat's experiment was successful. The company's productivity level increased, and during a ten-year period both Fiat and its competitors regarded the factory as a remarkable example of productivity and corporate efficiency. The experiment was named 'The Melfi Model'.

In 2004, however, there were unexpected problems. Both Fiat's employees and its suppliers went on strike, and the assembly line halted for several weeks. As a consequence, the Melfi factory's design was called into question, not least by the automotive media. When the company analysed what had happened, it was noted that tensions had been increasing among the Fiat workers since 2000. The analysis also revealed that the involvement of the unions created a situation where the unions were both the watchmen over, and the guarantors of, the company's productivity levels. Thus a situation arose where work quality and employee rights were spiralling downward.

The problem was that Fiat's traditional management model, with its hierarchical and authoritarian way of controlling production, was different than that used in the Melfi factory. The original committees, where the unions and management cooperated, had been abandoned. Many of the original employees had left the factory and the new employees were temporary. The result was high personnel turnover. At the same time, the speed of the assembly line increased. In the new work schedule, employees were expected to work 12 nights in a row. This changed way of managing the factory became a self-reproducing process. The conditions that had created continuous learning and contributed to the factory's successes had been destroyed (Lanzara and Patriotta, 2007).

Lanzara and Patriotta, 2007. A short description of the Melfi plant is provided at www.fiat.co.uk/Content/Article.aspx?id=22797 (retrieved 6 August 2010). Company information has been retrieved from www.fiat.com.

Questions

In realizing the vision of the learning factory, what are the major challenges facing managers?

Is it possible to build a culture, design formal structures, and adapt internal processes to facilitate and enhance learning in organizations?

What are the major theoretical perspectives on learning in general, and **organizational learning** in particular, that are applicable to the vision of creating a learning factory (organization)?

Introduction

The case description above shows how a well-known company addressed a major crisis using a learning approach. In the case, the task was to build a so-called learning factory, and it shows how a learning approach can help a company increase productivity and effectiveness. But the case also shows that there are many challenges involved in realizing the vision of a learning factory. A persistent focus on learning often makes it obvious that formal structures, internal routines, and standards are not adapted to this focus. The case furthermore shows that there are cultural elements involved in building a learning organization, and that a learning focus can challenge deeply held beliefs and patterns of understanding in organizations.

In the case description and the introduction above, the concept of learning was used without a clear definition. Considering the long history of learning and the rich variety of definitions and theoretical approaches available, it is obvious that the study of learning in organizations can take many forms depending on which theoretical standpoint is taken. The concept of learning also borrows from neighbouring concepts such as knowledge, knowledge acquisition, experience, and the like. This constitutes a rich and complex field of inquiry and it goes way beyond the scope of a textbook on organization theory to go in depth on all perspectives and neighbouring concepts, but the chapter will start with a brief introduction to different theoretical perspectives on learning. We will also introduce the concept of knowledge, which has gained widespread use in the field of organizational theory.

The field of learning theory is traditionally focused on the individual, and his/her ability to learn from experience. The situation becomes more complex and problematic when learning is used to understand groups of individuals, be it small and tightly knit groups, or larger and abstract groups such as organizations. In the second section of the chapter the focus is shifted to discuss learning in the context of organizations. This shift can take two different forms: either the focus is still on the individual and how he/she can learn together with others, or the focus is on how groups of individuals can learn. The first focus would still be consistent with the traditional focus on the individual as the actor of learning, but the second focus also means a shift of actor—from the individual to the group (often something larger than a small-group, e.g. the organization).

This chapter addresses a number of issues dealing with the problem of facilitating and enhancing learning in organizations. More specifically the following topics are covered:

- Definitions of learning and different theoretical perspectives,
- Learning in organizations,
- Knowledge and knowledge management,
- Learning from risk.

Theoretical perspectives on learning

Organizational learning is a concept that has gained widespread attention in the last few decades. With the pioneering work of Argyris and Schön (1978), organizational learning became a topic attracting practitioners and academics alike. In 2008, eight scientific journals were devoted to learning in an organizational context, which is astonishing growth considering the fact that in the early 1970s you couldn't even find eight scientific journals in the whole field of organizational theory (for an overview of the research on organizational learning see

Bapuji and Crossan, 2004). An additional 10, or more, journals are also devoted to the field of knowledge management, many of which are highly relevant for organizational theory. Considering the rapid growth and alleged importance of learning in the context of organizations, it is somewhat surprising to find a field marked by a lot of confusion and discussion concerning basic definitions of learning. On a general level, it is fairly easy to agree upon a basic definition of learning, but as soon as the discussion becomes more concrete, matters of definition become much more problematic. Traditionally, learning is defined as:

> Any relatively permanent change in behaviour resulting from past experience.
> (Encyclopaedia Britannica, 1964)

Important to notice in this definition is that learning is measured as a behavioural effect resulting from a cognitive process. It is often emphasized that this behavioural change must result from some kind of a mental act by the individual. Behaviour caused by mere chance, body reactions, instincts, or being forced by external pressure does not qualify as learning. In most theories of learning, there is usually assumed an element of deliberate activity by the individual. The emphasis on past experience in the definition above is a good example of viewing learning as a deliberate, conscious act of individuals. A more developed definition is provided in the definition box below.

DEFINITION BOX

Learning

'Learning refers to the change in a subject's behaviour or behaviour potential to a given situation brought about by the subject's experiences in that situation, provided that the behaviour change cannot be explained on the basis of the subject's native response tendencies, maturation, or temporary states (such as fatigue, drunkenness, drives, and so on) (Bower and Hilgard, 1981: 11).'

Both definitions above are generic enough to cover a wide variety of learning theories. They are also applicable to a wide range of learning situations. In order to create a better understanding of the concept of learning we will highlight the most important theoretical perspectives in the history of learning theory. Depending on which part of the definition above that is stressed, we end up with fundamentally different perspectives. The first part of the definition stresses the important role of behaviour in many learning theories. As will be clear below, the notion of changed behaviour as the measure of whether learning has taken place is very important in contemporary theories on learning in an organizational context. For lack of a better term we can label the different theories that emphasize behavioural change *behavioural theories*.

If the stress is rather put on the second part of the definition, interest is shifted towards the mechanisms of producing changes in behaviour. In the definition box, Bower and Hilgard also define learning as a change in *behaviour potential*, which indicates that cognitive changes are also a part of learning. Here we find a number of different theories and approaches, and they are often grouped together and referred to as *cognitive theories*. The cognitive theories emphasize that changed knowledge, experience, and understandings are outcomes of the learning process, and criticize the view that learning should only be defined as behavioural change. What is missing in the definitions above is a reference to the context in which learning takes place. This observation has paved the way for a new group of theories that will be referred to as *situational theories*. The distinction between the three groups of theories is often difficult to draw and there is considerable overlap between them, but as a simplified classification, it points to some of the conceptual challenges involved in defining and studying learning (see the definition box below).

DEFINITION BOX

Dimensions of learning

Theories on learning usually focus on one of the following three dimensions: Behaviour, cognition, and situation. The distinctions between the three perspectives are, however, not clear-cut and in many cases, theoretical perspectives borrow from more than one perspective, even though they have their major emphasis on one perspective.

The three basic perspectives also differ in terms of level of analysis, and they are, to varying degrees, applicable on all levels. For the purposes of this book we will make a difference between four levels—individual, small group, organization, and network of organizations. The focus on this chapter is on the organizational level and after introducing the three basic dimensions, the second part of the chapter concentrates on this level. The three perspectives are all visible in the Melfi case that introduced the chapter, as illustrated in the link box below.

LINK BOX

Learning in the Melfi plant

On the surface, it seems that Fiat, in the Melfi model above, is firmly rooted in a behavioural perspective on learning. It was emphasized that the workers spend time 'learning by doing', and thereby gained experience to increase their problem solving capacity. This would fit well with the encyclopaedic definition above—achieving a long term change in behaviour through an experience based process. This would come as no surprise since learning is also described as an experience based process in the cognitive and situated perspectives, even though the behavioural perspective makes behavioural change the very core of learning. A unique part of the learning process is the stress on creating a culture of learning and to increase commitment to the project and the company. The creation of a learning culture points towards a cognitive perspective, and it also emphasizes the social aspects of learning in organizations. An important aspect of both cognitive and situated perspectives is the achievement of higher-order learning, a capacity to reflect upon one's own learning and the creation of an organization where learning is inherent in the operations. In the Melfi model, a stated goal was that the workers should create a culture of continuous learning, and in order to achieve this, it is very important to create a culture where learning is understood and internalized by the employees and managers. Furthermore, it is clear from the case description that learning is more than a one-man task—it is something that concerns the whole organization and it requires dedicated management, which shifts the focus from individuals learning to learning in organizations. This will be discussed more in depth later in this chapter.

Reflection point: As this chapter has already indicated, there are numerous different perspectives and approaches to learning. In what ways does the Melfi model illustrate the different perspectives?

The behavioural and cognitive theories have, traditionally, been focused on individuals, and this reflects the strong roots in individual psychology. Within each of the two categories, we find a number of distinct theories and some of the more prominent are mentioned below. With the introduction of situational approaches, the interest has shifted more towards the small group as the unit/arena for learning, and this has led to a wide variety of theories and approaches that shed new light on learning *between* individuals. Based on insights from social psychology, education, and related areas, the small group has emerged as an important area for studies on learning. It is, for instance, obvious that relations between individuals in a class-room situation (for instance between teacher and pupil, and between pupils) in many ways influence the learning. To argue that the group as such can learn is more problematic, but for our purposes it is enough to conclude that the small group is an important arena for learning.

On the third level the organization as such is the focus of attention and a number of different theories have been proposed, drawing upon a wide variety of theoretical fields. A major problem with many proposed theories on organizational learning is that they turn organizations into actors that 'can learn'. This is especially evident in the stream of literature that deals with *learning organizations*. Inspired by Senge's book, *The fifth discipline*, a growing number of authors argue that it is possible to create an organization that can learn (e.g., Garvin, 1993; Wishart, Elam, and Robey, 1996). Even though a lot of research has shown that this assumption is highly problematic (Fiol and Lyles, 1985; Miller, 1996), it is growing in popularity. The final section of this chapter introduces the reader to the broad field of knowledge management.

On the fourth level the interest is shifted towards the interactions between organizations. It has been suggested that learning also can take place in the interaction between organizations and that collaboration between organizations can be an important arena for learning (Powell, Koput and Smith-Doerr, 1996).

 DEFINITION BOX

Levels of analysis in learning

Theories of learning usually have an analytical focus on either of the following levels of analysis: individual, small-group, organization, networks of organizations. As indicated above, the first level, individual learning contains two generic groups of theories/ approaches that are applicable to the other three levels.

Learning on the individual level

Behavioural perspectives

The early 20th century movement labelled *behaviourism* has its roots in the seminal work of Edward Lee Thorndike. In the book, *The Animal Intelligence*, Thorndike began a systematic work to launch an independent science of psychology based on comparative studies. It was obvious to Thorndike that learning goes beyond instincts, what he called *unlearned tendencies*. He launched the idea of learning as an *associative process*, where the individual moves from instincts to forming habits. This is basically a learning theory that puts repetition and recognition at the centre.

> '... any act which, in a given situation, produces satisfaction becomes associated with that situation, so that when the situation recurs, the act is more likely than before to recur also'
>
> (Thorndike, 1911: 203)

By a process of trial-and-error, the individual attempts different solutions to a problem until a satisfying solution is reached. The ideas of trial-and-error and associations were an important source of inspiration to the behaviourist movement that gained momentum in the first two decades of the 20th century. The main idea was that learning was a near automatic response to stimuli from the environment. The individual learned to associate certain, adequate, responses to a specific situation. Thorndike persistently argued that this was a process that did not involve ideas but was rather a mechanical trial-by-error like process.

Perhaps the most well-known of the early behaviourists is the Russian physiologist Ivan Petrovich Pavlov. Pavlov organized and led the work at the Department of Physiology at the Institute for Experimental Medicine in St Petersburg. Although Pavlov is commonly viewed as a psychologist, he was actually working in the field of physiology. In 1904 he received the Nobel price in Medicine for his studies on digestive glands. These studies eventually led Pavlov to investigate the so-called conditional reflexes. Pavlov's systematic studies on dogs were a major source of inspiration for the behaviourist movement. Pavlov (1927/2003) realized that learning must involve a more active process than the one envisioned by Thorndike. Pavlov was interested in uncovering the more specific process that led to adequate responses by individuals. The basic concept in Pavlov's thinking is *reflexes*, (this concept soon became known as *responses* in the behaviourist terminology) which he describes as the active component in the individual's strive to reach a balance in relation to the external forces acting upon him. The process of responding to external stimuli Pavlov called *conditioning*, which can be described as the individual's adaptation to stimuli. He was interested in understanding how certain reflexes could be conditioned to appear, beyond the 'automatic' reflexes he referred to as unconditioned. The distinction between conditioned and unconditioned reflexes is crucial to Pavlov's thinking. Conditioned reflexes are acquired through processes of education, training, and habit, and although Pavlov is not entirely explicit in this point, it is clear that conditioning is essentially a process of learning.

Pavlov conducted a number of often described experiments to examine how conditioned reflexes could be activated by arbitrary stimuli, what he labelled conditioned stimuli. The archetypical experiment consisted of following the processes of unconditioned reflexes to unconditioned stimuli, for instance a dog salivating when presented with a bowl of meat powder. By introducing an arbitrary signal before the food is presented to the dog (for instance the ringing of a bell), Pavlov wanted to see if the dog could be taught to respond to the bell (the conditioned stimulus) and thereby a conditioned reflex would be evoked. Pavlov realized that the conditioned reflexes soon faded out, and he became interested in the concept of *reinforcement*, that is, the process of stimulating certain behaviours to occur. Reinforcement later became a cornerstone in the model of behavioural change called *operant conditioning* (Skinner, 1974). In operant conditioning, compared to 'pavlovian' (or classical) conditioning, behaviour is strengthened through its consequences. Skinner (1974: 44) gives the following example:

> 'Thus, when a hungry organism exhibits behaviour that produces food, the behaviour is reinforced by that consequence and is therefore more likely to recur.'

Certain behaviours can thus be reinforced by introducing certain stimuli if the correct behaviour is exhibited. Reinforcers fall in different categories and for our purposes the most important are *secondary* reinforcers (any stimuli that is acquired through experience) and *social* reinforcers (stimuli whose effectiveness are derived from the behaviour of other individuals, for instance praise and attention). The concept of reinforcement is also an important part of the motivation theories launched in the 1950s (see Chapter 5 for an overview of motivation theories).

To summarize, the behavioural perspective stresses that the outcome of the learning processes is a behavioural change, making behaviour the ultimate measure of learning. Learning is also described as an experience-based process of association or conditioning, where the individual learns to choose appropriate responses to certain stimuli. Later research has pointed at a number of problems with the behaviourist view on learning. A major problem is the focus on behaviour as the measure of learning. It is hard to tell whether a behavioural change is actually the outcome of learning, and it is, furthermore, not necessary that behaviour is changed for learning to occur. In the generic definition of learning above, learning was rather described as a *potential* for behaviour. Modern cognitive theory also shows that the simple trial-by-error process is much more complex than envisioned by Pavlov and others. The early behaviourists, and not least the American psychologist John B Watson (1924/2007), were also heavily criticized for trying to reduce complex human behaviours to a simple stimulus-response process. Watson has been ridiculed for his strictly behaviourist thoughts on behavioural modification and child-rearing, and how a society can be shaped by applying the principles of the stimulus-response model.

Cognitive perspectives

The cognitive perspectives share the common feature of focusing on the 'inner' functioning of learning, that is, what happens in the human brain in learning processes. A typical definition of learning in the cognitive tradition is given by Morgan (2002: 12) below, with the major difference compared to the definitions above being the stress on behaviour *potential*:

> 'Learning is a relatively permanent change in behaviour potential brought about by practice or experience.'

The cognitive view on learning is often associated with the so called *information perspective*, which can be described as a sequential model of how individuals process information and respond to external stimuli. The well known stage model by Atkinson and Shiffrin (1968) summarizes some of the major components in the information perspective. The model starts with the *sensory stage* in which the individual comes in contact with information of any kind. All information passes through a sensory store in which a sensory receptor is stimulated by an external stimulus. In the next stage, information is processed in the working memory, the so-called *short-term store*. The short-term store contains any type of information content (words, numbers, pictures, images) that the individual is responding to in any given moment.

By repeating and rehearsing, information can be passed on to the next stage of the model—*the long-term store*. Cognitive theory is a rich and rapidly growing field and it is way beyond the scope of this chapter to capture every aspect relevant to our understanding of learning.

An important part of cognitive theory is the study of *conceptual behaviour*, that is, the process by which individuals manage to respond to objects or events by using general categories rather than the specific attributes of the objects and events. Without this capacity to see general patterns we would, literally, drown in stimuli that insist on our attention. Based on cognitive maps or schemes the individual learns how to classify and deal with information, and these maps can be viewed as representations of knowledge that the individual is using. A higher level of learning occurs in situations where the individual is forced to change his/her cognitive maps. Learning thus takes place within existing maps as well as in creating new maps and modifying existing ones.

The field of cognitive perspectives on learning is rich and rapidly growing and also contains perspectives that build on fundamentally different assumptions of human nature. A growing tradition emphasizes the role of humans as active creators of meaning where learning is rather described as an act of interpretation leading to increased *understanding*. This perspective is often referred to as a *sense-making perspective*, where the objectified view of learning in the information perspective gives way to a more active view of human nature. In this tradition Friedlander (1983: 194) describes learning in the following way:

'Change resulting from learning need not be visible behaviour. Learning may result in new significant insights and awareness that dictate no behavioural change.'

In the cognitive tradition we also find the so-called *constructionist perspective*, which shares a number of assumptions with the sense-making perspective. In the constructionist perspective, it is described how the individual builds his/her own mental structures in an interaction with the environment. Jean Piaget is perhaps the most well-known among constructionist psychologists, with his studies on cognitive development in children.

Situated perspectives

Both the sense-making and constructionist perspectives open up for a more deliberate focus on the situation in which learning takes place. The traditional behavioural and cognitive perspectives are often criticized for studying learning in artificial learning environments, far from the real-life situations in which learning takes place on a daily basis. The situated perspectives differ from the behavioural and cognitive perspectives in a number of respects, and emphasize the context of learning in a much more clear-cut way. The situated perspectives have been largely identified with the ideas of Jean Lave and Etienne Wenger, and the so-called *communities of practice* perspective.

MINICASE

Harvard Medical School (HMS)

Establishing and developing an organization that continuously manages to produce high quality research and education is a demanding task, and requires the combined efforts of many groups of researchers and teachers. It is far from the traditional view of the researcher as an isolated individual devoted to his or her dear research topic—it is more and more a group task and this is especially evident in research areas such as medicine, biotech, and physics which require huge resources and large teams of researchers. Creating a collaborative climate is crucial to modern research, and this is something the faculty at Harvard Medical School has fully understood. HMS is one of the most prestigious research institutions in the world and it is certainly number one in medicine in the United States. Founded 1782 in Boston, United States, it has, up to now, produced no less than 9 Nobel prizes (with awards given to 15 researchers), the most recent obtained in 2009. Researchers at HMS know what it takes to achieve excellence in research in the field of medicine, and working together in groups is certainly a part of the success story. This goes both for the work in the basic science departments as well as in the clinical departments at hospitals affiliated to HMS in the Boston area. The communities of practice perspective is elegantly captured in the stated mission of HMS: 'To create and nurture a diverse community of the best people committed to leadership in alleviating human suffering caused by disease'.

The communities of practice perspective borrows important features from the sensemaking perspective above and, in particular, the idea of humans experiencing their world as meaningful and acting as active constructors of meaning (Wenger, 1998). Learning, according to this perspective, takes place in social settings, *communities*, in which a shared world of practice is developed. The concept of practice is important since it emphasizes that learning takes place in concrete situations where individuals interact with others to solve day-to-day business.

The community of practice theory, and the broader movement of situated practice, is focusing on understanding learning in everyday situations. This perspective shifts the focus from the individual (his/her behaviour and cognition) to the surrounding environment of the learning individual which includes the social structure of the group(s) to which the individual belongs, and with which it interacts. This perspective has contributed a broader understanding of learning, where it is described as an integrated part of the social practice.

Illustrations of the situated perspective can also be found in the Melfi case, and this is discussed in the link box below.

LINK BOX

Situated learning in the learning factory

The Melfi model, described in the introductory case of the chapter, is clearly not designed to demonstrate either the behaviourist experiments on reinforcement and conditioned responses, or the cognitive view of humans as 'computers' as in the information perspective. There is a clear emphasis on learning-by-doing, and enabling a focus on learning and knowledge in the production process. The case description indicates that learning takes place in association with practice, when the employees encounter problems in the daily production process. With the problems encountered in 2004, it is also clear that the learning factory is embedded in a web of social relations that can hinder the future development of the Melfi model—in this case, the interface between the bottom-up and democratic ideal of the Melfi model and the traditional hierarchic and authoritarian production model of Fiat. The attempts at building a community of practitioners in the Melfi model emphasize the important roles of freely sharing ideas, discussing, and interacting to create a learning culture. This is directly in line with the ideas of the communities of practice perspective in its description of learning as arising from a socially and culturally structured world. For a community of practice to function it is highly important that there are few restrictions on the free flow of information and knowledge between individuals in the relevant context, and this is what eventually caused problems at Fiat. It is also important that there is a mutual understanding and a high degree of respect between the different actors and this can surely be difficult to achieve in a hierarchic and authoritarian structure.

Reflection point: How can an organization such as Fiat create the basis for a free and creative exchange of ideas?

Learning in organizations

In the first part of this chapter we have introduced and discussed the major perspectives of learning. We now turn to discussing learning in organizations. This is a crucial shift of level, and it is not unproblematic to describe learning on an organizational level. We can have different opinions on how to define learning, and few would question that learning is a relevant concept to use in understanding individuals. Applied on the organizational level things become trickier. As noticed by Popper and Lipshitz (2000), the interface between individual and organizational learning is highly problematic. In a strict, psychological, sense we cannot treat an organization as an actor, and therefore cannot assign it the capacity to learn. Individual learning is a process, regardless of whether we use behavioural, cognitive, or situational perspectives, that is formed in the individual's interaction with the external world, and it is only in a transferred sense that we can say that an organization can act and learn. Seen from this perspective it is obvious that the individual is the basic learning unit, and we must be careful in treating organizations, as such, as learning units. This is especially problematic if we are interested in the cognitive operations and processes involved in learning. The risk that organizations are assigned human qualities has been pointed out by many authors (e.g. Silverman, 1970), and this risk is apparent in the field of learning. In the literature on organizational learning, different solutions to this reification problem are proposed (Fiol and Lyles, 1985; Huber, 1991), and we identify three basic approaches to handle the shift from the individual to the organizational level.

The first approach tries to solve the problem by focusing on the *effects of learning* and thus not problematize the learning process as such. Furthermore, this approach does not assume the existence of the organization as an acting unit. In line with the behavioural approach presented above, organizational learning is often equated to change, and this shifts the focus away from the process of learning to emphasize the effects of learning, that is, change. Theoretically, this is not a satisfying solution, since it lacks a good description and analysis of the learning processes and mechanisms of learning. This perspective has been subject to a lot of criticism from researchers. Miller (1996) criticizes, in an influential article, the conceptual 'obscurity' of much of the organizational learning literature, and he suggested a more clear-cut focus on the acquisition of knowledge as the core in learning. A further problem with the focus on effects of learning is to decide whether the effect was due to learning or whether it would have happened 'anyway'. Despite the problems presented above the connection to change and effects is a very much alive genre in the managerial literature.

The second approach to solving the problem of studying learning on a group level is to *treat the organization (or other social unit) as an actor in itself.* It is often unclear whether the author is actually viewing the organization as an actor or if it is just a way of expression. In his book *On Organizational Learning*, Argyris (1992) introduced the topic of organizational learning by stating that 'the premise of this book is that organizational learning is a competence that all organizations should develop'. A deeper analysis of the literature shows that it is top management, rather than 'the organization' that learns. The quotation below is representative of this view:

'It is this kind of company that can more readily produce the adaptive response which helps an organization stay ahead of change'
(Moss Kanter, 1983: 130)

In much the same way as the first approach this view also has some obvious problems. Can we really treat the organization as an actor in itself? Isn't it rather the people in the organization who learn? It is, from a conceptual point of view, highly questionable if an organization can act and think. We find this theoretical focus well established in the semi-normative research on strategy and organizations, with authors such as Ghoshal and Bartlett (1997), Nonaka and Tackeuchi (1995), and Nohria and Goshal (1997), who all share the conviction that it is possible to create a learning organization.

The third approach describes learning as a social process, and puts the emphasis on organizations as *arenas for learning*, but where the learning, by definition, is something that is based on the actions of individuals. Within this approach a number of ideas have been proposed. A number of authors draw upon cultural and linguistic theories to describe learning (Crossan, Lane, and White, 1999; Gherardi, 2000; Popper and Lipshitz, 2000), whereas others take a more managerial view and argue that learning is a question of leading and managing knowledge. The concept of organizational learning is discussed in the link box below.

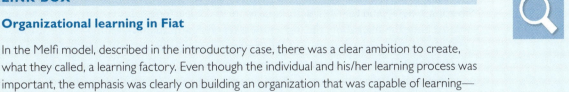

LINK BOX

Organizational learning in Fiat

In the Melfi model, described in the introductory case, there was a clear ambition to create, what they called, a learning factory. Even though the individual and his/her learning process was important, the emphasis was clearly on building an organization that was capable of learning—to build in a learning culture in the organization rather than just training individuals for their own individual working tasks. The notion of a learning factory implies consistent work to develop an organization that managed to not only deliver with high quality but also to develop its own operations. The latter point is important in an organizational learning perspective, since it points out the ability to anticipate problems and to self-adjust as important. This does not mean that individuals, and their learning, is not important. On the contrary, individuals are the agents in any learning organization. The point is rather to shift the focus from the individual to the organizational level, and ask how the organization, as a whole, can develop the capacity for learning. In the literature on organizational learning this 'higher-order' learning has been referred to as double-loop learning (Argyris and Schön, 1978), or as the ability to learn how to learn. The literature on learning in organizations has struggled over the years to understand how this capacity to learn how to learn could be created and upheld. In the Melfi model it was stressed that the workers should be able to reflect upon their own learning, and thereby contribute to build an organization that can learn from experience and avoid making mistakes. And up till the point where this collaborative model collided with the established hierarchic and authoritarian management model at Fiat, this proved to be a successful strategy.

Reflection point: Based on the example of Fiat and the Melfi model, what does it take to learn how to learn?

In line with the description of individual learning, different theories on organizational learning can be classified according to their roots in either behavioural or cognitive views on learning.

Behavioural theories on organizational learning

A common starting point for definitions of organizational learning is the assumption that *behavioural change* is the central result of the learning process. This assumes that 'the organization' has changed its way of operating, and it is very much in line with the second approach to solve the *reification* problem above—to treat the organization as an actor in itself. The cognitive process leading to this result is seldom problematized, which leaves the learning process a black box that we know little of. In the following, four basic views on organizational learning as a behavioural process are described.

Responses to external events: Organizational learning is often connected to the ability of the organization to meet external threats and meet opportunities with timely actions. Duncan and Weiss (1979) argue that organizational learning takes place when the organization experiences performance gaps between real and perceived environmental responses. Changes in the environment create pressure for change within the organization (Lant and Mezias, 1992). In this view, adaptation becomes a defining feature of the learning organization. The faster and more accurate the adaptation, the higher the level of organizational learning (Senge, 1990).

Reactions to new information: A similar approach stresses the collection and interpretation of new information as central to organizational learning (McGill, Slocum, and Lei, 1992). Both approaches have their roots in the contingency theory on organizations (see chapter 2), where the interaction between the organization and its environment is central (Donaldsson, 1985). Meeting the demands from the environment becomes central to learning, and it is no coincidence that the gathering of information becomes an important component. Even though the cognitive process of gathering and interpreting data is not described in depth it is obvious that this information processing view has links to a more cognitive view on learning. Since the stress is rather on the *action* based on information processing, we still classify both views as primarily behavioural.

Ability to innovate: A third theme stresses the ability to create new things, and Bouwen and Fry (1991) define organizational learning as the growing ability to be innovative. Stata (1989) describes organizational learning as the development of new insights and changed behaviour. A precondition for innovation is that new insights can develop and spread, and that old conceptions can be 'unlearned'.

Improve the performance of the organization: The final form of behavioural view of organizational learning is based on an experiential view of learning. Organizational learning is viewed

MINICASE

Learning at Shell

Learning and knowledge management are top priorities in many global companies, and they reflect the growing complexity and dynamics faced by modern companies. Without an inbuilt capacity to learn from experience, and the ability to reflect upon mistakes and learn from others, it would be very hard to survive in a highly competitive industry. One of the first companies to launch a deliberate focus on learning was Shell, and they are renowned for their persistent focus on training and learning initiatives. This would come as no surprise since the energy sector is one of the more competitive industries and the ability to adapt and learn is a prerequisite for success. This was understood early by Shell. The company has realized that talent management will be a competitive advantage for the future and that recruiting and retaining talented individuals will be even harder in the coming years. An important part of the learning initiatives is to provide employees with resources and expertise to develop their skills and abilities. The underlying rationale is that a consistent learning approach helps to attract and keep highly motivated and talented individuals. The learning initiatives at Shell consist of a wide variety of approaches and tools, including leadership development, technical/professional development, promoting diversity and inclusiveness, creating a state-of-the-art learning management system worldwide, working with blended learning approaches, and so on. The blended learning approach is a good example of the innovative learning approaches at Shell, where traditional classroom teaching is combined with learning at the workplace and face-to-face coaching activities.

Information on the learning focus of Shell is available at **www.shell.com**

as the improvement of performance, based on evaluating previous performance. Carmona and Perez-Casanova (1993: 31) define organizational learning as 'the process of improving actions through better knowledge and understanding'. A similar view is proposed by Fiol and Lyles (1985), and they view organizational learning as a process whereby the organization improves its performance by better knowledge and understanding. The minicase below illustrates how a company develops a consistent strategy to work with learning in the organization.

Cognitive theories on organizational learning

Among organizational scholars, the behavioural view has dominated the research agenda. Even though many authors touch upon the cognitive view, behavioural change is still the defining feature of organizational learning. There is, however, a growing recognition that the learning process needs to be viewed as a cognitive process. A number of authors acknowledge the central role of critical reflection in the learning process (Schön, 1983; Ventriss and Luke, 1988).

Huber (1991) has questioned the rationale of the behavioural view and he has proposed an alternative view on the link between learning and acting. What is interesting, according to Huber, is not the actual change in behaviour but rather the range of *potential behaviours*. He defines organizational learning in the following way:

'An entity learns if, through its processing of information, the range of its potential behaviours is changed.'
(Huber, 1991: 89)

Organizational learning can thus be viewed as increasing the potential for future action, which is more in line with a cognitive view of learning by stressing the capacity to change. In a theoretical paper Huber (1991) discusses four different processes that contribute to organizational learning. *Knowledge acquisition* is the process of obtaining information that is necessary for the survival of the organization, and involves activities such as experimenting and actively searching for information. *Information distribution* has to do with the piecing together of information to fit the needs of different units. In order to get the necessary breadth and diversity of learning, there is a need for distributing information in the organization. Once information is acquired and distributed a process of *information interpretation* starts. Daft and Weick (1984) describe interpretation as a process where information is given meaning by participants, and without this active component it is hard to make use of available information. Finally, *organizational memory* puts the emphasis on the processes of storing and retrieving information in the organization.

A number of authors have proposed a cultural/linguistic view of organizational learning as a way to put more emphasis on what is actually happening when learning takes place in an organization. Different authors argue that learning takes place in the interaction between individuals/groups of individuals, and that a cognitive view can shed more light on these processes. Crossan, Lane, and White (1999) have developed a model that describes four aspects of this process. Organizational learning can take place on three different levels (individual, group, and organization) and it contains four different subprocesses: *intuiting* and *interpreting* (take place primarily on the individual level), *integrating* (primarily on the group level), and *institutionalizing* (primarily on the organizational level).

Cook and Yanow (1993) sharply criticize the analogy between individual and organizational learning, and they argue that organizational learning is fundamentally different from individual learning. There is a growing recognition among organizational scholars that the concept of learning organizations is problematic and that the focus should be shifted towards *learning in organizations* (Popper and Lipshitz, 2000), where the organization constitutes an *arena* for learning processes that take place between individuals and groups of individuals.

With this shift of attention, it comes as no surprise that many authors emphasize communication and dialogue as central aspects of the learning processes between individuals. As indicated by Huber, above, the cognitive links (in terms of shared patterns of understanding) between individuals is an active process where ideas need to be expressed and transmitted, and language becomes the logical tool to use.

The concept of knowledge

In the previous sections of this chapter, we have introduced the concept of learning and put it in an organizational context. Learning, however, is not the only concept that can help us understand the challenges that were introduced in the Melfi case that started this chapter. The concept of knowledge management is a fairly recent term in the organization and management theory discourse. While for instance, organizational learning has been discussed since at least the late 1950s, influenced by what has been called the 'cognitive revolution' in psychology, knowledge management appeared as a systematic and coherent perspective on organizations, in the mid-1990s, when new seminal books and special issues addressed knowledge as perhaps the single most important production factor in organizations. However, the concept of knowledge, per se, has been used in organization studies from the outset. For instance, in the early 1960s and in the 1970s, sociologists spoke of the 'post-industrial society' and the 'knowledge society' as new forms of society increasingly relying on intellectual resources as the primary motor of the economy. Needless to say, long before such sociological musing, the concept of knowledge has been a standing concern and a perennial issue in philosophy. In fact, the entire discipline of epistemology (a term derived from the Greek term for knowledge, *episteme*) addresses how knowledge is accomplished or reached under determinate conditions. Plato's two dialogues *Meno* and *Thaeatetus*, written in the third century B.C., are two classic works addressing the nature of knowledge.

Given this strong emphasis on knowledge in the Western tradition of thinking, it is curious that the organization and management studies discipline has been relatively ignorant of the concept of knowledge until the 1990s. Today, there is a wide range of publications, journals, conferences, and consultancy firms and interests groups on the Internet and elsewhere, that address the nature of knowledge in organizations. In the 1960s, two works addressing the importance of knowledge in organizations were published. In his *Modern Organizations*, Etzioni (1964: 75) claimed that 'most knowledge is created in organizations and passed from generation to generation—i.e., preserved—by organizations' and two years earlier, Fritz Machlup (1962) published what is arguably the first knowledge management book, *The Production and Distribution of Knowledge in the United States*. Machlup sketches how knowledge is increasingly influencing organizations and the broader society. Machlup (1962: 21–22) distinguishes between five categories of knowledge:

1. *Practical knowledge* in which he includes 'professional knowledge', 'business knowledge', 'workman's knowledge', 'political knowledge', and 'household knowledge',

2. *Intellectual knowledge*, for instance, scientific skills and capabilities,

3. *Small-talk* and *pastime knowledge* that is used in everyday life to support social interaction and relationships,

4. *Spiritual knowledge*,

5. *'Unwanted knowledge'*, i.e., knowledge you possess but do not really care for, or would prefer not to be aware of.

Etzioni (1964), for his part, distinguishes between three types of organization in terms of their use of knowledge:

- *'Professional organizations* that hire at least fifty per cent (50%) of professionals that are capable of producing, applying, preserving, and communicating knowledge.

- *Service organizations* where professionals are subordinate to administrators.

- *Non-professional organizations*, such as manufacturing firms and the 'military establishment.'

(Etzioni, 1964: 77)

The contemporary knowledge management discourse includes a variety of perspectives and methodological orientations, and in the following section we describe three basic perspectives on knowledge in organizations.

Three views of knowledge in organizations

Amin and Cohendet (2004: 5–6) identify three complementary perspectives on knowledge. First, they speak of a strategic-management approach where concepts such as *core competencies, competitive advantage*, and *intellectual capital* are used to examine organizations and firms as repositories of knowledge. Second, they point to an *evolutionary-economics approach* represented by, for instance, Nelson and Winter's (1982) influential work where the knowledge of the firm is embodied in its routines and standard operating procedures. Third, a *social-anthropology-of-learning approach* is presented. The differences between the first two and the last approach are significant and we will, in the next section, specifically address the last perspective. In the first two approaches, knowledge is regarded as a fixed or semi-fixed stock of knowledge residing in routines, standard operation procedures, patents and other structured organizational resources. On the contrary, in the *social-anthropology-of-learning approach*, knowledge is no longer regarded as a fixed or semi-fixed asset that can be put into use when desired, but knowledge is instead, a form of social and collective accomplishment embedded in social practices and communal routines and rules. In this perspective, knowledge is not primarily examined as an entity but as a process, an outcome from certain collaborations and interactions.

We can here draw on a number of definitions of knowledge and knowledge work: Quinn (2005: 610) says that knowledge is the outcome of 'competent, goal-oriented activity'. Tsoukas (2005: 5) speaks of knowledge in the following terms: 'Knowledge is the outcome of an active knower who has a certain biological structure, follows certain historically shaped cognitive practices, and is rooted within a consensual domain and sociocultural practice'. Bourdieu (2004: 72) provides the following definition: 'Knowledge is based, not on the subjective self-evidence of an isolated individual, but on collective experience, regulated by norms of communication and argumentation'. Finally, Cornelius Castoriadis (1997: 345) emphasizes the 'co-production of knowledge': 'All knowledge is co-production; and, in nontrivial cases, we cannot truly separate out what 'comes from' the subject and what 'comes from' the object. This is what I would like to call the 'principle of undecidability of origin''. In all these four definitions, knowledge is not what is 'possessed' or 'controlled' by individuals but what resides in complex networks comprising individuals, routines, practices, norms, means of communication, and so forth.

Situated and local knowledge

Within the knowledge management literature, the situated perspectives presented above constitute a growing body of literature, which is highly relevant for understanding attempts at creating/managing learning environments at work. Sole and Edmondson (2002: 20) define situated knowledge accordingly:

> 'We define situated knowledge as knowledge embedded in the work practices of a particular organizational site. In a manufacturing facility, for example, situated knowledge might include special knowledge about a local supplier's reliability, about the performance of a particular piece of equipment or about who knows that.'
> (Sole and Edmondson, 2002: 20)

Knowledge is claimed to be situated when it is dependent on its context and the prevailing social conditions. Another way to express this idea is to say that knowledge is of necessity local and determined by the distribution of power and authority. Yanow (2004) here distinguishes between what she calls 'expert knowledge' and 'local knowledge'. While 'expert knowledge' is always self-enclosed and only occasionally open for negotiations, local knowledge is practice-based and embedded in existing social relations. The expert's knowledge is sealed for the non-expert but the local knowledge is always subject to negotiation and rearticulation.

What Yanow's distinction between expert and local knowledge is suggesting is that some forms of knowledge are institutionalized (for instance, scientific knowledge, anchored in complex technoscientific procedures and verified by sophisticated peer review procedures) while local knowledge draws its legitimacy from 'what works'. As a consequence, the institutionalized knowledge is protected by layers of procedures and routines that generally cannot be put into question by the layman. The expert knowledge is thus knowledge that is laden with power and authority, that is, the authority of the legitimizing bodies. To illustrate this line of reasoning, medical doctors, for instance obstetricians, are trained in controlling a domain of expertise knowledge. They have undergone long years of intense medical training and are experienced from working in their field of expertise. The authority of the obstetrician is not open for discussion during the work in the ward, but nurses and mid-wives are expected to submit to the authority of the obstetrician. However, in certain domains of the work, the mid-wives are just as or even more qualified than the medical doctor. Midwives are of course also in possession of a wide and deep body of expertise, but their work is closer to what Yanow (2004) calls 'local knowledge', knowledge that has 'proven to work' over time. As a consequence, the relationship between obstetricians and mid-wives is a telling example of how professional groups could struggle over professional jurisdiction and authority in a specific field. In general, medical doctors refuse to recognize the competencies of nurses because they claim medical treatment is of necessity the exclusive domain of authority of the medical doctor, while nurses and mid-wives point at the practical implications from adhering to such principles, for instance, in situations where patients suffer because of slow decision-making. The distinction between expert and the local models of knowledge is explored in the link box below.

LINK BOX

Local knowledge in the Melfi model

The discussion above pinpoints the major differences between the expert and the local models of knowledge, and even though the distinction is artificial it still points out two different models of knowledge. In the Melfi case the ambition was to create a local culture of learning that emphasized learning in the workplace, and to build capacity to act in a pro-active way, to anticipate future problems and to work with continuous improvement (see Chapter 9 for a discussion on improvement). The view of learning and knowledge management in the case clearly fits well with the local knowledge model, being firmly rooted in work practices and also based on communication and interaction between workers. It was stressed in the case description that the company had developed a 'learning to do things' model, firmly rooted in practice. It was also stressed that the knowledge developed through testing and experiment, and by solving practical problems, should be shared in the organization and put to use. This fits well with local knowledge being based on interaction. The two models, however, are described as opposites and in reality most groups would exhibit parts of both models. It is certainly possible to combine different aspects of the two models, and the real challenge for a company such as Fiat is how to manage and build their unique form of learning model. It is also clear that they borrowed elements from the expert model, for instance, through insisting upon knowledge being made public, or explicit, to borrow the term from the table. The ability to 'free' knowledge from the individual and put it to use in the organization is also something that characterizes a learning organization, as was discussed in the section on learning in organizations above.

Reflection point: Which of the two models do you think is most successful in creating a learning organization?

Knowledge management in organizations: Knowledge work and knowledge workers

In practice, knowledge management is the management of individuals that, in various ways, have expertise and know-how in specific domains. The work of such experts is at times, which should come as no surprise, called knowledge work. The very fact that knowledge workers are at least partially in control of their 'production resources', i.e., their experience and know-how, makes knowledge workers a somewhat complicated group to manage and control. Knowledge workers form 'a special class of white-collar workers. This class includes professionals, consultants, technicians, intellectuals, and managers' (Schultze 2000: 5). While other groups of workers are controlled through direct (e.g., the assembly line determining the speed of work) or bureaucratic (e.g., the reporting of work hours and the reporting or measuring of performance) mechanisms of control, knowledge workers are more complicated to manage because the output from their work is not always easily measured. Knowledge workers are instead managed primarily through the alignment of professional identities, ideologies, and work ethos, in what Alvesson and Kärreman (2004) call sociocultural forms of control. Knowledge workers also articulate that they are willing to take part in the executive work of the organization. Tam, Korczynski, and Frenkel (2002) write:

> 'They [knowledge workers] also desired more participation in the decision-making process of senior management. Promotion to higher-ranking positions along internal career ladders offered both recognition of their expertise and greater institutionalized and formal influence over relatively higher-level decisions in the corporation. Formal power in decision-making would enable knowledge workers to mobilize corporate resources to protect and advance their interests. Management in our cases, however, relied primarily on extrinsic rewards and job autonomy as the major levers to manage work motivation.'
> (Tam, Korczynski, and Frenkel, 2002: 795–796)

In practical terms, knowledge workers engage, by definition, in knowledge work having the following characteristics:

- It produces and reproduces information and knowledge.
- Unlike physical blue-collar work, knowledge work is cerebral ... and involves the manipulation of abstractions and symbols that both *represent the world* and are objects *in the world.*
- Unlike *service work*, which is frequently scripted ... knowledge work defies routinization and requires the use of creativity in order to produce idiosyncratic, esoteric knowledge.
- It requires formal education, i.e., abstract, technical, and theoretical knowledge.

  (Schultze, 2000: 5)

The minicase below illustrates how a company can organize knowledge work.

MINICASE

Knowledge management practices at Huawei

The Chinese telecom system producer, Huawei, has in a short time managed to take a strong position in the telecom market and now rival Ericsson. The company is growing at a very fast pace and, through partnerships throughout the world, they have managed to secure a position as one of the top players in the telecom industry. As with many Chinese companies the ownership and management structure can be hard to understand. The company is a fully owned subsidiary of an investment and holding company called Shenzhen Huawei Investment and Holding Co. It is stated that the company is solely owned by the employees of the company without any third parties owning the shares (this would also include the government) (www.huawei.com). In 2009 the company employed more than 61,000 persons, and through a so-called employee shareholding scheme they are able to exercise, through the union, a certain degree of control of the company. Huawei has a dedicated focus on empowering the employees to become true knowledge workers, and this is done through a strong focus on teams as arenas for improvement. Within teams, older and more experienced workers are encouraged to teach younger members of the team and to act as mentors. There is also a strong emphasis on performance evaluation and assessment, and one of the evaluation criteria of team leaders is the effort they put on learning and training in the team.

Information on the knowledge management practices at Huawei is available at www.huawei.com

For Heervagen *et al.*, (2004: 511), 'knowledge work tasks include planning, analyzing, interpreting, developing, and creating products and services using information, data or ideas as the raw materials'. Their work time is therefore characterized, just like any leader, by a certain discontinuity:

- Workers have small blocks of uninterrupted time, punctuated by frequent, brief conversations.

- At any given time, only a proportion of tasks are worked on, with multiple tasks being in a state of suspension.

- Task switching is common and results, to a large extent, from interruptions to ongoing work.

- People spend most of their time in face-to-face interactions.

- Most face-to-face interactions at work are opportunistic rather than planned.

  (Heervagen, *et al.*, (2004: 511–512)

Overall, knowledge workers produce and reproduce what Schultze (2000: 7) calls 'informational objects', that is, objects that are, in various ways, verified and tested and contain a significant amount of information. For instance, computer programmers provide computer software programs written in code that are thereafter tested and verified through predefined procedures. Similarly, pharmaceutical researchers provide molecules that are tested from a variety of perspectives including stability, the capacity to be distributed in the human body, and toxicological features. The computer program and the molecule are examples of informational objects produced within the communities of computer programmers and pharmaceutical researchers (i.e., synthesis chemists and pharmacologists). The challenge for all organizations is to coordinate the various individual and collective skills and competencies and transform them into useful resources. Pfeffer and Sutton (1999) speak of this transformation as the bridging of the 'knowing-doing gap'. Effective knowledge-intensive firms are capable of closing this gap.

Learning from risks

This chapter has, so far, presented and discussed the rapidly growing literature on learning and knowledge management. The chapter started with a presentation of the attempts by Fiat to create a so-called learning factory. The different theories and perspectives on learning and knowledge management have, in different ways, shed light on the challenges inherent in any attempt at managing processes of learning and knowledge development in organizations. In the concluding section of this chapter we turn to a more specific application of learning in organizations, linking the concept of *risk* with a learning perspective. In recent years, more attention has been paid to the area of risk and risk management, both as an issue on the agenda of companies and society and as a research question in various fields, including organization theory. This section contains the following:

• Background for the focus on risk and definitions of risk,
• Learning on risk coupled to decision-making,
• Organizational management of risk and disasters,
• Organizational learning from disaster management.

Risk in organizations: Background and definitions

The management of risk became an issue for companies after the Second World War as new ways of making effective probability calculations and safety analyses developed (Renn, 1998) and as new risks associated with insurance fraud, trade secrets theft, and infringement on patent rights arose (Barlow, 1993). This situation, in turn, led to the creation of a new professional group in the 1950s and 1960s called 'insurance managers' who would, for example, cover uninsured risks, suggest organizational changes to avoid and minimize risks, and provide insurance for financially advantageous risks (Barlow 1993).

Risk, as we understand it today, has its origin in the ideas from the Enlightenment that emphasised scientific and technical progress and innovations. In the Enlightenment, science and technology came to be used in new ways, leading to the rationalization and development of work and social change in new directions (Beck, 1986; Giddens, 1999). These ideas on rationality meant that people thought science could be a useful way to control and lead society (Bauman, 1991). While technical innovations meant new ways of creating prosperity and productivity in society, they also meant that the risk of accidents greatly increased (Beck, 1986; Giddens 1999).

The new risk situation for society has appeared in organizational theory in a number of different practices and in the area of research. Among these are research into risk management (Holt, 2004; Besley and Ghatak, 2005), risk taking in decision-making (Cyert and March, 1963; Bell, 1983; Harrison and March, 1984; March and Shapira, 1987; Baum *et al.*, 2005; Luhmann, 2005; Sine *et al.*, 2005), the aftermath of major accidents (Lanzara, 1983; Turner and Pidgeon, 1997; Jasanoff, 2005), the combination of organization and technical perspectives in the analyses of major accidents (Weick, 1988; 1990; 1993; Weick and Sutcliffe, 2001), and the management aspects of risk taking (Power, 2004; Power 2005).

In the risk literature (and in the English language), the term 'risk' is often synonymous with hazard and threat (Luhmann, 2005). Military theory, on the other hand, differentiates threat 'due to an intentional act of an external enemy' (Battistelli, quoted in Czarniawska, 2005: 81) from risk 'which might come as unintended consequences of good deed, which might come from the inside, and for which those damaged are responsible themselves, like in the case of environmental risks' (Czarniawska, 2005: 81). The external enemy is sometimes described as Nature. When people talk about natural threats, the term often used is 'disaster', which is different from risk, hazard, or threat since a disaster has already occurred. Disasters are further divided into natural disasters such as earthquakes, tsunamis, floods and locust attacks, and man-made disasters such as the consequences of war, automotive wrecks, drowning, explosions, fires, and biological and chemical accidents (Turner and Pidgeon, 1997).

The perspective of the involved actors and observers also determines whether a situation is described as a threat or as a risk (Renn, 1998). For example, researchers in the natural sciences and researchers in the social sciences have different perspectives on risk. While researchers in the natural sciences define the risk of an event occurring objectively using statistics and probability distributions, researchers in the social sciences think risk should be defined as what people actually experience as risk (Boholm, 1996; 2004). Thus, it is the researcher's perspective that determines whether risk is defined by an objective measurement or as something 'actual'.

An implicit idea in all research on risk and definitions of risk is that risk is something that should be avoided or at least minimized (Renn, 1998). This idea is reflected, for example, in the area of risk management where a recent definition proposes that the purpose of risk management is to reduce all aspects of risk (Besley and Ghatak, 2005). Previously risk management meant business advantages, such as improvement in customer focus, a better profile for profit maximization and a common frame of reference for process, product, and project integration (Holt, 2004). According to this latest definition, risk management doesn't mean focusing only on negative results and events.

Researchers have also questioned if risk management is a rational way of managing the unknown risks that confront people. Michael Power (2005), who researches organizations, claims, for example, that risk management may indicate that management lacks control in a complex environment. As risk management is used increasingly, it may become a smoke screen that allows a company to conceal the fact that it cannot manage the risk it faces, and that, *de facto*, people are alone in confronting risks before them.

Learning from risk management and disasters

Since the 1970s researchers in risk research have tried to use companies' risk prevention measures and analyses of disasters to learn how to better prepare for the future. As an introduction, we next discuss their insights in the area of decision-making and organizing related to risk management, and thereafter their learning related to disasters.

Risk and decision-making

In the decision-making school of research, researchers such as Herbert Simon, James March, and Richard Cyert, and their followers, have shown that organizations cannot make a number of decisions at the same time since these separate decisions must be coordinated. According to Luhmann (2005), this means that organizations must break down decisions into parts so that they can make the resulting smaller decisions in a sequential order. A consequence is that managers in organizations, in attempting to manage the uncertain future that risks pose, first and foremost make short-term decisions about matters that are most important (Cyert and March, 1963).

The management of future possibilities and risks, an important element in every decision-making situation, thus ends up on managers' desks. Early studies of decision-making have shown that managers would rather avoid risk than face it. In addition, research shows that managers prefer taking short-term actions to making long-term plans. Nevertheless, Cyert and March (1963) think that the responsibility of leadership is to weigh the possibilities that may follow a decision against the risks that may arise. They argue that the organization's decision-making process should be designed so that risks and possibilities are always taken into consideration. Such a process has consequences for managers. For example, McClelland (1961) states that the manager who fails to take risks should not be a manager, and March and Shapira (1987) found that middle managers prefer a supervising manager who takes risks over one who does not. A successful manager *discovers* and *accepts* risks rather than avoids unknown risks (Luhmann, 2005: 199).

There are also studies of how managers handle risk. According to the model of the organization as a rational tool, it is assumed that mangers choose among possible actions, recognizing their associated risks, in order to achieve certain goals (March and Shapira, 1987). Choice is a matter of picking the best action after evaluating the probable future values of each action. Nevertheless, there is always the risk that the manager will make the wrong choice (Bell, 1983), resulting in the so-called post-decision disappointment when managers have relied too heavily on the intelligent-designed calculation model (Harrison and March, 1984). Yet, the weakness with post-decision disappointment is that it is difficult to predict although, when given the opportunity to second-guess events, people are inclined to claim they already knew that the outcome would be different than it actually was. According to Goitein (1984), people manage surprise and disappointment by describing them in words.

Organizational learning from disasters and risk management

While studies of the decision-making process primarily reveal how individuals in organizations manage risk and learn from this activity, analyses of organizing and disasters show how both people and organizations teach themselves about their management of unforeseen events. Since the beginning of the 1970s, some research has focused on what happens after catastrophic events (Turner and Pidgeon, 1997). A problem encountered with this research is the possible bias in the interviews with the victims of disasters. Because of their post-traumatic feelings, affectations and stress, it is difficult to learn what really happened. As an alternative, Barry A. Turner believed that it was crucial to investigate the actual processes that lead to an accident. The concern is with examining both the technical course of events and people's influence on the accident, the so-called social-technical teamwork (see also Chapter 5, on Motivation).

Against this background, Turner studied 84 accidents that took place between 1 January 1965 and 31 December 1975, using data obtained from the British government (Turner and Pidgeon, 1997). Taking a process perspective, Turner and Pidgeon (1997) found a number of causal factors in major accidents. They concluded that an organization's political, cultural, symbolic, and institutional conditions create conditions where people act in ways such that certain threats cannot be avoided. This is further discussed in the minicase below.

The organizational process that risks leading to a major accident

A sensitive situation arises when different groups from one or two organizations work with a task that is complex, ill-defined, and lengthy. When the task is extensive, many people both inside and outside the organization have access to it, and there may be doubts about how best to manage it. This situation causes communication difficulties. Furthermore, in the drawn-out process of the project, its goals and administration may change. The people who work with the task during its long time frame may willingly assume new roles related to the task. The regulations that previously controlled management of the work may also be out-of-date and perhaps not carefully adhered to. At the same time, people working in the project may be busy in various ways with tasks following on from their previous positions in the organization.

In certain situations even the general public is involved when they are treated in a special way by those working with the task and belonging to the organization. Often organization members react stereotypically, for example, in informing the public as to how they are expected to behave on a boat trip or in a fire. If the public complains when its viewpoints are disregarded, the response is that they are not experts. Since the public does not have access to all the information, they cannot be trusted.

When the task encounters various threats some will be discovered and checked, while others will be neglected. Some neglected threats are threats not discovered, for example, in situations when people are dealing with other threats. On the other hand, some threats are discovered but require too many organizational resources in the form of time, money, and work to attend to them. In addition, other threats may be neglected when most people think it very improbable that they will develop into something really dangerous (Turner and Pidgeon, 1997).

MINICASE

It is clear from this example that in a number of ways a serious threat may arise where, in the worst case, a disaster will result. This may happen when information is wrong, when people outside the project or organization are involved, when previous safety regulations no longer apply, or when people try to minimize various potential dangers.

Another facet of learning related to disasters is that they give rise to 'ephemeral organizations'. According to Lanzara (1983), this learning has two aspects. The first aspect highlights organizations' own learning about organizing, and this in itself is related to their culture and the political climate that is decisive in determining whether alternative stories of the disaster shall be heard (Jasanoff, 2005). The second aspect is what disasters teach organization researchers about organizing. For example, Lanzara (1983) shows that formal organizations may be paralyzed by a disaster that creates insecurity and reveals that the structures of everyday routines for managing different problems may no longer work. In such situations, the so-called ephemeral organizations can organize preliminary assistance. This is illustrated in the minicase below.

Formal and ephemeral organizations for earthquake assistance

In Italy, an area was isolated by an earthquake in 1980, and it was three days before the official aid organization arrived. During this period an ephemeral organization for helping people sprang up. It began when one person saw the need to help people by serving free coffee, and so a temporary coffee kiosk was quickly set up. During the next three days more assistance activities developed around the kiosk as people gathered, exchanged information, and planned the rescue work. When the official rescue organization arrived, in this case the army, the temporary organizing activity disappeared (Lanzara, 1983). Projects and other types of temporary organizations are often assumed to be good examples of learning organizations, even though the passing on of experience between projects is subject to a heated discussion in the field of project management. A both interesting and intriguing question is how temporary organizations manage to solve complex situations and how the ability to do so can be 'stored' in different ways. In this particular case it is obvious that no formal management or organizational system supported the earthquake assistance. It is also clear that the people that joined in had little experience of formal rescue operations; still they managed to organize activities to solve immediate problems. Maybe the learning from this case is rather, that thanks to the lack of formal training, elaborate management systems, and complicated IT-systems, they managed to solve problems. This would certainly be something to think about for the field of organization and management theory.

In explaining why the ephemeral organization dissolved, Lanzara (1983) says that there was no one in charge of this temporary aid organization. This lack of authority clashed with the official organization's bureaucratic structure and the requirement that there had to be proper authorization for various tasks.

Karl Weick is another researcher who has studied organizing and crisis management. He believes crises in organizations are characterized by events that can be summarized by the relationship between low probability/high consistency (Weick, 1988). Like Turner, Weick studies the processes that cause a crisis. He thinks that by understanding these processes, potential problems can be discovered before they develop into major crises. He uses the concept of 'enactment', which he defines as follows:

'When people act, they bring events and structures into existence and set them in motion. People who act in organizations often produce structures, constraints, and opportunities that were not there before they took action.'

(Weick, 1988: 306–307)

According to Weick, it is important to distinguish between the process of enactment and the product that becomes 'an enacted environment'. A specific enactment of reality can contribute to making organizations more crisis-inclined. By understanding the process of enactment, risks can also be avoided.

Among the disasters that Weick has studied is the 1949 Mann Gulch fire in the USA where many fire-fighters died in a wildfire where they had poor equipment and conditions and were poorly prepared. He has also studied the 1972 airplane disaster where a plane with 43 passengers, including 16 football players from Uruguay, crashed in the Andes. Survivors were rescued after ten weeks in the treacherous mountain terrain (Weick, 1993). Other examples Weick describes are the 1984 gas explosion tragedy in Bhopal and the 1977 plane crash in Tenerife. In the latter disaster, a KLM Boeing 747 and a Pan Am Boeing 747 crashed on the runway resulting in the deaths of the 583 people on board (Weick, 1988; 1990). Here Weick showed how major accidents can be caused by small mistakes in minor actions. Enactment doesn't occur when something unexpected happens in an organization, for example, when a measurement tool displays a strange number. However, a crisis may arise when a person begins to manage the unexpected event in a situation where, for instance, people use complex, non-routine technologies. Crises can quickly escalate if such technologies are not completely understood by the people who work with them or by those who must coordinate their activities. When people do not understand their work, they themselves and their crisis management become part of the crisis. There is also a risk that the crisis will intensify before they have understood what must be done.

Another element that may contribute to the severity of a disaster is the bureaucratic organization itself. When a crisis is developing, a message is sent to everyone in upper management. However, the person with the most authority isn't necessarily the person most capable of managing the crisis. In such situations, the result is the person higher up in the hierarchy may do as little as possible—for example, making few attempts to prevent accidents or to issue warnings about them—or may create more confusion. Other aspects of the bureaucratic organization that worsen a crisis are understaffing and large turnover in personnel. If organizations are understaffed, they become more susceptible to crises because there are fewer knowledgeable people employed. If they have significant employee turnover, there are fewer people who remember early organizational experience (Weick and Sutcliffe, 2001).

Summary and conclusions

Learning and knowledge management have been hot topics for managers and academics for more than three decades. The interest in learning in organizations dates back to the seminal work of Argyris and Schön (1978) and their ideas of single-loop and double-loop learning. In a similar way the literature on knowledge and knowledge management has exploded over the last two decades. In this chapter we have captured a multitude of perspectives and concepts by the use of three theoretical perspectives: behavioural, cognitive, and situated perspectives. These three perspectives are very much alive in both the field of organizational learning and in knowledge management, even though the literature on learning makes more explicit references to the basic perspectives. It is clear that theoretical perspectives which describe learning and knowledge development as a situated activity, and emphasize the individual's active (and socially based) construction of reality, have gained ground the last decades. It also appears that the behaviourist version of behavioural perspectives, as well as the traditional cognitive view, has lost its most outspoken advocates. It is, in fact, a common practice in textbooks dealing with learning and knowledge, to take the criticism of these perspectives as a starting point for describing their own perspectives.

The behavioural perspectives have moved way beyond the traditional stimulus-response model of the early behaviourist, and it is nowadays a common feature in the more popular press on learning and knowledge management. Behavioural approaches on learning in organizations stress change and adaptation as important goals of learning. The cognitive perspectives are more apparent in the knowledge management literature, where the metaphors of computers, brains, and databases are commonly used to describe how knowledge is collected, stored, and utilized in organizations.

? Study questions

1. What are the major theoretical perspectives on learning?
2. What are the major differences between individual learning and learning in organizations?
3. What are the major differences between the concepts of learning and knowledge?

Literature recommendations and further readings

As indicated in this chapter the literature on learning and knowledge has exploded in recent decades, and numerous journals are focused on learning and knowledge management in organizations. For the interested reader, we still recommend reading the classical texts from the different theoretical perspectives. It is very interesting to read the *Conditioned Reflexes* by Pavlov, and Skinner's book, *About Behaviorism*, even though most readers probably will find them instrumentalistic and harsh in their view on human nature. For the traditional cognitive perspective we recommend reading a modern textbook on learning, for instance, the book *Learning, Behavior and Cognition* by Lieberman. For the situated perspective, the book, *Situated Learning* by Lave and Wenger is still important reading for anyone interested in learning.

Take your learning further

online
resource
centre

http://www.oxfordtextbooks.co.uk/orc/erikssonzetterquist/

Visit the Online Resource Centre which accompanies this book to enrich your understanding of this chapter.

Students: explore web links and further reading suggestions. Keep up to date with the latest developments via 'What happened next' updates to appropriate cases from within the book.

Lecturers: you will find seminar exercises and teaching notes, for use in class or assessment.

References

Abbott, A.D., (1988). *The System of Professions: An Essay on the Division of Expert Labor.* Chicago: Chicago University Press.

Abdulah, S.R.S. & Keenoy, T., (1995). Japanese managerial practices in the Malaysian electronics industry: Two case studies, *Journal of Management Studies*, 32(6): 747–766.

Acker, J. & Van Houten, D.R., (1974). Differential recruitment and control: The sex structuring of organizations. *Administrative Science Quarterly*, 19(2): 152–163.

Acker, J., (1990). Hierarchies, jobs, bodies: A theory of gendered organizations, *Gender and Society*, 4(2): 139–58.

Adams, S.J., (1965). Inequity in social exchange. In: L. Berkowitz, (ed.) *Advances in Experimental Social Psychology*. 2: 267–299. New York: Academic Press.

Adams, S.J., (1968). Effects of overpayment: Two comments on Lawler's paper, *Journal of Personality and Social Psychology*, 10(3): 315–316.

Adler, P., (1986). New technologies, New skills. *California Management Review*. XXIX(1): 9–28.

Adorno, T.W., (2000). *Introduction to Sociology.* Cambridge: Polity Press.

Ahl, H., (2004). *The Scientific Reproduction of Gender Inequality: A Discourse Analysis of Research Texts on Women's Entrepreneurship.* Stockholm: Liber.

Akrich, M., Callon, M. & Latour, B., (2002a). The key success in innovation part I: The art of interessement, *International Journal of Innovation Management*, 6(2): 187–206.

Akrich, M., Callon, M. & Latour, B., (2002b). The key success in innovation part II: The art of choosing good spokespersons, *International Journal of Innovation Management*, 6(2): 2067–225.

Aldag, R.J. & Brief, A.P., (1981). *Managing Organizational Behaviour.* St. Paul, MN: West Publishing.

Aldrich, H.E., (1972). Technology and organizational structure: A re-examination of the findings of the Aston group, *Administrative Science Quarterly*, 17: 26–43.

Allison, G.T., (1971). *Essence of Decision: Explaining the Cuban Missile Crises.* New York: Harper Collins.

Altman, M. & Lamontagne, L., (2003). On the natural intelligence of women in a world of constrained choice: How feminization of clerical work contributed to gender pay equality in early twentieth-century Canada, *Journal of Economic Issues*. XXXVII(4): 1045–1074.

Alvesson, M. & Billing, Y.D., (1997). *Gender and Organization.* London: Sage.

Alvesson, M. & Kärreman, D., (2004). Cages in tandem: Management control, social identity, and identification in a knowledge-intensive firm. *Organization*. 11: 149–175.

Alvesson, M. & Svenningsson, S., (2008). *Changing Organizational Culture: Cultural Change in Progress*, London & New York: Routledge.

Amin, A. & Cohendet, P., (2004). *Architecture of Knowledge. Firms, Capabilities, and Communities*, Oxford & New York: Oxford University Press.

Anderson, D.D., (2010). *Organization Development.* Los Angeles: Sage.

Angle, H.L. & Van de Ven, A.H.,(2000). *Research on the Management of Innovation: The Minnesota Studies.* Oxford: Oxford University Press.

Argyris, C., (1970). *Intervention Theory and Method.* Reading, Mass.: Addison-Wesley.

Argyris, C., (1992). *On Organizational Learning.* Cambridge, Mass.: Blackwell Publishers.

Argyris, C., (1998). Empowerment: The emperor's new clothes, *Harvard Business Review*, May–June: 98–105.

Argyris, C. & Schön, D., (1978). *Organizational Learning: A Theory of Action Perspective.* Reading, Mass: Addison-Wesley.

Argyres, N.S. & Silverman, B.S., (2004). R&D, organization structure, and the development of corporate technological knowledge, *Strategic Management Journal*, 25: 929–958.

Atkinson, R.C. & Shiffrin, R.M., (1968). Human memory: A proposed system and its control processes. In Spence, K.W. & Spence, J.T. (eds.), *The Psychology of Learning and Motivation*. Vol 2. New York: Academic Press.

Attali, J., (1985). *Noise: The Political Economy of Music*, Trans. by B. Massumi, Manchester: Manchester University Press.

Attewell, P., (1990). What is a skill? *Work and Occupations*, 17(4): 422–448.

Babbage, C., (1833). *On the Economy of Machinery and Manufactures.* Reprinted 1971. New York: Kelley.

Ball, K., (2005). Organization, surveillance and the body: Towards a politics of resistance. *Organization*. 12: 89–108.

Balogun, J., (2003). From blaming the middle to harnessing its potential: Creating change intermediaries, *British Journal of Management*, 14, 69–83.

Bapuji, H. & Crossan, M., (2004). From Questions to answers: Reviewing organizational learning research. *Management Learning.* 35: 397–417.

Barker, J.R., (1993). Tightening the iron cage: Concertive control in self-managing teams. *Administrative Science Quarterly.* 38: 408–437.

Barley, S.R. & Kunda, G., (1992). Design and devotion: Surges of rational and normative ideologies of control in managerial discourse, *Administrative Science Quarterly*, 37: 363–399.

Barley, S.R. & Tolbert, P., (1997). Institutionalization and structuration. Studying the links between action and institution, *Organization Studies*, 18(1): 93–117.

Barlow, D., (1993). The evolution of risk management. *Risk Management*, 40(4): 30–45.

Barnard, C., (1938). *The Functions of the Executive*, Cambridge, Mass.: Harvard University Press.

Bass, B.M., (1967). Social behavior and the orientation inventory: A review. *Psychological Bulletin.* 68: 260–292.

Bass, B.M., (1990). *Bass and Stogdill's Handbook of Leadership.* New York: Free Press.

Bass, B.M. & Avolio, B., (1994). *Improving Organizational Effectiveness through Transformational Leadership.* Thousand Oaks, CA: Sage Publications.

Baum, J.A.C., Rowley, T.J., Shipilov, A. & Chuang, Y., (2005). Dancing with strangers: Aspiration performance and the search for underwriting syndicate partners, *Administrative Science Quarterly*, 50: 536–575.

Bauman, Z., (1991). *Modernity and Ambivalence.* Cambridge: Polity Press.

Bauman, Z., (1999). *Culture as Praxis.* London, Thousand Oaks & New Delhi: Sage.

Bauman, Z., (2000). *Liquid Modernity.* Cambridge: Polity Press.

Beck, U., (1986). *Risksamhället. På väg mot en annan modernitet.* Göteborg: Daidalos.

Becker, H.S., Geer, B., Hughes, E.C. & Strauss, A.L., (1961). *Boys in White: Student Culture in Medical School.* Chicago: The University of Chicago Press.

Bell, D.E., (1983). Risk premiums for decision regret, *Management Science.* 29(10): 1156–1166.

Bennis, W. & Nanus, B., (1985/1997). *Leaders: Strategies for Taking Charge.* New York: Harper Business.

Bennis, W.G., (1966). *Changing Organizations: Essays on the Development and Evolution of Human Organization,* New York: McGraw-Hill.

Berger, P. & Luckmann, T., (1966). *The Social Construction of Reality.* London: Penguin Books.

Berger, P. & Luckmann, T., (1967). *The Social Construction of Reality. A Treatise in the Sociology of Knowledge.* New York: Doubleday.

Bergström, O., (1998). *Att passa in.* Göteborg: BAS.

Berle, A.A. Jr & Means, G.C., (1934). *The Modern Corporation and Private Property.* New York: Macmillan.

Bertalanffy, L. von., (1968). *General System Theory: Foundations, Development, Applications,* New York: Braziller.

Bertolotti, F., Macrì, D.M. & Tagliaventi, M.R., (2004). Social and organisational implications of CAD usage: A grounded theory in a fashion company, *New Technology, Work and Employment.* 19(2): 110–127.

Besley, T. & Ghatak, M., (2005). Incentives, risk and accountability in organizations. In: Hutter, B. & Power, M. (eds.) *Organizational Encounters with Risk.* Cambridge: Cambridge University Press.

Bhuiyan, N. & Baghel, A., (2005). An overview of continuous improvement: From the past to the present. *Management Decision.* 43: 761–771.

Bijker, W.E., Hughes, T.P., & Pinch, T.J., (1987/1989). (eds.) *The Social Construction of Technological Systems.* Cambridge, Massachusetts: The MIT Press.

Björkman, I., (1989). Factors influencing processes of radical change in organizational belief systems. *Scandinavian Journal of Management.* 5: 251–271.

Blake, R. & Mouton, J., (1964). *The Managerial Grid.* Houston, TX: Gulf.

Blau, P., (1963). *The Dynamics of Bureaucracy,* Chicago: University of Chicago Press.

Blauner, R., (1964). *Alienation and Freedom: The Factory Worker and his Industry.* Chicago: University Press.

Bloomfield, B.P., (1991). The role of information systems in UK National Health Service: Action at distance and the fetish of calculation, *Social Studies of Science*, 21: 701–734.

Bloomfield, B.P. & Hayes, N., (2009). Power and organizational transformation through technology: Hybrids of electronic government, *Organization Studies*, 30(5): 461–487.

Blyton, P. & Morris, J., (eds.) (1991). *A Flexible Future? Prospects for Employment and Organization.* Berlin: Walter de Gruyter.

Bogard, W., (1996). *The Simulation of Surveillance: Hypercontrol in Telematic Societies,* Cambridge: Cambridge University Press.

Boholm, Å., (1996). Risk perception and social anthropology. Critique of Cultural Theory, *Ethnos*, 61(1–2): 64–84.

Boholm, Å., (2004). Riskbedömningars ontologi och epistemologi. Ur Brink, Inger, Boholm, Åsa och Löfstedt, Ragnar E., (red.) *Facility Siting: Risk, Power and Identity in Land-use Planning*. London: Earthscan.

Bourdieu, P., (2004). *The Science of Science and Reflexivity*. Chicago & London: The University of Chicago Press.

Bouwen, R. & Fry, R., (1991). Organizational innovation and learning. *International Studies of Management and Organization*. 21: 37–51.

Bovey, W.H. & Hede, A., (2001). Resistance to organisational change: The role of defence mechanisms. *Journal of Managerial Psychology*. 16: 534–548.

Bower, G.H. & Hilgard, E.R., (1981). *Theories of Learning*. Englewood Cliffs, N.J.: Prentice-Hall.

Briscoe, F., (2007). From iron cage to iron shield? How bureaucracy enables temporal flexibility for professional service workers, *Organization Science*, 18(2): 297–314.

Brown, A.D. & Coupland, C., (2005). Sounds of silence: Graduate trainees, hegemony and resistance, *Organization Studies*, 26(7): 1049–1069.

Brown, R., (1992). *Understanding Industrial Organizations*. London: Routledge.

Brubakk, B. & Wilkinson, A., (1996). Changing roles of middle management? A case study of bank branch management. *Journal of Retailing and Consumer Services*. 3: 163–174.

Bruner, J., (1990). *Acts of Meaning*. Cambridge: Harvard University Press.

Brunsson, N., (1985). *The Irrational Organization: Irrationality as a Basis for Organizational Action and Change*. New York: Wiley.

Brunsson, N. & Jönsson, S., (1979). *Beslut och handling*. Stockholm: Liber.

Brunsson, N. & Olsen, J. P., (1990). Kan organisationsformer väljas? In: Brunsson N. & Olsen, J.P. (eds.) *Makten att reformera*. 11–26. Stockholm: Carlssons förlag.

Buckley, W., (1967). *Sociology and Modern Systems Theory*. Englewood Cliffs, N.J.: Prentice-Hall.

Burawoy, M., (1979). *Manufacturing Consent: Changes in the Labour Process under Monopoly Capitalism*. Chicago: University of Chicago Press.

Burke, P.J., (1966). Authority relations and disruptive behavior in small discussion groups. *Sociometry*, 29: 237–250.

Burke, W.W. (2008). *Organization Change: Theory and Practice*. London: Sage.

Burns, J.M., (1978). *Leadership*. New York: Harper & Row.

Burns, T. & Stalker, G.M., (1961). *The Management of Innovation*. London: Tavistock.

Burns, T. & Stalker, G.M., (1962). *The Management of Innovation*. Oxford: Oxford University Press.

Burris, B., (1998). Computerization of the workplace. *Annual Review of Sociology*. 24: 141–157.

Büssing, A., (2002). Motivation and satisfaction. In: A. Sorge., (ed.). *Organization*. London: Thomson Learning.

Calás, M. & Smircich, L., (1991). Voicing seduction to silence leadership, *Organization Studies*, 12(4): 567–602.

Campbell-Kelly, M., (2001). Information technology and organizational change in the British Census, 1801–1911. In: Yates, J. & Van Maanen, J. (eds.) *Information, Technology and Organizational Transformation. History, Rhetoric, and Practice*. 35–58. Thousand Oaks: Sage.

Canguilhem, G., (1989). *A Vital Rationalist: Selected Writings from George Canguilhem*. New York: Zone Books.

Carlson, S., (1951). *Executive Behavior: A Study of the Workload and Working Methods of Managing Directors*. Stockholm: Strömbergs.

Carmona, S. & Perez-Casanova, G., (1993). Organizational forgetting and information systems. *Scandinavian Journal of Management*. 9: 29–44.

Carruthers, B. & Espeland, W., (1991). Accounting for rationality; Double-entry book-keeping and the rhetoric of economic rationality, *American Journal of Sociology*, 97(1): 31–69.

Cartwright, D. & Zander, A., (1960). *Group Dynamics– Research and Theory*. Evansto, IL.: Row, Peterson.

Case, P., (1999). Remember re-engineering? The rhetorical appeal of a management salvation device, *Journal of Management Studies*, 36(4): 419–441.

Castoriadis, C., (1997). *World in Fragments*. Stanford: Stanford University Press.

Cavendish, R., (1982). *Women on the line*. London: Routledge and Kegan Paul.

Chandler, A.D., (1962). *Strategy and Structure*. Cambridge: MIT Press.

Chandler, A.D., (1962). *Strategy and Structure: Chapters in the History of the American Industrial Enterprise*. Washington, D.C.: Beard books.

Chandler, A.D., (1977). *The Visible Hand. The Managerial Revolution in American Business.* Cambridge, Massachusetts: The Belknap Press of Harvard University Press.

Chia, R., (1994). The concept of decision: A deconstructive analysis, *Journal of Management Studies*, 31(6): 781–806.

Child, J., (1972). Organizational structure, environment and performance: The role of strategic choice. *Sociology*, 6: 1–22.

Clawson, D., (1980). *Bureaucracy and the Labor Process: The Transformation of U.S. Industry, 1860–1920.* New York: Monthly Review Press.

Cockburn, C. & Ormrod, S., (1993). *Gender and Technology in the Making.* London: Sage.

Cockburn, Cynthia, (1983). *Brothers. Male Dominance and Technological Change.* London: Pluto Press.

Cohen, M.D., March, J.G. & Olsen, J.P., (1972). A garbage can model of organizational choice, *Administrative Science Quarterly*, 17: 1–25.

Cohen, P.S., (1969). Theories of myth, *Man*, 4(3), 337–353.

Collins, D., (1998). *Organizational Change.* London: Routledge.

Collinson, D.L., (1992). *Managing the Shopfloor: Subjectivity, Masculinity, and Workplace Culture.* Berlin: de Gruyter.

Colwill, N., (1995). Sex differences. In: Vinnicombe, S. & Colwill, N. (eds.) *The Essence of Women in Management.* London: Prentice Hall.

Conger, J.A., (1999). Charismatic and transformational leadership in organizations: An insider's perspective on these developing streams of research, *Leadership Quarterly*, 10: 145–79.

Conger, J.A. & Kanungo, Rabindra N., (1988). The empowerment process: Integrating theory and practice, *Academy of Management Review*, 13(3): 471–482.

Connell, R.W., (1995). *Masculinities.* Berkley and Los Angeles: University of California Press.

Cook, S. & Yanow, D. (1993). Culture and organizational learning. *Journal of Management Inquiry.* 2: 373–390.

Coppersmith, J., (2001). Texas politics and the fax revolution. In: Yates, J. & Van Maanen, J. (eds.) *Information, Technology and Organizational Transformation. History, Rhetoric, and Practice.* Thousand Oaks: Sage, pp. 59–85.

Craig, T., (1995). Achieving innovation through bureaucracy: Lessons from the Japanese brewing industry, *California Management Review*, 38(1): 8–36.

Crenshaw, K.W., (1989). Demarginalizing the intersection of race and sex: A black feminist critique of antidiscrimination doctrine, feminist theory and antiracist politics, University of Chicago Legal Forum 139–67. Quoted in D. Kairys, (ed.) (1990), *The Politics of Law: A Progressive Critique.*195–217 (2nd edn) New York: Pantheon.

Crenshaw, K.W., (1994). Mapping the margins: Intersectionality, identity politics, and violence against women of color. In: Fineman, M.A. & Mykitiuk, R. (eds.) *The Public Nature of Private Violence.* 93–118. New York: Routledge.

Crossan, M.M., Lane, Henry W. & White, R.E., (1999). An organizational learning framework: from intuition to institution, *Academy of Management Review*, 24: 522–537.

Cullen, J.B., Anderson, K.S. & Baker, D.D., (1986). Blau's theory of structural differentiation revisited: A theory of structural change or scale?, *Academy of Management Journal*, 29: 203–229.

Cusumano, M.A., (1985). *The Japanese Automobile Industry: Technology and Management at Toyota and Nissan*, Cambridge, Massachusetts: Harvard University Press.

Cyert, R.M. & March, J.G., (1963). *A Behavioral Theory of the Firm.* Englewood Cliffs, N.J.: Prentice-Hall.

Czarniawska, B., (2002). Organizing, process of. In: Sorge, A. (ed.) *Organization.* London: Thomson Learning.

Czarniawska, B., (2005). Networks, networking and nets: NCW from an Organization Theory perspective. In: Ydén, K. (ed.) *Directions in Military Organizing.* S 63–87. Stockholm: Försvarshögskolan, Publikationer.

Czarniawska, B. & Joerges, B., (1996). Travels of ideas. In: Czarniawska, B. & Sevón, G. (eds.) *Translating Organizational Change.* 13–48. Berlin: Walter de Gruyter.

Czarniawska, B. & Sevón, G., (1996)., (eds.) *Translating Organizational Change.* Berlin: Walter de Gruyter.

Czarniawska-Joerges, B., (1993). *The Three-Dimensional Organization.* Lund: Studentlitteratur.

Daft, R.L. & Weick, K.E., (1984). Toward a model of organizations as interpretation systems. *Academy of Management Review.* 9: 284–295.

Dalton, M., (1959). *Men Who Manage: Fusion of Feeling and Theory in Administration.* New York: Wiley.

Damanpour, F., (1992). Organziation size and innovation, *Organization Studies*, 13(3): 375–402.

Dawson, S. & Wedderburn, D., (1980). Introduction. Joan Woodward and the development of organization theory. In: Woodward, J. (1965/1980).

Industrial Organization: Theory and Practice. xiv-xl. Oxford: Oxford University Press.

Deal, T.E. & Kennedy, A.A., (1982). *Corporate Cultures: The Rites and Rituals of Corporate Life.* Reading, Mass.: Addison-Wesley.

De Cock, C. & Hipkin, I., (1997). TQM and BPR: Beyond the beyond myth, *Journal of Management Studies*, 34(5): 659–675.

Delbridge, R., (1998). *Life on the Line in Contemporary Manufacturing: The Workplace Experience of Lean Production and the 'Japanese Model'*, Oxford & New York: Oxford University Press.

Delbridge, R., Turnbull, P. & Wilkinson, B., (1992). Pushing back the frontiers: Managment control and work intensification under JIT/TQM factory regimes, *New Technology, Work and Employment*, 7(2): 9706.

Denham, N., Ackers, P. & Travers, C., (1997). Doing yourself out of a job? How middle managers cope with empowerment, *Employee Relations*, 19: 147–159.

Dent, E.B. & Goldberg, S.G., (1999). Challenging "Resistance to Change", *Journal of Applied Behavioral Science*, 35: 25–41.

Deutschman, A., (2001). *The Second Coming of Steve Jobs.* Milsons Point, N.S.W: Random House International.

Dierickx, I. & Cool, K., (1989). Asset stock acumulation and sustainability of competitive advantage, *Management Science*, 35(12): 1504–1511.

Dill, W.R., (1958). Environment as an influence on managerial autonomy, *Administrative Science Quarterly*, 2: 409–443.

Dillard, D., (1966). *Economic Development of the North Atlantic Community.* Englewood Cliffs, N.J.: Prentice-Hall.

Dillard, D., (1967). *Västeuropas och Förenta Staternas ekonomiska historia.* Malmö: Gleerups.

DiMaggio, P.J., (1983). State expansion and organizational fields. In: Hall, R.H. & Quinn, R.E. (eds.) *Organizational Theory and Public Policy.* 147–161. Beverly Hills: Sage Publications.

DiMaggio, P. & Powell, W.W., (1983). The iron cage revisited: Institutional isomorphism and collective rationality in organizational fields. *American Sociological Review*, 48(2): 147–160.

DiMaggio, P.J. & Powell, W.W., (1991). Introduction. In: Powell, W.W. & DiMaggio, P.J. (eds.) *The New Institutionalism in Organizational Analysis.* 1–38. Chicago: The University of Chicago Press.

DiMaggio, P.J. & Powell, W.W., (1983/1991). The iron cage revisited: Institutional isomorphism and collective rationality in organizational fields. In: Powell, W.W. & DiMaggio, P.J. (eds.) *The New Institutionalism in Organizational Analysis.* 63–82. Chicago: The University of Chicago Press.

Dogdson, M., (2000). *The Management of Technological Innovation.* Oxford & New York: Oxford University Press.

Dodgson, M., Gann D. & Salter, A., (2005). *Think, Play, Do: Technology, Innovation, and Organization*, Oxford & New York: Oxford University Press.

Donaldsson, L., (1985). *In Defence of Organization Theory.* Cambridge: Cambridge University Press.

Dosi, G., Nelson, R.R. & Winter, S.G., (2000). *The Nature and Dynamics of Organizational Capabilities*, Oxford: Oxford university press.

Dougherty, D., (1999). Organizing for innovation. In: Clegg, S.R., Hardy, C. & Nord, W.R. (eds.) *Managing Organizations*, London: Sage.

Dougherty, D. & Hardy, C., (1996). Sustained product innovation in large mature organizations: Overcoming innovation-to-organization problems, *Academy of Management Journal*, 39(5): 1120–1153.

Dougherty, D. & Heller, T., (1994). The Illegitimacy of successful product innovation in established firms. *Organization Science.* 5: 200–218.

Drejer, I. & Vinding, A.L., (2006). Organization, 'anchoring' of knowledge, and innovative activity in construction, *Building Research and Information*, 24: 921–931.

Drori, I., (2000). *The Seam Line: Arab Workers and Jewish Managers in the Israeli Textile Industry.* Stanford: Stanford University Press.

Drucker, P., (1955). *The Practice of Management.* London, Thousand Oaks & New Delhi: Sage.

Duncan, R.B., (1972). Characteristics of organizational environments and perceived environmental uncertainty, *Administrative Science Quarterly*, 17: 313–327.

Duncan, R. & Weiss, A., (1979). Organizational learning: Implications for organizational design. In Staw, B (ed.) *Research in Organizational Behavior.* 75–123.

Durkheim, É., (1912/1995). *The Elementary Form of Religious Life.* New York: Free Press.

Edwards, R., Collinson, M. & Rees, C., (1998). The determinants of employee responses to total quality management: Six case studies, *Organization Studies*, 19: 449–475.

Elger, T. & Smith, C., (1994). (eds.) *Global Japanization— The Transnational Transformation of the Labour Process.* London & New York: Routledge.

The New Encyclopaedia Britannica (1964). Chicago: Encyclopaedia Britannica.

Epstein, C., (1970*). Woman's Place*. Berkeley and Los Angeles: University of California Press.

Eriksson, U., (2000). *Det mangranna sällskapet. Om konstruktion av kön i företag.* (in Swedish) Göteborg: BAS Förlag.

Eriksson-Zetterquist, U., (2002). Construction of gender in corporations. In: Czarniawska, B. & Höpfl, H. (eds.) *Casting the Other*. London: Routledge.

Eriksson-Zetterquist, U., (2008). Gendered role modelling—A paradoxical construction process, *Scandinavian Journal of Management.* 24(3): 259–270.

Eriksson-Zetterquist, U. & Lindberg, K., (2002). *Organizational Effects on E-Business in Companies.* Göteborg University: School of Business.

Eriksson-Zetterquist, U. & Styhre, A., (2007). *Organisering och intersektionalitet (*in Swedish), Malmö: Liber.

Etzioni, A., (1964). *Modern Organizations*. Englewood Cliffs: Prentice-Hall.

Fagerberg, J., Mowery, D.C. & Nelson, R.R., (2005). (eds). *The Oxford Handbook of Innovation*, Oxford & New York: Oxford University Press.

Fanon, F., (1986). *Black Skin, White Masks*. London: Pluto Press.

Faulkner, W., (2007). 'Nuts and bolts and people': Gender-troubled engineering identities, *Social Studies of Science*, 37(3): 331–356.

Fayol, H., (1916/1949). *General and Industrial Management*. London: Pitman.

Feldman, D.C., (1994). Who's socializing whom? The impact of socializing newcomers on insiders, work groups, and organizations, *Human Resource Management Review.* 4(3): 213–233.

Feldman, D.C., Bearden, W.O. & Hardesty, D.M., (2006). Varying the content of job advertisements, *Journal of Advertising.* 35(1): 123–141.

Feldman, M.S., (1989). *Order Without Design: Information Production and Policy Making.* Stanford, Calif.: Stanford University Press.

Feldman, M.S., (2003). A performative perspective on stability and change in organizational routines. *Journal of Economic Geography.*12: 727–752.

Feldman, M.S. & Pentland, B.T., (2003). Reconceptualizing organization routines as a source of flexibility and change, *Administrative Science Quarterly*, 48: 94–118.

Feldman, M. & Pentland, B., (2005). Organizational routines and the macro-actors. In: Czarniawska, B. & Hernes, T. (eds). *Actor-Network Theory and Organizing*, 91–111. Malmö: Liber & Copenhagen: Copenhagen Business School Press.

Festinger, L., (1957). *A Theory of Cognitive Dissonance.* Stanford: Stanford University Press.

Fiedler, F., (1967). *A Theory of Leadership Effectiveness.* New York: McGraw-Hill.

Fiol, M.C. & Lyles, M.A., (1985). Organizational learning. *Academy of Management Review*, 10:803–813.

Fiol, M.C. & O'Connor, E.J., (2002). When hot and cold collide in radical change processes: Lessons from community development. *Organization Science.* 13: 532–546.

Fleming, P. & Sewell, G., (2002). Looking for the good soldier, Švejk: Alternative modalities of resistance in the contemporary workplace, *Sociology*, 36(4): 857–873.

Fleming P. & Spicer A., (2007). *Contesting the Corporation: Struggle, Power and Resistance in Organizations.* Cambridge: Cambridge University Press.

Foldy, E.G., (2002). 'Managing diversity'. Identity and power in organizations. In: Aaltio, I. & Mills, A.J. (eds.) *Gender, Identity and the Culture of Organizations.* London: Routledge.

Fondas, N., (1997). Feminization unveiled: Management qualities in contemporary writings. *Academy of Management Review.* 22/1: 257–282.

Frank, T., (1997). *The Conquest of Cool: Business Culture, Counterculture and the Rise of Hip Consumerism.* Chicago & London: The University of Chicago Press.

French, W.L. *et al.* (2005). *Organization Development and Transformation.* New York: McGraw-Hill.

Friedlander, F., (1983). Patterns of individual and organizational learning. In Shrivasta, S. (ed.) *The Executive Mind.* San Francisco: Jossey-Bass.

Friedman, A.L., (2004). Strawmanning and labour process analysis, *Sociology*, 38(3): 573–591.

Fucini, J.J. & Fucini, S., (1990). *Working for the Japanese*, Free Press, New York.

Galbraith, J., (1973). *Designing Complex Organizations*, Reading, Mass.: Addison-Wesley Publishing Company.

Galison, P., (1997). *Image and Logic: A Material Culture of Microphysics*, Chicago & London: The University of Chicago Press.

Gallo, C., (2010). *The Presentation Secrets of Steve Jobs.* New York: McGraw-Hill.

Gantt, H.L., (1919). *Work, Wages and Profits.* New York.

Garfinkel, H., (1968). *Studies in Ethnomethodology.* Englewood Cliffs N.J.: Prentice-Hall.

Garsten, C., (1999). Betwixt and between: Temporary employees as liminal subjects in flexible organizations, *Organization Studies*, 20(4): 601–617.

Garvin, D.A., (1993). Building a learning organization. *Harvard Business Review*, 71(4): 78–91.

George, C.S., (1972). *The History of Management Thought.* New Jersey: Prentice-Hall, Inc.

Gherardi, S., (1995). *Gender, Symbolism, and Organizational Cultures.* London, Thousand Oaks & New Delhi: Sage.

Gherardi, S., (2000). Practice-based theorizing on learning and knowing in organizations. *Organization*, 7: 211–223.

Gherardi, S., (2003). Feminist theory and organization theory: A dialogue on new bases. In: Knudsen, H. & Tsoukas, H. (eds.) *The Oxford Handbook of Organizational Theory: Meta-theoretical perspectives.* Oxford: Oxford University Press.

Ghoshal, S. & Bartlett, C.A., (1997). *The Individualized Corporation. A Fundamentally New Approach to Management.* New York: HarperCollins.

Ghoshal, S. & Bartlett, C.A., (1998). *Managing Across Borders.* London: Random House.

Giddens, A., (1999). *Runaway World. How Globalisation is Reshaping Our Lives.* London: Prolife Books Ltd.

Gillespie, R., (1991). *Manufacturing Knowledge.* New York: Cambridge University Press.

Gilson, M.B., (1940). Review of Roethlisberger and Dickson: Management and the Worker, *American Journal of Sociology*, 46: 98–101.

Gitelman, L., (1999). *Scripts, Grooves, and Writing Machines. Representing Technology in the Edison Era*, Stanford: Stanford University Press.

Goitein, B., (1984). The danger in disappearing postdecision surprise: Comment on Harrison and March, "Decision making and postdecision surprises", *Administrative Science Quarterly.* 29: 410–413.

Gouldner, A.W., (1954). *Patterns of Industrial Bureaucracy.* New York: The Free Press.

Graham, L., (1995). *On the Line at Subaru-Isuzu: The Japanese Model and the American Worker.* Ithaca: ILR press.

Greenwood, R., Oliver, C., Sahlin, K. & Suddaby, R., (2008). (eds.) *The Sage Handbook of Organizational Institutionalism.* 1–46. London, Thousand Oaks & New Delhi: Sage.

Greve, H.R. & Taylor, A., (2000). Innovations as catalysts for organizational change: Shifts in Organizational cognition and search, *Administrative Science Quarterly*, 45: 54–80.

Grey, C., (2001). Re-imaging relevance: A response to Starkey and Madan, *British Journal of Management*, 12, Special Issue, S27–S32.

Grey, C., (2004). Reinventing business schools: The contribution of critical management studies, *Academy of Management Learning and Education*, 3(2): 178–186.

Grint, K. & Case, P., (1999). The violent rhetoric of re-engineering? Management consultancy on the offence, *Journal of Management Studies*, 35(5): 557–577.

Grinyer, P.H. & Yasai-Ardekani, M., (1980). Dimensions of organizational structure: A critical replication, *Academy of Management Journal*, 23: 405–421.

Guest, D.E., (1987). Human Resource Management and Industrial Relations, *Journal of Management Studies*, 24(5): 503–521.

Guillén, M.F., (1994). *Models of Management: Work, Authority, and Organization in a Comparative Perspective.* Chicago & London: The University of Chicago Press.

Hackman, J.R. & Oldham, G.R., (1980). *Work Redesign.* Reading, Massachusetts: Addison-Wesley Publishing Company.

Hackman, R. & Wageman, R., (1995). Total quality management: Empirical, conceptual, and practical issues, *Administrative Science Quarterly*, 40: 309–342.

Haley, M.J., (1983). Relationship between internal-external locus of control beliefs, self-monitoring and leadership style adaptability, *Dissertation Abstracts International*, 44 (11B), 3563.

Hamel, G., (2000). *Leading the Revolution: How to Thrive in Turbulent Times by Making Innovation a Way of Life.* Boston: Harvard Business School Press.

Hammer, M., (2001). *The Agenda*, London: Random House.

Hammer, M. & Champy, J., (1993). *Reengineering the Corporation.* Harper Business, New York.

Handy, C., (1989). *The Age of Unreason.* London: Hutchinson Business Books.

Hansson, M. & Wigblad, R., (2006a). Recontextualizing the Hawthorne effect, *Scandinavian Journal of Management*, 22, 120–137.

Hansson, M. & Wigblad, R., (2006b). Pyrrhic victories–anticipating the closedown effect, *International Journal of Human Resource Management*, 17(5): 938–958.

Hargadon, A.B. & Douglas, Y., (2001). When innovations meet institutions; Edison and the design of the electric light, *Administrative Science Quarterly*, 46: 476–501.

Harrison, R.J. & March, J.G., (1984). Decision making and postdecision surprises. *Administrative Science Quarterly.* 29: 26–42.

Hatchuel, A., (2001). The two pillars of new management research, *British Journal of Management*, 12, Special Issue, S33–S39.

Heervagen, J.H., Kampschroer, K., Powell, K.M. & Loftness, V., (2004). Collaborative knowledge environments, *Building Research and Information*, 32(6): 510–528.

Heracleous, L. & Barrett, M., (2001). Organization change as discourse: Communicative actions and deep structures in the context of information technology implementation, *Academy of Management Journal*, 44(4): 755–778.

Herbst, P.G., (1974). *Socio-Technical Design.* London: Tavistock Publications.

Hersey, P. & Blanchard, K.H., (1969/1993). *Management of Organizational Behavior: Utilizing Human Resources.* Englewood Cliffs, NJ: Prentice-Hall.

Herzberg, F., (1966). *Work and the Nature of Man.* Cleveland and New York: The World Publishing Company.

Hindmarsh, J. & Pilnick, A., (2007). Knowing bodies at work: Embodiment and ephemeral teamwork in anaesthesia. *Organization Studies.* 28: 1395–1416.

Hinings, C.R. & Greenwood, R., (1988). *The Dynamics of Strategic Change.* Oxford: Basil Blackwell.

Hirschman, A.O., (1977). *The Passions and the Interests. Political Arguments for Capitalism before Its Triumph.* New Jersey: Princeton.

Hirst, P. & Zeitlin, J., (1991). Flexible specialization versus post-Fordism: Theory, evidence and policy implications, *Economy and Society*, 29(1): February.

Hodgkinson, G.P., Herriot, P. & Anderson, N., (2002). Re-aligning the stakeholders in management research: Lessons from industrial, work and organizational psychology, *British Journal of Management*, 12(Special Issue): S41–S48.

Hoffman, A., (1999). Institutional evolution and change: Environmentalism and the U.S. chemical industry, *Academy of Management Journal.* 42(4): 351–371.

Hofstede, G., (1980). *Cultural Consequences: International Differences in Work-Related Value.*, London: Sage.

Holt, R., (2004). Risk management: The talking cure, *Organization.* 11(2): 251–270.

Huber, G.P., (1991). Organizational learning: The contributing processes and the literatures, *Organization Science*, 2: 88–115.

Hughes, C., (2004). Class and other identification in managerial careers: The case of the lemon dress, Gender, *Work and Organization*, 11(5): 526–543.

Hung, S., (2004). Explaining the process of innovation: The dynamic reconciliation of action and structure. *Human Relations.* 57: 1479–1497.

Hutchinson, J.R. & Mann, H.S., (2004). Feminist praxis: Administering for a multicultural, multigendered public, *Administrative Theory & Praxis*, 26(1): 79–95.

Huy, Q.N., (1999). Emotional capability, emotional intelligence, and radical change. *Academy of Management Review.* 24: 325–345.

Hyman, R., (1988). Flexible specialisation: Miracle and myth. In: Hyman, R. & Streek, W. (eds.) (1988), *New Technology and Industrial Relations.* Oxford : Blackwell.

Iacono, S. & Kling, R., (2001). Computerization movements. The rise of the internet and distant forms of work. In: Yates, J. & Van Maanen, J. (eds.) *Information, Technology and Organizational Transformation. History, Rhetoric, and Practice.* 93–138. Thousand Oaks: Sage.

Iedema, R., (2003). *Discourses of Post-bureaucractic Organization.* Amsterdam & Philadephia: John Benjamins.

Ingelgård, A., Roth, J., Styhre, A. & Shani, A.B., (2002). Dynamic learning capability and actionable knowledge creation: Clinical R&D in a pharmaceutical company, *The Learning Organization*, 9(2): 65–77.

Inglehart, D., (1990). *Culture Shift.* Princeton, NJ: Princeton University Press.

Inglehart, D., (1997). *Modernization and Postmodernization.* Princeton, NJ: Princeton University Press.

International Journal of Project Management, January 2008, 26(1): 30–37.

Jacoby, S.M., (1985). *Employing Bureaucracy: Managers, Unions, and the Transformation of Work in American Industry, 1900–1945.* New York: Columbia University Press.

Jaques, E., (1951). *The Changing Culture of a Factory*. London: Tavistock Publications.

Jacques, R., (1996). *Manufacturing the Employee. Management Knowledge from the 19th to 21st Centuries*. London: Sage.

Jaeger, D. & Pekruhl, U., (1998). Participative company management in Europe: The new role of middle management. *New Technology, Work and Employment*. 13: 94–103.

Janis, I.L., (1982). *Groupthink: Psychological Studies of Policy Decisions and Fiascos*. 2nd edn. Boston: Houghton Mifflin.

Jarvenpaa, S.L. & Stoddard, D.B., (1998). Business process redesign: Radical and evolutionary change. *Journal of Business Research*. 41: 15–27.

Jasanoff, S., (2005), Restoring reason: causal narratives and political culture. In: Hutter, B. & Power, M. (eds.) *Organizational Encounters with Risk*. Cambridge: Cambridge University Press.

Jepperson, R.L., (1991). Institutions, institutional effects, and institutionalism. In: Powell, W.W. & DiMaggio, P.J. (eds.) *The New Institutionalism in Organizational Analysis*. 143–163. Chicago: The University of Chicago Press.

Jermier, J.M., Knights, D. & Nord, W.R., (1994). (eds.) *Resistance and Power in Organization*. London & New York: Routledge.

Joerges, B. & Czarniawska, B., (1998). The question of technology, or how organizations inscribe the world. *Organization Studies*, 19(3): 363–385.

Jones, G., (2010). *Organizational Theory, Design and Change*. Upper Saddle River: Pearson.

Kanter, R.M., (1977). *Men and Women of the Corporation*. New York: Basic Books.

Kärreman, D. & Alvesson, M., (2004). Cages in tandem: Management control, social identity, and identification in a knowledge-intensive firm, *Organization*, 11(1): 149–175.

Katz, D. & Kahn, R.L., (1966). *The Social Psychology of Organizations*. New York: John Wiley & Sons.

Kerfoot, D. & Knights, D., (1996). "The best is yet to come?": Searching for embodiment in management. In: Collinson, D. & Hearn, J. (eds.) *Masculinity and Management*. London: Sage.

Key, S., (1999). Toward a new theory of the firm: A critique of stakeholder "theory", *Management Decision*, 37(4): 317–328.

Kilduff, M. & Kelemen, M., (2001). The consolations of organization theory. *British Journal of Management*. 12: 55–59.

Kinnie, N., Hutchinson, S. & Purcell, J., (2000). 'Fun and surveillance': The paradox of high commitment management in call centres, *International Journal of Human Resource Management*, 11(5): 967–985.

Knights, D. & McCabe, D., (1998). 'What happens when the phone goes wild? Straff, stress, and spaces for escape in BPR telephone banking work regime,' *Journal of Management Studies*, 35(2): 163–194.

Knights, D. & McCabe, D., (1999). 'Are there no limits to authority?' TQM and organziational power, *Organization Studies*, 20(2): 197–224.

Knights, D. & Willmott, H., (2000): (eds.) *The Reengineering Revolution? Critical Studies of Corporate Change*. London, Thousand Oaks & New Delhi: Sage.

Koprowski, E.J., (1983). Cultural myths: Clues to effective management. *Organizational Dynamics*, Autumn, 39–51.

Korczynski, M. & Jones, K., (2006). Instrumental music? The social origins of broadcast music in British factories. *Popular Music*. 25: 145–164.

Kotter, J., (1978). *The General Managers*. New York: The Free Press.

Kotter, J.P. & Schlesinger, L.A., (1979). Choosing strategies for change. *Harvard Business Review*. 57: 106–114.

Krikman, B.L., Rosen, B., Tesluk, P.E. & Gibson, C.B., (2004). The impact of team empowerment on virtual team performance: The moderating role of face-to-face interaction, *Academy of Management Journal*, 47(2): 175–192.

Kunda, G., (1992). *Engineering Culture*. Philadelphia: Temple University Press.

Lam, A., (2007). Knowledge networks and careers. Academic scientists in industry-university links, *Journal of Management Studies*, 44(6): 993–1016.

Lant, T.K. & Mezias, S.J., (1992). An organizational learning model of convergence and reorientation. *Organization Science*. 3: 47–71.

Lanzara, G.F., (1983). Ephemeral organizations in extreme environments: Emergence, strategy, extinction, *Journal of Management Studies*. 20(1): 71–95.

Lanzara, G.F. & Patriotta, G., (2007). The institutionalization of knowledge in an automotive factory: Templates, inscriptions, and the problem of durability, *Organization Studies*, 28(5): 635–660.

Larson, M.S., (1977). *The Rise of Professionalism*. Berkeley: University of California Press.

Latour, B. & Woolgar, S., (1979). *Laboratory life*. New Jersey: Princeton University Press.

Latour, B., (1993). *Aramis, or the Love of Technology*. Cambridge, Massachusetts: Harvard University Press.

Latour, B., (1998). *Artefaktens återkomst*. Stockholm: Nerenius & Santerus.

Lave, J. & Wenger, E., (1991). *Situated Learning. Legitimate Peripheral Participation*. Cambridge: Cambridge University Press.

Law, J., (1987). Technology and heterogeneous engineering: The case of Portuguese expansion. In Bijker, Wiebe E., Hughes, Thomas P. & Pinch, Trevor J. (eds.) *The Social Construction of Technological Systems*. Boston, Mass.: MIT Press.

Law, J., (1991). Introduction: Monsters, machines and sociotechnical relations. In: Law, J. (ed.) *A Sociology of Monsters*. 1–23. London: Routledge.

Lawler, E.E., (1968). Effects of hourly overpayment on productivity and work quality, *Journal of Personality and Social Psychology*, 10(3): 306–313.

Lawrence, P.R. & Lorsch, J.W., (1967). *Organization and Environment: Managing Differentiation and Integration*. Boston, Mass.: Harvard University.

Legge, K., (1995). *Human Resource Management. Rhetorics and Realities*. Hampshire: Macmillan Press Ltd.

Leidner, R., (1993). *Fast Food, Fast Talk: Service Work and the Routinization of Everyday Life*. Berkeley: University of California Press.

Lewin, K., (1951/1997). *Resolving Social Conflict. Field Theory in Social Science*. Washington, DC: American Psychological Association.

Lieberman, D.A., (1993). *Learning: Behavior and Cognition*. Pacific Grove, Calif.: Brooks/Cole Pub. Co.

Liker, J.K., (2004). *The Toyota Way: 14 Management Principles from the World's Greatest Manufacturer*. Cambridge: Harvard Business School Press.

Lillrank, P., (1995). The transfer of management innovations from Japan, *Organization Studies*, 16(6): 971–989.

Lindgren, G., (1985). Kamrater, kollegor och kvinnor. PhD Thesis. Sociologiska institutionen, Umeå universitet, Sweden.

Litvin, D.R., (2002). The Business case for diversity and the 'Iron Cage'. In: Czarniawska, B. & Höpfl, H. (eds.) *Casting the Other. The Production and Maintenance of Inequalities in Work Organizations*. London: Routledge.

Llewellyn, S., (2001). 'Two-way windows'. Clinicians as medical managers, *Organization Studies*, 22(4): 593–623.

Lohan, M., (2000). Constructive tensions in feminist technology studies, *Social Studies of Science*. 3076: 895–916.

Luhmann, N., (2005). *Risk. A Sociological Theory*. New Jersey: Transaction Publishers.

Luhmann, N., (2005). The autopoesis of social systems. In: Seidl, D. & Becker, K.H. (eds.) *Niklas Luhmann and Organisation Studies*. 64–82. Copenhagen: Copenhagen Business School Press.

Lupton,To., (1963). *On the Shop Floor*. Pergamon Press.

Lyon, D., (1994). *The Electronic Eye: The Rise of Surveillance Society*. Cambridge: Polity Press.

MacDuffie, J.P., (1995). Human resource bundles and manufacturing performance: Organizational logic and flexible production systems in the world auto industry. *Industrial and Labor Relations Review*. 48: 197–221.

Machlup, F., (1962). *The Production and Distribution of Knowledge in the United States*. Princeton: Princeton University Press.

Maehr, M.L., (1974). Culture and achievement motivation, *American Psychologist*, December 1974: 887–896.

March, J.G. & Olsen, J., (1976). *Ambiguity and Choice in Organizations*. Oslo: Universitetsforlaget.

March, J.G. & Simon, H.A., (1958). *Organizations*. 2nd edn. Oxford: Blackwell.

March, J.G., (1994). *A Primer on Decision Making*. New York: Free Press.

March, J.G. & Shapira, Z., (1987). Managerial perspectives on risk and risk taking, *Management Science*, 33(11): 1404–1418.

Markides, C., (2007). In search of ambidextrous professors, *Academy of Management Journal*, 50(4): 762–768.

Markus, M.L., Manviolle, B. & Agres, C.E., (2000). What makes a virtual organization work?, *Sloan Management Review*, Fall: 13–26.

Marshall, J., (1984). *Woman Managers: Travellers in a Male World*. Chicago: John Wiley.

Martin, P.Y., (2003). Said and done versus saying and doing. Gendering practices, practicing gender at work, *Gender in Society* 17(3): 342–366.

Maslow, A.H., (1954). *Motivation and Personality*. New York: Harper and Row, Publishers.

Mason, D., Button, G., Lankshear, G. & Coates, S., (2002). Getting real about surveillance and privacy at work. In: Woolgar, S. (ed.) *Virtual society? Technology, Cyberbole, Reality.* Oxford & New York: Oxford University Press.

Mathews, B.P. & Redman, T., (1996). Getting personal in personnel recruitment. *Employee Relations.* 18(1): 68–78.

Mayo, E., (1933). *The Human Problems of an Industrial Civilization.* New York: Routledge.

Maznevsky, M.L. & Chudoba, K.M., (2000). Bridging space over time: Global virtual team dynamics and effectiveness, Organization Science, 11(5): 473–492.

McCabe, D., Knights, D., Kerfoot, D., Morgan, G. & Wilmott, H., (1998). 'Making sense of "quality?"- Toward a review and critique of quality initiatives in financial services', *Human Relations*, 31(3): 389–411.

McClelland, D.C. & Burnham, D.H., (1976). Power is the great motivator, *Harvard Business Review* 54(2): 100–111.

McClelland, D.C., (1961). *The Achieving Society.* Princeton: Van Nostrand.

McClelland, D.C., (1962). Business drive and national achievement, *Harvard Business Review* 40(4): 99–112.

McClelland, D.C., (1965). Achievement motivation can be developed, *Harvard Business Review* 43(6): 6–17.

McClelland, D.C., (1985). *Human Motivation.* Glenview, Illinois: Scott, Foresman and Company.

McGill, M.E., Slocum, J.W. Jr, & Lei, D., (1992). Management practicies in learning organizations. *Organizational Dynamics.* 21: 5–17.

McGregor, D., (1957). The human side of enterprise. *The Management Review* 46(11): 22–28.

McGregor, D., (1966). *Leadership and Motivation.* Cambridge: The M.I.T. Press.

Merton, R.K., (1968). *Social Theory and Social Structure.* New York: The Free Press.

Meyer, J.W. & Rowan, B., (1977). Institutionalized organizations: Formal structure as myth and ceremony, *American Journal of Sociology.* 83(2): 340–363.

Miles, R.E. & Snow, C.C., (1978). *Organizational Strategy, Structure, and Process.* Stanford, California: Stanford business books.

Miller, D., (1986). Configurations of strategy and structure: Towards a synthesis, *Strategic Management Journal*, 7: 233–249.

Miller, D., (1996). A preliminary typology of organizational learning: Synthesizing the literature, *Journal of Management*, 22: 485–505.

Miller, D. & Friesen, P.H., (1978). Archetypes of Strategy Formulation. *Management Science.* 24: 921–933.

Miller, P., (1992). The Tavistock Mission: A review essay. *Human Relations*, 45(4): 411–426.

Mills, C.W., (1951). *White Collars: The American Middle Class.* Oxford: Oxford University Press.

Mills, P.K. & Ungson, G., (2003). Reassessing the limits of structural empowerment: Organizational constitution and trust as controls, *Academy of Management Review.* 28(1): 143–153.

Mintzberg, H., (1973). *The Nature of Managerial Work.* New York: Harper & Row.

Mintzberg, H., (1978). Patterns in strategy formation. *Management Science.* 24: 934–948.

Mintzberg, H., (1979). *The Structuring of Organizations.* Englewood Cliffs, N.J.: Prentice-Hall.

Mintzberg, H., (1983). *Structure in Fives: Designing Effective Organizations.* Englewood Cliffs, N.J.: Prentice-Hall.

Morgan, D.L., (2002). *Essentials of Learning and Cognition.* Waveland Press.

Morris, P.W.G. & Pinto, J.K., (2007). (eds.) *The Wiley Guide to Project, Program and Portfolio Management.* Hoboken, N.J: Wiley.

Moss Kanter, R.,(1983). *The Change Masters.* London: George Allen &Unwin.

Mueller, F. & Carter, C., (2005). 'The scripting of Total Quality Management within its organizational biography', *Organization Studies*, 26: 221–247.

Müllern, T. & Elofsson, A., (2006). *Den karismatiska chefen* (in Swedish). Lund: Studentlitteratur.

Mumby, D.K., (2005). Theorizing resistance in organization studies. A diacritical approach, *Management Communication Quarterly*, 19(1): 19–44.

Münsterberg, H., (1913). *Psychology and Industrial Efficiency.* Boston and New York: Mifflin.

Murray, H., (1990). The transformation of selection procedures. In: Trist, E.L. & Murray, H. (eds.) *The Social Engagement of Social Science.* London: Free Association Books.

Nadler, D.A. & Tushman, M.L., (1990). Beyond the charismatic leader: Leadership and organizational change, *California Management Review*, 32: 77–97.

Narayandas, D., Dessain, V., Beyersdorfer, D. & Sjöman, A., (2007). Ericsson: Leading in times of change, *Harvard Business Review.*

Nelson, R.R. & Winter, S.G., (1982). *An Evolutionary Theory of the Economic Change*. Cambridge: Belknap.

Nkomo, S.M. & Cox, T., (1996). Diverse identities in organizations. In: Clegg, S.R., Hardy C. & Nord, W.R. (eds.) *Handbook of Organizational Studies*. London: Sage.

Nohria, N. & Ghoshal, S., (1997). *The Differentiated Network*. San Francisco: Jossey-Bass.

Nonaka, I. & Takeuchi, H., (1995). *The Knowledge-Creating Company*. Oxford: Oxford University Press.

Nye, D.E., (1990). *Electrifying America: Social Meanings of a New Technology, 1880–1940*. Cambridge: The MIT Press.

Nye, D.E., (2006). *Technology Matters: Questions to Live With*. Cambridge & London: The MIT Press.

O'Doherty, D. & Willmott, H., (2001). Debating labour process theory: The issue of subjectivity and the relevance of poststructuralism, *Sociology*, 35(2): 457–476.

O'Connor, E., (1999). Minding the workers: The meaning of 'human' and 'human relations' in Elton Mayo, *Organization* 6(2): 223–246.

Ohno, T., (1988). *Toyota Production System*. Cambridge, Mass: Productivity press.

Omanovic, V., (2003). Perspectives on diversity research. In: Leijon, S., Lillhanuus, R. & Widell, G. (eds.) *Reflecting Diversity: Viewpoints from Scandinavia*. Göteborg: Bas förlag.

Omanovic, V., (2004). *Negotiating and Naturalizing "Diversity": A Swedish Manufacturing Case*. A paper for EGOS Colloquium, Ljubljana, Slovenia, July 1st–3rd, 2004.

Orlikowski, W.J., (2007). Sociomaterial practices: Exploring technology at work, *Organization Studies*. 28(9): 1435–1448.

Pardo del Val, M. & Fuentes, C.M., (2003). Resistance to change: A literature review and empirical study, *Management Decision*. 41: 148–155.

Parker, M., (1999). Capitalism, subjectivity and ethics: Debating labour process analysis, *Organization Studies*, 20(1): 25–45.

Parker, M., (2000). *Organization, Culture and Identity: Unity and Division at Work*. London, Thousand Oaks & New Delhi: Sage.

Parsons, T., (1990). Prolegomena to a theory of social institutions, *American Sociological Review*, 55(3): 319–333.

Pavitt, K., (2005). Innovation processes. In: Fagerberg, J., Mowery, D.C. & Nelson, R.R. (eds.) *The Oxford Handbook of Innovation*. 86–114. Oxford & New York: Oxford University Press.

Pavlov, I.P., (1927/2003). *Conditioned Reflexes*. Mineola, New York: Dover Publications.

Pennings, J.M., (1975). The relevance of the structural-contingency model for organizational effectiveness, *Administrative Science Quarterly*, 20: 393–411.

Pentland, B.T. & Rueter, H.H., (1994). Organization routines as grammars of action, *Administrative Science Quarterly*, 39(3): 484–510.

Perrow, C., (1986). *Complex Organizations. A Critical Essay*. New York: McGraw-Hill.

Perrow, C., (1986). *Complex Organizations: A Critical Perspective*. 2nd edn. New York: McGraw-Hill.

Pettigrew, A.M., (1973). *The Politics of Organizational Decision-making*. London: Tavistock.

Pettigrew, A. & Massini, S., (2003). Innovative forms of organizing: Trends in Europe, Japan and the USA in the 1990s, In: Pettigrew, A.M. et al., (eds.) *Innovative Forms of Organizing* London: Sage.

Pettigrew, A., Massini, S. & Numagami, T., (2000). Innovative forms of organizing in Europe and Japan, *European Journal of Management*, 18: 259–273.

Pettigrew, A., et al. (2003). *Innovative Forms of Organizing*. London: Sage.

Pfeffer, J., (1993). Barriers to the advance of organizational science: Paradigm development as a dependant variable, *Academy of Management Review*, 18(4): 599–620.

Pfeffer, J., (2008). What ever happened to pragmatism? *Journal of Management Inquiry*, 17(1): 67–60.

Pfeffer, J. & Fong, C.T., (2002). The end of business schools: Less success than meets the eye, *Academy of Management Learning and Education*, 1(1): 78–95.

Pfeffer, J. & Salancik, G.R., (1978). *The External Control of Organizations: A Resource Dependence Perspective*. New York: Harper and Row.

Pfeffer, J. & Sutton, R.I., (1999). *The Knowing-Doing Gap: How Smart Companies Turn Knowledge into Action*. Cambridge, Mass.: Harvard University Press.

Pfeffer, J. & Sutton, R.L., (2006). *Hard Facts, Dangerous Half-truths and Total Nonsense*. Boston, Mass.: Harvard Business School Press.

Pillai, R., (1995). Context and charisma: The role of organic structure, collectivism and crisis in the emergence of charismatic leadership, *Academy of Management Journal*. Best papers proceedings: 332–336.

Pinsonneault, A. & Kraemer, K.L., (1993). The impact of information technology on middle managers. *MIS Quarterly*. 17: 271–292.

Pinsonneault, A. & Kraemer, K., (1997). Middle management downsizing: An empirical investigation of the impact of information technology, *Management Science*, 43: 5.

Piore, M.J. & Sabel, C.F., (1984). *The Second Industrial Divide—Possibilities for Prosperity*, Basic Books, New York.

Plant, S., (1997). *Zeros + Ones. Digital Women + The New Technoculture*. London: Fourth Estate.

Polanyi, K., (1944). *Den stora omdaningen. Marknadsekonomins uppgång och fall*. Lund: Studentlitteratur.

Pollert, A., (1981). *Girls, Wives, Factory Lives*. London: MacMillan.

Popper, M. & Lipshitz, R., (2000). Organizational learning. Mechanisms, culture, and feasibility. *Management Learning*, 31: 181–196.

Porter, L.W. & Lawler, E.E., (1968). *Managerial Attitudes and Performance*. Homewood. Ill.: Richard D. Irwin.

Porter, M.I., (1985). *Competitive Advantage: Creating and Sustaining Superior Performance*. New York: Free Press.

Powell, W.W. & Grodal, S., (2005). Networks of innovation. In: Fagerberg, J., Mowery, D.C. & Nelson, R.R. (eds.) *The Oxford Handbook of Innovation*. 56–85. Oxford & New York: Oxford University Press.

Powell, W.W., Koput, K.W. & Smith-Doerr, L., (1996). Interorganizational collaboration and the locus of innovation: Networks of learning in biotechnology, *Administrative Science Quarterly*, 41: 116–145.

Power, M., (2004). *The Risk Management of Everything. Rethinking the Politics of Uncertainty*. London: Demos.

Power, M., (2005). Organizational responses to risk: The rise of the chief risk officer. In: Hutter, B. & Power, M. (eds.) *Organizational Encounters with Risk*. Cambridge: Cambridge University Press.

Pugh, D.S., Hickson, D.J., Hinings, C.R., Macdonald, K.M., Turner, C. & Lupton, T., (1963). A conceptual scheme for organizational analysis, *Administrative Science Quarterly*, 8: 289–315.

Pugh, D.S., Hickson, D.J., Hinings, C.R. & Turner, C., (1968). Dimensions of organization structure. *Administrative Science Quarterly*. 13: 65–105.

Quinn, R.W., (2005). Flow in knowledge work: High performance experience in the design of national security technology, *Administrative Science Quarterly*, 50: 610–641.

Radcliffe-Brown, A.R., (1958). *Methods in Social Anthropology*. Chicago: The University of Chicago Press.

Ramirez, P. & Tylecote, A., (2004). Hybrid corporate governance and its effects on innovation. A case study of AsraZeneca, *Technology Analysis & Strategic Management*, 16(1): 97–119.

Ratnasingam, P., (2001). Interorganizational trust in EDI adoption: The case of Ford Motor Company and PBR Limited in Australia. *Internet Research*. 11(3).

Rehman A.A., (2008). *Dubai & Co*. New York: McGraw-Hill.

Reich, R., (2000). *Introduction*. In: A. Smith, *The Wealth of Nations*. 1776. New York: The Modern Library.

Renn, O., (1998). Three Decades of Risk Research: Accomplishments and New Challenges *Journal of Risk Research*. 1:1 49–71.

Rice, A.K., (1951/1990). The use of unrecognized cultural mechanisms in an expanding machine shop. In: Trist, E.L. & Murray, H. (eds.) *The Social Engagement of Social Science*. London: Free Association Books.

Robertson, M. & Swan, J., (2004). Going public: The emergence and effects of soft bureaucracy within a knowledge-intensive firm. *Organization*. 11: 123–148.

Robertson, E., Korczynski, M. & Pickering, M., (2007). Harmonious relations? Music at work in the Rowntree and Cadbury factories. *Business History*. 49: 211–234.

Roethlisberger, F.J. & Dickson, W.J., (1934). *Management and the Worker. Technical vs. Social Organization in an Industrial Plant*. Harvard University. Graduate School of Business Administration. Division of Research. Business Research Studies No. 9.

Roethlisberger, F.J. & Dickson, W.J., (1939). *Management and the Worker*. Cambridge, Massachusetts: Harvard University Press.

Rombach, B. & Solli, R., (2006). *Constructing Leadership. Reflections on Film Heroes as Leaders*. Stockholm: Santérus förlag.

Roscigo, V.J. & Hodson, R., (2004). The organizational and social foundations of worker resistance, *American Sociological Review*, 69: 14–39.

Rowley, C., (1995). The illustration of flexible specialization: The case of the domestic ware sector of the British ceramics industry, *New Technology, Work, and Employment*, 9(2).

Roy, D., (1952). Quota restriction and goldbricking in a machine shop. *The American Journal of Sociology.* 57: 427–442.

Samad, S.A., (2005). *AstraZenecas Growth Strategies*, India: IBSCDC.

Saxenian, A., (1994). *Regional Advantage: Culture and Competition in Silicon Valley and Route 128.* Cambridge & London: Harvard University Press.

Schein, E.H., (1965/1980). *Organizational Psychology.* 3rd edn. New Jersey: Prentice Hall.

Schein, E.H., (1978). *Career Dynamics: Matching Individual and Organizational Needs.* MA: Addison-Wesley.

Scheuer, S., (2000). *Social and Economic Motivation at Work.* Copenhagen Business School Press: Handelshøjskolens Forlag.

Schleef, D.J., (2006). *Managing Elites: Professional Socialization in Law and Business Schools*, Lanham: Rowman & Littlefield.

Schön, D., (1983). *The Reflective Practitioner.* Basic Books.

Schoonhoven, C.B., (1981). Problems with contingency theory: Testing assumptions hidden within the language of contingency 'theory', *Administrative Science Quarterly*, 26: 349–377.

Schroeder, R.G., Ven de Ven, A.H., Scudder, G.D. & Polley, D., (2000). The development of innovation ideas. In: Van de Ven, A., Angle, H.L. & Poole, M.S. (eds.) *Research on the Management of Innovation.* 107–134. Oxford & New York : Oxford University Press.

Schultze, U., (2000). A confessional account of an ethnography about knowledge work, *MIS Quarterly*, 24(1): 3–41.

Schumpeter, J.A., (1939). *Business Cycles.* Vol. 1. New York: McGraw-Hill.

Schumpeter, J.A., (1942). *Capitalism, Socialism, and Democracy.* New York: Harper & Row.

Scott, R.W., (2004). Reflections on a half-century of organizational sociology, *Annual Review of Sociology*, 30: 1–21.

Scott, W.R., (1987). The adolescence of institutional theory. *Administrative Science Quarterly.* 32: 493–511.

Scott, W.R., (1995). *Institutions and Organizations.* London, Thousand Oaks and New Delhi: Sage.

Scott, W.R., (2004). Reflections on a half-century of organizational sociology, *Annual Review of Sociology*, 30: 1–20.

Selznick, P., (1949). *TVA and the Grassroots.* Berkely: University of California Press.

Selznick, P., (1957). *Leadership in Administration: A Sociological Interpretation*, Berkeley: University of California Press.

Selznick, P., (1996). Institutionalism 'old' and 'new', *Administrative Science Quarterly*, 40: 270–277.

Senge, Peter M., (1990). *The Fifth Discipline.* New York: Doubleday.

Sewell, G., (1998). The discipline of teams: The control of team-based industrial work through electronic and peer surveillance, *Administrative Science Quarterly*, 43: 397–428.

Sewell, G., (2001). What goes around, comes around: Investigating a mythology of teamwork and empowerment, *Journal of Applied Behavioral Science*, 37(1): 70–79.

Sewell, G. & Barker, J.R., (2006). Coercion versus care: Using irony to make sense of organizational surveillance, *Academy of Management Review*, 31(4): 934–961.

Shamir, B. & Howell, J.M., (1999). Organizational and Contextual Influences on the Emergence and Effectiveness of Charismatic Leadership, *Leadership Quarterly*, 10: 257–283.

Shamir, B., House, R.J. & Arthur, M.B., (1993). The motivational effects of charismatic leadership: a self-concept based theory, *Organization Science*, 4: 577–594.

Sharma, A., (1999). Central dilemmas of managing innovation in large firms, *California Management Review*, 41(3): 146–164.

Shenhav, Y., (1999). *Manufacturing Rationality.* Oxford: Oxford University Press.

Sherman, S.W. & Garland, G.E., (2007). Where to bury the survivors? Exploring possible *ex post* effects of resistance to change. *S.A.M. Advanced Management Journal.* 72: 52–62.

Silverman, D., (1970). *The Theory of Organizations.* New York: Basic Books.

Simon, H.A., (1957). *Models of Man.* New York: Wiley.

Simon, H.A., (1976). *Administrative Behavior.* 3rd. edn. New York: Free Press.

Sine, W.D., Haveman, H.A. & Tolbert, P.S., (2005). Risky business? Entrepreneurship in the new independent-power sector, *Administrative Science Quarterly*, 50: 200–232.

Sinter, R., (1998). *Jack Welch & the G.E. Way: Management Insights and Leadership Secrets of the Legendary CEO.* New York: McGraw-Hill.

Skinner, B.F., (1974). *About Behaviorism.* New York: Vintage Books.

Slappendel, C., (1996). Perspectives on innovation in organizations, *Organization Studies*, 17(1): 107–129.

Smith, A., (1776). *The Wealth of Nations*. New York: The Modern Library.

Smith, C., (1989). Flexible specialisation, automation and mass production, *Work, Employment, and Society*, 3(2): 203–220.

Smircich, L., (1983). Concepts of culture and organizational analysis. *Administrative Science Quarterly*. 28: 339–358.

Sole, D. & Edmondson, A., (2002). Situated knowledge and learning in disperse teams, *British Journal of Management*, 13: S17–S34.

Spector, P.E. *et al.* (2002). Locus of control and well-being at work: How generalizable are western findings? *Academy of Management Journal*. 45: 453–466.

Spufford, F. & Uglow, J., (1996). *Cultural Babbage. Technology. Time and Invention*. London: Faber and Faber.

Stata, R., (1989). Organizational learning—The key to management innovation. *Sloan Management Review*. Spring, 63–79.

Stjernberg, T., (1977). *Organizational Change and Quality of Life. Individual and Organizational Perspective on Democratization of Work in an Insurance Company*. Stockholm: EFI.

Strauss, A., Schatzman, L., Bucher, R., Ehrlich, D. & Sabshin, M., (1964). *Psychiatric Ideologies and Institutions*. 2nd edn. New Brunswick & London: Transaction Books.

Styhre, A. & Eriksson-Zetterquist, U., (2008). Thinking the multiple in gender and diversity studies: Examining the concept of intersectionality, *Gender in Management*, 23(8): 567–582.

Tam, Y.M., Korczynski, M. & Frenkel, S.J., (2002). Organizational and occupational commitment: Knowledge workers in large corporations. *Journal of Management Studies*. 39: 775–801.

Tannenbaum, A.S., (1968). *Control in Organizations*. New York: MacGraw-Hill.

Taylor, F.W., (1998/1911). *The Principles of Scientific Management*. Mineola, New York: Dover Publications, Inc.

Taylor, P., Hyman, J., Mulvey, G. & Bain, P., (2002). Work organization, control and the experience of work in call centers, *Work, Organization and Society*, 16(1): 133–150.

Tengblad, S., (2000). Vad innebär Human Resource Management? In: Bergström, O. & Sandoff, M. (eds.) *Handla med människor—perspektiv på Human Resource Management*. Lund: Academia Adacta.

Thomas, R. & Dunkerley, D., (1999). Careering downwards? Middle managers' experiences in the downsized organization, *British Journal of Management*, 10: 157–169.

Thompson, J.D., (1967). *Organizations in Action*. New York: McGraw-Hill.

Thompson, V.A., (1969). *Bureaucracy and Innovation*, Alabama: The University Press of Alabama.

Thompson, P., Smith, C. & Ackroyd, S., (2000). If ethics is the answer, you are asking the wrong questions. A reply to Martin Parker, *Organization Studies*, 20(6): 1149–1158.

Thorndike, E.L., (1911). *The Elements of Psychology*. New York: A.G. Seiler.

Thrift, N., (1998). Virtual capitalism: The globalization of reflexive business knowledge. In: Carrier, J.G. & Miller, D. (eds.) *Virtualism: A New Political Economy*. Oxford & New York: Berg.

Thrift, N., (2005). *Knowing Capitalism*. London: Sage.

Todorov, T., (1984). *Mikhail Bakhtin: The Dialogical Principle*. Trans. by Wlad Godzich, Manchester: Manchester University Press.

Tolbert, P.S. & Zucker, L.G., (1996). The institutionalization of institutional theory. In: Clegg, S.R., Hardy, C., & Nord, W.R. (eds.) *Handbook of Organizational Studies*. London, Thousand Oaks and New Delhi: Sage.

Townley, B., (1994). *Reframing Human Resource Management*. London: Sage.

Townley, B., Cooper, D. & Oakes, L., (2003). Performance measures and the rationalization of organizations, *Organization Studies*, 24: 1045–1071.

Trice, H.M. & Beyer J.M., (1993). *The Cultures of Work Organizations*. New Jersey: Prentice-Hall, Inc.

Trist, E., (1981). *The Evolution of the Socio-technical System*. Occasional Paper no, 2, June 1981. Ontario Ministry of Labour. Ontario Quality of Working Life Centre.

Trist, E.L. & Bamforth, K.W., (1951). Some social and psychological consequences of the Longwall method of coal-getting. *Human Relations*, 4: 3–38.

Trist, E.L. & Murray, H., (1990). Historical overview: The foundation and the development of the Tavistock Institute. In: Trist, E.L. & Murray, H. (eds.) *The Social Engagement of Social Science*. London: Free Association Books.

Tsoukas, H., (2005). *Complex Knowledge: Studies in Organizational Epistemology*. Oxford & New York: Oxford University Press.

Tuckman, A., (1994). 'The yellow brick road: Total Quality Management and the restructuring of organizational culture', *Organization Studies*, 15(5): 727–751.

Turner, B.A. & Pidgeon, N.F., (1997). *Man-made Disasters*. Oxford: Heinemann.

Tushman, M.L. & O'Reilly, C.A., (1996). Ambidextrous organizations: Managing evolutionary and revolutionary change, *California Management Review*, 38(4): 8–30.

Van de Ven, A., (1986). Central problems in the management of innovation, *Management Science*, 32(5): 590–607.

Van Maanen, J. & Katz, R., (1976). Individuals and their careers: Some temporal considerations for work satisfaction. *Personnel Psychology*. 29: 601–616.

Ven de Ven, A.H. & Poole, M.S., (2000). Methods for studying innovation processes. In: Van de Ven, A., Angle, H.L. & Poole, M.S. (eds.) (2000). *Research on the Management of Innovation*. 31–54. Oxford & New York: Oxford University Press.

Ventriss, C. & Luke, J., (1988). Organizational learning and public policy: Towards a substantive perspective. *The American Review of Public Policy*. 18: 337–357.

Volberda, H.W., (1998). *Building the Flexible Firm*. Oxford: Oxford University Press.

Vroom, V.H., (1964). *Work and Motivation*. New York: John Wiley & Sons, Inc.

Wagner-Tsukamoto, S., (2007). An Institutional economic reconstruction of scientific management: On the lost theoretical logic of taylorism. *Academy of Management Review*. 32: 105–117.

Wajcman, J., (2004). *TechnoFeminism*. Cambridge: Polity Press.

Waldo, D., (1961). Organization theory: An elephantine problem. *Public Administration Review*. 21: 210–225.

Walsh, J.P., Meyer, A.D. & Schoonhoven, C.B., (2006). A future for organization theory: Living in and living with changing organizations, *Organization Science*, 17: 657–671.

Walton, R.E., (1980). Establishing and maintaining high commitment work systems. In: Kimberly, J., Miles, R.H. *et al*. *The Organizational Life Cycle*. San Francisco: Jossey-Bass Publishers.

Wanous, J.P., (1992). *Organizational, Entry: Recruitment, Selection, Orientation and Socialization of Newcomers*. New York: Addison-Wesley Publ.

Watanabe, S., (1991). "The Japanese quality control circle: Why it works", *International Labour Review*, 130(1): 57–80.

Watson, J.B., (1924/2007). *Behaviorism*. New Brunswick: Transaction Publishers.

Watson, T.J., (2002). *Organising and Managing Work*. Harlow, England: Prentice Hall.

Weber, M., (1978). *Economy and Society: An Outline of an Interpretive Sociology*. Berkeley, California: University of California Press.

Weber, M., (1904/2009). *The Protestant Ethic and the Spirit of Capitalism*. New York: W.W. Norton.

Weick, K.E., (1969). *The Social Psychology of Organizing*. Reading, Mass.: Addison-Wesley.

Weick, K., (1988). Enacted sensemaking in crisis situations, *Journal of Management Studies*. 25(4): 305–317.

Weick, K., (1990). The vulnerable system: An analysis of the Tenerife air disaster, *Journal of Management*. 16(3): 571–593.

Weick, K.E., (1993). The collapse of sensemaking in organizations: The Mann Gulch disaster, *Administrative Science Quarterly*. 38: 628–652.

Weick, K.E. & Sutcliffe, K.M., (2001). *Managing the Unexpected. Assuring High Performance in an Age of Complexity*. San Francisco: Jossey-Bass.

Wenger, E., (1998). *Communities of Practice. Learning, Meaning, and Identity*. Cambridge: Cambridge University Press.

Werth, B., (1994). *The One Billion Molecule: One Company's Quest for the Perfect Drug*. New York: Simon & Schuster.

Westley, F.R., (1990). Middle managers and strategy: Microdynamics of inclusion. *Strategic Management Journal*. 11: 337–351.

White, M., (2007). Who'll stop the ring tones?, *New York Times*, November 18, 2007.

Whittington, R. & Pettigrew, A., (2003). Complementarities in action: Organizational change and performance in BP and Unilever 1985–2002. In Pettigrew, A. *et al*. (eds.) *Innovative Forms of Organizing*. London: Sage.

Whittington, R., Pettigrew, A., Peck, S., Fenton, E. & Conyon, M., (1999). Change and complementarities in the new competitive landscape: A european panel study, 1992–1996, *Organization Science*, 10: 583–600.

Whyte, W.H., (1956). *The Organization Man*. New York: Simon and Schuster.

Wiener, N., (1948). *Cybernetics, or Control and Communication in the Animal Machine*. New York: John Wiley.

Wiener, N., (1950). *The Human Use of Human Beings*. London: Eyre and Spottiswoode.

Wilkinson, A., Godfrey, G. & Marchington, M., (1997). Bouquets, brickbats and blinkers: Total Quality Management and employee involvement in practice, *Organization Studies*, 18(5): 799–819.

Wilkinson, B., Morris, J. & Munday, M., (1995). The iron fist and the velvet glove: Management and organization in Japanese manufacturing transplants in Wales," *Journal of Management Studies*, 32(6): 819–830.

Winch, G., (1998). Zephyrs of creative destruction: Understanding the management of innovation in construction, *Building Research & Information*, 26(4): 268–297.

Winter, S.J. & Taylor, L.S., (2001). The role of information technology in the transformation of work. In: Yates, J. & Van Maanen, J. (eds.) *Information, Technology and Organizational Transformation. History, Rhetoric, and Practice*. 7–33. Thousand Oaks: Sage.

Wishart, N.A., Elam, J.J. & Robey, D., (1996). Redrawing the portrait of a learning organization: Inside Knight-Ridder, Inc. *Academy of Management Executive*. 10: 7–20.

Wolfe, R.A., (1994). Organization innovation: Review, critique and suggested research directions, *Journal of Management Studies*, 31(3): 405–431.

Woodward, J., (1965). *Industrial Organization*. Oxford: Oxford University Press.

Woolgar, S., (1991). The turn to technology in social studies of science, *Science, Technology & Human Values*, 16(1): 20–50.

Womack, J.P., Jones, D.T. & Roos, D., (1990). *The Machine that Changed the World*. London: Simon & Schuster.

Wren, D.A., (1972). *The Evolution of Management Thought*. New York: The Ronald Press Company.

Yagil, D., (1998). Charismatic leadership and organizational hierarchy: Attribution of charisma to close and distant leaders. *Leadership Quarterly*. 9: 161–176.

Yanow, D., (2004). Translating local knowledge at organizational peripheries, *British Journal of Management*, 15: S9–S25.

Yates, J. & Van Maanen, J., (2001). Introduction. In: Yates, J. & Van Maanen, J. (eds.) *Information, Technology and Organizational Transformation. History, Rhetoric, and Practice*. Thousand Oaks: Sage.

Yoder, J.D., (1991). Rethinking tokenism: Looking beyond numbers, *Gender and Society*, 5(2): 178–192.

Yoder, J.D., (1994). Looking beyond numbers: The effect of gender status, job prestige, and occupational gender-typing on tokenism processes, *Social Psychology Quarterly*, 57(2): 150–159.

York, R.O. & Hastings, T., (1985). Worker maturity and supervisory leadership behavior, *Administration in Social Work*. 9: 37–47.

Young, A.P., (2000). 'I'm just me': A study of managerial resistance, *Journal of Organization Change Management*, 13(4). 375–388.

Zaleznik, A., Christensen, C.R., Roethlisberger, F.J., with the assistance and collaboration of Homans, George C., (1958). *The Motivation, Productivity, and Satisfaction of Workers*. Boston: Harvard University, Division of Research, Graduate School of Business Administration.

Zammuto, R.F., Griffith, T.L., Majchrzak, A., Dougherty, D.J. & Faraj, S., (2007). Information technology and the changing fabric of organization, *Organization Science*, 19(5): 749–762.

Zbaracki, M.J., (1998). The rhetoric and reality of total quality management, *Administrative Science Quarterly*, 43: 602–636.

Zuboff, S., (1988). *In the Age of the Smart Machine*. London & New York: Basic Books.

Zucker L.G., (1987). Institutional theories of organizations, *Annual Review of Sociology*, 13: 443–464.

Glossary

Behaviourism A perspective on learning that defines behavioural change as the core of learning. The behaviouristic perspective tries to understand how individuals learn how to deal with situations, and it depicts learning as an experience-based process. Within the behaviourist perspective there was also a focus on how certain behaviours can be trained: a process called conditioning.

Bounded rationality A term proposed by Herbert Simon to denote the capacity of human beings to only take into account a limited amount of relevant data in decision-making processes at the same time as rational decision-making. I.e., linear processes where information is collected, alternatives considered, and decisions are finally made serve as the ideal decision-making situation for humans. Simon thus suggests that humans seek to act rationally but are only capable of being so to a limited extent, i.e., their decision-making is characterized by a 'bounded rationality'.

Bureaucracy Described by Max Weber as an ideal type of organization with certain features, amongst which Weber specifically mentioned the use of goal- or value-based rules, systems of rules rather than piecemeal rules, legal authority as superior to other forms of authority (e.g., traditional authority), and obedience based on membership.

Business process reengineering A set of managerial and organizational principles aimed at eliminating non-value adding activities in the product development, production, and distribution process. The term was widely popular in the 1990s and today the concept of *Lean*, originally developed in the Toyota production system, represents a similar ambition to eliminate unnecessary procedures.

Change management An area within Organizational Behaviour and Organizational Development that covers methods and techniques for managing organizational change processes.

Charismatic leadership Charisma is seen as a source of authority. Charismatic leadership is expected to grow out of situations of crisis in which the charismatic manager lifts the organization out of the predicament. Even though the crisis is a temporary state, charisma tends to be routinized.

Cognitive theory A broad grouping of approaches to understanding processes of thinking, primarily on the individual level. The concept has been applied within the learning field, and it contains a number of influential perspectives, for instance the information perspective, which can be described as a sequential model of how individuals process information and respond to external stimuli.

Commitment An idea based on the belief that an employee's dedication to work is built-in as a fundamental part of the work structure.

Communities of practice A perspective on learning that argues that learning takes place in social settings (*communities*) in which a shared world of practice is developed. The concept of practice is important since it emphasizes that learning takes place in concrete situations in which individuals interact with others to resolve day-to-day business.

Conditioning A concept in learning theory describing how individuals respond to external stimuli. In the behaviourist tradition researchers such as Pavlov studied how certain reflexes could be conditioned to emerge. Conditioned reflexes are acquired through processes of education, training, and habit.

Configurational approach The configurational approach seeks to describe the complementarities between strategy, structure, and environments, and how organizations can be described as design types, configurations, or archetypes.

Content-oriented motivation theories Theories which examine the fundamentals of human needs, for instance Maslow's Hierarchy of Needs from 1954.

Contingency theory A theory in which contingent factors such as technology, market position, product diversity, rate of change, and size affect the efficiency of the organization. An efficient organization is designed to adapt to all situational demands coming from the various contingent factors. For instance, the technologies used in production have effects on organization structure as well as the success of the organization.

Continuous change A change model that focuses on change as a process that takes place on a daily basis. A central argument is that organizations can benefit from working with change in many small steps, rather than making large-scale changes.

Decision-making Decision-making is an intellectual, cognitive, and behavioural social process wherein one or a number of actors make conscious selections between alternatives. Decisions are based on a perceived problem, access to various resources enabling various actions, and desirable outcomes. While rationalist images of decision-making emphasize the information collection and information evaluation processes, behavioural theories of decision-making emphasize the political, emotional, and cultural embedding of all decision-making in organizations.

Deskilling relates to the degradation of an occupation due to decreased needs of skills and decreased economic status resulting in lower wages.

Diversity Different ways of dealing with organization members' identities. Diversity includes gender, ethnicity, age, personal history, education, personality, lifestyle, sexual preferences, geographic origins, organizational position, among others.

Downsizing Attempts at reducing the number of workers, for instance through delayering within an organization.

Emergent change A theoretical perspective on change focusing on change as a social process. In contrast to planned change this perspective tries to understand how change is happening in organizations, and how it is situated in cultural and institutional patterns.

Empowerment A concept challenging Taylor's idea of separating intellectual work tasks from manual tasks. Empowerment is thought to improve the work group or the individual employee at lower levels of the hierarchy by giving them increased responsibilities in the form of administrative tasks and planning.

Enlightenment philosophy An idea from the eighteenth and nineteenth centuries based on scientific reasoning and rational thinking. According to Enlightenment philosophers it is believed that a modern society can be designed rationally and hereby directed and controlled. This concept has been the impetus for extensive technological rationalizations.

Environment A central concept in the open system view and contingency theory, describing the external factors that influence the organization. The environment includes both the more narrow business environment and the broader environment (including society at large).

Figureheads CEOs who play important communicative roles externally and internally, for instance as symbols of their companies.

Group thinking A phenomenon observed by industry psychologists wherein a group or a community fails to take into account factors and conditions that affect the outcomes of their decisions. Group thinking suggests that many groups are collectively imposing intellectual and cultural barriers, blindfolding the decision-making at times, leading to decisions that in hindsight or from the outside appear inadequate.

Hard HRM A philosophy arguing for strategically incorporating personnel management in line with the overall goals and strategies of the organization as a way for the organization to achieve higher efficiency.

Hawthorne Effect When employees are selected and treated as special, productivity is believed to increase. A contributing factor is benevolent management and humane treatment of employees. In addition, informal groups are found to influence the norms that relate to productivity.

Hawthorne Study One of the most extensive empirical studies undertaken in organizational theory. It was carried out between 1926 and 1932 in the US company the Hawthorne Electrical Works, Chicago.

Homosocial reproduction A term explaining why primarily men are recruited to top organizational positions. Homosocial reproduction is founded on the male preference for identifying and socializing with other men. Recruiting someone who is similar in work habits, social background, education, and general behaviour is expected to secure trustworthiness, loyalty, and achievement orientation.

Human Resource Management Strategically maximizing the integration of employee and organizational goals, increasing the employee's work involvement. In addition, it also defines the nature and flexibility of the workforce.

Human-centred perspective on technology Taking people as the starting point and assuming people engage with technology in different ways, this perspective advocates technology having different meanings in different contexts.

Information technology A definition provided by Yates and Van Maanen (2001: xxi) is 'mechanisms used to organize, store, manipulate, present, send, and review information'. It also includes everything from the library to blackboards to calculators and computers.

Innovation Innovation refers to new products, services, or procedures that are being developed by organizations and companies either to be sold on the market or to enhance organizational activities (so-called 'process innovations'). Innovative work commonly includes a broad set of competencies and expertise and in many cases departments, companies, or even industries are collaborating to produce innovations.

Institution A set of beliefs, routines, or standardized procedures how to both legitimately perceive social reality and how to act upon it. Institutions denote tangible organizational arrangements such as technology standards and procedural routines, as well as intangible norms and beliefs guiding social action.

Intersectionality A research vein claiming the simultaneous effect of categories such as gender, ethnicity, social class, sexuality, religion, and age. A person's superior or subordinate position in an organization has an effect on these various categories.

Isomorphisms (coercive, mimetic, normative) A tendency of organizations and organizational practices and routines to become standardized and predictable across relatively heterogeneous organizational fields. 'Isomorphism' is derived from the Greek words *iso* (meaning 'similar') and *morphe* ('form') thus meaning 'similar form-ness'. Institutional theorists perceive isomorphisms as indications of strong institutional pressures on organizations to conform to widely enacted beliefs and norms.

Job enlargement A process in which an employee's normal work tasks are increased in scope.

Job enrichment A process in which an employee's work tasks are expanded to include planning and control.

Knowledge A broad concept used in a number of fields to describe the outcome of a knowledge-acquiring/-creating process. The concept has a long tradition and there are a large number of perspectives on knowledge, and it has grown to become an important concept within organization theory.

Knowledge management Knowledge management is the management of individuals that in various ways have expertise and know-how in specific domains. It has evolved into a rich field of studies, influenced by a number of different theoretical perspectives.

Labour process theory A branch within sociology (at times referred to as *industry sociology*) studying work and work relations. Traditionally, labour process theory has examined the manufacturing industry, but more recently the service industry and creative industries have also been regarded from a labour process theory perspective.

Leadership as contextual Leadership takes place in a spatial and temporal context (including for instance formal structures, people, relations, culture, legislation, and technology). Simultaneously, leadership is part of shaping this very context.

Learning The concept is broadly defined as the change in a subject's behaviour or behaviour potential to a given situation brought about by the subject's experiences in that situation, provided that the behaviour change cannot be explained on the basis of the subject's native response tendencies, maturation, or temporary states (such as fatigue, drunkenness, drives, and so on).

Management control A wide variety of activities and procedures for controlling and safeguarding the output from organizational activities. Management control includes both formal and tangible procedures such as accounting routines, as well as more subtle and indirect forms of control such as corporate cultures and professional policies.

Open system The idea of the organization being an open system sees the organization as vulnerable to influence from its surroundings. Hereby the organization lives with uncertainty. The major sources of organizational uncertainty are technology and the environment.

Operative decentralization People with operative tasks that take on decision-making authority concerning their specific tasks.

Organization culture Organization cultures are the residual components guiding and structuring human action in organizations, that is, shared norms, beliefs, and preferences collectively enacted by organization members or imposed on workers that influence their actions. The concept of organization culture was widely endorsed in the 1980s to explain how the Japanese manufacturing industry had established an egalitarian and participative culture that contributed to the elimination of non-value-adding activities.

Organizational boundaries A concept derived from the open systems view of organizations, which depicts the organization as delimited from its environment, and where the boundaries are described as the interface between the organization and its environment.

Organizational change The process of initiating and managing change in organizational structures, processes, and technology. Organizational change encompasses a number of different perspectives, from the view that change is movement between two steady states, to the view that change is an integrated part of the daily work in organizations.

Organizational learning A rapidly growing part of the literature on organizations, which contains a number of different perspectives. Traditionally the view is that organizations, *per se*, can learn. Recent research suggests that learning is actually a process that takes place within and around organizations.

Organizational structure The prescribed order of coordinating human effort in organizations. This order is assumed to be stable and explicit, and it usually contains elements such as centralization, standardization, formalization, number of hierarchic layers, and flexibility. The overall organizational structure is often depicted in an organizational chart.

Outsourcing Moving certain functions or activities from the company to its suppliers.

Planned change A group of theories on change that emphasize that change is something initiated by managers, and where the change process can be deliberately managed and controlled. There are a number of models trying to identify the necessary steps an organization needs to take in order to successfully carry out change.

Process-oriented motivation theories Theories considering human needs and exterior factors relating to working conditions as well as other parts of the environment of an individual in order to understand what motivates people.

Psychological contract Part of the results of a successful recruitment process, describing the reciprocal commitments and expectations between the individual and the organization.

Radical change A change model focusing on large-scale, company-wide changes. This model argues that organizations are often facing complex demands that make it necessary to carry out large change projects.

Recruitment A strategic activity in order to supply organizations with talented employees.

Recruitment process A process including identifying the future needs of the organization, advertising (in print or online) to attract and prepare suitable applicants, painting a realistic picture of the future workplace, testing applicants' reactions to various situations, simultaneously giving applicants time to gradually adapt to the future employer, hereby establishing commitment between employer and future employee.

Resistance Resistance is a broad term denoting a variety of practices aimed at undermining managerial objectives. Resistance can appear in many forms, ranging from outright protests and quarrels between managers and workers to more subtle methods including forms of sabotage and ignoring of enacted rules.

Routines Routines are predictable, widely shared scripted behaviours that constitute everyday work in organizations. At the same time, routines are flexible and adaptable to emerging situations and contingencies, enabling organization actors to adapt to a variety of situations and demands.

Scientific management A system of managerial and organizational principle formulated and implemented in industry by Frederick W. Taylor based on engineering sciences and aiming at a transparency of performance and win–win agreements between labourers and owners. At times also referred to as Taylorism.

Situated learning A perspective on learning that argues that learning always takes place in concrete situations. The perspective also describes the social aspects of learning.

Situational leadership An idea advocating that managers differ in their leadership behaviour exhibited in interactions with employees. If employees display a low level of maturity, a task-oriented style is used by the leader. If employees display a high level of maturity, the leader exhibits low levels of task- and relations-orientation.

Sociomaterial practices A perspective on technology and organizations based on the idea that social and material worlds are intertwined. In order to understand technology in organizations, both the social and the material have to be examined and described simultaneously.

Sociotechnical system The *social system* consisting of people, communication, and knowledge is seen as integrated, complexly interwoven, and interdependent with the *technical system*, consisting of machines, equipment, tools, and other artefacts. Developed at the Tavistock Institute in England.

Soft HRM A philosophy according to which employees are seen as a critical resource to be involved in and motivated by various normative control measures. An efficient organization is believed to be founded upon motivated, enthusiastic, and satisfied employees.

Style approach to leadership focusing on what managers are doing. Leadership styles are separated into leadership focus on people (relations, people, group maintenance, consideration) or tasks (goal achievement, task initiating of structure, production) or variations of these two themes.

Technological determinism Technology is seen as exogenous, homogenous, predictable, stable, and independent of time and space. As such it becomes a lever for human action. Criticized for ignoring economic, legal, social, cultural, political, and institutional conditions when studying how technology changes organizations.

Tokenism Seeing a person as a symbol for a group rather than as an individual person.

Total Quality Management A set of managerial and organizational principles developed within the Toyota production system aimed at (1) eliminating quality problems by establishing zero-defect policies and involving the workers in the work, (2) reducing the stock of components through just-in-time logistics, (3) instituting routines through continuously improving the activities on the shop floor.

Trait approach Emphasizing the personality traits of the manager. An approach whereby personality traits are used to characterize successful managers and potential leaders.

Transactional leadership Seeing leadership as an exchange situation in which the manager uses different incentives in exchange for, for instance, money, working conditions, or praise, for the effort of the worker.

Transformational leadership A mutual effort by the manager and worker who go beyond the realm of self-interest in order to work for a common cause or value. Based on the notion of intrinsic motivation this concept focuses on the inner motives of people as important drivers for human effort.

Uncertainty A central concept in the open systems view and contingency theory. Contingency theory describes uncertainty as emanating from the environment, and more specifically from heterogeneity and dynamics. It is argued that the more heterogeneous and dynamic the environment, the higher the perceived uncertainty.

Upskilling Changes to work which enable workers to learn to carry out operation processes using new system tools.

Women-in-management literature Literature claiming that women have a different management style than men. This literature has been severely criticized for being founded on popular assumptions about men and women rather than nuanced scientific studies.

Index

A

accidents, learning from 265–7
accounting procedures as
    institutions 183–4
Acker, J. and Van Houten, D., on
    Hawthorne Study 117
acquisitions, integration
    process 231
activity approach to
    leadership 146–7
Actor Network Theory (ANT)
    51, 68
Adams, S.J., Equity Theory 124–5
adaptation 40
Adler, P., on effects of
    computerization 66
Administrative Behaviour,
    Herbert Simon 169
Adorno, Theodore W., on
    institutions 177
advertisements, recruitment 110
aesthetical considerations 143
affiliation, need for 124
agriculture, enclosure movement 8
Akrich, M., Callon, M., and Latour, B.,
    interessement 205–6
Alienation and Freedom, Robert
    Blauner 88
Allison, Graham T., study of Cuba
    crisis 171–3
Altman, M. and Lamontagne, L., on
    deskilling of female clerical
    workers 67
Alvesson, M. and Svenningsson, S.,
    on shop floor culture 87
'ambidextrous' professors 195
Amin, A. and Cohendet, P.,
    perspectives on
    knowledge 257–8
Andes plane crash (1972) 267
Angle, H.L. and Van de Ven, A.
    on innovation phases 202
    on innovative capacity 203
Animal Intelligence, The, Edward
    Lee Thorndike 247
Any Given Sunday (movie), depiction
    of motivation 126
Apple
    introduction of iPad 68
    Steve Jobs' leadership 151
apprenticeship programme,
    Primo 107–8
    comparison with Hawthorne
    Study 118
    motivational factors 122

Archer Daniels Midland Company
    (ADM)
    impact of Hawthorne Study 112–13
arenas for learning 252
Argyres, N.S. and Silverman, B.S.,
    on R&D structure and
    innovation 211
Argyris, Chris
    definition of interventions 237
    On Organizational Learning 252
assembly lines 61
    stress exposure 88
assimilation of tokens 155
associative processes, learning 247
Aston School 30
AstraZeneca
    decision-making 170
    portfolio selection 165–7, 177
    sub-cultures 187
    tensions 184
Atkinson, R.C. and Shiffrin, R.M.,
    stage model 249
attitude measurement 126
autopoiesis theory of social
    systems 177
Awakening Giant, The, A.M.
    Pettigrew 232

B

Babbage, Charles 11–12, 64–5
    on division of labour 78
Balogun, J., study of change
    implementation 160–1
Bamforth, Ken 58
Barley, S.R. and Tolbert, P., on
    institutions 178
Barnard, Chester
    The Functions of the Executive 28
    theory of organizations 222
Bass, B.M. and Avolio, B., *Full Range
    of Leadership Model* 151
Bauman, Z., on organizational
    culture 185
Bay of Pigs invasion 174
Beck, Ulrich, on risks of technological
    development 50
Bedaux system 80
behavioural theories of decision-
    making 170–1
behavioural theories of learning 244,
    246, 253–5
behaviourism 247–8
belief systems, link to radical
    change 230–1
belonging, sense of 143

Bennis, Warren and Nannus, Burt,
    Leaders 147
bias in recruitment 111
Blau, Peter M., *The Dynamics of
    Bureaucracy* 28
Blauner, Robert, *Alienation and
    Freedom* 88
Bloomfield, R.P. and Hayes, N., on
    impact of IT 142
Body Shop, Anita Roddick's
    leadership 148–9
boredom, employees 14
boundary crossing, Sony
    Ericsson 142–3
boundaryless organization 43
bounded rationality 169
Bovey, W.H. and Hede, A., on
    defence mechanisms 237–8
Bradley, Glen, Ciba Vision 217, 218
*Brothers: Male Dominance and
    Technological Change*, Cynthia
    Cockburn 66–7
Brunsson, N., on hypocrisy in
    institutions 183
Brunsson, N. and Olsen, J.P., on
    Scandinavian
    institutionalism 228
Burawoy, Michael, shop floor
    study 89
bureaucracy 27–8
bureaucratic control 97
bureaucratic organizations 100
    innovation 209–11
    susceptibility to crises 267
Burke, W.W., on change 232
Burns, James, on leadership 149–50
Burns, T. and Stalker, G.M.,
    mechanistic and organic
    organizational systems 36
business process
    re-engineering 94–5
    definition 94
business school research,
    relevance 2, 3–4
business schools, growth in student
    numbers 3
business titles, growth 2–3

C

Cadbury, use of singing 85
call centres
    'culture of fun' 186
    management control 97
Calvin, John 10
Canguilhem, G., on institutions 178

career development, Rolls-Royce
    Motor Cars 121
career models, Primo apprenticeship
    programme 108
Carlson, Rachel, *Silent Spring* 227
Carlson, Sune, study of
    leadership 146
case studies 5
    minicases 7
Castoriadis, Cornelius, on
    knowledge 258
Catholic Church, hierarchical
    structure 8
Census Office, data processing 64–5
Chalmers University of Technology,
    research centres 195, 212,
    214
Chandler, A.D.
    *Strategy and Structure: Chapters in the
        History of American Industrial
        Enterprise* 37
    'structure follows strategy'
        formula 211
change
    as a feature of innovation 199
    keeping up 22
    see also organizational change
change implementation, role of
    middle managers 160–1
change management 219–20
Chaplin, Charlie, *Modern Times* 82
charismatic/transformational
    leadership 148–9
    contextual factors 152
Chia, Robert, on decision-
    making 175–6
Chicago sociology group 86
chief executive officers (CEOs)
    at Ericsson 135–6
    figure-head role 138
    Irene Rosenfeld 137–8
    stereotypes 137
Child, John, strategic-choice
    approach 37
child labour, in Industrial
    Revolution 11
Ciba Vision
    organizational change 217–19, 221
        continuous improvement 229
        unfreezing stage 223–4
        resistance to change 236
Cisco, integration strategy 231
Clawson, Dan, on Taylorism 83
clerical work, deskilling 66, 67
clinical pathways 94–5
closedown threat, effect on
    productivity 159
close-mindedness 174

cloth industry, industrialization 8–9
coal mining, sociotechnical
    perspective 58
CocaCola, sustainable
    structures 40–1
Cockburn, Cynthia, *Brothers: Male
    Dominance and Technological
    Change* 66
coercive isomorphisms 182, 226–7
cognitive dissonance 174
cognitive revolution 170
cognitive theories of learning 244–5,
    246, 248–9
    organizational learning 255–6
Cohen, P.S., on myths 70
collectivism 131
commitment 127
communities of practice perspective
    of learning 250
community building 42–3
compensation systems, Hawthorne
    Study 116
compensation theories
    Achievement Motivation
        Theory 123–4
    Equity Theory 124–5
    Expectancy Theory 124
    Expectancy Theory and Equity
        Theory in combination 125
    see also motivation
competition 42
    on shop floor 89
complementarities in action 41
complex product systems 209
computerization
    deskilling/upskilling debate 66–7
    see also information technology (IT)
computerization movements 70–1
conceptual behaviour 249
concertive control 97–8
conditioned reflexes 247–8
configurational approach 37–8
conflicting demands 22
'congealed action', institutions as 177
Conger, J.A., on charismatic/
    transformational
    leadership 150
'conquest of cool' 186
consideration 146
construction industry, complex
    product systems 209
constructionist perspective of
    learning 249
contact lens products, Ciba
    Vision 217–18
content-oriented motivation
    theories 119, 126–7
    job characteristics model 122–3

Maslow's Hierarchy of
    Needs 119–20
    Theory X and Theory Y 120
    Two-Factor Theory 121–2
contingency factors 24
contingency theory 23–4, 33–7,
    60–2
    criticisms 37
    definition 140
continuous improvement 229,
    232–3
    in Ciba Vision 221
    combination with radical change 233
    Jönköping county council 233
contrast of tokens 155
Cook, S. and Yannow, D., on
    organizational learning 256
cooperation 42
'co-optation', Tennessee Valley
    Authority 179–80
co-production of knowledge 258
'Copy Exactly' strategy, Intel 20
corporate culture 184–6
corporate identity 143
corporate social responsibility (CSR)
    strategies 181
cottage industries 8–9
counterdependent personality
    type 203
craft system 8, 10
Craig, T., on innovation in Japanese
    brewing industry 210–11
creative destruction 197–8
crises, charismatic leadership 152
    at Ericsson 152–3
crisis management 266–7
Crossan, MM, Lane, H.W. and
    White, R.E., model of
    organizational learning 255
Cuba crisis
    decision-making 171–3
    depiction in movies 173
cultural influences 168
culture 184–6
    Israeli textile factory, incorporation
        of traditional family values 190
    Japanese 'transplants' 189–90
    national differences 186–7
    professional and occupational 188–9
    shop floor work 87
    sub-cultures in pharmaceutical
        industry 187
'culture of fun' 186
cybernetic theory 176
Cyert, R.M. and March, J.G., on
    decision-making 264
Czarniawska, B. and Joerges, B., on
    organizational change 228

D

Daft, R. and Weick, K.,
    on interpretation
        systems 230
Dalton, M., *Men Who Manage* 88
Damanpur, F., on organization size
        and innovation 211
decentralization 140–1
decision-making 167–71, 191
    in AstraZeneca 170
    behavioural theory 170–1
    conclusions 175–6
    group thinking 174–5
    Herbert Simon's work 169–70
    risk management 264
decision-making models 171–3
defence mechanisms 237–8
delayering, impact on middle
        managers 159
Deming, W. Edwards, on quality
        improvement 232–3
Dent, E.B. and Goldberg, S.G., on
        resistance to change 238
deskilling 11
    in clerical work 66, 67
    as criticism of Taylorism 80, 83
    as effect of computerization 66–7
development, difference from
        research 200–1
Dierickx, I. and Cool, K., time-
        compression
        diseconomies 196
differentiation, definition 29
Dill, W.R. 35
DiMaggio, P.J. and Powell, W.W., on
        isomorphisms 182, 226
dimensions of structural factors 30
    Intel Corporation 30–1
direct control 97, 98
disasters 263
    formation of ephemeral
        organizations 266
    learning from 265–7
discontinuous change 229
diversity 131–2
    intersectionality 157–8
diversity initiatives 131
diversity management, McKinsey &
        Company 132
diversity training 131
division of labour 55, 78
    Babbage principle 64
    in coal mining 58
    historical origins 9, 12
divisional structure
    definition 33
    Intel Corporation 19–20
        dividing by output 26

doctors
    demarcation disputes with
        nurses 81, 259
    normative isomorphism 182–3
    organizational culture 185–6
double-entry book-keeping 11,
        183–4
Dougherty, D.
    definition of innovation 200
    on innovation phases 202
Dougherty, D. and Hardy, C., on
        innovation 210
Dougherty, D. and Heller, T., on
        innovation 206–7
downsizing 127
    impact on middle managers 159
    in Ericsson 161
Drori, Israel, study of Israeli textile
        factory 190
Drucker, Peter
    The Practice of Management 128–9
    on Taylorism 83
drug development 175
Dubai, radical change 234
Durkheim, Émile 86
    institutions concept 177
Dynamics of Bureaucracy, The,
        Peter M. Blau 28

E

e-Business
    benefits 70
    introduction at Ford and Volvo Car
        Company 47, 50–1, 71
Edison, Thomas Alva
    innovative genius 206
    invention of phonograph 207–8
effects of learning approach 252
Emerson, Harrington, staff and line
        organization 25
Emirates airline, organizational
        change 234
employees
    challenge vs monotony problem 14
    conflict with managers 13
    historical perspectives 10
    welfare 13
    see also workers
empowerment
    of middle managers 159
    of workers 84, 127–8
        in decentralization 140–1
enabling 150
enactment 267
enclosure movement 8
energizing 150
engineering profession,
        development 78

Enlightenment 7, 8
    risk of accidents 262–3
Enlightenment philosophers 49, 50
environmental enactment 38
environmental influences 34–7, 43
    adaptation to 253–4
environmental issues, as driver of
        change 227
Environmental Protection Agency
        (EPA) 227
envisioning 150
ephemeral organizations 266
epistemology 256
equipment, variables of 82
Equity Theory 124–5
    combination with Expectancy
        Theory 125
Ericsson
    crisis, role in charismatic
        leadership 152–3
    downsizing, impact on middle
        managers 161
    gender issues 154–5
    leadership philosophies 135–6
Erie Canal construction 12
'et cetera clauses' 101
ethical considerations 143
Etzioni, A.
    Modern Organizations 256
    types of organizations 257
evidence-based approach 3
evolutionary-economics approach to
        knowledge 257
Expectancy Theory 124
    combination with Equity Theory 125
expert knowledge 258–9
expert work, separation from
        standard work 81
external demands 22

F

Fab 32 manufacturing unit, Intel 20
factory observers 11–12
factory system 8, 10, 55
    organization 11
Fanon, Franz, on culture 185
fashions and fads in management 95
Fayol, Henri, basic functions of
        administration 222
Feldman, M., on management
        control 96
Feldman, M. and Pentland, B., on
        organizational routines 100
female workers
    impact on organizations 85
    see also gender issues; women
feminine expressions,
        interpretations 157

Festinger, Leon, on cognitive
    dissonance 174
Fiat's Melfi Model 241–2, 245–6
    organizational learning 253
    situated learning 251
Fiedler, Fred, contingency
    theory 140
Fifth Discipline, The, Peter Senge 246
figure-heads 138
First World War, productivity
    levels 14
Fleming, P. and Sewell, G., on
    resistance 99–100
Fleming, P. and Spicer, A., on
    'culture of fun' 186
flexibility, impact of IT 69
flexible specialization 90
Fog of War (movie) 173
Foldy, E.G., on diversity
    programmes 131–2
followership 139
force fields, Lewin 223
Ford Motor Company
    introduction of e-Business 47, 48,
        50–1, 71
    purchasing function 59
foremen, functional foremanship 25
formal structures see organizational
    structures
Frank, Thomas, on 'conquest of cool'
    186
free trade 9
freezing stage of change 223
French Revolution 7
frequency structures 155
Friedlander, F., on learning 249
Full Range of Leadership Model 151
functional foremanship, definition 25
Functions of the Executive, The,
    Chester Barnard 28
fuzzy boundaries 142

G
Galbraith, J., on information
    processing 36
Gantt, Henry, refinement of
    Taylorism 80–1
Gantt-charts 203
garbage-can decision-making 171
Garfinkel, Harold, on 'et cetera
    clause' 101
gender issues
    at Ericsson 154–5
    feminine expressions and their
        interpretations 157
    in organizational culture 185–6
    recent ideas on leadership 156–7
    intersectionality 157–8

women and leadership in
    the 1970s 153–6
Women-in-Management (WIM) 156
see also female workers; women
General Electric, as a boundaryless
    organization 43
general system theory 23
generic roles 42
Germany, industrialization 13–14
Gerstner, Lou, shared vision 148
Gherardi, S., on organizational
    culture 185–6
Giddens, Anthony, on risks of
    technological
    development 50
Gilbreth, Frank and Lillian 81–2
Gilson, M.B., criticism of Hawthorne
    Study 117
GLAM (Gay, Lesbian, Bisexual, and
    Transgender) network 132
globalization, impact of IT 69–70
goal achievement versus group
    maintenance 146
goals 27
    formal and informal 87
goal-setting, Primo apprenticeship
    programme 108
Good Soldier Švejk, The, Jaromir
    Hašek 99–100
Google, innovation 211–12
Gotein, B., on post-decision
    disappointment 264
Gouldner, Alvin
    on change 223
    Patterns of Industrial Bureaucracy 28
    study of 'mock-bureaucracy' 88
Governmental Politics model of
    decision-making 173
'gravy jobs' 87
Greve, H.R. and Taylor, A., on
    innovation 214
Grey, C. 2
group thinking 174–5
    in pharmaceutical industry 175
grouping into units 31–2
guild system 55
Guillén, M.F., on Bedaux system 80

H
Hackman, J.R. and Oldham, G.R., job
    characteristics model 122–3
Hackman, R. and Wageman, R., on
    Total Quality
    Management 92
Hammer, M. and Champy, J., business
    process re-engineering 94–5
Hard Facts, J. Pfeffer and R.L.
    Sutton 3

hard HRM 130
    definition 129
Harvard Medical School,
    communities of practice
    perspective 250
Hawthorne effect 56
Hawthorne Study 55–6, 111–12, 133
    Bank Wiring Observation
        Room 115–17
    comparison with Primo
        apprenticeship
        programme 118
    impact on ADM 112–13
    Interview Study 114–15
    Relay Assembly Room 113–14
    results and criticisms 117–18
health care, continuous
    improvement 233
Heervagen, J.H. *et al.*, on knowledge
    work 261
Hellström, Kurt, leadership of
    Ericsson 135–6
Hersey, P. and Blanchard, K.H.,
    theory of situational
    leadership 139
Herzberg, F.
    on motivation 126
    Two-Factor Theory 121–2
hierarchy 30
    in organizational charts 31
Hofstede, Geert, on national cultural
    differences 187
holistic view 101
homogeneous–heterogeneous
    (simple–complex)
    dimension 35
homosocial reproduction 111
horizontal grouping 30
hotels, Total Quality
    Management 92
Huawei, knowledge management
    practices 261
Huber, G.P., on organizational
    learning 255
Hughes, Christina, study of identity
    categorisation 158
human-centred perspective 54
Human Relations School 25–6, 85
Human Resource Management
    128–9, 133
    IKEA 128
    impact on organizations 130–1
    at Primo 130
    at Rolls-Royce Motor Cars 121
humanist values, singing as
    psychical exercise 85
hygiene factors, in Two-Factor
    Theory of motivation 121

I

Iacono, S. and Kling, R.
   on impact of the Internet 70, 71
IBM, Lou Gerstner's shared
     vision 148
ICT investments 171
identity categorization 158
IKEA, HRM practices 128
In Search of Excellence, Tom Peters
     and Robert Waterman 184
incremental change 229
Industrial Organization, Joan
     Woodward 30
Industrial Revolution 10, 55
industrial sociology 86
   shop floor studies 86–9
industrialization 8–10
   organization 10–12
industry–university
     collaboration 195–6, 197,
     204–5
informal rewards 88
information distribution, in
     organizational learning 255
information interpretation, in
     organizational learning 255
information perspective of
     learning 249
information processing 36
information technology (IT) 72
   definition 64
   deskilling/upskilling debate 66–7
   e-Business, introduction at Ford and
     Volvo Car Company 47–8
   historical development 64–5
   impact on leadership 141–2
   impact on middle managers 159–60
   myths 68–70
   role in organization 52
informational objects 261–2
'infusion with values', Tennessee
     Valley Authority 179
initiating of structure 146
Innform (Innovative forms of
     organizing) study 32–3, 140
innovation 214
   in Ciba Vision 217–18
   in definition of organizational
     learning 254
   definitions 197–200
   differences between research and
     development 200–1
   establishment of new
     technologies 204
   at Google 211–12
   industry–university
     collaboration 195–6, 204–5
   invention of recorded music 207–8

   in networks 212, 213–14
   at Nokia 199
   perspectives 201
   relationship to organization
     forms 209–13
   social nature 203–7
   systemic view 208–9
innovation phases 202–3
innovation systems 208
innovative capacity 203
instituted rules
   efficiency costs 182
institutional fields, pharmaceutical
     industry 179
institutional order 53
institutional theory 168, 176–7,
     225–6
   corporate social responsibility (CSR)
     strategies 181
   isomorphism 181–3, 226–7
   old and new 180
   organizational fields 226
   study of Tennessee Valley
     Authority 179–80
institutionalism, Scandinavian 227–8
institutionalization 178
   Ronald Jepperson's definition 225–6
institutionalized knowledge 258
institutions 28–9, 177–8, 222
   accounting procedures 183–4
   Ronald Jepperson's definition 225–6
insurance industry, use of IT 65
insurance managers 262
integrated action 229
integration
   definition 29
   Karolinska University Hospital 32
integration strategy, Cisco 231
Intel Corporation
   crossing the boundaries of the formal
     organization 39–40
   dimensions of structural
     factors 30–1
   division by output 26
   formal structure 19–20
   interorganizational relations 41
   keeping up with change 22
intellectual knowledge 257
intellectual work, separation from
     manual labour 79, 84
intensive technology 62
interdependencies, influence on
     outcome of change 223
interessement 205–6
interest charges, introduction 55
internal work motivation 123
Internet presence 70–1
internships, ADM 112–13

interorganizational relations 41, 143
interpretation systems, organizations
     as 230
intersectionality 157–8
interviews, recruitment 110
iPad 68
isomorphism 181–3, 226–7
Israeli textile factory, incorporation
     of traditional family
     values 190

J

Janis, Irving, study of political
     fiascos 174
Japanese brewing industry,
     innovation 210–11
Japanese companies
   operations management 75–6
   organization culture 184
Japanese management models 102
   secrets of success 101
Japanese 'transplants'
   cultural issues 93, 189–90
   implementation of management
     systems 88
Jaques, E., definition of culture 185
Jarvenpaa, S. and Stoddard, D.B., on
     radical change 230, 233
Jepperson, Ronald, definition of
     institutions 225–6
job characteristics model of
     motivation 122–3
job enlargement 127
job enrichment 127
Jobs, Steve, leadership of
     Apple 151
Joerges, B. and Czarniawska, B. 53
Jönköping county council, continuous
     improvement 233
just-in-time logistics 75–6, 91
jute weaving industry, sociotechnical
     perspective 57

K

kaizen 75, 90
Kanter, Rosabeth Moss, *Men and
     Women of the
     Corporation* 153–6
Karolinska University Hospital,
     grouping by knowledge and
     skills 32
Kärreman, D. and Alvesson, M., on
     management control 96
Katz, D. and Kahn, R.L., *The Social
     Psychology of
     Organizations* 224
Kennedy, John F., management of
     Cuba crisis 171–3

'knowing-doing gap' 262
knowledge
    contemporary perspectives 257–8
    definitions 258
    in Melfi model 259
    situated and local 258–9
knowledge acquisition 255
knowledge and skills, as basis for
        grouping 31, 32
knowledge categories 257
knowledge management 256–7
    practice 260–2
        at Huawei 261
    summary and conclusions 267–8
knowledge workers 260–2
Koprowski, E.J., on myths about
        technology 70
Kotter, J. and Schlesinger, L.
    reasons for resistance to change 236
    study of leadership 146–7
Kraft Foods, Irene Rosenfeld 137–8
Kunda, G., on culture of Tech 185

L
labour process theory 85–9, 102
laissez-faire doctrine 9, 10
Lam, A., on industry–university
        collaboration 195
land enclosure movement 55
Lang, Fritz, *Metropolis* 82
Lanzara, G.F., on learning from
        disasters 266
Lanzara, G.F. and Patriotta, G., on
        institutionalization 178
large batch production systems 61
Lave, Jean, situated perspective of
        learning 250
law students, professional
        socialization 188
Lawler, E.E., compensation
        theory 125
Lawrence, P.R., on response to
        resistance to change 236
Lawrence, P.R. and Lorsch, J.W.,
        *Organization and
        Environment* 29
Leaders, Warren Bennis and Burt
        Nanus 147
leadership 137–8, 162
    at Ericsson 135–6
    at Kraft Foods 137–8
    middle managers 158–61
    organizational context 138–9
        influence of organizational
            structures 139–43
        post-materialist values 143–4
    recent ideas on gender 156–7
        intersectionality 157–8

situational 139
Women-in-Management (WIM) 156
women's role in 1970s 153–6
Leadership in Administration, Philip
        Selznick 222–3
Leadership in Organizations, Philip
        Selznick 28–9
leadership theory 144, 144–5, 146
    activity approach 146–7
    charismatic/transformational
        approach 147–51
    contextual factors 152
'lean', as generic term 95
lean production 91, 127
learning 243, 244, 267–8
    behavioural perspectives 247–8
    cognitive perspectives 248–9
    dimensions 245
    levels of analysis 246
    in organizations 251–2
    situated perspectives 250
    theoretical perspectives 243–6
    see also knowledge
learning factory, Fiat's Melfi
        Model 241–2, 245–6
    organizational learning 253
    situated learning 251
learning organizations 246
Lewin, Kurt
    on change 223
    on resistance to change 235
life quality 127
lighting levels, Hawthorne
        Study 111–12
line organization 25
link boxes 7
local knowledge 258–9
    in Melfi model 259
lock-in effects, innovation 203
long-linked technology 62
long-term store 249
Lovelace, Ada 64
LPC (Least Preferred Coworker)
        score 140
Luhmann, N., on decision-
        making 264
Lupton, T., study of piece-rate
        system 87

M
machine bureaucracy, definition 27
Machlup, Fritz, *The Production and
        Distribution of Knowledge in
        the United States* 256–7
management attention, effect on
        motivation 118
management control 96
    forms 97–8

minicase 98
    resistance 99–100
    surveillance 98–9
managers
    conflict with employees 13
    historical origins 11, 12–13
    role in radical change 232
    see also middle managers
Mann Gulch fire (1949) 267
manual labour, separation from
        intellectual work 79, 84
March, J.G., on decision-making 176
March, J.G. and Olsen, J.P., theory of
        decision-making 171
March, J.G. and Shapira, Z., on
        decision-making 264
March, J.G. and Simon, H.,
        Organizations 29
Markides, C., 'ambidextrous'
        professors 195
marriage, as an institution 178
Marx, Karl, on sociological
        implications of capitalism 86
masculinity 157
Maslow's Hierarchy of
        Needs 119–20
mass production systems 61
    introduction 13
'mavericks', innovative capacity 203
McCallum, Daniel 12
McClellan, J., on decision-
        making 264
McClelland, D., Achievement
        Motivation Theory 123–4
McGregor, D., Theory X and Theory
        Y 120
McKinsey & Company, diversity
        management 132
mechanistic organizational
        systems 36
mediating technology 62
Melfi Model 241–2, 245–6
    local knowledge 259
    organizational learning 253
    situated learning 251
Men and Women of the Corporation,
        Rosabeth Moss Kanter 153–6
Men who Manage, M. Dalton 88
mentoring programmes 131–2
mercantilism 8, 9
mergers, integration process 231
Merton, Robert 86
    Social Theory and Social Structure 28
'me-too-drugs' 175
Metropolis, Fritz Lang 82
Meyer, J.W. and Rowan, B.
    on isomorphism 181–2
    on ritual aspects of institutions 180

micro systems 233
microwave oven, unintended
        uses 67–8
middle managers 138, 158–9
    impact of delayering 159
    impact of downsizing in Ericsson 161
    impact of IT 69, 142, 159–60
    role in change
        implementation 160–1
    role in radical change 232
midwives, demarcation
        disputes 81, 259
Miles, R.E. and Snow, C.C.,
        configurational approach 38
military, officer selection 57
military organization 7
Miller, D., bridges between strategy
        and structure 38
Mills, Charles Wright 86
mimetic isomorphism 182, 227
mind-guarding 174
minicases 7
minimum level of acceptable
        performance 28
Mintzberg, Henry
    definition of machine
        bureaucracy 27
    on logic of organization 31
    The Rise and Fall of Strategic
        Planning 168–9
    study of CEOs 138
mock-bureaucracy 88
Models of Man, Herbert Simon 169
Modern Organizations, A. Etzioni 256
Modern Times, Charlie Chaplin 82
Mon Oncle, Jacques Tati 82
monocratic bureaucracy 27
Montgomery, James 11
Moore's law 20
Morgan, J.L., on learning 248
morphogenesis 225
motion, variables of 82
motivation 29, 118–19, 133
    attitude measurement approach 126
    content-oriented theories 126–7
        job characteristics model 122–3
        Maslow's Hierarchy of
            Needs 119–20
        Theory X and Theory Y 120
        Two-Factor Theory 121–2
    in movies 125–6
    new theories 127–8
    in Primo 122
    process-oriented theories 123
        Achievement Motivation
            Theory 123–4
        Equity Theory 124–5
        Expectancy Theory 124

        Expectancy Theory and Equity
            Theory in combination 125
        Taylor's conception 84
    see also Hawthorne Study
motivation theory, classification 119
movies
    depiction of Cuban crisis 173
    motivation 125–6
moving stage of change 223
Multifactor Leadership
        Questionnaire (MLQ) 151
Münsterberg, Hugo, criticism of
        Taylorism 80
music 85
music recording 207–8
myths
    about information
        technology 68–70
    purposes 70

N
NAch people 124
Nadler, D.A. and Tushman, M.L., on
        charismatic leadership 150
NAff people 124
Nasser, Jacques, introduction of
        e-Business at Ford 47
national cultures 186–7
natural disasters 263
needs
    Achievement Motivation
        Theory 123–4
    Maslow's Hierarchy 119–20
Nelson, R.R. and Winter, S.G., on
        knowledge 257
neo-institutional theory 43, 180
networks
    role in innovation 212, 213–14
    role in management 147
new organizational research,
        definition 33
new technologies
    challenges 50–1
        jute weaving industry example 57
    role in organization 52
Nissan, Total Quality Management
        (TQM) 93–4
Nokia, innovation 199
non-professional organizations 257
normative isomorphism 182–3, 227
norms
    in Hawthorne Study 116
    shop floor work 87
NPow people 124
nurses, demarcation disputes 81,
        259
Nye, D.E., on establishment of new
        technologies 204

O
objective rationality 169
obstetricians, expert knowledge 259
occupational cultures 188–9
Ohio State Leadership Studies 146
On Organizational Learning, Chris
        Argyris 252
open system theory 23–4, 26, 41–2,
        62
    view of organizational change 224–5
operant conditioning 248
operations management 77, 102
    Toyota 75–6
operative decentralization 140
opportunity structures 154
    at Ericsson 154–5
Oracle corporation, acquisition of
        Sun Microsystems 1
organic organizational systems 36
Organization and Environment, P.R.
        Lawrence and J.W. Lorsch 29
organization culture 184–6
organization forms, relationship to
        innovation 209–13
Organization Process model of
        decision-making 172–3
organization theory, historical
        origins 7–8, 14–15
    1900s 13–14
    growth of large and modern
        corporation 12–13
    industrialization 8–10, 10–12
    technological innovation 10
organization types 257
organizational change 220
    in Ciba Vision 217–18
    continuous improvement 232–3
    defence mechanisms 237–8
    definition 219
    institutional theory view 225–6
    perspectives 221
    radical change 230–2
        Dubai 234
    related to environmental issues 227
    resistance 234–8
    Scandinavian institutionalism 227–8
    summary 238
    systems view 224–5
    traditional views 221–3
    types of change 228–30
organizational characteristics
    relationship to technology 60–1
organizational charts 23, 31
organizational culture
    Israeli textile factory, incorporation
        of traditional family values 190
    Japanese 'transplants' 189–90
    role in radical change 231

Organizational Development (OD)
    perspective 229
  interventions 237
organizational fields 226
organizational learning 243–6, 251–2
  behavioural theories 253–5
  cognitive theories 255–6
  from disasters 265–7
  in Fiat 253
  at Shell 254
  see also learning
organizational memory 255
organizational structures 21–2
  definition 24
  determinants of 26
  effect of technological change 60–2
  elements 27–38
  influence on leadership 139–43
  role and importance 23–7
  Walmart 24
organizations
  definition 4
  features 23
  as systems 4–5
Organizations, J. March and H.
    Simon 29, 169
Orlikowski, Wanda, on
    technology 53–4
outsourcing 127
  AstraZeneca 165–6
Ovi Store 199
Owen, Robert 11
ownership, separation from
    control 12–13, 15

P
Pardo del Val, M. and Fuentes, C.M.,
    on resistance to change 236
Parker, M., on organizational
    culture 185, 186
Parsons, Talcott, on institutional
    theory 178
pastime knowledge 257
path-dependencies, innovation 203
Patterns of Industrial Bureaucracy,
    Alvin Gouldner 28, 223
Patton, Walter, Ciba Vision 217
Pavitt, K.
  on innovation 198
  on innovation phases 202
Pavlov, Ivan Petrovich 247–8
peer-based control 97–8
Pennings, J.M., criticism of
    contingency theory 37
performance improvement, in
    definition of organizational
    learning 254–5
Perrow, Charles 63

personality tests, use in
    recruitment 110–11
personalized medicine 175
personnel management 128–9
  historical origins 14
  involvement of women 130
  see also Human Resource
    Management
Peters, Tom and Waterman, Robert,
    In Search of Excellence 184
Petrobras, CSR strategy 181
Pettigrew, A.M., on radical
    change 232
Pfeffer, J. and Salancik, G.R
  on institutionalization 178
  on open system view 42
Pfeffer, J. and Sutton, R.I., Hard
    Facts 3
Pfeffer, J. et al., on business school
    research 2
pharmaceutical industry
  group thinking 175
  innovation 213
  institutional patterns 179
  portfolio selection 165–7
  sub-cultures 187
  tensions 184
phonograph, invention and
    application 207–8
Piaget, Jean 249
piece-rate system
  Donald Roy's study 86–7
  Michael Burawoy's study 89
Pillai, R., on charismatic
    leadership 152
pin factory example, Adam Smith 9
Pinsonneault, A. and Kraemer, K., on
    impact of IT 142, 159–60
Piore, Michael and Sabel, Charles,
    The Second Industrial
    Divide 90
Plato
  on knowledge 256
  Republic 222
political decision-making 171–2
  Bay of Pigs invasion 174
  Cuba crisis 171–3
politicized processes, role in radical
    change 231–2
Politics of Organizational Decision-
    Making, The, A.M.
    Pettigrew 232
Poor, Henry Varnum 12
Porter, Michael, value chain model 40
portfolio selection, pharmaceutical
    industry 165–7, 177
post-decision disappointment 264
post-materialist values 143–4

Powell, W.W. et al., on networks,
    value in innovation 213–14
power, need for 124
Power, Michael, on risk
    management 263
power distance 187
power structures 155
practical knowledge 257
Practice of Management, The, Peter
    Drucker 128–9
practices 100–1
prescriptive design principles 26
Primo apprenticeship
    programme 107–8
  comparison with Hawthorne
    Study 118
  hard and soft human resource
    management 130
  motivational factors 122
  recruitment 109–10
Principles of Scientific Management,
    Frederick Taylor 79
procedures 182
process-oriented motivation
    theories 119, 123
  Achievement Motivation
    Theory 123–4
  Equity Theory 124–5
  Expectancy Theory 124
  Expectancy Theory and Equity
    Theory in combination 125
process production systems 61
product innovation 200
Production and Distribution of
    Knowledge, The, Fritz
    Machlup 256–7
production systems 61
productivity levels
  maximization 14
  see also Hawthorne Study
professional cultures 188–9
professional organizations 257
professional socialization 188
professional training, normative
    isomorphism 182–3
profit-sharing systems, historical
    origins 12
project managers 138
projects 141
psychological contract 110
psychological tests, use in
    recruitment 110–11

Q
quality see Total Quality
    Management (TQM)
quality improvement, Deming's
    work 232–3

Quality Leadership program,
    Nissan 93–4
Quinn, R.W., on knowledge 258

R
Radcliffe-Brown, A.R., definition of
    institutions 177
radical change 229, 230
    changes in belief systems 230–1
    in Ciba Vision 221
    combination with continuous
        improvement 233
    Dubai 234
    in mergers and acquisitions 231
    political perspective 231–2
    resistance 235
    role of managers 232
railroad companies, organizational
    structure 12–13
Ramirez, P. and Tylecote, A., study of
    AstraZeneca 165–7
Rational Actor model of decision-
    making 172
rational choice theory 169
recruitment 109–11, 132–3
    Primo apprenticeship
        programme 107–8, 109–10
reflexes, conditioned 247–8
regulation, pharmaceutical
    industry 165
reification problem of organizational
    learning 253
reinforcement 248
research, difference from
    development 200–1
research and development
    (R&D) 202
    organization structure, relationship
        to innovation 211
research centres 195–6
    Chalmers University of
        Technology 212
resistance 99–100
resistance to change 87, 234–5
    in Ciba Vision 236
    interventions 237
    reasons 235, 236
    responses 236
resource-dependency theory 177
responses (reflexes) 247
revolutionary change 229
rewards, informal 88
Rise and Fall of Strategic Planning, The,
    Henry Mintzberg 168–9
risk 262–3
risk management 263–4
    decision-making 264
    learning from disasters 265–7

Roddick, Anita, leadership of Body
    Shop 148–9
Roethlisberger, F.J. and Dickson, W.J.,
    Hawthorne Study 114–15
Rolls-Royce Motor Cars, HRM
    practices 121
Rombach, B. and Solli, R., on
    motivation in movies 126
Roosevelt, Franklin D., 'New Deal'
    programme 179
Rosenfeld, Irene 137–8
routines 100–1
Rowntree, use of singing 85
Roy, Donald, study of piece-rate
    system 86–7
rules 28, 100–1
    in Hawthorne Study 116
    institutions 182
    mock-bureaucracy 88
Rutherford, Jonathan, on 'zombie
    institutions' 178

S
Saxenian, AnnaLee, study of Silicon
    Valley 189
Scandinavia, institutionalism 227–8
Schleef, Debra
    on professional identities 188
    study of 'managing elites' 97
Schoonhoven, C.B., criticism of
    contingency theory 37
Schroeder, R.G. *et al.*, systemic view
    of innovation 208–9
Schumpeter, Joseph, on
    innovation 197–8, 210
scientific management 14, 25, 26, 55,
    77, 102
    Taylorism 78–9, 79
        criticisms 80
        followers 80–2
        legacy 82–4
scientific studies of work 85–6
Scott, Richard, on institutional
    theory 225
Second Industrial Divide, The, Michael
    Piore and Charles Sabel 90
secondary reinforcers 248
segmentalism 229
self-concept 150
Selznick, Philip
    on change 222–3
    Leadership in Organizations 28–9
    study of Tennessee Valley
        Authority 179–80
Senge, Peter, *The Fifth Discipline* 246
sense-making perspective of
    learning 249
service organizations 257

sex discrimination 132
Shamir, B. and Howell, J.M., on
    charismatic leadership 152
shared vision 147
    Lou Gerstner 148
Sharma, A., on innovation in large
    organizations 209–10
Shell, focus on learning 254
Shimano, change management 220
shop floor studies 86–9
Shop Management, Frederick
    Taylor 79
short-term store 249
Silent Spring, Rachel Carlson 227
Silicon Valley, culture 189
Simon, Herbert, work on decision-
    making 168, 169–70
simple–complex (homogeneous–
    heterogeneous)
    dimension 35
singing, as psychical exercise 85
situated knowledge 258
situated learning 250
    in Melfi model 251
situational leadership, definition 139
situational theories of learning 245,
    246
size of organizations, relationship to
    innovation 209–11, 213
Skinner, B.F., on operant
    conditioning 248
Slappendel, C., definition of
    innovation 200
small batch production systems 61
small-talk 257
Smircich, L., on organizational
    culture 185
Smith, Adam, *The Wealth of
    Nations* 9–10, 78
social behaviour, Hawthorne
    Study 115–17
Social Psychology of Organizations, The,
    D. Katz and R.L. Kahn 224
social reinforcers 248
social systems, autopoiesis theory 177
Social Theory and Social Structure,
    Robert Merton 28
social-anthropology-of-learning
    approach to
    knowledge 257–8
socio-ideological control 97, 98
sociology 86
sociomaterial practices 54
sociotechnical perspective 55, 56, 72
    Ford/VCC purchasing function
        changes 59
    studies 56–8
        results 58–9

sociotechnical system, definition 56
soft HRM 130
   definition 129
'soldiering' 86–7
Sole, D. and Edmondson, A.,
      definition of situated
      knowledge 258
solidarity groups 131
Sony Ericsson, boundary
      crossing 142–3
span of control 30
specialization, historical origins 9
Spinning Jenny 55
spiritual knowledge 257
stable–dynamic dimension 35
staff and line organization 25
stage-gate models of innovation 203
stage model, Atkinson and
      Shiffrin 249
stakeholder management
      approach 41–2, 177
standard work, separation from
      expert work 81
steam engines 55
'stinkers' 87
strategic agendas 147
strategic-choice approach 37
strategic decentralization 140–1
strategic-management approach to
      knowledge 257
strategic types 38
Strategy and Structure: Chapters in the
      History of American Industrial
      Enterprise, A.D. Chandler 37
stress, assembly line work 88
structural dimensions 30
   Intel Corporation 30–1
'structure follows strategy'
      formula 211
student numbers, growth 3
students, transition to work life 111
Studies of Science and Technology
      research 67–8
studies of work
   scientific studies 85–6
   shop floor studies 86–9
style approach to leadership 146
sub-cultures 185
   in pharmaceutical industry 187
subjectification 89
subjective rationality 169
Sun Microsystems, acquisition by
      Oracle Corporation 1
surface cynicism 188
surroundings, variables of 82
surveillance 98–9
survivor syndrome 159
sustainable structures 40–1

Svanberg, Carl-Henric, leadership of
      Ericsson 136
Švejk mode of resistance 99–100
systems theory 176

T
Tam, M., Korczynski, M., and Frenkel,
      S.J., on knowledge
      workers 260
Tannenbaum, A., on management
      control 96
task environment 35
task versus relations-orientation 146
Tata Motors, uncertainty and
      heterogeneity 35–6
Tati, Jacques, Mon Oncle 82
Tavistock Institute 56
   studies 57–9
Taylor, Frederick 55
   followers 80–2
   legacy 82–4
   scientific approach (Taylorism) 25,
      77–9, 102
   criticisms 80
team-based control 97–8
team-based work 75
Tech, culture 185
technical control 97, 98
technical determinism 54
technocratic utopianism 142
technological change,
      challenges 50–1
technological innovation 10
technological rationalizations
      49–50, 72
technologies, multiple use 63
technology
   definitions 51–3
   impact on pharmaceutical
      industry 165–6
   implementation 53–4
   related organizational
      characteristics 60–1
   transformation of organizational
      structure 60–2
   unintended uses 67–8
   see also information technology;
      innovation
technology types 62–3
temporarily employed workers
      ('temps') 90
temporary forms of organization 141
Tenerife plane crash (1977) 267
Tennessee Valley Authority (TVA)
      179–80
theoretical areas addressed 6
Theory X and Theory Y 120, 122
Thirteen Days (movie) 173

Thompson, James 62–3
   on dealing with uncertainty 36
Thompson, V.A., definition of
      innovation 199
Thorndike, Edward Lee, The Animal
      Intelligence 247
time and motion studies
   Gantt's use 80
   historical origins 11–12
time-compression diseconomies 196
Todorov, Tzvetan, on culture 185
tokenism 155, 156
tools, variables of 82
Total Quality Management (TQM)
      75, 91–3
   definition 91
   growth outside manufacturing
      industry 92
   isomorphism 181
   at Nissan 93–4
Toyota
   lean production 95
   operations management 75–6, 77
      use of Taylorist ideas 84
trained incapacity 28
training, historical perspective 11
trait approach to leadership 146
transactional leadership 149, 229
transformational leadership 149–51,
      229
translation 228
trial-and-error processes 247
Trist, Eric 56, 58
Tsoukas, H., on knowledge 258
Turner, B.A. and Pidgeon, B.F., study
      of accidents 265
Two-Factor Theory 121–2
typesetting, impact of
      computerization 66–7

U
uncertainty 35
   influential studies 36
   Tata Motors 35–6
understanding 249
unfreezing stage of change 223
   in Ciba Vision 223–4
unit production systems 61
United States, industrialization 12–13
unwanted knowledge 257
upskilling, as effect of
      computerization 66

V
value chain model 40
values 148–9
   influence on leadership 143–4
   shop floor work 87

Van de Ven, A., on
    innovation 199–200
Van de Ven, A. and Poole, M.S.,
    systemic view of
    innovation 208
Vanderbilt, Cornelius 13
variables, F. and L. Gilbreth 82
virtual organizations 141
visibility, tokenism 155
Volvo Car Company
    introduction of e-Business 47–8,
        50–1, 71
    purchasing function changes
        sociotechnical perspective 59
    use of multiple technologies 63–4
Vroom, V., Expectancy Theory 124

W
wages, in Industrial Revolution 10
Wajcman, J., on introduction of word
    processors 66
Walmart, organizational
    structure 24
Watson, Tony, on change
    management 219–20
ways-of-working, Industrial
    Revolution 10
Wealth of Nations, The, Adam
    Smith 9–10, 78
Weber, Max 86
    on bureaucratic organization 27, 100
    on charismatic leadership 149, 152
    on Industrial Revolution 10

Weick, Karl
    definition of technology 51–2
    environmental enactment idea 38
    study of crises 266–7
Welch, Jack, leadership of General
    Electric 43
Wenger, Etienne, situated
    perspective of learning 250
Whittington, R. and Pettigrew, A.,
    interorganizational
    relations 41
Whyte, William H. 86
Winch, G., complex product
    systems 209
Winter, S.J. and Taylor, L.S., on
    impact of information
    technology 69
Wolfe, R.A., perspectives of
    innovation 201
women
    CEOs 137–8
    deskilling in clerical work 66, 67
    involvement in personnel
        management 130
    leadership in the 1970s 153–6
    see also female workers; gender
        issues
Women-in-Management (WIM) 156
Woodward, Joan 60–2
    definition of formal structures 24
    Industrial Organization 30
word processors, impact on office
    workers 66

work organization 89–90, 102
    business process
        re-engineering 94–5
    flexible specialization 90
    Total Quality Management
        (TQM) 91–3
workers
    empowerment 84
    measurement of attitudes 126
    variables of 82
    see also employees
workers' potentials, Taylor's
    negativity 83
working conditions, in Industrial
    Revolution 11
World Values Survey
    (WVS) 144
    data 145
World War II, reconstruction of
    Japanese industry 76

Y
Yagil, D., on charismatic
    leadership 152
Yanow, D., on knowledge 258

Z
Zara, on-line store
    development 65
Zbaracki, M.J., on Total Quality
    Management 92
zero degree defect rate 91
'zombie institutions' 178